THE SACRED BOOKS OF THE EAST

TRANSLATED BY

VARIOUS ORIENTAL SCHOLARS

EDITED BY

F. MAX MÜLLER

VOLUME 28

SACRED BOOKS OF THE EAST

(50 VOLUMES)

Series Editor : *F. Max-Müller*

ISBN: 978-81-208-0101-1 (Set) Rs. 11000 (Each Vol. Rs. 250)

These volumes of the Sacred Books of the East series include translations of all the most important works of the seven non-Christian religions that have exercised a profound influence on the civilisations of the continent of Asia. The Vedic Brahmanic system claims 21 volumes, Buddhism 10, and Jainism 2; 8 volumes comprise Sacred Books of the Parsis; 2 volumes represent Islam; and 6 the two main indigenous systems of China. Translated by twenty leading authorities in their respective fields, the volumes have been edited by the late F. Max Müller. The inception, publication and the compilation of these books cover almost 34 years.

I. BUDDHISM

Vol. 49: Buddhist Mahayana Texts (2 Parts)
Vol. 11: Buddhist Suttas
Vol. 10: The Dhammapada and Sutta Nipata
Vols. 35 & 36: The Questions of King Milinda (2 Parts)
Vol. 21: The Saddharma Pundarika or the Lotus of the True Law
Vols. 13, 17 & 20: Vinaya Texts (3 Parts)

II. CHINESE

Vol. 19: The Fo-Sho-Hing-Tsan-King
Vols. 3, 16, 27, 28, 39 & 40: The Sacred Books of China (6 Parts)

III. A GENERAL INDEX

Vol. 50: A General Index to the Names and Subject-matter of the Sacred Books of the East

IV. ISLAM

Vols. 6 & 9: The Qur'an (2 Parts)

V. JAINISM

Vols. 22 & 45: The Jaina Sutras (2 Parts)

VI. PARSIS

Vols. 5, 18, 24, 37 & 47: Pahlavi Texts (5 Parts)
Vols. 4, 23 & 31: The Zend-Avesta (3 Parts)

VII. VEDIC-BRAHMANIC SYSTEM

Vol. 8: The Bhagavadgita with the Sanatsujatiya and the Anugita
Vols. 29 & 30: The Grihya-Sutras: Rules of Vedic Domestic Ceremonies (2 Parts)
Vol. 42: Hymns of the Atharva Veda together with Extracts from the Ritual Books and the Commentaries
Vol. 7: The Institutes of Vishnu
Vol. 25: The Laws of Manu
Vol. 33: The Minor Law Books
Vols. 2 & 14: The Sacred Laws of the Aryas as Taught in the Schools of Apastamba, Gautama, Vasishtha and Baudhayana (2 Parts)
Vols. 12, 26, 41, 43 & 44: The Satapatha Brahmana According to the Text of the Madhyandina School (5 Parts)
Vols. 1 & 15: The Upanishads (2 Parts)
Vols. 34 & 38: The Vedanta Sutras (2 Parts)
Vol. 48: The Vedanta-Sutras (with the commentary by Ramanuja)
Vols. 32 & 46: Vedic Hymns (2 Parts)

THE SACRED BOOKS OF CHINA

The texts of Confucianism

Translated by

James Legge

Part IV

The LĪ KĪ, XI—XLVI

MOTILAL BANARSIDASS PUBLISHERS
PRIVATE LIMITED • DELHI

Reprint: Delhi, 1964, 1967, 1970, 1976, 1986, 1992, 2001, 2008
First published by the Oxford University Press, 1885

ISBN: 978-81-208-0129-5

MOTILAL BANARSIDASS
41 U.A. Bungalow Road, Jawahar Nagar, Delhi 110 007
8 Mahalaxmi Chamber, 22 Bhulabhai Desai Road, Mumbai 400 026
203 Royapettah High Road, Mylapore, Chennai 600 004
236, 9th Main III Block, Jayanagar, Bangalore 560 011
Sanas Plaza, 1302 Baji Rao Road, Pune 411 002
8 Camac Street, Kolkata 700 017
Ashok Rajpath, Patna 800 004
Chowk, Varanasi 221 001

UNESCO COLLECTION OF REPRESENTATIVE WORKS— Indian Series
This book has been accepted in the Indian Translation Series of the UNESCO Collection of Representative Works, jointly sponsored by the United Nations Educational Scientific and Cultural Organization (UNESCO) and the Government of India

PRINTED IN INDIA
BY JAINENDRA PRAKASH JAIN AT SHRI JAINENDRA PRESS,
A-45 NARAINA, PHASE-I, NEW DELHI 110 028
AND PUBLISHED BY NARENDRA PRAKASH JAIN FOR
MOTILAL BANARSIDASS PUBLISHERS PRIVATE LIMITED,
BUNGALOW ROAD, DELHI 110 007

RASHTRAPATI BHAVAN,
NEW ḌELHI 4
June 10, 1962

I am very glad to know that the Sacred Books of the East, published years ago by the Clarendon Press, Oxford, which have been out of print for a number of years, will now be available to all students of religion and philosophy. The enterprise of the publishers is commendable and I hope the books will be widely read.

S. RADHAKRISHNAN

PREFATORY NOTE TO THE NEW EDITION

Since 1948 the United Nations Educational, Scientific and Cultural Organization (UNESCO), upon the recommendation of the General Assembly of the United Nations, has been concerned with facilitating the translation of the works most representative of the culture of certain of its Member States, and, in particular, those of Asia.

One of the major difficulties confronting this programme is the lack of translators having both the qualifications and the time to undertake translations of the many outstanding books meriting publication. To help overcome this difficulty in part, UNESCO's advisers in this field (a panel of experts convened every other year by the International Council for Philosophy and Humanistic Studies), have recommended that many worthwhile translations published during the 19th century, and now impossible to find except in a limited number of libraries, should be brought back into print in low-priced editions, for the use of students and of the general public. The experts also pointed out that in certain cases, even though there might be in existence more recent and more accurate translations endowed with a more modern apparatus of scholarship, a number of pioneer works of the greatest value and interest to students of Eastern religions also merited republication.

This point of view was warmly endorsed by the Indian National Academy of Letters (Sahitya Akademi), and the Indian National Commission for UNESCO.

It is in the spirit of these recommendations that this work from the famous series "Sacred Books of the East" is now once again being made available to the general public as part of the UNESCO Collection of Representative Works.

PUBLISHER'S NOTE

First, the man distinguished between eternal and perishable. Later, he discovered within himself the germ of the Eternal. This discovery was an epoch in the history of the human mind and the *East was the first to discover it.*

To watch in the Sacred Books of the East the dawn of this religious consciousness of man, must always remain one of the most inspiring and hallowing sights in the whole history of the world. In order to have a solid foundation for a comparative study of the Religions of the East, we must have before all things, complete and thoroughly faithful translation of their Sacred Books in which some of the ancient sayings were preserved because they were so true and so striking that they could not be forgotten. They contained eternal truths, expressed for the first time in human language.

With profoundest reverence for Dr. S. Radhakrishnan, President of India, who inspired us for the task; our deep sense of gratitude for Dr. C. D. Deshmukh & Dr. D. S. Kothari, for encouraging assistance, esteemed appreciation of UNESCO for the warm endorsement of the cause; and finally with indebtedness to Dr. H. Rau, Director, Max Müller Bhawan, New Delhi, in procuring us the texts of the Series for reprint, we humbly conclude.

THE LÎ *K*Î.

A COLLECTION OF TREATISES ON THE RULES OF PROPRIETY OR CEREMONIAL USAGES.

BOOK XI. YU ƷÂO

OR

THE JADE-BEAD PENDANTS OF THE ROYAL CAP[1].

SECTION I.

1. The son of Heaven, when sacrificing[2], wore (the cap) with the twelve long pendants of beads of jade hanging down from its top before and behind, and the robe embroidered with dragons.

2. When saluting the appearance of the sun[3] outside the eastern gate[4], he wore the dark-coloured square-cut robes; and (also) when listening to the notification of the first day of the month[5] outside the southern gate.

---

[1] See introductory notice, vol. xxvii, pp. 27, 28.

[2] Probably, to Heaven; *K*ăng thought it was to the former kings. Many try to unite both views.

[3] At the vernal equinox. Callery has 'Quand de bon matin il sacrifie au soleil.' Probably there was a sacrifice on the occasion; but the text does not say so. The character 朝 (*kh*iâo) means 'to appear at audience.'

[4] Probably, of the city; many say, of the Hall of Distinction.

[5] This announcement was to the spirits of his royal ancestors in the first place. Compare Analects III, 16.

3. If the month were intercalary, he caused the left leaf of the door to be shut, and stood in the middle of that (which remained open)[1].

4. He wore the skin cap at the daily audience in the court, after which he proceeded to take the morning meal in it. At midday he partook of what was left in the morning. He had music at his meals. Every day a sheep and a pig were killed and cooked; and on the first day of the month an ox in addition. There were five beverages:—water, which was the principal; rice-water, spirits, must, and millet-water.

5. When he had done eating, he remained at ease in the dark-coloured square-cut robes[2]. His actions were written down by the recorder of the Left, and his utterances by the recorder of the Right. The blind musician in attendance judged whether the music were too high or too low[3].

6. If the year were not good and fruitful, the son of Heaven wore white and plain robes, rode in the plain and unadorned carriage, and had no music at his meals.

---

[1] This is not easy to understand, nor easy to make intelligible. An intercalary month was an irregular arrangement of the year. It and the previous month formed one double month. The shutting half the door showed that one half of the time was passed. There remained the other leaf to be given—in the temple or in the palace—to the king for all the ceremonies or acts of government appropriate in such a position for the whole intercalary month. Something like this is sketched out as the meaning by the *Kh*ien-lung editors.

[2] These were so named from the form in which they were made, the cloth being cut straight and square.

[3] And judged, it is said, of the character of the measures of government; but this is being 'over-exquisite' to account for the custom.

7. The princes of states, in sacrificing, wore their dark-coloured square-cut robes. At court-audiences (of the king), they wore the cap of the next inferior degree of rank to their own [1]. They wore the skin-cap, when listening to the notification of the first day of the month in the Grand temples; and their court robes when holding their daily audience in the inner court-yard.

8. (Their ministers and officers) entered (the palace) as soon as they could distinguish the dawning light [2], and the ruler came out daily (to the first court, inside the Khû gate), and received them. (After this audience), he retired, and went to the great chamber, there to listen to their proposals about the measures of government. He employed men to see whether the Great officers (were all withdrawn) [3]; and when they had left, he repaired to the smaller chamber, and put off his (court) robes.

9. He resumed his court robes, when he was about to eat. There was a single animal, with three (other) dishes of meat, the lungs forming the sacrificial offering. In the evening he wore the long robe in one piece, and offered some of the flesh of the animal. On the first day of the moon,

[1] So it seems to be said; but why it was done so, does not clearly appear.

[2] Several pieces in the Shih allude to this early attendance at court. See Book II, ii, 8; iii, 8, et al.

[3] They sat or waited, not inside the chamber, but outside. Some Great officer might wish to bring a matter before the ruler which he had not ventured to mention in public. The ruler, therefore, would give him a private audience; and did not feel himself free from business till all had withdrawn.

a sheep and a pig were killed, and there were five (other) dishes of meat, and four of grain. On 3ze and Mâo days[1] there were only the glutinous rice and vegetable soup. His wife used the same kitchen as the ruler[2].

10. Without some cause for it, a ruler did not kill an ox, nor a Great officer a sheep, nor a lower officer a pig or a dog. A superior man had his shambles and kitchen at a distance (from the) house; he did not tread wherever there was such a thing as blood or (tainted) air[3].

11. When the eighth month came without rain, the ruler did not have full meals nor music. If the year were not abundant, he wore linen, and stuck in his girdle the tablet of an officer[4]. Duties were not levied at the barrier-gates and dams; the prohibitions of the hills and meres were enforced, but no contributions were required (from hunters and fishermen). No earthworks were undertaken, and Great officers did not make (any new) carriages for themselves.

12. The officer of divination by the tortoise-shell fixed the shell (to be used); the recorder applied the ink; and the ruler determined the figures (produced by the fire)[5].

---

[1] See vol. xxvii, p. 180.

[2] That is, the wife was supplied with what was left from the ruler's meals.

[3] Lû Tien says, 'He would not tread on ants.' The *Kh*ien-lung editors characterise this as 'a womanish remark.'

[4] A ruler's tablet was of ivory; an officer's only of bamboo, tipt with ivory.

[5] See the *K*âu Lî, Book XXII, 25. The *Kh*ien-lung editors say that the methods of this divination are lost.

13. (The cross-board in front of) the ruler was covered with lambskin, edged with tiger's fur; for his sacred carriage and court-carriage a Great officer had a covering of deer skin, edged with leopard's fur; as also had an ordinary officer for his sacred carriage[1].

14. The regular place for a gentleman was exactly opposite the door, (facing the light). He slept with his head to the east. When there came violent wind, or rapid thunder, or a great rain, he changed (countenance). It was the rule for him then, even in the night, to get up, dress himself, put on his cap, and take his seat.

15. He washed his hands five times a day. He used millet-water in washing his head, and maize-water in washing his face. For his hair (when wet) he used a comb of white-grained wood, and an ivory comb for it when dry. (After his toilet), there were brought to him the (usual) cup and some delicacy; and the musicians came up[2] and sang.

In bathing he used two towels; a fine one for the upper part (of his body), and a coarser for the lower part. When he got out of the tub, he stepped on a straw mat; and having next washed his feet with hot water, he stepped on the rush one. Then in his (bathing) robe of cloth, he dried his body (again), and put on his shoes; and a drink was then brought into him.

16. When he had arranged to go to the ruler's,

[1] 'The sacred carriage' was one used for going in to some temple service that required previous fasting. The paragraph is strangely constructed. It is supposed that the ruler's carriage at the beginning of it was also a sacred one.

[2] Came up on the raised hall, that is.

he passed the night in vigil and fasting, occupying an apartment outside his usual one. After he had washed his head and bathed, his secretary brought him the ivory tablet, on which were written his thoughts (which he should communicate to the ruler), and how he should respond to orders (that he might receive). When he was dressed he practised deportment and listened to the sounds of the gems (at his girdle pendant). When he went forth, he bowed to all in his own private court elegantly, and proceeded to mount his carriage (to go to the ruler's) in brilliant style.

17. The son of Heaven carried in his girdle the thing tablet, showing how exact and correct he should be in his relations with all under heaven. The feudal lords had the shû, rounded at the top and straight at the bottom, showing how they should give place to the son of Heaven. The tablet of the Great officers was rounded both at the top and the bottom; showing how they should be prepared to give place in all positions [1].

18. When (a minister) is sitting in attendance on his ruler, the rule was that he should occupy a mat somewhat behind him on one side. If he did not occupy such a mat, he had to draw the one assigned to him back and keep aloof from the ruler's kindred who were near him [2].

One did not take his place on his mat from the

---

[1] It is not clear what the tablets of this paragraph were, and whether they were carried in the hand or inserted in the girdle. The character 搢 (Ʒin) seems to imply the latter.

[2] The *Kh*ien-lung editors say that after these two sentences; the subject of the rest of the paragraph is a student before his teacher.

front, to avoid seeming to step over it. When seated and unoccupied he did not take up the whole of the mat by at least a cubit. If he were to read any writings or to eat, he sat forward to the edge. The dishes were put down a cubit from the mat [1].

19. If food were given (to a visitor), and the ruler proceeded to treat him as a guest, he would order him to present the offering, and the visitor would do so. If he took the precedence in eating, he would take a little of all the viands, drink a mouthful, and wait (for the ruler to eat) [2]. If there were one in attendance to taste the viands, he would wait till the ruler ate, and then eat himself. After this eating, he would drink (a mouthful), and wait (again).

20. If the ruler ordered him to partake of the delicacies, he took of that which was nearest to him. If he were told to take of all, he took of whatever he liked. In all cases, in tasting of what was some way off, they began with what was near.

(The visitor) did not dare to add the liquid to his rice till the ruler had touched the corners of his mouth with his hands and put them down [3]. When the ruler had done eating, he also took of the rice in this fashion, repeating the process three times. When the ruler had the things removed, he took his rice and sauces, and went out and gave them to his attendants.

21. Whenever pressed (by his host) to eat, one should not eat largely; when eating at another's,

[1] And also any tablets or other things to be referred to.

[2] Tasting the things before the ruler to see that they were good and safe.

[3] That is, touched those parts with his fingers to see that no grains were sticking to them.

one should not eat to satiety. It was only of the water and sauces that some was not put down as an offering;—they were accounted too trivial for such a purpose.

22. If the ruler gave a cup (of drink) to an officer, he crossed over from his mat, bowed twice, laid his head to the ground, and received it. Resuming his place, he poured a portion of it as an offering, drank it off, and waited. When the ruler had finished his cup, he then returned his empty.

The rule for a superior man in drinking (with the ruler) was this:—When he received the first cup, he wore a grave look; when he received the second, he looked pleased and respectful. With this the ceremony stopped. At the third cup, he looked self-possessed and prepared to withdraw. Having withdrawn, he knelt down and took his shoes, retired out of the ruler's (sight) and put them on. Kneeling on his left knee, he put on the right shoe; kneeling on the right knee, he put on the left one[1].

23. (At festive entertainments), of all the vases that with the dark-coloured liquor (of water) was considered the most honourable[2]; and only the ruler sat with his face towards it. For the uncultivated people in the country districts, the vases all con-

[1] The subject in the two parts of this paragraph does not appear to be the same. The officer in the former was merely an attendant we may suppose; in the latter, one of a superior rank. The cup in the one case was of special favour; in the second the cups were such as were drunk with the ruler at certain times, but were always confined to three.

[2] 'Mindful,' says *K*ăng, 'of the ways of antiquity.' See Book VII, i, 10, 11, et al. on the honour paid to water at sacrifices and feasts, and the reasons for it.

tained prepared liquors[1]. Great officers had the vase on one side of them upon a tray without feet; other officers had it in a similar position on a tray with feet[2].

Section II.

1. At the ceremony of capping, the first cap put on was one of black linen. The use of this extended from the feudal lords downwards. It might, after having been thus employed, be put away or disused[3].

2. The dark-coloured cap, with red strings and tassels descending to the breast, was used at the capping of the son of Heaven. The cap of black linen, with strings and tassels of various colours, was used at the capping of a feudal prince. A dark-coloured cap with scarlet strings and tassels was worn by a feudal lord, when fasting. A dark-coloured cap with gray strings and tassels was worn by officers when similarly engaged.

3. A cap of white silk with the border or roll of a dark colour was worn (? at his capping) by a son or grandson (when in a certain stage of mourning)[4]. A similar cap with a plain white edging, was worn after the sacrifice at the end of the year's mourning. (The same cap) with strings hanging down five inches,

---

[1] The gratification of their taste was the principal thing at festive entertainments of the common people.

[2] On the two trays mentioned here,—the yü (composed of 木, and 於 on the right of it) and the *k*in (禁),—see Book VIII, i, 12.

[3] Such a cap had been used anciently; and it was used in the ceremony, though subsequently disused, out of respect to the ancient custom.

[4] When his grandfather was dead, and his father (still alive) was in deep mourning for him.

served to mark the idle and listless officer[1]. A dark-coloured cap with the roll round it of white silk was worn by one excluded from the ranks of his compeers[2].

4. The cap worn in private, with the roll or border attached to it, was used by all from the son of Heaven downwards. When business called them, the strings were tied and their ends allowed to hang down.

5. At fifty, one did not accompany a funeral with his sackcloth hanging loose. When his parents were dead, (a son) did not have his hair dressed in tufts (any more). With the large white (cap) they did not use strings hanging down. The purple strings with the dark-coloured cap began with duke Hwan of Lû[3].

6. In the morning they wore the dark-coloured square-cut dress; in the evening, the long dress in one piece. That dress at the waist was thrice the width of the sleeve; and at the bottom twice as wide as at the waist. It was gathered in at each side (of the body). The sleeve could be turned back to the elbow.

7. The outer or under garment joined on to the sleeve and covered a cubit of it[4]. The collar was 2 inches wide; the cuff, a cubit and 2 inches long; the border, $1\frac{1}{2}$ inch broad. To wear silk under or inside linen was contrary to rule.

8. An (ordinary) officer did not wear anything woven of silk that had been first dyed[5]. One who had left the service of his ruler wore no two articles of different colours.

---

[1] By way of punishment or disgrace.

[2] Also in punishment. See Book III, iv, 2–5. [3] B.C. 711–694.

[4] If we could see one dressed as in those early days, we should understand this better than we do.

[5] Because of its expensiveness.

If the upper garment were of one of the correct colours, the lower garment was of the (corresponding) intermediate one[1].

9. One did not enter the ruler's gate without the proper colours in his dress; nor in a single robe of grass-cloth, fine or coarse; nor with his fur robe either displayed outside, or entirely covered.

10. A garment wadded with new floss was called *k*ien; with old, phâo. One unlined was called *k*iung; one lined, but not wadded, tieh.

11. The use of thin white silk in court-robes began with *K*î Khang-ȝze. Confucius said, 'For the audience they use the (regular) court-robes, which are put on after the announcement of the first day of the month (in the temple).' He (also) said, 'When good order does not prevail in the states and clans, (the officers) should not use the full dress (as prescribed)[2].'

12. Only a ruler wore the chequered fur robe[3] in addressing (his troops or the multitudes), and at the autumnal hunts[4]. (For him) to wear the Great fur robe was contrary to ancient practice.

13. When a ruler wore the robe of white fox-fur, he wore one of embroidered silk over it to display it[5].

---

[1] The five 'correct' colours were azure (靑; of varying shade), scarlet (赤; carnation, the colour of the flesh), white, black, and yellow. The 'intermediate' were green (綠), red (紅), jade-green (碧), purple (紫), and bay-yellow (騮黃).

[2] See the concluding article in the 'Narratives of the School.' The words of Confucius are understood to intimate a condemnation of *K*î Khang-ȝze.

[3] Made of black lamb's fur and white fox-fur.

[4] Or, according to many, in giving charges about agriculture.

[5] Of one colour, worn by the king, at a border sacrifice.

When (the guards on) the right of the ruler wore tigers' fur, those on the left wore wolves' fur. An (ordinary) officer did not wear the fur of the white fox.

14. (Great and other) officers wore the fur of the blue fox, with sleeves of leopard's fur, and over it a jacket of dark-coloured silk to display it; with fawn's fur they used cuffs of the black wild dog[1], with a jacket of bluish yellow silk, to display it; with lamb's fur, ornaments of leopard's fur, and a jacket of black silk to display it; with fox-fur, a jacket of yellow silk to display it. A jacket of embroidered silk with fox-fur was worn by the feudal lords.

15. With dog's fur or sheep's fur[2], they did not wear any jacket of silk over it. Where there was no ornamentation, they did not use the jacket. The wearing the jacket was to show its beauty.

When condoling, they kept the jacket covered, and did now show all its ornamental character; in the presence of the ruler, they showed all this.

The covering of the dress was to hide its beauty. Hence, personators of the deceased covered their jackets of silk. Officers holding a piece of jade or a tortoise-shell (to present it) covered it; but if they had no (such official) business in hand, they displayed the silken garment, and did not presume to cover it.

16. For his memorandum-tablet, the son of Heaven used a piece of sonorous jade; the prince of a state, a piece of ivory; a Great officer, a piece of bamboo, ornamented with fishbone[3]; ordinary

---

[1] Or foreign dog. An animal like the tapir or rhinoceros is called by the same name, but cannot be meant here.

[2] 'The dress,' says *K*ăng, 'worn by the common people.'

[3] The bone seems to be specified; 須, read pan. What bone and of what fish, I do not know.

officers might use bamboo, adorned with ivory at the bottom.

17. When appearing before the son of Heaven, and at trials of archery, there was no such thing as being without this tablet. It was contrary to rule to enter the Grand temple without it. During the five months' mourning, it was not laid aside. When engaged in the performance of some business, and wearing the cincture, one laid it aside. When he had put it in his girdle, the bearer of it was required to wash his hands; but afterwards, though he had something to do in the court, he did not wash them (again).

When one had occasion to point to or draw anything before the ruler, he used the tablet. When he went before him and received a charge, he wrote it down on it. For all these purposes the tablet was used, and therefore it was ornamental.

18. The tablet was 2 cubits and 6 inches long. Its width at the middle was 3 inches; and it tapered away to 2½ inches (at the ends).

19. (A ruler) wore a plain white girdle of silk, with ornamented ends; a Great officer, a similar girdle, with the ends hanging down; an ordinary officer, one of dyed silk, with the edges tucked in, and the ends hanging down; a scholar waiting to be employed, one of embroidered silk; and young lads, one of white silk[1].

---

[1] From this paragraph to the end of the part, the text is in great confusion; with characters missing here and there, and sentences thrown together without natural connexion. *Kh*ăn Hâo has endeavoured to readjust them; but I have preferred to follow the order of the imperial and other editions. The *Kh*ien-lung editors advise the reader to do so, and make the best he can of them by means of *K*ăng Hsüan's notes. *Kh*ăn Hâo's order is—

20. For all these the buttons and loops were made of silk cords.

21. The knee-covers of a ruler were of vermilion colour; those of a Great officer, white; and of another officer, purple:—all of leather; and might be rounded, slanting, and straight. Those of the son of Heaven were straight (and pointed at all the corners); of the prince of a state, square both at bottom and top; of a Great officer, square at the bottom, with the corners at the top rounded off; and of another officer, straight both at bottom and top.

22. The width of these covers was 2 cubits at bottom, and 1 at top. Their length was 3 cubits. On each side of (what was called) the neck were 5 inches, reaching to the shoulders or corners. From the shoulders to the leathern band were 2 inches[1].

23. The great girdle of a Great officer was 4

paragraphs—25, 19, 20, 27, 23, 21, 22, 24, 26, 28, 29. By this arrangement something like a train of thought can be made out.

[1] The knee-covers of the prince of a state are represented thus—

; and of a Great officer,

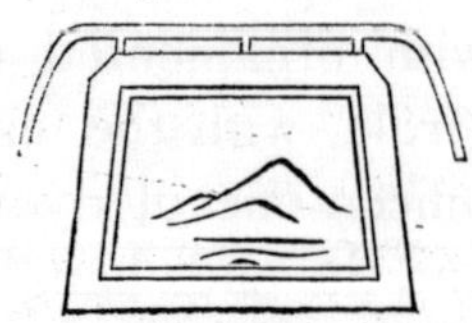

The middle suspender joined on to the top strap at the neck; the two others at the shoulders. On the central portions of the cover were represented certain of the emblems of distinction, according to the rank of the wearer:—dragons on the king's; flames on a prince's; and mountains on a Great officer's. But I do not think the makers of these figures had distinct ideas of the articles which they intended to represent. They certainly fail in giving the student such ideas. The colours, &c., moreover, appear to have varied with the occasions on which they were worn.

inches (wide)[1]. In variegated girdles, the colours for a ruler were vermilion and green; for a Great officer, cerulean and yellow; for an (ordinary) officer, a black border of 2 inches, and this, when carried round the body a second time, appeared to be 4 inches. On all girdles which were tucked in there was no needlework.

24. (An officer) who had received his first commission wore a cover of reddish-purple, with a black supporter for his girdle-pendant. One who had received the second commission wore a scarlet cover, (also) with a black supporter for the pendant; and one who had received the third commission, a scarlet cover, with an onion-green supporter for the pendant[2].

25. The son of Heaven wore a girdle of plain white silk, with vermilion lining, and ornamented ends.

26. The queen wore a robe with white pheasants embroidered on it; (a prince's) wife, one with green pheasants[3].

27. (The cords that formed the loops and buttons) were 3 inches long, equal to the breadth of the girdle. The rule for the length of the sash (descending from the girdle) was, that, for an officer, it should

---

[1] This, according to the *Kh*ien-lung editors, was the girdle or sash of 'correct dress,' and white. The variegated girdles, they say, were worn in private and when at leisure.

[2] The character for a knee-cover here (韍, fû) is different from that in paragraph 21 (韠, pî); but the *Kh*ien-lung editors say their significance is exactly the same. How the knee-covers and the supporter or balance-yard (衡, hăng) of the girdle pendant are spoken of together, I do not know.

[3] The pheasants here referred to are described as I have done in the *R*-Ya. The 'wife' is supposed also to include the ladies called the king's 'three helpmates' in Book I, ii, Part ii, 1.

be 3 cubits; for one discharging a special service, 2½. 3ze-yû said, 'Divide all below the girdle into three parts, and the sash will be equal to two of them. The sash, the knee-covers, and the ties are all of equal length[1].'

28. (The wife of a count or baron) who had received a degree of honour from the ruler[2] wore a pheasant cut out in silk on her robe; (the wife of the Great officer of a count or baron), who had received two degrees, wore a robe of fresh yellow; (the wife of a Great officer), who had received one degree, a robe of white; and the wife of an ordinary officer, a robe of black.

29. Only the ladies of honour[3] received their degree of appointment, when they presented their cocoons. The others all wore the dresses proper to them as the wives of their husbands.

---

[1] *Kh*ăn Hâo says, 'Man's length is 8 cubits; below the waist 4½ (= 45 inches). A third of this is 15 inches. 2 × 15 = 30 or 3 cubits, the length of the sash, and of the covers in par. 22.' The cubit must have been shorter than the name now indicates. I do not know what the 'ties' were.

[2] *K*ăng Hsüan took the ruler here to be feminine, and to mean 'the queen;' and, notwithstanding the protest of the *Kh*ien-lung editors, I think he was right. This paragraph and the next speak of the queen and ladies who were brought around her by their work in silk. Why may we not suppose that in her department she could confer distinction on the deserving as the king did in his? This passage seems to show that she did so.

[3] These ladies—'hereditary wives'—occur also in Bk. I, ii, Part ii, 1. It is commonly said that there were twenty-seven members of the royal harem, who had each that title; but there is much vagueness and uncertainty about all such statements. 'The others' must refer to the ladies, wives of the feudal lords and Great officers, whose rank gave them the privilege to co-operate with the queen in her direction of the nourishing of the silkworms and preparation of silk.

SECTION III.

1. All (officers) in attendance on the ruler let the sash hang down till their feet seemed to tread on the lower edge (of their skirt)[1]. Their chins projected like the eaves of a house, and their hands were clasped before them low down. Their eyes were directed downwards, and their ears were higher than the eyes. They saw (the ruler) from his girdle up to his collar. They listened to him with their ears turned to the left[2].

2. When the ruler called (an officer) to his presence, he might send three tokens. If two of them came to him, he ran (to answer the message); if (only) one, he yet walked quickly. If in his office, he did not wait for his shoes; if he were outside elsewhere, he did not wait for his carriage.

3. When an officer received a visit from a Great officer, he did not venture to bow (when he went) to meet him[3]; but he did so when escorting him on his departure. When he went to visit one of higher rank than himself, he first bowed (at the gate) and then went into his presence. If the other bowed to him in replying, he hurried on one side to avoid (the honour).

4. When an officer was speaking before the ruler, if he had occasion to speak of a Great officer who was dead, he called him by his posthumous epithet, or by the designation of his maturity; if of an officer

[1] See vol. xxvii, page 100, note 1.

[2] They were on the right of the ruler, and turned their ears to the left to hear him.

[3] That the more honourable visitor might not have the trouble of responding with a bow.

(who was similarly dead), he called him by his name. When speaking with a Great officer, he mentioned officers by their name, and (other) Great officers by their designation.

5. In speaking at a Great officer's, he avoided using the name of the (former) ruler, but not that of any of his own dead. At all sacrifices and in the ancestral temple, there was no avoiding of names. In school there was no avoiding of any character in the text.

6. Anciently, men of rank did not fail to wear their girdle-pendants with their precious stones, those on the right giving the notes *K*ih and *K*io, and those on the left Kung and Yü[1].

When (the king or ruler) was walking quickly (to the court of audience), he did so to the music of the Ʒhâi *Kh*î; when walking more quickly (back to the reception-hall), they played the Sze hsiâ[2]. When turning round, he made a complete circle; when turning in another direction, he did so at a right angle. When advancing, he inclined forward a little; he held himself up straight; and in all these movements, the pieces of jade emitted their tinklings. So also the man of rank, when in his carriage, heard the harmonious sounds of its bells; and, when walking, those of his pendant jade-stones; and in this way evil and depraved thoughts found no entrance into his mind.

7. When the ruler was present, (his son and heir)

[1] *K*ih and *K*io were the fourth and third notes of the musical scale, corresponding to our D and B; Kung and Yü, the first and fifth, corresponding to G and E. See the Chinese Classics, vol. iii, p. 84, note.

[2] Ʒhâi *Kh*î is taken as another name for the Khû Ʒhze, Chinese Classics, vol. iii, pp. 317-318.

did not wear the pendant of jade-stones. He tied it up on the left of his girdle, and left free the pendant (of useful things) on the right. When seated at ease, he wore the (jade) pendant; but in court, he tied it up[1].

In fasting and vigil they wore it, but the strings were turned round, and fastened at the girdle. They wore then the purple knee-covers[1].

8. All wore the jade-stone pendant at the girdle, excepting during the mourning rites. (At the end of the middle string) in it was the tooth-like piece, colliding with the others. A man of rank was never without this pendant, excepting for some sufficient reason; he regarded the pieces of jade as emblematic of the virtues (which he should cultivate).

9. The son of Heaven had his pendant composed of beads of white jade, hung on dark-coloured strings; a duke or marquis, his of jade-beads of hill-azure, on vermilion strings; a Great officer, his of beads of aqua-marine, on black strings; an heir-son, his of beads of Yü jade, on variegated strings; an ordinary officer, his of beads of jade-like quartz, on orange-coloured strings.

Confucius wore at his pendant balls of ivory[2], five inches (round), on gray strings.

10. According to the regulations for (the dress of) a lad[3], his upper garment was of black linen,

---

[1] There were three pendants from the girdle:—the jade-stone in the middle, called the pendant of 'virtue;' and two others of useful things on the left and right, of which we shall read by and by. The subject of the first two sentences is said, correctly as I think, to be the heir-son of a ruler; while the last two have a more general application.

[2] Or 'an ivory ring.' [3] One who had not yet been capped.

with an embroidered edging. His sash was embroidered, and (also) the strings for the button-loops (of his girdle). With such a string he bound up his hair. The embroidered border and strings were all red.

11. When the ends of fastening strings reached to the girdle, if they had any toilsome business to do, they put them aside. If they were running, they thrust them in the breast[1].

12. A lad did not wear furs, nor silk, nor the ornamental points on his shoes. He did not wear the three months' mourning. He did not wear the hempen band, when receiving any orders. When he had nothing to do (in mourning rites), he stood on the north of the principal mourner, with his face to the south. When going to see a teacher, he followed in the suite of others, and entered his apartment.

13. When one was sitting at a meal with another older than himself, or of a different (and higher) rank, he was the last to put down the offering[2], but the first to taste the food. When the guest put down the offering, the host apologised, saying that the food was not worthy of such a tribute. When the guest was enjoying the viands, the host apologised for their being scanty and poor. When the host himself put down the pickle (for the guest), the guest himself removed it. When the members of a household ate together, not being host and guests, one of them removed the dishes; and the same was done when a company had eaten together. At all festival meals, the women (of the house) did not remove the dishes.

---

[1] This paragraph seems to be out of place. *K*ăng thought should follow the first sentence of paragraph 27 in the last part.

[2] By way of thanksgiving to the father of Cookery.

14. When eating dates, peaches, or plums, they did not cast the stones away (on the ground)[1]. They put down the first slice of a melon as an offering, ate the other slices, and threw away the part by which they held it. When others were eating fruits with a man of rank, they ate them after him; cooked viands they ate before him[2]. At meetings of rejoicing, if there were not some gift from the ruler, they did not congratulate one another; at meetings of sorrow[3], ...

15. If one had any toilsome business to do, he took them in his hand. If he were running, he thrust them in his breast[4].

16. When Confucius was eating with (the head of) the *K*î family, he made no attempt to decline anything, but finished his meal with the rice and liquid added to it, without eating any of the flesh[5].

17. When the ruler sent (to an officer) the gift of a carriage and horses, he used them in going to give thanks for them. When the gift was of clothes, he wore them on the same occasion. (In the case of similar gifts to a commissioner from the king), until his (own) ruler had given him orders to use them, he did not dare at once to do so[6]. When the ruler's

[1] Compare vol. xxvii, page 81, paragraph 62.

[2] Fruits were the productions of nature, and there could be no poison in them. Cooked food might have been tampered with, and those in attendance on a superior man first tasted it as a precaution for his safety.

[3] The conclusion is evidently lost.

[4] A mistaken and meaningless repetition of part of paragraph 11.

[5] To express, it is supposed, his dissatisfaction with some want of courtesy in his host.

[6] This sentence is perplexing, and there are different views in interpreting it. I have followed *K*ăng Hsüan.

gift reached him, he bowed his head to the ground with his two hands also, laying one of them over the other. A gift of liquor and flesh did not require the second expression of thanks (by the visit).

18. Whenever a gift was conferred on a man of rank, nothing was given to a small man on the same day.

19. In all cases of presenting offerings to a ruler, a Great officer sent his steward with them, and an ordinary officer went with them himself. In both cases they did obeisance twice, with their heads to the ground as they sent the things away; and again the steward and the officer did the same at the ruler's[1]. If the offerings were of prepared food for the ruler, there were the accompaniments of ginger and other pungent vegetables, of a peach-wood and a sedge-broom[2]. A Great officer dispensed with the broom, and the officer with the pungent vegetables. (The bearers) went in with all the articles to the cook. The Great officer did not go in person to make obeisance, lest the ruler should come to respond to him.

20. When a Great officer went (next day) to do obeisance for the ruler's gift, he retired after performing the ceremony. An officer, (doing the same), waited to receive the ruler's acknowledgment (of his visit), and then retired, bowing again as he did so; but (the ruler) did not respond to his obeisance.

When a Great officer gave anything in person to an ordinary officer, the latter bowed on receiving

[1] This translation seems to make too much out of the text; but it is after Khung Ying-tâ, *Kh*ăn Hâo, and others.

[2] Such presents might decompose or become offensive, and therefore these accompaniments were sent with them.

it; and also went to his house to repeat the obeisance. He did not, however, wear the clothes (which might have been the gift), in going to make that obeisance.

(In interchanges between) equals, if (the recipient) were in the house (when the gift arrived), he went and made his obeisance in the house (of the donor).

21. When any one presented an offering to his superior in rank, he did not dare to say directly that it was for him[1].

An ordinary officer did not presume to receive the congratulations of a Great officer; but a Great officer of the lowest grade did so from one of the highest.

When one was exchanging courtesies with another, if his father were alive, he would appeal to his authority; if the other gave him a gift, he would say, in making obeisance for it, that he did so for his father.

22. If the ceremony were not very great, the (beauty of the) dress was not concealed. In accordance with this, when the great robe of fur was worn, it was without the appendage of one of thin silk to display it, and when (the king) rode in the grand carriage, he did not bend forward to the cross-bar (to show his reverence for any one beyond the service he was engaged on)[2].

---

[1] He would say, for instance, that it was for some member of his household.

[2] There are only fifteen characters in this paragraph, nor is there any intricacy in its structure, but few passages in the collection perplex a translator more. If we leave out the negatives in the former sentence, the meaning becomes clear. The grand carriage and grand fur-robe were used at the greatest of all ceremonies, the solstitial sacrifice to Heaven, which itself so occupied the mind

23. When a father's summons came to him, a son reverently obeyed it without any delay. Whatever work he had in hand, he laid aside. He ejected the meat that was in his mouth, and rân, not contenting himself with a measured, though rapid pace. When his parents were old and he had gone away, he did not go to a second place, nor delay his return beyond the time agreed on; when they were ailing, his looks and manner appeared troubled:—these were less-important observances of a filial son.

24. When his father died, he could not (bear to) read his books;—the touch of his hand seemed still to be on them. When his mother died, he could not (bear to) drink from the cups and bowls that she had used;—the breath of her mouth seemed still to be on them.

25. When a ruler, (visiting another ruler), was about to enter the gate, the attendant dusted the low post (at the middle of the threshold). The Great officers stood midway between the side-posts and this short post (behind their respective rulers). An officer, acting as an attendant, brushed the side-posts.

(A Great officer) on a mission from another court, did not enter at the middle of (either half of) the gate, nor tread on the threshold. If he were come on public business, he entered on the west of the short post; if on his own business, on the east of it.

26. A ruler and a representative of the dead brought their feet together step by step when they walked; a Great officer stepped along, one foot after the other; an ordinary officer kept the length of his

---

of the sovereign that he was supposed to think of nothing else. The paragraph might have had a more appropriate place in the seventh Book or the ninth.

foot between his steps. In walking slowly, they all observed these rules. In walking rapidly, while they wished to push on (and did so), they were not allowed to alter the motion either of hands or feet. In turning their feet inwards or outwards, they did not lift them up, and the edge of the lower garment dragged along, like the water of a stream. In walking on the mats it was the same.

When walking erect, (the body was yet bent, and) the chin projected like the eaves of a house, and their advance was straight as an arrow. When walking rapidly, the body had the appearance of rising constantly with an elevation of the feet. When carrying a tortoise-shell or (a symbol of) jade, they raised their toes and trailed their heels, presenting an appearance of carefulness.

27. In walking (on the road), the carriage of the body was straight and smart; in the ancestral temple, it was reverent and grave; in the court, it was exact and easy.

28. The carriage of a man of rank was easy, but somewhat slow;—grave and reserved, when he saw any one whom he wished to honour. He did not move his feet lightly, nor his hands irreverently. His eyes looked straightforward, and his mouth was kept quiet and composed. No sound from him broke the stillness, and his head was carried upright. His breath came without panting or stoppage, and his standing gave (the beholder) an impression of virtue. His looks were grave, and he sat like a personator of the dead[1]. When at leisure and at ease, and in conversation, he looked mild and bland.

[1] See vol. xxvii, page 62, paragraph 6, and note 2.

29. At all sacrifices, the bearing and appearance (of the worshippers) made it appear as if they saw those to whom they were sacrificing.

30. When engaged with the mourning rites, they had a wearied look, and an aspect of sorrow and unrest. Their eyes looked startled and dim, and their speech was drawling and low.

31. The carriage of a martialist was bold and daring; his speech had a tone of decision and command; his face was stern and determined; and his eyes were clear and bright.

32. He stood with an appearance of lowliness, but with no indication of subserviency. His head rose straight up from the centre of the neck. He stood (firm) as a mountain, and his movements were well timed. His body was well filled with the volume of his breath, which came forth powerfully like that of nature. His complexion showed (the beauty and strength of) a piece of jade[1].

33. When they spoke of themselves, the style of the son of Heaven was, 'I, the One man,' a chief of regions described himself as 'The strong minister

[1] On the translation of this, and many of the paragraphs immediately preceding, Callery says:—'The Chinese text contains dissyllabic expressions very difficult to translate, because they are a sort of onomatopœias, which have nothing in common with the nature of the things to which they are applied. We could do nothing better with them than adopt the sense given by the commentators.' But these binomial combinations, which are often repetitions of the same character, are only onomatopoietic in the sense in which all words, sensuously descriptive at first, are applied by the mind to express its own concepts; metaphorical rather than onomatopoietic. They are very common in the Shih, or Book of Poetry, and in all passionate, descriptive composition. So it is in other languages as well as Chinese.

of the son of Heaven;' the relation of a feudal lord expressed itself by 'So and So, the guardian of such and such a territory.' If the fief were on the borders, he used the style—'So and So, the minister in such and such a screen.' Among his equals and those below him, he called himself 'The man of little virtue.' The ruler of a small state called himself 'The orphan.' The officer who answered for him (at a higher court) also styled him so[1].

34. A Great officer of the highest grade (at his own court), called himself 'Your inferior minister;' (at another court), his attendant who answered for him, described him as 'The ancient of our poor ruler.' A Great officer of the lowest grade (at his own court), called himself by his name; (at another court), his attendant described him as 'Our unworthy Great officer.' The son and heir of a feudal prince (at his own court), called himself by his name; (at another court), his attendant described him as 'The rightful son of our unworthy ruler.'

35. A ruler's son (by an inferior lady) called himself 'Your minister, the shoot from the stock.' An (ordinary) officer styled himself 'Your minister, the fleet courier;' to a Great officer, he described himself as 'The outside commoner.' When a Great officer went on a mission about private affairs, a man of his private establishment went with him as his spokesman, and called him by his name.

36. When an officer belonging to the ruler's establishment acted (at another court for a Great officer), he spoke of him as 'Our unworthy Great officer,' or 'The ancient of our unworthy ruler.'

[1] So, most commentators; but this last sentence is not clear.

When a Great officer went on any mission, it was the rule that he should have such an officer from the ruler's establishment with him, to answer for him.

PLAN OF THE HALL OF DISTINCTION.

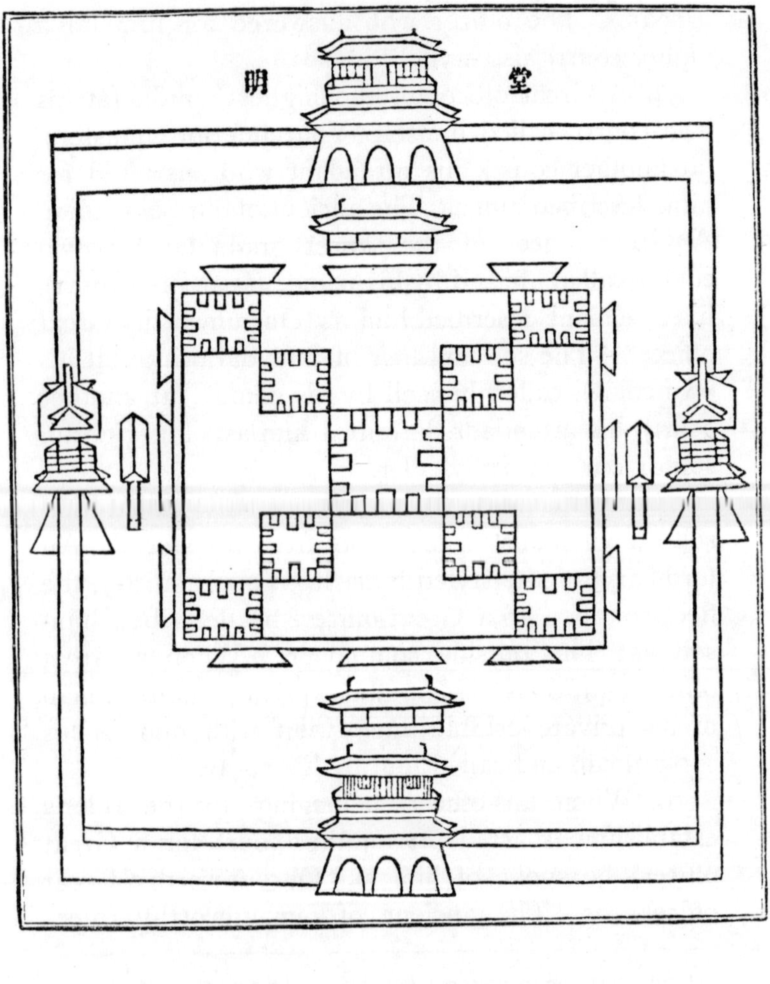

BOOK XII. MING THANG WEI

OR

THE PLACES IN THE HALL OF DISTINCTION[1].

1. Formerly, when the duke of *K*âu gave audience to the feudal princes in their several places in the Hall of Distinction, the son of Heaven stood with his back to the axe-embroidered screen[2], and his face towards the south[3].

2. The three dukes[4] were in front of the steps, in the middle, with their faces to the north, inclining to the east as the most honourable position[5]. The places of the marquises were at the east of the

---

[1] See introductory notice, vol. xxvii, pp. 28–30. On the opposite page there is the plan of the Hall, as given in Morrison's Dictionary, vol. i, part i, page 512. Compare it with the less complicated figure in vol. xxvii, page 252.

[2] See vol. xxvii, page 111, paragraph 11.

[3] Many chronological and other perplexing questions arise in connexion with the great audience described in this and the paragraphs that immediately follow. The time should be referred, I think, to the inauguration of Lo as the eastern capital of *K*âu, probably in B.C. 1109, at the close of the duke of *K*âu's regency for the young king *Kh*ăng; see the Shû, V, xiii. That 'the son of Heaven' must be understood of king *Kh*ăng himself, and not of the duke of *K*âu, is a point, it seems to me, that no Chinese commentator should ever have called in question.

[4] The three Kung, I suppose, mentioned in vol. iii, page 227, paragraph 3. The duke of *K*âu was himself one of them; but perhaps, during his regency, another had been appointed in his place.

[5] The text here simply = 'the east the upper.' The nearer one was to the king, the more honourable was his position.

eastern steps, with their faces to the west, inclining to the north as the most honourable position. The lords of the earldoms were at the west of the western steps, with their faces to the east, inclining also and for the same reason to the north. The counts were on the east of the gate, with their faces to the north, inclining to the east as the more honourable position. The barons were on the west of the gate, with their faces to the north, inclining also and for the same reason to the east.

3. The chiefs of the nine Î[1] were outside the eastern door, with their faces to the west, inclining to the north as the position of honour; those of the eight Mân were outside the door on the south, with their faces to the north, inclining for the same reason to the east; those of the six *Z*ung were outside the door on the west, with their faces to the east, inclining for the same reason to the south; and those of the five Tî were outside the door on the north, with their faces to the south, inclining for the same reason to the east.

4. The chiefs of the nine 3hâi were outside the Ying gate, with their faces to the north, inclining to the east as the position of honour for them; those of the four Sâi (also) came, who had only once in their time to announce their arrival (at the court). These were the places of the lords in the Hall of Distinction (when they appeared before) the duke of *K*âu[2].

---

[1] Î was the general name for the wild tribes of the east; Mân, for those of the south; *Z*ung, for those of the west; and Tî, for those of the north.

[2] It is so difficult to explain what is meant by 'the nine 3hâi,' and again by 'the four Sâi,' that I am inclined to doubt, with Wang Yen (王炎) and others, the genuineness of this paragraph.

5. The Hall of Distinction was so called, because in it the rank of the princes was clearly shown as high or low[1].

6. Formerly, when *K*âu of Yin was throwing the whole kingdom into confusion, he made dried slices of (the flesh of) the marquis of Kwei[2], and used them in feasting the princes. On this account the duke of *K*âu assisted king Wû in attacking *K*âu. When king Wû died, king *Kh*ăng being young and weak, the duke took the seat of the son of Heaven[3], and governed the kingdom. During six years he gave audience to all the princes in the Hall of Distinction; instituted ceremonies, made his instruments of music, gave out his (standard) weights and measures[4], and there was a grand submission throughout the kingdom.

7. In the seventh year, he resigned the government to king *Kh*ăng; and he, in consideration of the duke's services to the kingdom, invested him with (the territory about) *Kh*ü-fû[5], seven hundred lî square, and sending forth a thousand chariots of

---

[1] See the introduction, vol. xxvii, page 28.

[2] 'The marquis of Kwei' appears in Sze-mâ *Kh*ien's history of Yin (near the end), as the marquis of *Kh*iû (九侯), and is made into pickle. The reference, no doubt, is to some act of atrocious and wanton cruelty on the part of *K*âu.

[3] This can only mean that the duke, as regent, administered the government, though the compiler of the Book wanted to exalt his personality beyond the bounds of truth.

[4] The text is—measures of length and of capacity.

[5] *Kh*ü-fû is still a district city in the department of Yen-*k*âu, Shan-tung. It was the capital of Lû; and is called by foreigners 'the city of Confucius.' It contains the great temple of the sage, and is the residence of his representative-descendant, with thousands of other Khungs.

war[1]. He (also) gave charge that (the princes of) Lû, from generation to generation, should sacrifice to the duke of *K*âu with the ceremonies and music proper at a sacrifice by the son of Heaven.

8. Thus it was that the rulers of Lû, in the first month of spring, rode in a grand carriage, displaying the banner, suspended from its bow-like arm, with the twelve streamers, and having the sun and moon emblazoned on it, to sacrifice to God in the suburb of their metropolis, associating Hâu *K*î as his assessor in the service;—according to the ceremonies used by the son of Heaven[2].

9. In the last month of summer, the sixth month, they used the ceremonies of the great sacrifice in sacrificing to the duke of *K*âu in the great ancestral temple, employing for the victim to him a white bull. The cups were those with the figure of a victim bull, of an elephant, and of hills and clouds that for the fragrant spirits was the one with gilt eyes on it. For libations they used the cup of jade with the handle made of a long rank-symbol. The dishes with the offerings were on stands of wood, adorned with jade and carved. The cups for the personator were of jade carved in the same way. There were also the plain cups and those of horn, adorned with round pieces of jade; and for the meat-stands, they used those with four feet and the cross-binders.

10. (The singers) went up to the hall (or stage),

[1] This is one of the gross exaggerations in the Book. The marquisate of Lû was only a hundred lî square on its first constitution.

[2] Of this and many of the statements in the paragraphs that follow, see the fourth of the 'Praise Odes of Lû,' in the Shih, Metrical version, pp. 379-383.

and sang the *Kh*ing Miâo; (in the court) below, (the pantomimes) performed the Hsiang dance[1], to the accompaniment of the wind instruments. With their red shields and jade-adorned axes, and in their caps with pendants, they danced to the music of the Tâ Wû[2]; in their skin caps, and large white skirts gathered at the waist, and jacket of silk, they danced the Tâ Hsiâ[3]. There (were also) the Mei, or music of the wild tribes of the East; and the *Z*ăn, or music of those of the South. The introduction of these two in the grand temple was to signalise the distinction of Lû all over the kingdom.

11. The ruler, in his dragon-figured robe and cap with pendants, stood at the eastern steps; and his wife, in her head-dress and embroidered robe, stood in her room. The ruler, with shoulder bared, met the victim at the gate; his wife brought in the stands for the dishes. The ministers and Great officers assisted the ruler; their wives[4] assisted his wife. Each one discharged the duty proper to him or her. Any officer who neglected his duty was severely punished; and throughout the kingdom there was a great acknowledgment of, and submission to, (the worth of the duke of *K*âu).

12. (In Lû) they offered (also) the sacrifices of summer, autumn, and winter (in the ancestral temple); with those at the altars of the land and grain in spring, and that at the autumnal hunt, going on to the great sacrifice of thanksgiving at

[1] See vol. xxvii, page 361, paragraph 21.

[2] Attributed to king Wû. [3] Said to be of the Hsiâ dynasty.

[4] 'The commissioned wives;' including, according to *Kh*ăn Hâo, the ruler's 'ladies of honour,' as well as the wives of his ministers and Great officers.

the end of the year:—all (after the pattern of) the sacrifices of the son of Heaven.

13. The grand temple (of Lû) corresponded to the Hall of Distinction of the son of Heaven, the Khû gate of the (marquis's palace) to the Kâo (or outer) gate of the king's, and the *K*ih gate to the Ying[1]. They shook the bell with the wooden clapper in the court as was done in the royal court, in announcing governmental orders.

14. The capitals of the pillars with hills carved on them, and the pond-weed carving on the small pillars above the beams; the second storey and the great beams projecting under the eaves; the polished pillars and the windows opposite to one another; the earthen stand on which the cups, after being used, were placed; the high stand on which the jade tokens were displayed aloft; and the slightly carved screen:—all these were ornaments of the temple of the son of Heaven[2].

15. (The princes of Lû) had, as carriages, that of (Shun), the lord of Yü, furnished with bells; that of the sovereign of Hsiâ, with its carved front; the Great carriage (of wood), or that of Yin; and the carriage (adorned with jade), or that of *K*âu.

16. They had, as flags or banners, that of (Shun), the lord of Yü; the yak's tail of the sovereign of Hsiâ; the great white flag of Yin; and the corresponding red one of *K*âu.

---

[1] The five gates of the royal palace, beginning with the outermost, were the Kâo (皐), the Khû (庫), the *K*ih (雉), the Ying (應), and the Lû (路); the palaces of the princes wanted the Kâo and Ying gates. The grand temples appear to have been constructed on a similar plan, to the east of the palace.

[2] And in the temple of Lû, also, it is implied.

17. They had the white horses of the sovereign of Hsiâ, with their black manes; the white horses of Yin, with their black heads; and the bay horses of *K*âu, with red manes. The sovereigns of Hsiâ preferred black victims; those of Yin, white; and those of *K*âu, victims which were red and strong.

18. Of jugs for liquor, they had the earthenware jug of the lord of Yü; the jug of Hsiâ, with clouds and hills figured on it; the *k*o of Yin, with no base, which rested directly on the ground; and the jugs of *K*âu, with a victim-bull or an elephant on them.

19. For bowls or cups they had the *k*ân[1] of Hsiâ; the *k*iâ of Yin[2]; and the *k*io of *K*âu[3].

20. For libations they had the jug of Hsiâ, with a cock on it; the *k*iâ of Yin; and that of *K*âu, with gilt eyes on it.

For ladles they had that of Hsiâ, with the handle ending in a dragon's head; that of Yin, slightly carved all over; and that of *K*âu, with the handle like plaited rushes.

21. They had the earthen drum, with clods for the drumstick and the reed pipe,—producing the music of Î-*kh*î[4]; the pillow-like bundles of chaff,

---

[1] Made of jade, or adorned with it.

[2] With plants of grain figured on it.

[3] Also made of, or adorned with, jade.

[4] Î-*kh*î is said by *K*ăng to be 'the dynastic title of an ancient son of Heaven.' Many identify him with Shăn Năng, who generally follows Fû-hsî in the chronology, and who cannot be placed later than the thirty-first century B. C., if we can speak at all of so distant dates. Evidently the compiler is putting down the names of the most ancient instruments which he had heard of. There is in the *Kh*ien-lung edition of our collection, chapter 81, page 5, a representation of the drum and its handle; with a collection of the views about them, contradictory and fantastical,

which were struck[1]; the sounding stone of jade; the instruments rubbed or struck, (to regulate the commencement and close of the music)[2]; the great lute and great cithern; the medium lute and little cithern[3]:—the musical instruments of the four dynasties.

22. The temple of the duke of Lû was maintained from generation to generation like that of (king) Wăn (in the capital of *K*âu), and the temple of duke Wû in the same way like that of (king) Wû[4].

23. They had the hsiang (school) of the lord of Yü, in connexion with which were kept the stores of (sacrificial) rice[5]; the hsü school of the sovereign of Hsiâ; the school of Yin, in which the blind were

---

so that it is not worth while to reproduce them here. There is a figure also of the reed pipe, which can only have been something a little superior to the early 'oaten pipe' of the west.

[1] This also is represented in the *Kh*ien-lung edition; but how anything like music could be brought from the pillows I do not know. The two characters, supposed to give the name, are found, perhaps, in the Shu, II, iv, 9, used with verbal force of playing on the lute.

[2] The *K*û and Yü, see vol. xxvii, pages 219 and 273.

[3] The invention of the lute and cithern is ascribed to Fû-hsî. They are represented thus—

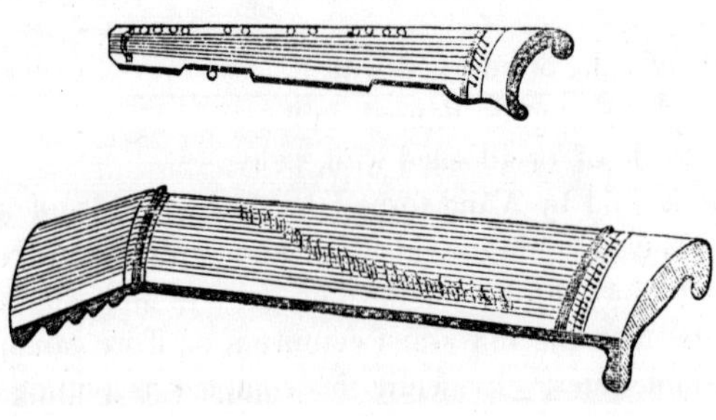

[4] The duke of Lû here is the first duke, Po-*kh*in (B.C. 1115–1063). Duke Wû was the ninth duke (B.C. 826–817).

[5] As a lesson, it is said, of filial duty.

honoured[1]; and the college of *K*âu, with its semicircle of water.

24. They had the tripods of *Kh*ung[2] and Kwan[2]; the great jade hemisphere; and the tortoise-shell of Făng-fû[3]:—all articles (properly) belonging to the son of Heaven. They (also) had the lance of Yüeh[3]; and the great bow,—military weapons of the son of Heaven.

25. They had the drum of Hsiâ supported on four legs; that of Yin supported on a single pillar; the drums of *K*âu, pendent from a stand; the peal of bells of Sui[4]; the differently toned *kh*ing (sonorous stones) of Shû[5]; and the organ of Nü-kwâ[6], with its tongues.

26. They had the music-stand of Hsiâ, with its face-board and posts, on which dragons were carved; that of Yin, with the high-toothed face-board; and that of *K*âu, with its round ornaments of jade, and feathers (hung from the corners).

---

[1] The father of Music, it is said, was here sacrificed to, or had offerings presented to him. All this is very uncertain. Blind men were used as musicians.

[2] These are names of states mentioned in the Shû, with which we find king Wăn at war.

[3] Făng-fû must also be the name of an ancient state; but where it was I do not know. Yüeh was a great state, south of Wû, on the seaboard.

[4] See the Shû, II, i, 21, and note.

[5] Shû was also called Wû-kâu (無句).

[6] Nü-kwâ is placed between Fû-hsî and Shăn Năng. Various fabulous marvels are related of him or her (for many hold the name to be that of a female) in the account of the five Tîs, prefixed to Sze-mâ *Kh*ien's histories. The organ is represented thus—

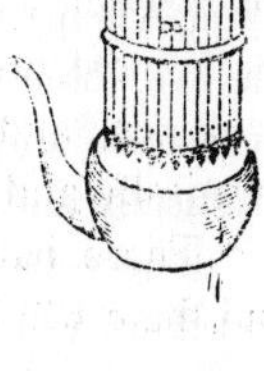

27. They had the two tui of the lord of Yü (for holding the grain at sacrifices); the four lien of Hsiâ; the six hû of Yin; and the eight kwei of *K*âu[1].

28. They had for stands (on which to set forth the flesh of the victims), the khwan of Shun; the *k*üeh of Hsiâ; the *k*ü of Yin; and the room-like stand of *K*âu. For the tall supports of the dishes, they used those of Hsiâ of unadorned wood; those of Yin, adorned with jade; and those of *K*âu, with feathers carved on them.

29. They had the plain leather knee-covers of Shun; those of Hsiâ, with hills represented on them; those of Yin, with flames; and those of *K*âu, with dragons.

30. They used for their sacrificial offerings (to the father of Cookery), like the lord of Yü, (portions of) the head; like the sovereigns of Hsiâ, (portions of) the heart; as they did under Yin, (portions of) the liver; and as they did under *K*âu, (portions of) the lungs[2].

31. They used the bright water preferred by Hsiâ; the unfermented liquor preferred by Yin; and the completed liquor preferred by *K*âu[3].

---

[1] Figures of all these are given. The number of the vessels in the different dynasties is thought to have been regulated by the number of the kinds of grain; but most of this is conjecture.

[2] *K*ăng Hsüan, in explanation of these practices, has only three characters, which I confess I do not fully comprehend. Khung Ying-tâ says nothing about them, nor the *Kh*ien-lung editors. Fang *K*üeh writes, on the relation between the five elements and the five colours, and the symbolical colours adopted by the different dynasties, and of the different members of the victims; very mystically and darkly, and failing to elucidate the passage.

[3] There have been various references to these points already, and there will be more hereafter.

32. They used (the names) of the 50 officers of the lord of Yü; of the 100 of the sovereigns of Hsiâ; of the 200 of Yin; and of the 300 of *K*âu[1].

33. (At their funerals) they used the feathery ornaments of the lord of Yü; the wrappings of white silk (about the flag-staffs) of the sovereigns of Hsiâ; (the flags) with their toothed edges of Yin; and the round pieces of jade and plumes of *K*âu[2].

34. Lû (thus) used the robes, vessels and officers of all the four dynasties, and so it observed the royal ceremonies. It long transmitted them everywhere. Its rulers and ministers never killed one another. Its rites, music, punishments, laws, governmental proceedings, manners and customs never changed. Throughout the kingdom it was considered the state which exhibited the right ways; and therefore dependence was placed on it in the matters of ceremonies and music[3].

---

[1] Compare the Shû, V, xx, 3. Various attempts are made to reconcile the statements there and those of this paragraph; 'all,' says *Kh*ăn Hâo, 'mere conjectures.'

[2] Compare paragraph 22, page 139, vol. xxvii.

[3] Much of what is said here is glaringly false; and justifies what is said of the Book in the introduction, page 29.

BOOK XIII. SANG FÛ HSIÂO *K*Î

OR

RECORD OF SMALLER MATTERS IN THE DRESS OF MOURNING[1].

Section I.

1. When wearing the unhemmed sackcloth (for a father), (the son) tied up his hair with a hempen (band), and also when wearing it for a mother. When he exchanged this band for the cincture (in the case of mourning for his mother)[2], this was made of linen cloth.

(A wife)[3], when wearing the (one year's mourning) of sackcloth with the edges even, had the girdle (of the same), and the inferior hair-pin (of hazel-wood), and wore these to the end of the mourning.

2. (Ordinarily) men wore the cap, and women the hair-pin; (in mourning) men wore the cincture, and women the same after the female fashion.

---

[1] See the introductory notice, vol. xxvii, page 30.

[2] This was done after the slighter dressing of the corpse. The cincture (wăn, 免) is mentioned in the first paragraph of the Than Kung (vol. xxvii, page 120). The hempen band being removed, one of linen cloth, about the breadth of which there are different accounts, was put round the hair on the crown, taken forward to the forehead, there crossed, taken back again, and knotted at the back of the hair.

[3] The text does not mention 'the wife' here; but a comparison of different passages shows that this sentence is only applicable to her.

The idea was (simply) to maintain in this way a distinction between them [1].

3. The dark-coloured staff was of bamboo; that pared and fashioned (at the end) was of eleococca wood [2].

4. When the grandfather was dead, and afterwards (the grandson) had to go into mourning for his grandmother, he, being the representative of the family (through the death of his father), did so for three years.

5. The eldest son, (at the mourning rites) for his father or mother, (before bowing to a visitor who had come to condole with him), first laid his forehead to the ground (as an expression of his sorrow).

When a Great officer came to condole (with an ordinary officer), though it might be (only) in a case of the three months' mourning, (the latter first) laid his forehead to the ground [3].

A wife, at the rites for her husband or eldest son, bowed her head to the ground before she saluted

---

[1] Anciently, it is said, there was no distinction between these two cinctures, but in the name. There probably came to be some difference between them; but what it was I cannot discover.

[2] This is found also in the Î Lî, XXXII, 5; but the interpretation there is as difficult as here. The translation of the first character (苴, ȝhü) by 'dark-coloured' is from Khung Ying-tâ. The paring away the end of the dryandria branch was to make it square. The round bamboo was carried in mourning for a father, and was supposed to symbolise heaven; the other was carried in mourning for a mother, and its square end symbolised earth. What heaven and earth were to nature that the father and mother were to a child. I can make nothing more or better of the passage.

[3] We do not see how this instance coheres with the former one; nor why the two are brought together.

a visitor; but in mourning for others, she did not do so[1].

6. The man employed to preside (at the mourning rites) was required to be of the same surname (as the deceased parent); the wife so employed, of a different surname[2].

7. The son who was his father's successor (as now head of the family) did not wear mourning for his mother who had been divorced.

8. In counting kindred (and the mourning to be worn of them), the three closest degrees become expanded into five, and those five again into nine. The mourning diminished as the degrees ascended or descended, and the collateral branches also were correspondingly less mourned for; and the mourning for kindred thus came to an end[3].

9. At the great royal sacrifice to all ancestors, the first place was given to him from whom the founder of the line sprang, and that founder had the place of assessor to him. There came thus to be established four ancestral shrines[4]. In the

[1] The 'others,' according to *K*ăng, must be understood of her own parents. She was now identified with a family of another surname; and her husband's relatives were more to her than her own.

[2] The son and his wife who should have presided are supposed to be dead. The wife elected for the office would be the wife of some other member of the family, herself therefore of a different surname.

[3] The three closest degrees are 'father, son, and son's son.' Add the grandfather and grandson (counting from the son), and we have five; great-grandfather and great-grandson (here omitted), and we have seven. Then great-great-grandfather and great-great-grandson, make nine; and the circle of kindred, for whom mourning should be worn, is complete. See Appendix, Book II, vol. xxvii.

[4] This statement about the four shrines has given occasion to much writing.

case of a son by another than the queen coming to be king, the same course was observed.

10. When a son other than (the eldest) became the ancestor (of a branch of the same line), his successor was its Honoured Head, and he who followed him (in the line) was its smaller Honoured Head. After five generations there was a change again of the Honoured Head; but all in continuation of the High Ancestor.

11. Hence the removal of the ancestor took place high up (in the line), and the change of the Honoured Head low down (in it). Because they honoured the ancestor, they reverenced the Honoured Head; their reverencing the Honoured Head was the way in which they expressed the honour which they paid to the ancestor and his immediate successor [1].

12. That any other son but the eldest did not sacrifice to his grandfather showed that (only he was in the direct line from) the Honoured Head (of their branch of the family). So, no son but he wore the (three years') unhemmed sackcloth for his eldest son, because the eldest son of no other continued (the direct line) of the grandfather and father [2].

13. None of the other sons sacrificed to a son

[1] The subject imperfectly described in these two paragraphs,—the manner in which a family, ever lengthening its line and multiplying its numbers, was divided into collateral branches, will come before the reader again in the next Book.

[2] It is difficult to catch exactly the thought in the writer of these, and several of the adjacent, sentences. Even the native critics, down to the *Kh*ien-lung editors, seem to experience the difficulty.

(of his own) who had died prematurely, or one who had left no posterity. (The tablet of) such an one was placed along with that of his grandfather, and shared in the offerings made to him.

14. Nor could any of them sacrifice to their father; showing that (the eldest son was the representative of) the Honoured Head.

15. (In the distinctions of the mourning) for the kindred who are the nearest, the honoured ones to whom honour is paid, the elders who are venerated for their age, and as the different tributes to males and females; there are seen the greatest manifestations of the course which is right for men.

16. Where mourning would be worn from one's relation with another for parties simply on the ground of that affinity, when that other was dead, the mourning ceased. Where it would have been worn for them on the ground of consanguinity, even though that other were dead, it was still worn[1].

When a concubine had followed a ruler's wife to the harem, and the wife came to be divorced, the concubine, (following her out of the harem), did not wear mourning for her son[2].

17. According to the rules, no one but the king offered the united sacrifice to all ancestors[3].

---

[1] Khung Ying-tâ specifies six cases coming under the former of these cases, and four under the second. It is not necessary to set them forth. The *Kh*ien-lung editors say that the paragraph has reference only to the practice of the officer; for a Great officer did not wear mourning either for his wife or mother's kin.

[2] This concubine would be either of the near relatives of the wife, who had gone with her on her marriage.

[3] This paragraph is out of place. It should have formed part, probably, of paragraph 9.

18. The heir-son (of the king or a feudal lord) did not diminish the mourning for the parents of his wife. For his wife he wore the mourning which the eldest and rightful son of a Great officer did for his [1].

19. When the father was an officer, and the son came to be king or a feudal prince, the father was sacrificed to with the rites of a king or a lord; but the personator wore the dress of an officer. When the father had been the son of Heaven, or a feudal lord, and the son was (only) an officer, the father was sacrificed to with the rites of an officer, but his personator wore only the dress of an officer [2].

20. If a wife were divorced while wearing the mourning (for her father or mother-in-law), she put it off. If the thing took place while she was wearing the mourning for her own parents, and before she had completed the first year's mourning, she continued to wear it for the three years; but if that term had been completed, she did not resume the mourning.

If she were called back before the completion of the year, she wore it to the end of that term; but if that term had been completed before she was called back, she went on wearing it to the regular term of mourning for parents.

21. The mourning which lasted for two complete years was (held to be) for three years; and that

---

[1] The sackcloth for one year, without carrying the staff.

[2] Both the cases in this paragraph can hardly be taken as anything more than hypothetical. On the concluding statement, the *Kh*ien-lung editors ask how the robes of a king could be exhibited in the ancestral temple of an officer.

which lasted for one complete year for two years[1]. The mourning for nine months and that for seven months[2] was held to be for three seasons; that for five months for two; and that for three months for one. Hence the sacrifice at the end of the completed year was according to the prescribed rule; but the putting off the mourning (or a part of it) then was the course (prompted by natural feeling). The sacrifice was not on account of the putting off of the mourning[3].

22. When the interment (for some reason) did not take place till after the three years, it was the rule that the two sacrifices (proper at the end of the first and second years) should then be offered. Between them, but not all at the same time, the mourning was put off[4].

23. If a relative who had himself to wear only the nine months' mourning for the deceased took the direction of the mourning rites in the case of any who must continue their mourning for three years, it was the rule that he should offer for them the two annual terminal sacrifices. If one who was merely a friend took that direction, he only offered

---

[1] See the introduction on Book XXXV, vol. xxvii, page 49.

[2] We have not met before with this mourning term of seven months. It occurs in the Î Lî, Book XXIV, 6, as to be worn for those who had died in the second degree of prematurity between the age of twelve and fifteen inclusive.

[3] 'This remark is made by the compiler,' say the *Kh*ien-lung editors, 'to guard against the sudden abandonment of their grief by the mourners, as if they had done with the deceased when the mourning was concluded.'

[4] After the first, it is said, men put off the mourning headband, and women that of the girdle. After the second they both put off their sackcloth.

the sacrifice of Repose, and that at the placing of the tablet in the shrine [1].

24. When the concubine of an officer had a son, he wore the three months' mourning for her. If she had no son, he did not do so [2].

25. When one had been born (in another state), and had had no intercourse with his grand-uncles and aunts, uncles and cousins, and his father, on hearing of the death of any of them, proceeded to wear mourning, he did not do so.

26. If one did not (through being abroad) hear of the death of his ruler's father or mother, wife or eldest son, till the ruler had put off his mourning, he did not proceed to wear any.

27. If it were a case, however, where the mourning was reduced to that of three months, he wore it [3].

28. (Small) servants in attendance on the ruler, (who had followed him abroad), when he assumed mourning (on his return, for relatives who had died when he was away), also put it on. Other and (higher officers in his train) also did so; but if the proper term for the mourning in the case were past, they did not do so. (Those who had remained at home), though the ruler could not know of their doing so, had worn the (regular) mourning.

---

[1] Because of the youth of the son, or of some other reason existing in the case. The director would himself be a cousin.

[2] But Great officers wore the three months' mourning for the relatives who had accompanied their wives to the harem, though they might have had no son. No such relatives accompanied the wife of an officer.

[3] This, it is supposed, should follow paragraph 25. There are doubts as to the interpretation of it.

Section II.

1. (The presiding mourner), after the sacrifice of Repose, did not carry his staff in proceeding to his apartment; after the placing of the tablet of the deceased (in the shrine of the grandfather), he did not carry it in going up to the hall[1].

2. The (son of another lady of the harem), who had been adopted as the child of the (childless) wife of the ruler, when that wife died, did not go into mourning for her kindred[2].

3. The sash was shorter (than the headband), by one-fifth of the length (of the latter). The staff was of the same length as the sash[3].

4. For the ruler's eldest son a concubine wore

---

[1] See vol. xxvii, p. 170. I have met with 'the Pacifying sacrifice,' instead of 'the sacrifice of Repose,' which I prefer for 虞 in this application. The character is explained by 安, the symbol of 'being at rest.' The mourners had done all they could for the body of the deceased. It had been laid in the grave; and this sacrifice of Repose was equivalent to our wish for a departed friend, 'Requiescat in pace.' It was offered in the principal apartment of the house. It remained only to place with an appropriate service the tablet of the deceased in its proper shrine in the ancestral temple next day. The staff was discarded by the mourner, it is said, to show that his grief was beginning to be assuaged. He and the others would pass from the principal apartment to others more private; and on leaving the temple, would have to mount the steps to the hall.

[2] The *Kh*ien-lung editors argue, and, I think, correctly, that this paragraph should say the opposite of what it does. They think it has been mutilated.

[3] The purely native staff in China is very long. At temples in the interior of the country I have often been asked to buy choice specimens as long as a shepherd's crook, or an alpenstock.

mourning for the same time as his wife, (the son's mother).

5. In putting off the mourning attire, they commenced with what was considered most important. In changing it, they commenced with what was considered least important.

6. When there was not the (regular) occasion for it, they did not open the door of the temple [1]. All wailed in the (mourning) shed (at other times).

7. In calling the dead back, and writing the inscription (to be exhibited over the coffin), the language was the same for all, from the son of Heaven to the ordinary officer. A man was called by his name. For a wife they wrote her surname, and her place among her sisters. If they did not know her surname, they wrote the branch-name of her family.

8. The girdle of dolychos cloth assumed with the unhemmed sackcloth (at the end of the wailing), and the hempen girdle worn when one (first) put on the hemmed sackcloth (of one year's mourning), were of the same size. The girdle of dolychos cloth assumed (as a change) in the hemmed sackcloth mourning, and that of hempen cloth at the (beginning of the) nine months' mourning, were of the same size. When the occasion for assuming the girdle of the lighter mourning occurred, a man wore both it and the other together [2].

---

[1] This is not the ancestral temple; but the apartment where the body was kept in the coffin, entered regularly for wailing in the morning and evening.

[2] So far as I can understand this paragraph, it describes the practice of a man (not of a woman), when, while he was wearing

9. An early interment was followed by an early sacrifice of repose. But they did not end their wailing till the three months were completed.

10. When the mourning rites for both parents occurred at the same time, the sacrifices of repose and of the enshrining of the tablet, for the (mother) who was buried first, did not take place till after the burial of the father. The sackcloth worn at her interment was the unhemmed and jagged[1].

11. A Great officer reduced the (period of) mourning for a son by a concubine[2]; but his grandson, (the son of that son), did not reduce his mourning for his father.

12. A Great officer did not preside at the mourning rites for an (ordinary) officer.

13. For the parents of his nurse[3] a man did not wear mourning.

14. When the husband had become the successor and representative of some other man (than his own father), his wife wore the nine months' mourning for his parents-in-law[4].

15. When the tablet of an (ordinary) officer was placed in the shrine of (his grandfather who had been) a Great officer, the victim due to him (as an officer) was changed (for that due to a Great officer).

16. A son who had not lived with his step-father (did not wear mourning for him). (They) must

deep mourning, a fresh death in his circle required him to add to it something of a lighter mourning.

[1] Compare vol. xxvii, page 315, paragraph 6.

[2] To nine months.

[3] A concubine of his father's.

[4] Her husband's own parents. But the paragraph is a difficult one; nor have the commentators elucidated it clearly.

have lived together and both be without sons to preside at their mourning rites; and (the step-father moreover) must have shared his resources with the son, and enabled him to sacrifice to his grandfather and father, (in order to his wearing mourning for him);—under these conditions they were said to live together. If they had sons to preside at the mourning rites for them, they lived apart.

17. When people wailed for a friend, they did so outside the door (of the principal apartment), on the left of it, with their faces towards the south [1].

18. When one was buried in a grave already occupied, there was no divination about the site (in the second case).

19. The tablet of an (ordinary) officer or of a Great officer could not be placed in the shrine of a grandfather who had been the lord of a state; it was placed in that of a brother of the grandfather who had been an (ordinary) officer or a Great officer. The tablet of his wife was placed by the tablet of that brother's wife, and that of his concubine by the tablet of that brother's concubine.

If there had been no such concubine, it was placed by the tablet of that brother's grandfather; for in all such places respect was had to the rules concerning the relative positions assigned to the tablets of father and son [2]. The tablet of a feudal lord could not be placed in the shrine of the son of Heaven (from whom he was born or descended); but that of the son of Heaven, of a feudal lord, or

[1] See vol. xxvii, page 134, paragraph 10.

[2] See vol. xxvii, page 223, paragraph 4, and note.

of a Great officer, could be placed in the shrine of an (ordinary) officer (from whom he was descended)[1].

20. For his mother's mother, who had been the wife proper of her father, if his mother were dead, a son did not wear mourning[2].

21. The son who was the lineal Head of his new branch of the surname, even though his mother were alive, (his father being dead), completed the full period of mourning for his wife[3].

22. A concubine's son who had been reared by another, might act as son to that other; and she might be any concubine of his father or of his grandfather[4].

23. The mourning went on to the than ceremony for a parent, a wife, and the eldest son[5].

24. To a nursing mother, or any concubine who was a mother, sacrifice was not maintained for a second generation.

25. When a grown-up youth had been capped, (and died) though his death could not be considered premature; and a (young) wife, after having worn

[1] A descendant in a low position could not presume on the dignity of his ancestors; but those who had become distinguished glorified their meaner ancestors.

[2] It is difficult to say exactly what is the significance of the 君母 in the text here.

[3] Meaning, say some, performed the than sacrifice at the end of twenty-seven months for her. I cannot think this is the meaning. Even for such a wife there could not be the 'three years' mourning.' According to Wang Yüan (汪琬), the mourning for one year terminated with a than sacrifice in the fifteenth month. This must be what is here intended.

[4] This is the best I can do for this paragraph, over which there is much conflict of opinion.

[5] Here is the same difficulty as in paragraph 21.

the hair-pin, (died), though neither could her death be said to be premature; yet, (if they died childless), those who would have presided at their rites, if they had died prematurely, wore the mourning for them which they would then have done [1].

26. If an interment were delayed (by circumstances) for a long time, he who was presiding over the mourning rites was the only one who did not put off his mourning. The others having worn the hempen (band) for the number of months (proper in their relation to the deceased), put off their mourning, and made an end of it [2].

27. The hair-pin of the arrow-bamboo was worn by (an unmarried daughter for her father) to the end of the three years' mourning [3].

28. That in which those who wore the sackcloth with even edges for three months, and those who wore (it) for all the nine months' mourning agreed, was the shoes made of strings (of hemp).

29. When the time was come for the sacrifice at the end of the first year's mourning, they consulted the divining stalks about the day for it, and the individual who was to act as personator of the deceased. They looked that everything was clean, and that all wore the proper girdle, carried their staffs, and had on the shoes of hempen-string. When the officers charged with this announced that all was ready, (the son) laid aside his staff, and assisted at the divinations for the day and for the

[1] Another difficult paragraph, about the interpretation of which there seem to be as many minds as there are commentators.

[2] Yet they would keep it by them till the interment took place, and then put it on again for the occasion.

[3] Should form part of the first paragraph of Section i.

personator. The officers having announced that these were over, he resumed his staff, bowed to the guests (who had arrived in the meantime), and escorted them away. At the sacrifice for the end of the second year, (the son) wore his auspicious (court) robes, and divined about the personator.

30. The son of a concubine, living in the same house with his father, did not observe the sacrifice at the end of the mourning for his mother.

Nor did such a son carry his staff in proceeding to his place for wailing.

As the father did not preside at the mourning rites for the son of a concubine, that son's son might carry his staff in going to his place for wailing. Even while the father was present, the son of a concubine, in mourning for his wife, might carry his staff in going to that place.

31. When a feudal prince went to condole on the death of a minister of another state[1], (being himself there on a visit), the ruler of that state received him and acted as the presiding mourner. The rule was that he should wear the skin cap and the starched sackcloth. Though the deceased on account of whom he paid his condolences had been interred, the presiding mourner wore the mourning cincture. If he had not yet assumed the full mourning dress, the visitor also did not wear that starched sackcloth.

32. One who was ministering to another who was ill did not do so in the mourning clothes (which he might be wearing); and (if the patient died), he might go on to preside at the mourning rites for him. But if another relative, who had not ministered

[1] That is, if the visit were made before the removal of the coffin.

to the deceased in his illness, came in to preside at the rites for him, he did not change the mourning which he might be wearing. In ministering to one more honourable than himself, the rule required a person to change the mourning he might be wearing, but not if the other were of lower position[1].

33. If there had been no concubine of her husband's grandmother by whose tablet that of a deceased concubine might be placed, it might be placed by that of the grandmother, the victim offered on the occasion being changed.

34. In the mourning rites for a wife, at the sacrifices of repose and on the ending of the wailing, her husband or son presided; when her tablet was put in its place, her father-in-law presided.

35. An (ordinary) officer did not take the place of presiding (at the mourning rites) for a Great officer. It was only when he was the direct descendant of the Honoured Head of their branch of the surname that he could do so.

36. If a cousin arrived from another state (to take part in the rites), before the presiding mourner had put off his mourning, the latter received him in the part of host, but without the mourning cincture[2].

37. The course pursued in displaying the articles, (vessels to the eye of fancy, to be put into the grave)[3], was this:—If they were (too) many as dis-

---

[1] If the other, it is said, in the former case were elder, an uncle or elder cousin; in the latter, a younger cousin.

[2] If the ruler came to condole after the interment, the presiding mourner would resume his cincture to receive him, out of respect to his rank; but this was not required on the late arrival of a relative.

[3] These articles were the contributions of friends and those

played, a portion of them might be put into the grave; if they were comparatively few as displayed, they might all be put into it.

38. Parties hurrying to the mourning rites for a brother or cousin (whose burial had taken place) first went to the grave and afterwards to the house, selecting places at which to perform their wailing. If the deceased had (only) been an acquaintance, they (first) wailed in the apartment (where the coffin had been), and afterwards went to the grave.

39. A father (at the mourning rites) for any of his other sons did not pass the night in the shed outside (the middle door, as for his eldest son by his wife).

40. The brothers and cousins of a feudal prince wore the unhemmed sackcloth (in mourning for him)[1].

41. In the five months' mourning for one who had died in the lowest stage of immaturity, the sash was of bleached hemp from which the roots were not cut away. These were turned back and tucked in.

42. When the tablet of a wife was to be placed by that of her husband's grandmother, if there were three (who could be so denominated), it was placed by that of her who was the mother of her husband's father[2].

43. In the case of a wife dying while her husband

prepared by the family. They were displayed inside the gate of the temple on the east of it when the body was being moved, and in front of the grave, on the east of the path leading to it.

[1] Even though they might not be in the same state with him.

[2] We must suppose that the grandfather had had three wives; not at the same time, but married one after another's death. Some suppose the three to be a mistake for two. 'The mother of her husband's father' is simply 'the nearest' in the text.

was a Great officer, and his ceasing, after her death, to be of that rank; if his tablet were placed (on his death) by that of his wife, the victim on the occasion was not changed (from that due to an ordinary officer). But if her husband (who had been an officer) became a Great officer after her death, then the victim at the placing of his tablet by hers was that due to a Great officer[1].

44. A son who was or would be his father's successor did not wear mourning for his divorced mother. He did not wear such mourning, because one engaged in mourning rites could not offer sacrifice[2].

45. When a wife did not preside at the mourning rites and yet carried the staff, it was when her mother-in-law was alive, and she did so for her husband. A mother carried the eleococca staff with its end cut square for the oldest son. A daughter, who was still in her apartment unmarried, carried a staff for her father or mother. If the relative superintending the rites did not carry the staff, then this one child did so[3].

---

[1] We must suppose that the appointment of the husband, whether as officer or Great officer, had been so recent that there had been no time for any tablets of an elder generation to get into his ancestral temple. His wife's had been the first to be placed in it.

[2] That is, he might have to preside at the sacrifices in the ancestral temple of his own family, and would be incapacitated for doing so, if he were mourning for her. The reader should bear in mind that there were seven justifiable causes for the divorce of a wife, without her being guilty of infidelity, or any criminal act.

[3] It is supposed there was no brother in the family to preside at the rites, and a relative of the same surname was called in to do so. But it was not in rule for him to carry the staff, and this daughter therefore did so, as if she had been a son.

46. In the mourning for three months and five months, at the sacrifice of repose and the ending of the wailing, they wore the mourning cincture.

After the interment, if they did not immediately go to perform the sacrifice of repose, they all, even the presiding mourner, wore their caps; but when they came to the sacrifice of repose, they all assumed the cincture.

When they had put off the mourning for a relative, on the arrival of his interment, they resumed it; and when they came to the sacrifice of repose and the ending of the wailing, they put on the cincture. If they did not immediately perform the sacrifice, they put it off.

When they had been burying at a distance, and were returning to wail, they put on their caps. On arriving at the suburbs, they put on the cincture, and came back to wail.

47. If the ruler came to condole with mourners, though it might not be the time for wearing the cincture, even the president of the rites assumed it, and did not allow the ends of his hempen girdle to hang loose. Even in the case of a visit from the ruler of another state, they assumed the cincture. The relatives all did so.

48. When they put off the mourning for one who had died prematurely, the rule was that at the (accompanying) sacrifice, the dress should be dark-coloured. When they put off the mourning for one fully grown, they wore their court robes, with the cap of white, plain, silk.

49. A son, who had hurried to the mourning rites of his father (from a distance), bound up his hair in the raised hall, bared his chest, descended to

the court, and there performed his leaping. (The leaping over, he reascended), covered his chest, and put on his sash in an apartment on the east.

If the rites were for his mother, he did not bind up his hair. He bared his chest, however, in the hall, descended to the court, and went through his leaping. (Reascending then), he covered his chest, and put on the cincture in the apartment on the east.

In the girdle (or the cincture), he proceeded to the appointed place, and completed the leaping. He then went out from the door (of the coffin-room), and went to (the mourning shed). The wailing commencing at death had by this time ceased. In three days he wailed five times, and thrice bared his chest for the leaping.

50. When an eldest son and his wife could not take the place hereafter of his parents, then, (in the event of her death), her mother-in-law wore for her (only) the five months' mourning[1].

---

[1] The scope of this paragraph is plain enough; but the construing of it is difficult. I have translated after *Kh*ăn Hâo's text, which contains a character more than that of the *Kh*ien-lung edition. The son and his wife could not become the representatives of the family. Various reasons are suggested by the commentators for the fact. The text supposes the death of the wife to take place before that of her mother-in-law.

BOOK XIV. TÂ KWÂN

OR

THE GREAT TREATISE[1].

1. According to the rules, only the king offered the united sacrifice to all ancestors. The chief place was then given to him from whom the founder of the line sprang, and that founder had the place of assessor to him[2].

The sacrifices of the princes of states reached to their highest ancestor. Great officers and other officers, who had performed great services, when these were examined (and approved) by the ruler, were able to carry their sacrifices up to their high ancestor.

2. The field of Mû-yeh was the great achievement of king Wû. When he withdrew after the victory, he reared a burning pile to God, prayed at the altar of the earth; and set forth his offerings in the house of Mû[3]. He then led all the princes of the kingdom, bearing his offerings in their various stands, and hurrying about, and carried the title of king back to Thâi who was Than-fû, *K*î-lî, and king Wăn who was *Kh*ang;—he would not approach his honourable ancestors with their former humbler titles.

---

[1] See the introductory notice, vol. xxvii, pages 30, 31.

[2] See the last Book, I, paragraphs 9, 17, et al.

[3] I suppose that all which is here described was done by king Wû after his victory at Mû, under the advice of his brother, known to us as the duke of *K*âu; see the *K*ung Yung, paragraphs 54, 55. 'The house of Mû' would be a building converted for the occasion into a temple.

3. Thus he regulated the services to be rendered to his father and grandfather before him;—giving honour to the most honourable. He regulated the places to be given to his sons and grandsons below him;—showing his affection to his kindred. He regulated (also) the observances for the collateral branches of his cousins;—associating all their members in the feasting. He defined their places according to their order of descent; and his every distinction was in harmony with what was proper and right. In this way the procedure of human duty was made complete.

4. When a sage sovereign stood with his face to the south, and all the affairs of the kingdom came before him, there were five things which for the time claimed his first care, and the people were not reckoned among them. The first was the regulating what was due to his kindred (as above); the second, the reward of merit; the third, the promotion of worth; the fourth, the employment of ability; and the fifth, the maintenance of a loving vigilance. When these five things were all fully realised, the people had all their necessities satisfied, all that they wanted supplied. If one of them were defective, the people could not complete their lives in comfort.

It was necessary for a sage on the throne of government to begin with the (above) procedure of human duty.

5. The appointment of the measures of weight, length, and capacity; the fixing the elegancies (of ceremony); the changing the commencement of the year and month; alterations in the colour of dress; differences of flags and their blazonry; changes in vessels and weapons, and distinctions in dress:—

these were things, changes in which could be enjoined on the people. But no changes could be enjoined upon them in what concerned affection for kin, the honour paid to the honourable, the respect due to the aged, and the different positions and functions of male and female.

6. Members of the same surname were united together in the various ramifications of their kinship, under the Heads of their different branches[1]. Those of a different surname[2] had their mutual relations regulated principally by the names assigned to them. Those names being clearly set forth, the different positions of males and females were determined.

When the husband belonged to the class of fathers [or uncles][3], the wife was placed in that of mothers [or aunts]; when he belonged to the class of sons [or cousins], the wife was placed in that of (junior) wives[4]. Since the wife of a younger brother was (thus) styled (junior) wife, could the wife of his elder brother be at the same time styled mother [or aunt]? The name or appellation is of the greatest

---

[1] That is, the males all called by the surname of the family.

[2] That is, the females, married into the family from other families of different surnames, and receiving different names or appellations from the places of their husbands in the family roll.

[3] 'Fathers' and 'mothers' here are really uncles and aunts, the 父 for the former being equivalent to 伯 叔 父; and the 母 for the latter to 伯 叔 母. The uncles were of the same category as the father in respect to age, and the aunts in the same category as the mother.

[4] Fû, the character here for wife, does not in itself contain the idea of this inferiority in point of age. That idea was in the mind of the writer, arising from the subject of which he was treating.

importance in the regulation of the family;—was not anxious care required in the declaration of it?

7. For parties four generations removed (from the same common ancestor) the mourning was reduced to that worn for three months, and this was the limit of wearing the hempen cloth. If the generations were five, the shoulders were bared and the cincture assumed; and in this way the mourning within the circle of the same was gradually reduced. After the sixth generation the bond of kinship was held to be at an end.

8. As the branch-surnames which arose separated the members of them from their relatives of a former time, and the kinship disappeared as time went on, (so far as wearing mourning was concerned), could marriage be contracted between parties (so wide apart)[1]? But there was that original surname tying all the members together without distinction, and the maintenance of the connexion by means of the common feast[2];—while there were these conditions, there could be no intermarriage, even after a hundred generations. Such was the rule of *K*âu[3].

9. The considerations which regulated the mourning worn were six:—first, the nearness of the kinship[4];

---

[1] *Kh*ăn Hâo says that under the Yin dynasty intermarriages were allowed after the fifth generation in a family of the same surname. The same statement is referred to by Khung Ying-tâ, from whom *Kh*ăn, probably, took it; but the *Kh*ien-lung editors discard it, as being 'without proof.'

[2] 'The feast' given to all the kindred after the seasonal sacrifices in the ancestral temple.

[3] *Kh*ăn Hâo refers to this prohibition of intermarriages by *K*âu as the grand distinction of the dynasty, marking clearly 'for the first time the distinction between man and beast.'

[4] As between parents and children.

second, the honour due to the honourable[1]; third, the names (as expressing the position in the relative circle)[2]; fourth, the cases of women still unmarried in the paternal home, and of those who had married and left it[3]; fifth, age[4]; and sixth, affinity, and external relationship[5].

10. Of the considerations of affinity and external relationship there were six cases:—those arising from inter-relationship[6]; those in which there was no inter-relationship[7]; those where mourning should be worn, and yet was not; those where it should not be worn, and yet was; those where it should be deep, and yet was light; and those where it should be light, and yet was deep.

11. Where the starting-point was affection, it began from the father. Going up from him by degrees it reached to the (high) ancestor, and was said to diminish. Where the starting-point was the consideration of what is right, it began with the ancestor. Coming down by natural degrees from him, it reached to the father, and was said to increase. In the diminution and the increase, the considerations of affection and right acted thus.

12. It was the way for the ruler to assemble and feast all the members of his kindred. None of

[1] As to the ruler, Great officers, and ministers.

[2] See paragraph 6.

[3] Spinsters and married aunts, cousins, sisters, &c.

[4] Relatives dying as minors, and after maturity.

[5] See next paragraph.

[6] Mother's kin; husband's kin; wife's kin.

[7] As when a minister wore mourning for his ruler's kindred; a concubine for the kindred of the wife, &c. The reader must task himself to imagine cases in which the other four conditions would apply.

them could, because of their mutual kinship, claim a nearer kinship with him than what was expressed by the places (assigned to them).

13. Any son but the eldest, (though all sons of the wife proper), did not sacrifice to his grandfather,—to show there was the Honoured Head (who should do so). Nor could he wear mourning for his eldest son for three years, because he was not the continuator of his grandfather[1].

14. When any other son but the eldest became an ancestor of a line, he who succeeded him became the Honoured Head (of the branch); and his successor again became the smaller Head[1].

15. There was the (great) Honoured Head whose tablet was not removed for a hundred generations. There were the (smaller) Honoured Heads whose tablets were removed after five generations. He whose tablet was not removed for a hundred generations was the successor and representative of the other than the eldest son (who became an ancestor of a line); and he was so honoured (by the members of his line) because he continued the (High) ancestor from whom (both) he and they sprang; this was why his tablet was not removed for a hundred generations. He who honoured the continuator of the High ancestor was he whose tablet was removed after five generations. They honoured the Ancestor, and therefore they reverenced the Head. The reverence showed the significance of that honour.

16. There might be cases in which there was a smaller Honoured Head, and no Greater Head (of

[1] See the last Book, I, paragraphs 10–12.

a branch family); cases in which there was a Greater Honoured Head, and no smaller Head; and cases in which there was an Honoured Head, with none to honour him. All these might exist in the instance of the son of the ruler of a state[1].

The course to be adopted for the headship of such a son was this; that the ruler, himself the proper representative of former rulers, should for all his half-brothers who were officers and Great officers appoint a full brother, also an officer or a Great officer, to be the Honoured Head. Such was the regular course.

17. When the kinship was no longer counted, there was no further wearing of mourning. The kinship was the bond of connexion (expressed in the degree of mourning).

18. Where the starting-point was in affection, it began with the father, and ascended by steps to the ancestor. Where it was in a consideration of what was right, it began with the ancestor, and descended in natural order to the deceased father. Thus the course of humanity (in this matter of mourning) was all comprehended in the love for kindred.

19. From the affection for parents came the honouring of ancestors; from the honouring of the

---

[1] Suppose a ruler had no brother by his father's wife, and appointed one of his brothers by another lady of the harem, to take the headship of all the others, this would represent the first case. If he appointed a full brother to the position, but could not appoint a half-brother to the inferior position, this would represent the second; and if the younger brothers of the ruling house were reduced to one man, he would represent the third case, having merely the name and nothing more. Such is the explanation of the text, so far as I can apprehend it.

ancestor came the respect and attention shown to the Heads (of the family branches). By that respect and attention to those Heads all the members of the kindred were kept together. Through their being kept together came the dignity of the ancestral temple. From that dignity arose the importance attached to the altars of the land and grain. From that importance there ensued the love of all the (people with their) hundred surnames. From that love came the right administration of punishments and penalties. Through that administration the people had the feeling of repose. Through that restfulness all resources for expenditure became sufficient. Through the sufficiency of these, what all desired was realised. The realisation led to all courteous usages and good customs; and from these, in fine, came all happiness and enjoyment :—affording an illustration of what is said in the ode :—

'Glory and honour follow Wăn's great name,
And ne'er will men be weary of his fame[1].'

---

[1] See vol. iii, page 314, the last two lines of ode 1; Metrical Version, page 351.

BOOK XV. SHÂO Î

OR

SMALLER RULES OF DEMEANOUR[1].

1. I have heard (the following things):—

When one wished to see for the first time another of character and position, his language was, 'I, so and so, earnestly wish my name to be reported to the officer of communication[2].' He could not go up the steps directly to the host. If the visitor were of equal rank with the host, he said, 'I, so and so, earnestly wish to see him.' If he were an infrequent visitor, he asked his name to be reported. If he were a frequent visitor, he added, 'this morning or evening.' If he were blind[3], he asked his name to be reported.

2. If it were on an occasion of mourning, the visitor said he had come as a servant and helper; if he were a youth, that he had come to perform whatever might be required of him. If the visit were at the mourning rites for a ruler or high minister, the language was, 'I am come to be employed by the chief minister of the household[4].'

---

[1] See the introductory notice, vol. xxvii, pages 31, 32.

[2] The visitor did not dare to send even a message directly to the master of the establishment where he was calling.

[3] That is, an officer of music, high or low.

[4] The name of the minister here is generally translated by 'Minister of Instruction.' But that can hardly be its meaning here; and there were officers so called also in the establishments of Great officers; see vol. xxvii, page 154, paragraph 20.

3. When a ruler was about to go out of his own state[1], if a minister were presenting to him money or pieces of jade, or any other article, the language was, 'I present this to the officer for the expenses of his horses.' To an equal in a similar case it was said, 'This is presented for the use of your followers.'

4. When a minister contributed a shroud to his ruler, he said, 'I send this laid-aside garment to the valuers[2].' An equal, sending such a gift to another equal, simply said, 'a shroud.' Relatives, such as brothers, did not go in with the shrouds which they presented.

5. When a minister was contributing articles or their value to his ruler who had mourning rites on hand for the previous ruler, he said, 'I present these products of my fields to the officers[3].'

6. A carriage and horses presented for a funeral, entered the gate of the ancestral temple. Contributions of money and horses with the accompanying presents of silk, the white flag (of a mourning carriage) and war chariots, did not enter the gate of the temple[4].

7. When the bearer of the contribution had

[1] About to proceed to the royal court.

[2] In the *K*âu Lî, Book I, 35, we find that among the functionaries attached to the 'Treasury of Jade,' there were eight men thus denominated 'valuers.' There were officers, probably, performing a similar duty in the department to which the charge of the offering in this paragraph would be consigned.

[3] The things presented here are called 'articles (coarse), shells' (貨 貝), the meaning being, I think, what I have given. The things were not the produce of the donor's land; but that land being held by him from the ruler, he so expressed himself.

[4] It is difficult for us to appreciate the reasons given for the distinction made between these contributions.

delivered his message, he knelt down and left the things on the ground. The officer of communication took them up. The presiding mourner did not himself receive them.

8. When the receiver stood, the giver stood, neither knelt. Parties of a straightforward character might, perhaps, do so.

9. When (the guest was) first entering, and it was proper to give the precedence to him, the officer of communication said (to the host), 'Give precedence.' When they proceeded to their mats, he said to them, 'Yes; be seated.'

When the leaves of the door were opened, only one man could take off his shoes inside the door. If there were already an honourable and elderly visitor, parties coming later could not do so.

10. When asking about the various dishes (of a feast), they said, 'Have you enjoyed such and such a dish?'

When asking one another about their (various) courses[1] and accomplishments[2], they said, 'Have you practised such and such a course? Are you skilful at such and such an accomplishment?'

11. (A man sought to) give no occasion for doubt about himself, nor to pass his judgment on the articles of others. He did not desire the (possessions of) great families, nor speak injuriously of the things which they valued.

12. Sweeping in general was called sâo. Sweep-

---

[1] There was the threefold course of aim, diligence, and filial duty, in filialness, friendship, and obedience.

[2] The accomplishments were six:—ceremonies, music, archery, charioteering, writing, mathematics.

ing up in front of a mat was called phân. In sweeping a mat they did not use a common broom[1]. The sweeper held the dust-pan with its tongue towards himself.

13. There was no divining (twice about the same thing) with a double mind. In asking about what had been referred to the tortoise-shell or the stalks, two things were to be considered, whether the thing asked about were right, and what was the diviner's own mind. On the matter of right he might be questioned, but not on what was in his own mind.

14. When others more honourable and older than one's self took precedence of him, he did not presume to ask their age. When they came to feast with him, he did not send to them any (formal) message. When he met them on the road, if they saw him, he went up to them, but did not ask to know where they were going. At funeral rites for them, he waited to observe the movements (of the presiding mourner), and did not offer his special condolences. When seated by them, he did not, unless ordered to do so, produce his lutes. He did not draw lines on the ground; that would have been an improper use of his hand. He did not use a fan. If they were asleep, and he had any message to communicate to them, he knelt in doing so.

15. At the game of archery, the inferior carried his four arrows in his hand. At that of throwing darts, he carried the four together in his breast. If he conquered, he washed the cup and gave it to the other, asking him to drink. If he were defeated, the elder went through the same process with him. They

[1] It might be dirty, having been used to sweep the ground.

did not use the (large) horn; they did not remove the (figure of a) horse (for marking the numbers)[1].

16. When holding the reins of the ruler's horses, the driver knelt. He wore his sword on his right side with his back to the best strap (for the ruler). When handing this to him, he faced him and then drew the strap towards the cross-bar. He used the second or inferior strap to help himself in mounting. He then took the reins in hand, and began to move on.

17. One asked permission to appear at court, but not to withdraw.

One was said to withdraw from court; to return home from a feast or a ramble; to close the toils of a campaign.

18. When sitting by a person of rank, if he began to yawn and stretch himself, to turn round his tablet, to play with the head of his sword, to move his shoes about, or to ask about the time of day, one might ask leave to retire.

19. For one who (wished to) serve his ruler, (the rule was) first to measure (his abilities and duties), and then enter (on the responsibilities); he did not enter on these, and then measure those. There was the same rule for all who begged or borrowed from others, or sought to engage in their service. In this way superiors had no ground for offence, and inferiors avoided all risk of guilt.

20. They did not spy into privacies nor form intimacies on matters aside from their proper business. They did not speak of old affairs, nor wear an appearance of being in sport.

[1] See in Book XXXVII.

21. One in the position of a minister and inferior might remonstrate (with his ruler), but not speak ill of him; might withdraw (from the state), but not (remain and) hate (its Head); might praise him, but not flatter; might remonstrate, but not give himself haughty airs (when his advice was followed). (If the ruler were) idle and indifferent, he might arouse and assist him; if (the government) were going to wreck, he might sweep it away, and institute a new one. Such a minister would be pronounced as doing service for the altars (of the state).

22. Do not commence or abandon anything hastily. Do not take liberties with or weary spiritual Beings. Do not try to defend or cover over what was wrong in the past, or to fathom what has not yet arrived. A scholar should constantly pursue what is virtuous, and amuse himself with the accomplishments.

A workman should follow the rules (of his art), and amuse himself with the discussion (of their application). One should not think about the clothes and elegant articles (of others), nor try to make good in himself what is doubtful in words (which he has heard)[1].

23. The style prized in conversation required that it should be grave and distinct. The demeanour prized in the court required that it should be

[1] These cautions are expressed enigmatically in the text. The expurgated edition gives only the third and fourth, which P. Callery translates thus:—'L'homme de lettres s'applique à la vertu par-dessus tout, et ne s'adonne que d'une façon secondaire à la culture des arts libéraux, semblable en cela à l'ouvrier qui suit d'abord les procédés fondamentaux de son art, et ne discute qu'après les changements à introduire dans leur application.'

well regulated and urbane; that at sacrifices was to be grave, with an appearance of anxiety. The horses of the chariot were to be well-paced and matched. The beauty of their bells was that they intimated dignity and harmony[1].

24. To a question about the age of a ruler's son, if he were grown up, it was said, 'He is able to attend to the business of the altars.' If he were still young, it was said, 'He is able to drive,' or 'He is not yet able to drive.' To the same question about a Great officer's son, if he were grown up, it was said, 'He is able to take his part in music;' if still young, it was said, 'He is able to take lessons from the music-master,' or 'He is not yet able to do so.' To the same question about the son of an ordinary officer, if he were grown up, it was said, 'He is able to guide the plough;' if he were still young, it was said, 'He is able to carry firewood,' or 'He is not yet able to do so[2].'

25. When carrying a symbol of jade, a tortoise shell, or the divining stalks, one did not walk hastily. Nor did he do so in the raised hall, or on a city wall. In a war chariot he did not bow forward to the cross-bar. A man in his mail did not try to bow[3].

26. A wife, on festive occasions, even though it were on receiving a gift from the ruler, (only) made

[1] This paragraph is in the expurgated edition, in the commentary to which, however, the whole is understood with reference to the heir-son of the kingdom or a state; and P. Callery translates accordingly:—'(L'héritier présomptif du trône) doit avoir,' &c.

[2] Compare vol. xxvii, page 115, paragraph 4.

[3] Compare vol. xxvii, page 72, paragraph 30; page 96, paragraph 39; et al.

a curtsy[1]. When seated as a personatrix (of the deceased grandmother of her husband), she did not bow with her head to her hands, but made the curtsy[2]. When presiding at the mourning rites, she did not bow with her head to her hands lowered to the ground.

27. (After the sacrifice of repose), her head-band was of dolychos cloth, and her girdle of hempen.

28. When taking meat from a stand or putting meat on it, they did not kneel.

29. An empty vessel was carried (with the same care) as a full one, and an empty apartment entered (with the same reverence) as if there were people in it.

30. At all sacrifices, whether in the apartment or in the hall, they did not have their feet bare. At a feast they might.

31. Till they had offered a portion in the temple, they did not eat of a new crop.

32. In the case of a charioteer and the gentleman whom he was driving, when the latter mounted or descended, the other handed him the strap. When the driver first mounted, he bowed towards the cross-bar. When the gentleman descended to walk, (he also descended), but (immediately) returned to the carriage and stood.

33. The riders in an attendant carriage (to court or temple), bowed forward to the bar, but not if it were to battle or hunt. Of such attendant carriages, the ruler of a state had seven; a Great officer of

[1] In Chinese fashion, an inclination of the head towards the hands.

[2] Some interpret this as saying that she did not even make the curtsy.

the highest grade, five; and one of the lowest grade, three[1].

34. People did not speak of the age of the horses or of the carriages of those who pos sessed such attendant carriages; nor did they put a value on the dress, or sword, or horses of a gentleman whom they saw before them.

35. In giving (to an inferior) or offering to a superior, four pots of spirits, a bundle of dried meat, and a dog, (the messenger) put down the liquor, and carried (only) the dried meat in his hand, when discharging his commission, but he also said that he was the bearer of four pots of spirits, a bundle of dried meat, and a dog. In presenting a tripod of flesh, he carried (one piece) in his hand. In presenting birds, if there were more than a couple, he carried a couple in his hand, leaving the others outside.

36. The dog was held by a rope. A watch dog or a hunting dog was given to the officer who was the medium of communication; and on receiving it, he asked its name. An ox was held by the tether, and a horse by the bridle. They were both kept on the right of him who led them; but a prisoner or captive, who was being presented, was kept on the left.

37. In presenting a carriage, the strap was taken off and carried in the hand of the messenger. In presenting a coat of mail, if there were other things to be carried before it, the messenger bore them. If there were no such things, he took off its covering, and bore the helmet in his hands. In the case of a

[1] Compare vol. xxvii, page 125, paragraph 4.

vessel, he carried its cover. In the case of a bow, with his left hand he stript off the case, and took hold of the middle of the back. In the case of a sword, he opened the cover of its case, and placed it underneath. Then he put into the case a silken cloth, on which he placed the sword.

38. Official tablets; writings; stalks of dried flesh; parcels wrapped in reeds; bows; cushions; mats; pillows; stools; spikes; staffs; lutes, large and small; sharp-edged lances in sheaths; divining stalks; and flutes:—these all were borne with the left hand upwards. Of sharp-pointed weapons, the point was kept behind, and the ring presented; of sharp-edged weapons, the handle was presented. In the case of all sharp-pointed and sharp-edged weapons, the point was turned away in handing them to others.

39. When leaving the city, in mounting a war-chariot, the weapon was carried with the point in front; when returning and entering it again, the end. The left was the place for the general and officers of an army; the right, for the soldiers.

40. For visitors and guests the principal thing was a courteous humility; at sacrifices, reverence; at mourning rites, sorrow; at meetings and reunions, an active interest. In the operations of war, the dangers had to be thought of. One concealed his own feelings in order to judge the better of those of others.

41. When feasting with a man of superior rank and character, the guest first tasted the dishes and then stopt. He should not bolt the food, nor swill down the liquor. He should take small and frequent mouthfuls. While chewing quickly, he did not make faces with his mouth. When he

proceeded to remove the dishes, and the host declined that service from him, he stopt[1].

42. The cup with which the guest was pledged was placed on the left; those which had been drunk (by the others) on the right. Those of the guest's attendant, of the host himself, and of the host's assistant;—these all were placed on the right[2].

43. In putting down a boiled fish to be eaten, the tail was laid in front. In winter it was placed with the fat belly on the right; in summer with the back. The slices offered in sacrifice (to the father of the fish-diet were thus more easily cut[3]).

44. All condiments were taken up with the right (hand), and were therefore placed on the left.

45. He who received the presents offered (to the ruler) was on his left; he who transmitted his words, on the right.

46. A cup was poured out for the driver of a personator of the dead as for the driver of the ruler. In the carriage, and holding the reins in his left hand, he received the cup with his right; offered a little in sacrifice at the end of the axle and cross-

[1] Compare vol. xxvii, pages 80, 81, paragraphs 54, 57, et al. The writer passes in this paragraph from the indicative to the imperative mood.

[2] The guest sat facing the south, so that the east and west were on his left and right respectively. The cups were set where they could be taken up and put down most conveniently.

[3] The fish, as a sacrificial offering and on great occasions, was placed lengthways on the stand. As placed in this paragraph, it was more convenient for the guest. It may be correct that the belly is the best part of a fish in winter, and the back in summer. Let gastronomers and those who are fond of pisciculture decide and explain the point.

bar on the right and left (to the father of charioteering), and then drank off the cup.

47. Of all viands which were placed on the stands, the offering was put down inside the stand.

A gentleman did not eat the entrails of grain-fed animals[1].

A boy[2] ran, but did not walk quickly with measured steps. When he took up his cup, he knelt in offering (some of the contents) in sacrifice, and then stood up and drank (the rest). Before rinsing a cup, they washed their hands. In separating the lungs of oxen and sheep, they did not cut out the central portion of them[3]; when viands were served up with sauce, they did not add condiments to it.

In selecting an onion or scallion for a gentleman, they cut off both the root and top.

When the head was presented among the viands, the snout was put forward, to be used as the offering.

48. He who set forth the jugs considered the left of the cup-bearer to be the place for the topmost one. The jugs and jars were placed with their spouts towards the arranger.

The drinkers at the ceremonies of washing the head and cupping, in presence of the stand with the divided victims on it, did not kneel. Before the common cup had gone round, they did not taste the viands.

---

[1] Dogs (bred to be eaten) and pigs. The reason for not eating their entrails can hardly be stated.

[2] A waiting-boy.

[3] That it might easily be taken in hand and put down as an offering of thanksgiving.

49. The flesh of oxen, sheep, and fish was cut small, and made into mince. That of elks and deer was pickled; that of the wild pig was hashed:—these were all sliced, but not cut small. The flesh of the muntjac was alone pickled, and that of fowls and hares, being sliced and cut small. Onions and shalots were sliced, and added to the brine to soften the meat.

50. When the pieces of the divided body were on the stand, in taking one of them to offer and in returning it[1], they did not kneel. So it was when they made an offering of roast meat. If the offerer, however, were a personator of the dead, he knelt.

51. When a man had his robes on his person, and did not know their names (or the meaning of their names), he was ignorant indeed.

52. If one came late and yet arrived before the torches were lighted, it was announced to him that the guests were all there, and who they were. The same things were intimated to a blind musician by the one who bid him. At a drinking entertainment, when the host carried a light, or bore a torch before them, the guests rise and decline the honour done to them. On this he gave the torch to a torch-bearer, who did not move from his place, nor say a word, nor sing[2].

53. When one was carrying in water or liquor and food to a superior or elder, the rule was not to

---

[1] The lungs.

[2] In the Ȝo *K*wân we have many accounts of these entertainments. The singing was almost always of a few lines from one of the pieces of the Shih King, expressing a sentiment appropriate to the occasion. The custom was like our after-dinner speeches and toasts.

breathe on it; and if a question was asked, to turn the mouth on one side.

54. When one conducted sacrifice for another, (and was sending to others the flesh of the victim), the message was, 'Herewith (the flesh of) blessing.' When sending of the flesh of his own sacrifice to a superior man, the party simply announced what it was.

If it were flesh of the sacrifice on placing the tablet of the deceased in the temple, or at the close of the first year's mourning, the fact was announced. The principal mourner spread out the portions, and gave them to his messenger on the south of the eastern steps, bowing twice, and laying his head to the ground as he sent him away; when he returned and reported the execution of his commission, the mourner again bowed twice and laid his head to the ground.

If the sacrifice were a great one, consisting of the three victims, then the portion sent was the left quarter of the ox, divided into nine pieces from the shoulder. If the sacrifice were the smaller, the portion sent was the left quarter, divided into seven pieces. If there were but a single pig, the portion was the left quarter, divided into five portions.

55. When the revenues of a state were at a low ebb, the carriages were not carved and painted; the buff-coats were not adorned with ribbons and cords; and the dishes were not carved; the superior man did not wear shoes of silk; and horses were not regularly supplied with grain.

BOOK XVI. HSIO *K*Î

OR

RECORD ON THE SUBJECT OF EDUCATION[1].

1. When a ruler is concerned that his measures should be in accordance with law, and seeks for the (assistance of the) good and upright, this is sufficient to secure him a considerable reputation, but not to move the multitudes.

When he cultivates the society of the worthy, and tries to embody the views of those who are remote (from the court), this is sufficient to move the multitudes, but not to transform the people.

If he wish to transform the people and to perfect their manners and customs, must he not start from the lessons of the school?

2. The jade uncut will not form a vessel for use; and if men do not learn, they do not know the way (in which they should go). On this account the ancient kings, when establishing states and governing the people, made instruction and schools a primary object;—as it is said in the Charge to Yüeh, 'The thoughts from first to last should be fixed on learning[2].'

3. However fine the viands be, if one do not eat, he does not know their taste; however perfect the course may be, if one do not learn it, he does not know its goodness. Therefore when he learns, one

---

[1] See the introductory notice, vol. xxvii, page 32.

[2] Vol. iii, page 117.

knows his own deficiencies; when he teaches, he knows the difficulties of learning. After he knows his deficiencies, one is able to turn round and examine himself; after he knows the difficulties, he is able to stimulate himself to effort. Hence it is said, 'Teaching and learning help each other;' as it is said in the Charge to Yüeh, 'Teaching is the half of learning[1].'

4. According to the system of ancient teaching, for the families of (a hamlet)[2] there was the village school; for a neighbourhood[2] there was the hsiang; for the larger districts there was the hsü; and in the capitals there was the college.

5. Every year some entered the college, and every second year there was a comparative examination. In the first year it was seen whether they could read the texts intelligently, and what was the meaning of each; in the third year, whether they were reverently attentive to their work, and what companionship was most pleasant to them; in the fifth year, how they extended their studies and sought the company of their teachers; in the seventh year, how they could discuss the subjects of their studies and select their friends. They were now said to have made some small attainments. In the ninth year, when they knew the different classes of subjects and had gained a general intelligence, were firmly established and would not fall back, they

---

[1] Vol. iii, page 117.

[2] The hamlet was supposed to contain twenty-five families; the neighbourhood 500; and the district 2,500. For the four institutions, P. Callery adopts the names of school, college, academy, and university. It would be tedious to give the various explanations of the names Hsiang and Hsü.

were said to have made grand attainments. After this the training was sufficient to transform the people, and to change (anything bad in) manners and customs. Those who lived near at hand submitted with delight, and those who were far off thought (of the teaching) with longing desire. Such was the method of the Great learning; as is said in the Record, 'The little ant continually exercises the art (of amassing)[1].'

6. At the commencement of the teaching in the Great college, (the masters) in their skin caps presented the offerings of vegetables (to the ancient sages), to show their pupils the principle of reverence for them; and made them sing (at the same time) the (first) three pieces of the Minor Odes of the Kingdom, as their first lesson in the duties of officers[2]. When they entered the college, the drum was beaten and the satchels were produced, that they might begin their work reverently. The cane and the thorns[3] were there to secure in them a proper awe. It was not till the time for the summer sacrifice[4] was divined for, that the testing examination was held;—to give composure to their minds. They were continually under inspection, but not spoken to,—to keep their minds undisturbed. They listened, but they did not ask questions; and

---

[1] See the note of Callery in loc. The quotation is from some old Record; it is not known what.

[2] The three pieces were the Lû Ming, the Ʒze Mâu, and the Hwang-hwang *K*ê hwâ, the first three pieces in the first decade of the Shih, Part II; showing the harmony and earnestness of officers.

[3] Callery calls these 'la latte et la baguette.'

[4] Khung Ying-tâ thought this was the quinquennial sacrifice. See the *Kh*ien-lung editors on the point.

they could not transgress the order of study (imposed on them). These seven things were the chief regulations in the teaching. As it is expressed in the Record, 'In all learning, for him who would be an officer the first thing is (the knowledge of) business; for scholars the first thing is the directing of the mind.'

7. In the system of teaching at the Great college, every season had its appropriate subject; and when the pupils withdrew and gave up their lessons (for the day), they were required to continue their study at home.

8. If a student do not learn (at college) to play in tune, he cannot quietly enjoy his lutes; if he do not learn extensively the figures of poetry, he cannot quietly enjoy the odes; if he do not learn the varieties of dress, he cannot quietly take part in the different ceremonies; if he do not acquire the various accomplishments, he cannot take delight in learning.

9. Therefore a student of talents and virtue pursues his studies, withdrawn in college from all besides, and devoted to their cultivation, or occupied with them when retired from it, and enjoying himself. Having attained to this, he rests quietly in his studies and seeks the company of his teachers; he finds pleasure in his friends, and has all confidence in their course. Although he should be separated from his teachers and helpers, he will not act contrary to the course;—as it is said in the Charge to Yüeh, 'Maintain a reverent humility, and strive to be constantly earnest. In such a case the cultivation will surely come[1].'

[1] Vol. iii, p. 117. But the quotation is a little different from the text of the Shû.

10. According to the system of teaching now-a-days, (the masters) hum over the tablets which they see before them, multiplying their questions. They speak of the learners' making rapid advances, and pay no regard to their reposing (in what they have acquired). In what they lay on their learners they are not sincere, nor do they put forth all their ability in teaching them. What they inculcate is contrary to what is right, and the learners are disappointed in what they seek for. In such a case, the latter are distressed by their studies and hate their masters; they are embittered by the difficulties, and do not find any advantage from their (labour). They may seem to finish their work, but they quickly give up its lessons. That no results are seen from their instructions :—is it not owing to these defects?

11. The rules aimed at in the Great college were the prevention of evil before it was manifested; the timeliness of instruction just when it was required; the suitability of the lessons in adaptation to circumstances; and the good influence of example to parties observing one another. It was from these four things that the teaching was so effectual and flourishing.

12. Prohibition of evil after it has been manifested meets with opposition, and is not successful. Instruction given after the time for it is past is done with toil, and carried out with difficulty. The communication of lessons in an undiscriminating manner and without suitability produces injury and disorder, and fails in its object. Learning alone and without friends makes one feel solitary and uncultivated, with but little information. Friendships of festivity

lead to opposition to one's master. Friendships with the dissolute lead to the neglect of one's learning. These six things all tend to make teaching vain.

13. When a superior man knows the causes which make instruction successful, and those which make it of no effect, he can become a teacher of others. Thus in his teaching, he leads and does not drag; he strengthens and does not discourage; he opens the way but does not conduct to the end (without the learner's own efforts). Leading and not dragging produces harmony. Strengthening and not discouraging makes attainment easy. Opening the way and not conducting to the end makes (the learner) thoughtful. He who produces such harmony, easy attainment, and thoughtfulness may be pronounced a skilful teacher.

14. Among learners there are four defects with which the teacher must make himself acquainted. Some err in the multitude of their studies; some, in their fewness; some, in the feeling of ease (with which they proceed); and some, in the readiness with which they stop. These four defects arise from the difference of their minds. When a teacher knows the character of his mind, he can save the learner from the defect to which he is liable. Teaching should be directed to develope that in which the pupil excels, and correct the defects to which he is prone.

15. The good singer makes men (able) to continue his notes, and (so) the good teacher makes them able to carry out his ideas. His words are brief, but far-reaching; unpretentious, but deep; with few illustrations, but instructive. In this way he may be said to perpetuate his ideas.

16. When a man of talents and virtue knows the difficulty (on the one hand) and the facility (on the other) in the attainment of learning, and knows (also) the good and the bad qualities (of his pupils), he can vary his methods of teaching. When he can vary his methods of teaching, he can be a master indeed. When he can be a teacher indeed, he can be the Head (of an official department). When he can be such a Head, he can be the Ruler (of a state). Hence it is from the teacher indeed that one learns to be a ruler, and the choice of a teacher demands the greatest care; as it is said in the Record, 'The three kings and the four dynasties were what they were by their teachers[1]'

17. In pursuing the course of learning, the difficulty is in securing the proper reverence for the master. When that is done, the course (which he inculcates) is regarded with honour. When that is done, the people know how to respect learning. Thus it is that there are two among his subjects whom the ruler does not treat as subjects. When one is personating (his ancestor), he does not treat him as such, nor does he treat his master as such. According to the rules of the Great college, the master, though communicating anything to the son of Heaven, did not stand with his face to the north. This was the way in which honour was done to him.

[1] 'The three kings' are of course the Great Yü, founder of the Hsiâ dynasty; Thang the Successful, founder of the Shang; and Wăn and Wû, considered as one, founders of *K*âu. The four dynasties is an unusual expression, though we shall meet with it again, as we have met with it already. They are said to be those of Yü (the dynasty of Shun), Hsiâ, Shang, and *K*âu. But how then have we only 'the three kings?' I should rather take them to be Hsiâ, Shang (considered as two, Shang and Yin), and *K*âu.

18. The skilful learner, while the master seems indifferent, yet makes double the attainments of another, and in the sequel ascribes the merit (to the master). The unskilful learner, while the master is diligent with him, yet makes (only) half the attainments (of the former), and in the sequel is dissatisfied with the master. The skilful questioner is like a workman addressing himself to deal with a hard tree. First he attacks the easy parts, and then the knotty. After a long time, the pupil and master talk together, and the subject is explained. The unskilful questioner takes the opposite course. The master who skilfully waits to be questioned, may be compared to a bell when it is struck. Struck with a small hammer, it gives a small sound. Struck with a great one, it gives a great sound. But let it be struck leisurely and properly, and it gives out all the sound of which it is capable[1]. He who is not skilful in replying to questions is the opposite of this. This all describes the method of making progress in learning.

19. He who gives (only) the learning supplied by

[1] P. Callery makes this sentence refer to the master, and not to the bell, and translates it:—'(Mais quelle que soit la nature des questions qu'on lui adresse, le maître) attend que l'élève ait fait à loisir toutes ses demandes, pour y faire ensuite une réponse complète.' He appends a note on the difficulty of the passage, saying in conclusion that the translation which he has adopted was suggested by a citation of the passage in the Pei-wăn Yun-fû (佩文韻府), where there is a different reading of (學), 'instruction,' for (聲), 'sound.' I have not been able to find the citation in the great Thesaurus, to which he refers. Yen Yüan does not mention any different reading in his examination of the text (皇清經解, chapter 917); and I do not see any reason for altering the translation which I first made.

his memory in conversations is not fit to be a master. Is it not necessary that he should hear the questions (of his pupils)? Yes, but if they are not able to put questions, he should put subjects before them. If he do so, and then they do not show any knowledge of the subjects, he may let them alone.

20. The son of a good founder is sure to learn how to make a fur-robe. The son of a good maker of bows is sure to learn how to make a sieve. Those who first yoke a (young) horse place it behind, with the carriage going on in front of it. The superior man who examines these cases can by them instruct himself in (the method of) learning[1].

21. The ancients in prosecuting their learning compared different things and traced the analogies between them. The drum has no special relation to any of the musical notes; but without it they cannot be harmonised. Water has no particular relation to any of the five colours; but without it they cannot be displayed[2]. Learning has no particular relation to any of the five senses; but without it they cannot be regulated. A teacher has no

[1] The *Kh*ien-lung editors say that this paragraph is intended to show that the course of learning must proceed gradually. So far is clear; but the illustrations employed and their application to the subject in hand are not readily understood. In his fifth Book (towards the end), Lieh-ȝze gives the first two illustrations as from an old poem, but rather differently from the text:—'The son of a good maker of bows must first learn to make a sieve; and the son of a good potter must first learn to make a fur-robe.' In this form they would more suitably have their place in paragraph 18.

[2] That is, in painting. The Chinese only paint in water colours. 'Water itself,' says Khung Ying-tâ, 'has no colour, but the paint requires to be laid on with water, in order to its display.' I cannot follow the text so easily in what it says on the other illustrations.

special relation to the five degrees of mourning; but without his help they cannot be worn as they ought to be.

22. A wise man has said, 'The Great virtue need not be confined to one office; Great power of method need not be restricted to the production of one article; Great truth need not be limited to the confirmation of oaths; Great seasonableness accomplishes all things, and each in its proper time.' By examining these four cases, we are taught to direct our aims to what is fundamental.

When the three sovereigns sacrificed to the waters, they did so first to the rivers and then to the seas; first to the source and then to its result. This was what is called 'Paying attention to the root.'

BOOK XVII. YO *K*Î

OR

RECORD OF MUSIC[1]

Section I.

1. All the modulations of the voice arise from the mind, and the various affections of the mind are produced by things (external to it). The affections thus produced are manifested in the sounds that are uttered. Changes are produced by the way in which those sounds respond to one another; and those changes constitute what we call the modulations of the voice. The combination of those modulated sounds, so as to give pleasure, and the (direction in harmony with them of the) shields and axes[2], and of the plumes and ox-tails[2], constitutes what we call music.

2. Music is (thus) the production of the modulations of the voice, and its source is in the affections of the mind as it is influenced by (external) things.

---

[1] See the introductory notice, vol. xxvii, pages 32–34.

[2] There was a pantomimic exhibition of scenes of war, in which the performers brandished shields and axes; and another of scenes of peace, in which they waved plumes and ox-tails. What I have rendered by 'the modulations of the voice' is in the text the one Chinese character yin (音), for which Callery gives 'air musical,' and which *K*ăng Hsüan explains as meaning 'the five full notes of the scale.' See the long note of Callery prefixed to this record, concluding:—'La musique Chinoise, telle que l'ont entendue les anciens, avait tous les caractères d'une représentation théatrale ayant pour but de parler tout à la fois aux yeux, aux oreilles, à l'esprit, et au cœur.'

When the mind is moved to sorrow, the sound is sharp and fading away; when it is moved to pleasure, the sound is slow and gentle; when it is moved to joy, the sound is exclamatory and soon disappears; when it is moved to anger, the sound is coarse and fierce; when it is moved to reverence, the sound is straightforward, with an indication of humility; when it is moved to love, the sound is harmonious and soft. These six peculiarities of sound are not natural[1]; they indicate the impressions produced by (external) things. On this account the ancient kings were watchful in regard to the things by which the mind was affected.

3. And so (they instituted) ceremonies to direct men's aims aright; music to give harmony to their voices; laws to unify their conduct; and punishments to guard against their tendencies to evil. The end to which ceremonies, music, punishments, and laws conduct is one; they are the instruments by which the minds of the people are assimilated, and good order in government is made to appear.

4. All modulations of the voice spring from the minds of men. When the feelings are moved within, they are manifested in the sounds of the voice; and when those sounds are combined so as to form compositions, we have what are called airs. Hence, the airs of an age of good order indicate composure and enjoyment. The airs of an age of disorder indicate dissatisfaction and anger, and its government is per-

[1] Or, 'are not the nature;' that is, the voice does not naturally, when the mind is not moved, from without itself, give such peculiar expressions of feeling. What belongs to man by his nature is simply the faculty of articulate speech, slumbering until he is awakened by his sensations and perceptions.

versely bad. The airs of a state going to ruin are expressive of sorrow and (troubled) thought. There is an interaction between the words and airs (of the people) and the character of their government.

5. (The note) kung represents the ruler; shang, the ministers; *k*io, the people; *k*ih, affairs; and yü, things. If there be no disorder or irregularity in these five notes, there will be no want of harmony in the state. If kung be irregular, (the air) is wild and broken; the ruler of the state is haughty. If shang be irregular, (the air) is jerky; the offices of the state are decayed. If *k*io be irregular, (the air) expresses anxiety; the people are dissatisfied. If *k*ih be irregular, (the air) expresses sorrow; affairs are strained. If yü be irregular, (the air) is expressive of impending ruin; the resources (of the state) are exhausted. If the five notes are all irregular, and injuriously interfere with one another, they indicate a state of insolent disorder; and the state where this is the case will at no distant day meet with extinction and ruin[1].

6. The airs of *K*ăng[2] and Wei were those of an age of disorder, showing that those states were near such an abandoned condition. The airs near the river Pû, at the mulberry forest, were those of a state going to ruin[3]. The government (of Wei) was in a state of dissipation, and the people were unsettled, calumniating their superiors, and pursuing their private aims beyond the possibility of restraint.

[1] On those notes, see Chinese Classics, vol. iii, page 48.

[2] See Confucian Analects, XV, 10, 6.

[3] This place was in the state of Wei. See the ridiculous incident which gave rise to this account of the airs in Sze-mâ *Kh*ien's monograph on music, pages 13, 14.

7. All modulations of sound take their rise from the mind of man; and music is the intercommunication of them in their relations and differences. Hence, even beasts know sound, but not its modulations; and the masses of the common people know the modulations, but they do not know music. It is only the superior man who can (really) know music.

8. On this account we must discriminate sounds in order to know the airs; the airs in order to know the music; and the music in order to know (the character of) the government. Having attained to this, we are fully provided with the methods of good order. Hence with him who does not know the sounds we cannot speak about the airs, and with him who does not know the airs we cannot speak about the music. The knowledge of music leads to the subtle springs that underlie the rules of ceremony. He who has apprehended both ceremonies and music may be pronounced to be a possessor of virtue. Virtue means realisation (in one's self)[1].

9. Hence the greatest achievements of music were not in the perfection of the airs; the (efficacy) of the ceremonies in the sacrificial offerings was not in the exquisiteness of the flavours. In the lutes for the *Kh*ing Miâo the strings were of red (boiled) silk, and the holes were wide apart; one lute began, and

[1] Virtue (德) and getting or realising (得) have the same name or pronunciation (teh) in Chinese. This concluding sentence, as Callery points out, is only a sort of pun on that common name. And yet 'virtue' is the 'realisation' in one's self 'of what is good.' The next paragraph expands the writer's thought. The greatest achievement of music in its ancient perfection was the softening and refining of the character, and that of the services of the temple was the making men reverent, filial, and brotherly.

(only) three others joined it; there was much melody not brought out. In the ceremonies of the great sacrifices, the dark-coloured liquor took precedence, and on the stands were uncooked fish, while the grand soup had no condiments: there was much flavour left undeveloped.

10. Thus we see that the ancient kings, in their institution of ceremonies and music, did not seek how fully they could satisfy the desires of the appetite and of the ears and eyes; but they intended to teach the people to regulate their likings and dislikings, and to bring them back to the normal course of humanity.

11. It belongs to the nature of man, as from Heaven, to be still at his birth. His activity shows itself as he is acted on by external things, and developes the desires incident to his nature. Things come to him more and more, and his knowledge is increased. Then arise the manifestations of liking and disliking. When these are not regulated by anything within, and growing knowledge leads more astray without, he cannot come back to himself, and his Heavenly principle is extinguished.

12. Now there is no end of the things by which man is affected; and when his likings and dislikings are not subject to regulation (from within), he is changed into the nature of things as they come before him; that is, he stifles the voice of Heavenly principle within, and gives the utmost indulgence to the desires by which men may be possessed. On this we have the rebellious and deceitful heart, with licentious and violent disorder. The strong press upon the weak; the many are cruel to the few; the knowing impose upon the dull; the bold make it bitter for

the timid; the diseased are not nursed; the old and young, orphans and solitaries are neglected:—such is the great disorder that ensues.

13. Therefore the ancient kings, when they instituted their ceremonies and music, regulated them by consideration of the requirements of humanity. By the sackcloth worn for parents, the wailings, and the weepings, they defined the terms of the mourning rites. By the bells, drums, shields, and axes, they introduced harmony into their seasons of rest and enjoyment. By marriage, capping, and the assumption of the hair-pin, they maintained the separation that should exist between male and female. By the archery gatherings in the districts, and the feastings at the meetings of princes, they provided for the correct maintenance of friendly intercourse.

14. Ceremonies afforded the defined expression for the (affections of the) people's minds; music secured the harmonious utterance of their voices; the laws of government were designed to promote the performance (of the ceremonies and music); and punishments, to guard against the violation of them. When ceremonies, music, laws, and punishments had everywhere full course, without irregularity or collision, the method of kingly rule was complete[1].

---

[1] With this paragraph ends the first portion of the treatise on music, called Yo Păn (樂本), or 'Fundamental Principles in Music.' The *Kh*ien-lung editors divide it into four chapters:—the first setting forth that music takes its character as good or bad from the mind of man, as affected by what is external to it; the second, that the character of the external things affecting the mind is determined by government as good or bad; the third, that the ceremonies and music of the ancient kings were designed to

15. Similarity and union are the aim of music; difference and distinction, that of ceremony. From union comes mutual affection; from difference, mutual respect. Where music prevails, we find a weak coalescence; where ceremony prevails, a tendency to separation. It is the business of the two to blend people's feelings and give elegance to their outward manifestations.

16. Through the perception of right produced by ceremony, came the degrees of the noble and the mean; through the union of culture arising from music, harmony between high and low. By the exhibition of what was to be liked and what was to be disliked, a distinction was made between the worthy and unworthy. When violence was prevented by punishments, and the worthy were raised to rank, the operation of government was made impartial. Then came benevolence in the love (of the people), and righteousness in the correction (of their errors); and in this way good government held its course.

17. Music comes from within, and ceremonies from without. Music, coming from within, produces the stillness (of the mind); ceremonies, coming from without, produce the elegancies (of manner). The highest style of music is sure to be distinguished by its ease; the highest style of elegance, by its undemonstrativeness.

18. Let music attain its full results, and there would be no dissatisfactions (in the mind); let ceremony do so, and there would be no quarrels. When

---

regulate the minds of men in their likings and dislikings; and the fourth, that that regulation was in harmony with the will of Heaven, as indicated in the nature of man.

bowings and courtesies marked the government of the kingdom, there would be what might be described as music and ceremony indeed. Violent oppression of the people would not arise; the princes would appear submissively at court as guests; there would be no occasion for the weapons of war, and no employment of the five punishments[1]; the common people would have no distresses, and the son of Heaven no need to be angry:—such a state of things would be an universal music. When the son of Heaven could secure affection between father and son, could illustrate the orderly relation between old and young, and make mutual respect prevail all within the four seas, then indeed would ceremony (be seen) as power.

19. In music of the grandest style there is the same harmony that prevails between heaven and earth; in ceremonies of the grandest form there is the same graduation that exists between heaven and earth. Through the harmony, things do not fail (to fulfil their ends); through the graduation we have the sacrifices to heaven and those to earth. In the visible sphere there are ceremonies and music; in the invisible, the spiritual agencies. These things being so, in all within the four seas, there must be mutual respect and love.

20. The occasions and forms of ceremonies are different, but it is the same feeling of respect (which they express). The styles of musical pieces are different, but it is the same feeling of love (which they

[1] The 'five punishments' were branding on the forehead, cutting off the nose, other various dismemberments, castration, and death; see Mayers' 'Chinese Readers' Manual,' page 313. But the one word 'punishment' would sufficiently express the writer's meaning.

promote). The essential nature of ceremonies and music being the same, the intelligent kings, one after another, continued them as they found them. The occasions and forms were according to the times when they were made; the names agreed with the merit which they commemorated.

21. Hence the bell, the drum, the flute, and the sounding-stone; the plume, the fife, the shield, and the axe are the instruments of music; the curvings and stretchings (of the body), the bending down and lifting up (of the head); and the evolutions and numbers (of the performers), with the slowness or rapidity (of their movements), are its elegant accompaniments. The dishes, round and square, the stands, the standing dishes, the prescribed rules and their elegant variations, are the instruments of ceremonies; the ascending and descending, the positions high and low, the wheelings about, and the changing of robes, are their elegant accompaniments.

22. Therefore they who knew the essential nature of ceremonies and music could frame them; and they who had learned their elegant accompaniments could hand them down. The framers may be pronounced sage; the transmitters, intelligent. Intelligence and sagehood are other names for transmitting and inventing.

23. Music is (an echo of) the harmony between heaven and earth; ceremonies reflect the orderly distinctions (in the operations of) heaven and earth. From that harmony all things receive their being; to those orderly distinctions they owe the differences between them. Music has its origin from heaven; ceremonies take their form from the appearances of earth. If the imitation of those appearances were

carried to excess, confusion (of ceremonies) would appear; if the framing of music were carried to excess, it would be too vehement. Let there be an intelligent understanding of the nature and interaction of (heaven and earth), and there will be the ability to practise well both ceremonies and music.

24. The blending together without any mutual injuriousness (of the sentiments and the airs on the different instruments) forms the essence of music; and the exhilaration of joy and the glow of affection are its business. Exactitude and correctness, without any inflection or deviation, form the substance of ceremonies, while gravity, respectfulness, and a humble consideration are the rules for their discharge.

25. As to the employment of instruments of metal and stone in connexion with these ceremonies and this music, the manifestation of them by the voice and its modulations, the use of them in the ancestral temple, and at the altars to the spirits of the land and grain, and in sacrificing to (the spirits of) the hills and streams, and to the general spiritual agencies (in nature);—these are (external demonstrations), natural even to the people[1].

26. When the (ancient) kings had accomplished their undertakings, they made their music (to commemorate them); when they had established their

---

[1] The eleven paragraphs ending with this form the second chapter of the Book, called by Liû Hsiang Yo Lun (樂論), while the third chapter, extending to the end of the section, is called Yo Lî (樂理), as if the two were an expansion of the statement in the seventh paragraph, that music is 'the intercommunication of the modulated sounds and the mind in their relations and differences.'

government, they framed their ceremonies. The excellence of their music was according to the greatness of their undertakings; and the completeness of their ceremonies was according to the comprehensiveness of their government. The dances with shields and axes did not belong to the most excellent music[1], nor did the sacrifices with cooked flesh mark the highest ceremonies[1].

27. The times of the five Tîs were different, and therefore they did not each adopt the music of his predecessor. The three kings belonged to different ages, and so they did not each follow the ceremonies of his predecessor. Music carried to an extreme degree leads to sorrow, and coarseness in ceremonies indicates something one-sided. To make the grandest music, which should bring with it no element of sorrow, and frame the completest ceremonies which yet should show no one-sidedness, could be the work only of the great sage.

28. There are heaven above and earth below, and between them are distributed all the (various) beings with their different (natures and qualities):—in accordance with this proceeded the framing of ceremonies. (The influences of) heaven and earth flow forth and never cease; and by their united action (the phenomena of) production and change ensue:—in accordance with this music arose. The processes of growth in spring, and of maturing in summer (suggest the idea of) benevolence; those of in-gathering in autumn and of storing in winter, suggest

[1] As being, I suppose, commemorative of the achievements of war, and not the victories of peace; and as marking a progress of society, and a departure from the primitive era of innocent simplicity and reverence.

righteousness. Benevolence is akin to music, and righteousness to ceremonies.

29. Harmony is the thing principally sought in music:—it therein follows heaven, and manifests the spirit-like expansive influence characteristic of it. Normal distinction is the thing aimed at in ceremonies:—they therein follow earth, and exhibit the spirit-like retractive influence characteristic of it. Hence the sages made music in response to heaven, and framed ceremonies in correspondence with earth. In the wisdom and completeness of their ceremonies and music we see the directing power of heaven and earth[1].

30. (The relation) between ruler and minister was determined from a consideration of heaven (conceived of as) honourable, and earth (conceived of as) mean. The positions of noble and mean were fixed with a reference to the heights and depths displayed by the surface (of the earth). The regularity with which movement and repose follow each other (in the course of nature) led to the consideration of affairs as small

[1] On the first of these two paragraphs, P. Callery says:—'The celebrated Encyclopædist, Mâ Twan-lin (Book 181), says that this passage is one of the most marvellous that ever were written, and he draws from it the proof that the work could not have been written later than the Han, "because reckoning from that dynasty, there did not appear any author capable of conceiving ideas so profound, and expressing them in language so elevated."' P. Callery adds, 'As regards the origin of the Lî Kî, the reasoning of the Encyclopædist appears to me passably (passablement) false; as to the intrinsic worth of the passage, I leave it to the reader to form his judgment from the translation, which I have endeavoured to render as faithful as possible.'

In the passage of Mâ Twan-lin, however, that author is simply quoting the words of Kû Hsî (Tâ Kwân, Book 37), and expresses no opinion of his own.

and great. The different quarters (of the heavens) are grouped together, and the things (of the earth) are distinguished by their separate characteristics; and this gave rise to (the conception of) natures and their attributes and functions. In heaven there are formed its visible signs, and earth produces its (endless variety of) things; and thus it was that ceremonies were framed after the distinctions between heaven and earth.

31. The breath (or influence) of earth ascends on high, and that of heaven descends below. These in their repressive and expansive powers come into mutual contact, and heaven and earth act on each other. (The susceptibilities of nature) are roused by the thunder, excited by the wind and rain, moved by the four seasons, and warmed by the sun and moon; and all the processes of change and growth vigorously proceed. Thus it was that music was framed to indicate the harmonious action of heaven and earth.

32. If these processes took place out of season, there would be no (vigorous) life; and if no distinction were observed between males and females, disorder would arise and grow:—such is the nature of the (different qualities of) heaven and earth.

33. When we think of ceremonies and music, how they reach to the height of heaven and embrace the earth; how there are in them the phenomena of retrogression and expansion, and a communication with the spirit-like (operations of nature), we must pronounce their height the highest, their reach the farthest, their depth the most profound, and their breadth the greatest.

34. Music appeared in the Grand Beginning (of all things), and ceremonies had their place on the com-

pletion of them. Their manifestation, being ceaseless, gives (the idea of) heaven; and again, being motionless, gives (the idea of) earth. Through the movement and repose (of their interaction) come all things between heaven and earth. Hence the sages simply spoke of ceremonies and music.

SECTION II.

1. Anciently, Shun made the lute with five strings, and used it in singing the Nan Făng. Khwei was the first who composed (the pieces of) music to be employed by the feudal lords as an expression of (the royal) approbation of them[1].

2. Thus the employment of music by the son of Heaven was intended to reward the most virtuous among the feudal lords. When their virtue was very great, and their instructions were honoured, and all the cereals ripened in their season, then they were rewarded by (being permitted) the use of the music. Hence, those of them whose toils in the government of the people were conspicuous, had their rows of pantomimes extended far; and those of them who had been indifferent to the government of the people

[1] Nan Făng, 'the South wind,' was the name of a poetical piece made by Shun, and celebrating the beneficent influence of rulers and parents as being like that of the south wind. Four lines of it are found in the Narratives of the School (Article 35):—

'The south wind's genial balm
Gives to my people's sorrows ease;
Its breath amidst the season's calm,
Brings to their wealth a large increase.'

The invention of the *kh*in or lute, here ascribed to Shun, is also attributed to the more ancient Tîs, Shăn Năng and Fû-hsî. Perhaps Shun was the first to make it with five strings. Khwei was his minister of music; see vol. iii, pages 44, 45.

had those rows made short. On seeing their pantomimes, one knew what was (the degree of) their virtue, (just as) on hearing their posthumous designations, we know what had been (the character of) their conduct.

3. The Tâ *K*ang expressed the brilliance (of its author's virtue); the Hsien *K*ih, the completeness (of its author's); the Shâo showed how (its author) continued (the virtue of his predecessor); the Hsiâ, the greatness (of its author's virtue); the music of Yin and *K*âu embraced every admirable quality[1].

4. In the interaction of heaven and earth, if cold and heat do not come at the proper seasons, illnesses arise (among the people); if wind and rain do not come in their due proportions, famine ensues. The instructions (of their superiors) are the people's cold and heat; if they are not what the time requires, an injury is done to society. The affairs (of their superiors) are the people's wind and rain; if they are not properly regulated, they have no success. In accordance with this, the object of the ancient kings in their practice of music was to bring their government into harmony with those laws (of heaven and earth). If it was good, then the conduct (of the people) was like the virtue (of their superiors).

5. (The feast on) grain-fed animals, with the adjunct of drinking, was not intended to produce evil, and yet cases of litigation are more numerous in consequence of it:—it is the excessive drinking which produces the evil. Therefore the former kings framed

[1] Tâ *K*ang was the name of Yâo's music; Hsien *K*ih, that of Hwang Tî's; Shâo, that of Shun's; and Hsiâ, that of Yü's. Pages would be required to condense what is said about the pieces and their names.

the rules to regulate the drinking. Where there is (but) one presentation of the cup (at one time), guest and host may bow to each other a hundred times, and drink together all the day without getting drunk. This was the way in which those kings provided against evil consequences.

Such feasts served for the enjoyment of the parties at them. The music was intended to illustrate virtue; the ceremonies to restrain excess.

6. Hence the former kings, on occasions of great sorrow, had their rules according to which they expressed their grief; and on occasions of great happiness, they had their rules by which they expressed their pleasure. The manifestations, whether of grief or joy, were all bounded by the limits of these rules[1].

7. In music the sages found pleasure, and (saw that) it could be used to make the hearts of the people good. Because of the deep influence which it exerts on a man, and the change which it produces in manners and customs, the ancient kings appointed it as one of the subjects of instruction.

8. Now, in the nature of men there are both the energy of their physical powers and the intelligence of the mind; but for their (affections of) grief, pleasure, joy, and anger there are no invariable rules. They are moved according to the external objects which excite them, and then there ensues the manifestation of the various faculties of the mind.

9. Hence, when a (ruler's) aims are small, notes

[1] With this paragraph ends the fourth division of the Book, called Yo Shih (樂施), meaning 'The grant of Music,' or the principles on which the ancient kings permitted their music to be used by the feudal princes, to signify their approval of what was good, and stimulate all to virtue.

that quickly die away characterise the music, and the people's thoughts are sad; when he is generous, harmonious, and of a placid and easy temper, the notes are varied and elegant, with frequent changes, and the people are satisfied and pleased; when he is coarse, violent, and excitable, the notes, vehement at first and distinct in the end, are full and bold throughout the piece, and the people are resolute and daring; when he is pure and straightforward, strong and correct, the notes are grave and expressive of sincerity, and the people are self-controlled and respectful; when he is magnanimous, placid, and kind, the notes are natural, full, and harmonious, and the people are affectionate and loving; when he is careless, disorderly, perverse, and dissipated, the notes are tedious and ill-regulated, and the people proceed to excesses and disorder.

10. Therefore the ancient kings (in framing their music), laid its foundations in the feelings and nature of men; they examined (the notes) by the measures (for the length and quality of each); and adapted it to express the meaning of the ceremonies (in which it was to be used). They (thus) brought it into harmony with the energy that produces life, and to give expression to the performance of the five regular constituents of moral worth. They made it indicate that energy in its Yang or phase of vigour, without any dissipation of its power, and also in its Yin or phase of remission, without the vanishing of its power. The strong phase showed no excess like that of anger, and the weak no shrinking like that of pusillanimity. These four characteristics blended harmoniously in the minds of men, and were similarly manifested in their conduct. Each occupied quietly

in its proper place, and one did not interfere injuriously with another.

11. After this they established schools for (teaching their music), and different grades (for the learners). They marked most fully the divisions of the pieces, and condensed into small compass the parts and variations giving beauty and elegance, in order to regulate and increase the inward virtue (of the learners). They gave laws for the great and small notes according to their names, and harmonised the order of the beginning and the end, to represent the doing of things. Thus they made the underlying principles of the relations between the near and distant relatives, the noble and mean, the old and young, males and females, all to appear manifestly in the music. Hence it is said that 'in music we must endeavour to see its depths.'

12. When the soil is worn out, the grass and trees on it do not grow well. When water is often troubled, the fish and tortoises in it do not become large. When the energy (of nature) is decayed, its production of things does not proceed freely. In an age of disorder, ceremonies are forgotten and neglected, and music becomes licentious.

13. In such a case the notes are melancholy but without gravity, or joyous without repose. There is remissness (in ceremonies), and the violation of them is easy. One falls into such a state of dissoluteness that he forgets the virtue properly belonging to his nature. In great matters he is capable of treachery and villainy; in small matters he becomes greedy and covetous. There is a diminution in him of the enduring, genial forces of nature, and an extinction of the virtue of satisfaction and harmony. On this

account the superior man despises such (a style of music and ceremonies)[1].

14. Whenever notes that are evil and depraved affect men, a corresponding evil spirit responds to them (from within); and when this evil spirit accomplishes its manifestations, licentious music is the result. Whenever notes that are correct affect men, a corresponding correct spirit responds to them (from within); and when this correct spirit accomplishes its manifestations, harmonious music is the result. The initiating cause and the result correspond to each other. The round and the deflected, the crooked and the straight, have each its own category; and such is the character of all things, that they affect one another severally according to their class.

15. Hence the superior man returns to the (good) affections (proper to his nature) in order to bring his will into harmony with them, and compares the different qualities (of actions) in order to perfect his conduct. Notes that are evil and depraved, and sights leading to disorder, and licentiousness, are not allowed to affect his ears or eyes. Licentious music and corrupted ceremonies are not admitted into the mind to affect its powers. The spirit of idleness, indifference, depravity, and perversity finds no exhibition in his person. And thus he makes his ears, eyes, nose, and mouth, the apprehensions of his mind, and the movements of all the parts of his body, all follow the course that is correct, and do that which is right.

---

[1] This and the six previous paragraphs form the fifth division of the Book, and are called Yo Yen (樂言), 'Words about Music.' The *Kh*ien-lung editors, however, propose changing the Yen (言) into Hsing (形), so that the meaning would be 'Manifestations of Music.'

16. After this there ensues the manifestation (of the inward thoughts) by the modulations of note and tone, the elegant accompaniments of the lutes, small and large, the movements with the shield and battle-axe, the ornaments of the plumes and ox-tails, and the concluding with the pipes and flutes[1]. All this has the effect of exhibiting the brilliance of complete virtue, stirring up the harmonious action of the four (seasonal) energies; and displaying the true natures and qualities of all things.

17. Hence in the fine and distinct notes we have an image of heaven; in the ample and grand, an image of earth; in their beginning and ending, an image of the four seasons; in the wheelings and revolutions (of the pantomimes), an image of the wind and rain. (The five notes, like) the five colours, form a complete and elegant whole, without any confusion. (The eight instruments of different materials, like) the eight winds, follow the musical accords, without any irregular deviation. The lengths of all the different notes have their definite measurements, without any uncertainty. The small and the great complete one another. The end leads on to the beginning, and the beginning to the end. The key notes and those harmonising with them, the sharp and the bass, succeed one another in their regular order.

[1] Thus:—

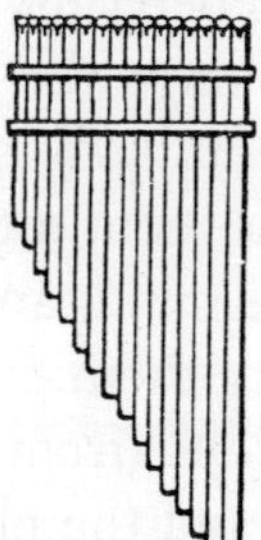

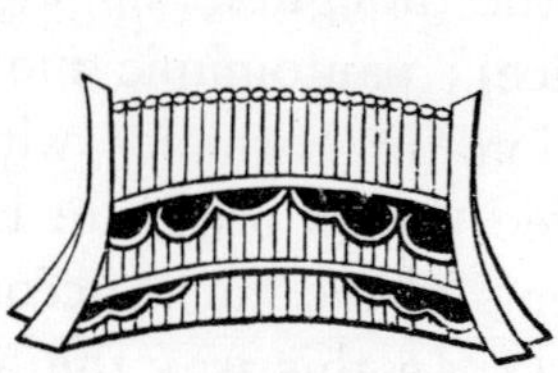

18. Therefore, when the music has full course, the different relations are clearly defined by it; the perceptions of the ears and eyes become sharp and distinct; the action of the blood and physical energies is harmonious and calm; (bad) influences are removed, and manners changed; and all under heaven there is entire repose.

19. Hence we have the saying, 'Where there is music there is joy.' Superior men rejoice in attaining to the course (which they wish to pursue); and smaller men in obtaining the things which they desire. When the objects of desire are regulated by a consideration of the course to be pursued, there is joy without any disorder. When those objects lead to the forgetfulness of that course, there is delusion, and no joy.

20. It is for this purpose that the superior man returns to the (good) affections (proper to his nature), in order to bring his will into harmony with them, and makes extensive use of music in order to perfect his instructions. When the music has free course, the people direct themselves to the quarter (to which they should proceed), and we can see (the power of) his virtue.

21. Virtue is the strong stem of (man's) nature, and music is the blossoming of virtue. Metal, stone, silk, and bamboo are (the materials of which) the instruments of music (are made). Poetry gives expression to the thoughts; singing prolongs the notes (of the voice); pantomimic movements put the body into action (in harmony with the sentiments). These three things originate in the mind, and the instruments of the music accompany them.

22. In this way the affections (from which comes the music) are deeply seated, and the elegant display

of them is brilliant. All the energies (of the nature) are abundantly employed, and their transforming power is mysterious and spirit-like. A harmonious conformity (to virtue) is realised within, and the blossoming display of it is conspicuous without, for in music, more than other things, there should be nothing that is pretentious or hypocritical.

23. Music springs from the movement of the mind; the notes are the manifestation of the music; the elegant colours and various parts are the ornaments of the notes. The superior man puts its fundamental cause in movement, makes its manifesting notes into music, and regulates its ornaments.

24. Thus they first strike the drum to warn (the performers) to be in readiness, and (the pantomimes) take three steps to show the nature of the dance. This is done a second time and they begin to move forward; and when they have completed their evolutions, they return and dress their ranks. However rapid their movements may be, there is nothing violent in them; however mysterious they may be, they are not beyond the power of being understood. One, studying them alone, finds pleasure in the object of them, and does not tire in his endeavours to understand them. When he has fully understood them, he does not keep what he desires to himself. Thus the affections (of joy) are displayed; the (ideal) of righteousness is established; and when the music is ended, the (due) honour has been paid to virtue. Superior men by it nourish their love of what is good; small men in it hear the (correction of) their errors. Hence it is said, that 'for the courses to be pursued by men the influence of music is great.'

25. In music we have the outcome and bestowal

(of what its framers felt); in ceremonies a return (for what their performers had received). Music expresses the delight in what produces it, and ceremonies lead the mind back to (the favours) which originate them. Music displays the virtue (of the framer); ceremonies are a return of the feelings (which led to them), as carrying the mind back to what originated them.

26. What is called 'a Grand carriage' is one which is (the gift) of the son of Heaven; the flag with dragons, and a nine-scolloped border, was the banner (conferred by) the son of Heaven; that with the azure and black edging exhibited the precious tortoises, and was (also the gift of) the son of Heaven, and when these were followed by herds of oxen and sheep, they were the gifts bestowed on the feudal lords[1].

Section III.

1. In music we have the expression of feelings which do not admit of any change; in ceremonies that of principles which do not admit of any alteration. Music embraces what all equally share; ceremony distinguishes the things in which men differ. Hence the theory of music and ceremonies embraces the whole nature of man.

2. To go to the very root (of our feelings) and know the changes (which they undergo) is the province of music; to display sincerity and put away all that is hypocritical is the grand law of ceremonies. Ceremonies and music resemble the nature of Heaven and Earth, penetrate to the virtues of the spiritual Intelligences, bring down the spirits from above, and

[1] With this ends the sixth chapter of the Book, called Yo Hsiang (樂象), meaning the natural symbols of music

raise up those whose seat is below. They give a sort of substantial embodiment of what is most subtle as well as material, and regulate the duties between father and son, ruler and subject.

3. Therefore, when the Great man uses and exhibits his ceremonies and music, Heaven and Earth will in response to him display their brilliant influences. They will act in happy union, and the energies (of nature), now expanding, now contracting, will proceed harmoniously. The genial airs from above and the responsive action below will overspread and nourish all things. Then plants and trees will grow luxuriantly; curling sprouts and buds will expand; the feathered and winged tribes will be active; horns and antlers will grow; insects will come to the light and revive; birds will breed and brood; the hairy tribes will mate and bring forth; the mammalia will have no abortions, and no eggs will be broken or addled,—and all will have to be ascribed to the power of music[1].

4. When we speak of music we do not mean the notes emitted by the Hwang *K*ung, Tâ Lü, (and the other musical pipes), the stringed instruments and the singing, or the (brandishing of the) shields and axes. These are but the small accessories of the music; and hence lads act as the pantomimes. (In

[1] There is extravagance in this description. The Great man is the sage upon the throne. The imagination of the eloquent writer runs riot as he dwells on the article of his creed, that 'Heaven, Earth, and Man' are the 'Three Powers (三才),' intended by their harmonious co-operation to make a happy and flourishing world. That would indeed be wonderful music which should bring about such a result. Compare the words of the Hebrew prophet in Hosea ii. 21, 22. Callery's translation of the concluding clause is:—'Tout cela n'est autre chose que l'harmonie de la musique rejaillissant (sous tous les êtres de la nature).'

the same way), the spreading of the mats, the disposing of the vases, and the arranging of the stands and dishes, with the movements in ascending and descending, are but the small accessories of ceremonies; and hence there are the (smaller) officers who direct them. The music-masters decide on the tunes and the pieces of poetry; and hence they have their places with their stringed instruments, and their faces directed to the north. The prayer-officers of the ancestral temple decide on the various ceremonies in it, and hence they keep behind the representatives of the deceased. Those who direct the mourning rites after the manner of the Shang dynasty[1], have their places (for the same reason) behind the presiding mourner.

5. It is for this reason that the practice of virtue is held to be of superior worth, and the practice of any art of inferior; that complete virtue takes the first place, and the doing of anything, (however ingenious, only) the second. Therefore the ancient kings had their distinctions of superior and inferior, of first and last; and so they could frame their music and ceremonies for the whole kingdom[2].

6. The marquis Wăn of Wei[3] asked Ʒze-hsiâ, saying, 'When in my square-cut dark robes and cap I listen to the ancient music, I am only afraid that I shall go to sleep. When I listen to the music of

---

[1] Which was distinguished for the plain simplicity of its observances.

[2] With this ends the seventh chapter, called Yo *Kh*ing (樂情), 'The attributes of Music.'

[3] The marquis Wăn ruled in Wei from B.C. 425 to 387. He is said to have received the classical books from Ʒze-hsiâ, when that disciple of Confucius must have been a hundred years old, and was blind, in B.C. 407.

*K*ăng and Wei, I do not feel tired; let me ask why I should feel so differently under the old and the new music.'

7. 3ze-hsiâ replied, 'In the old music, (the performers) advance and retire all together; the music is harmonious, correct, and in large volume; the stringed instruments (above) and those made from gourd shells with the organs and their metal tongues (below), are all kept waiting for the striking of the drum. The music first strikes up at the sound of the drum; and when it ends, it is at the sound of the cymbals. The close of each part of the performance is regulated by the Hsiang[1], and the rapidity of the motions by the Yâ[1]. In (all) this the superior man speaks of, and follows, the way of antiquity. The character is cultivated; the family is regulated; and peace and order are secured throughout the kingdom. This is the manner of the ancient music.

8. 'But now, in the new music, (the performers) advance and retire without any regular order; the music is corrupt to excess; there is no end to its vileness. Among the players there are dwarfs like monkeys, while boys and girls are mixed together, and there is no distinction between father and son. Such music can never be talked about, and cannot be said to be after the manner of antiquity. This is the fashion of the new music.

9. 'What you ask about is music; and what you like is sound. Now music and sound are akin, but they are not the same.'

---

[1] These are names of musical instruments, of which figures are given in the plates to the *Kh*ien-lung edition; but there is much uncertainty about them.

10. The marquis asked him to explain, and 3ze-hsiâ replied, 'In antiquity, Heaven and Earth acted according to their several natures, and the four seasons were what they ought to be. The people were virtuous, and all the cereals produced abundantly. There were no fevers or other diseases, and no apparitions or other prodigies. This was what we call "the period of great order." After this arose the sages, and set forth the duties between father and son, and between ruler and subject, for the guidance of society. When these guiding rules were thus correctly adjusted, all under heaven, there was a great tranquillity; after which they framed with exactness the six accords (upper and lower), and gave harmony to the five notes (of the scale), and the singing to the lutes of the odes and praise-songs; constituting what we call "the virtuous airs." Such virtuous airs constituted what we call "Music," as is declared in the Book of Poetry (III, i, ode 7, 4),

"Silently grew the fame of his virtue,
His virtue was highly intelligent;
Highly intelligent, and of rare discrimination;
Able to lead, able to rule,—
To rule over this great country,
Rendering a cordial submission, effecting a cordial union.
When (the sway) came to king Wăn,
His virtue left nothing to be dissatisfied with.
He received the blessing of God,
And it was extended to his descendants."

11. 'May I not say that what you love are the vile airs?' The marquis said, 'Let me ask where the vile airs come from?' 3ze-hsiâ replied, 'The

airs of *K*ăng go to a wild excess, and debauch the mind; those of Sung tell of slothful indulgence and women, and drown the mind; those of Wei are vehement and rapid, and perplex the mind; and those of *Kh*î are violent and depraved, and make the mind arrogant. The airs of those four states all stimulate libidinous desire, and are injurious to virtue;—they should therefore not be used at sacrifices.

12. 'It is said in the Book of Poetry (IV, i [Part ii] ode 5),

"In solemn unison (the instruments) give forth their notes;
Our ancestors will hearken to them."

That solemn unison denotes the grave reverence and harmony of their notes:—with reverence, blended with harmony, what is there that cannot be done?

13. 'A ruler has only to be careful of what he likes and dislikes. What the ruler likes, his ministers will practise; and what superiors do, their inferiors follow. This is the sentiment in the Book of Poetry (III, ii, ode 10, 6),

"To lead the people is very easy."

14. 'Seeing this, and after (the repose of the people was secured), the sages made hand-drums and drums, the stopper and the starter, the earthen whistle and the bamboo flute,—the six instruments which produced the sounds of their virtuous airs. After these came the bell, the sounding-stone, the organ with thirty-six pipes, and the large lute, to be played in harmony with them; the shields, axes, ox-tails, and plumes, brandished by the pantomimes in time and

tune. These they employed at the sacrifices in the temple of the former kings, at festivals in offering and receiving the pledge cup; in arranging the services of officers (in the temple) according to the rank due to each, as noble or mean, and in showing to future ages how they observed the order due to rank and to age.

15. 'The bells give out a clanging sound as a signal. The signal is recognised by all, and that recognition produces a martial enthusiasm. When the ruler hears the sound of the bell, he thinks of his officers of war.

'The sounding-stones give out a tinkling sound, as a summons to the exercise of discrimination. That discrimination may lead to the encountering of death. When the ruler hears the sounding-stone, he thinks of his officers who die in defence of his frontiers.

'The stringed instruments give out a melancholy sound, which produces the thought of purity and fidelity, and awakens the determination of the mind. When the ruler hears the sound of the lute and cithern, he thinks of his officers who are bent on righteousness.

'The instruments of bamboo give out a sound like that of overflowing waters, which suggests the idea of an assembly, the object of which is to collect the multitudes together. When the ruler hears the sound of his organs, pipes, and flutes, he thinks of his officers who gather the people together.

'The drums and tambours give out their loud volume of sound, which excites the idea of movement, and tends to the advancing of the host. When the ruler hears the sounds of his drums and tambours, he thinks of his leaders and commanders. When a superior man thus hears his musical instruments, he does not hear only the sounds which they emit. There are associated ideas which accompany these[1].'

16. Pin-mâu *K*iâ[2] was sittting with Confucius. Confucius talked with him about music, and said, 'At (the performance of) the Wû, how is it that the preliminary warning (of the drum) continues so long?' The answer was, 'To show (the king's) anxiety that all his multitudes should be of one mind with him.'

'How is it that (when the performance has commenced) the singers drawl their notes so long, and the pantomimes move about till they perspire?' The answer was, 'To show his apprehension that some (princes) might not come up in time for the engagement.'

'How is it that the violent movement of the arms and stamping fiercely with the feet begin so soon?' The answer was, 'To show that the time for the engagement had arrived.'

'How is it that, (in the performance of the Wû,) the pantomimes kneel on the ground with the right

---

[1] With this fifteenth paragraph ends the eighth chapter of the Book called simply 'Marquis Wan of Wei's Chapter' (魏文侯章); and the *Kh*ien-lung editors say nothing more about it.

[2] Pin-mâu *K*iâ must have been a scholar of Confucius' time. a master of music; but, so far as I have read, nothing is known about him beyond what appears here. The *Kh*ang Hung at the end of the paragraph was a historiographer of *K*âu, with whom Confucius is said to have studied music. The Wû was the dance and music which king Wû is said to have made after his conquest of Shang or Yin.

knee, while the left is kept up?' The answer was, 'There should be no kneeling in the Wû.'

'How is it that the words of the singers go on to speak eagerly of Shang?' The answer was, 'There should be no such sounds in the Wû.'

'But if there should be no such sound in the Wû, where does it come from?' The answer was, 'The officers (of the music) failed to hand it down correctly. If they did not do so, the aim of king Wû would have been reckless and wrong.'

The Master said, 'Yes, what I heard from *Kh*ang Hung was to the same effect as what you now say.'

17. Pin-mâu *K*iâ rose up, left his mat, and addressed Confucius, saying, 'On the long-continued warning (of the drum) in the Wû, I have heard your instructions; but let me ask how it is that after that first delay there is another, and that a long one?'

The Master said, 'Sit down, and I will tell you. Music is a representation of accomplished facts. The pantomimes stand with their shields, each erect and firm as a hill, representing the attitude of king Wû. The violent movements of the arms and fierce stamping represent the enthusiasm of Thâi-kung. The kneeling of all at the conclusion of the performance represents the government (of peace, instituted) by (the dukes of) *K*âu and Shâo.

18. 'Moreover, the pantomimes in the first movement proceed towards the north (to imitate the marching of king Wû against Shang); in the second, they show the extinction of Shang; in the third, they show the return march to the south; in the fourth, they show the laying out of the Southern states; in the fifth, they show how (the dukes of) *K*âu and Shâo were severally put in charge of the states on the

left and right; in the sixth, they again unite at the point of starting to offer their homage to the son of Heaven. Two men, one on each side of the performers, excite them with bells, and four times they stop and strike and thrust, showing the great awe with which (king Wû) inspired the Middle states. Their advancing with these men on each side shows his eagerness to complete his helpful undertaking. The performers standing long together show how he waited for the arrival of the princes.

19. 'And have you alone not heard the accounts of Mû-yeh? King Wû, after the victory over Yin, proceeded to (the capital of) Shang; and before he descended from his chariot he invested the descendants of Hwang Tî with *Kî*; those of the Tî Yâo with *K*û; and those of the Tî Shun with *Kh*ăn. When he had descended from it, he invested the descendant of the sovereign of Hsiâ with *Kî*; appointed the descendants of Yin to Sung; raised a mound over the grave of the king's son, Pî-kan; released the count of *Kh*î from his imprisonment, and employed him to restore to their places the officers who were acquainted with the ceremonial usages of Shang. The common people were relieved from (the pressure) of the (bad) government which they had endured, and the emoluments of the multitude of (smaller) officers were doubled.

'(The king then) crossed the Ho, and proceeded to the west. His horses were set free on the south of mount Hwâ, not to be yoked again. His oxen were dispersed in the wild of the Peach forest, not to be put to the carriages again. His chariots and coats of mail were smeared with blood, and despatched to his arsenals, not to be used again. The shields and spears were turned upside down and conveyed away, wrapped in tiger skins, which were styled "the appointed cases." The leaders and commanders were then constituted feudal lords; and it was known throughout the kingdom that king Wû would have recourse to weapons of war no more[1].

20. 'The army having been disbanded (the king commanded) a practice of archery at the colleges in the suburbs. At the college on the left (or east) they shot to the music of the Lî-shâu[2]; at that on the right (or west) they shot to the music of the 3âu-yü; and (from this time) the archery which consisted in going through (so many) buffcoats ceased. They wore (only) their civil robes and caps, with their ivory tokens of rank stuck in their girdles; and the officers of the guard put off their swords. (The king) offered sacrifice in the Hall of Distinction, and the people learned to be filial. He gave audiences at court, and the feudal lords knew how they ought to demean themselves. He ploughed in the field set apart for that purpose, and the lords learned what should be the object of reverence to them (in their states). These five things constituted great lessons for the whole kingdom.'

21. In feasting the three (classes of the) old and the five (classes of the) experienced in the Great college, he himself (the son of Heaven) had his

---

[1] See the account of all these proceedings after the victory of Mû in the Shû, V, iii, 9, though it is difficult to reconcile the two accounts in some of their details.

[2] See the *K*âu Lî, Book 22, 32. The ode Lî-shâu was used at the archery celebrations of the feudal lords, and is now lost. The 3âu-yü is the last ode in the second Book of the Shih, Part I. It was used at contests where the king presided.

breast bared and cut up the animals. He (also) presented to them the condiments and the cups. He wore the royal cap, and stood with a shield before him. In this way he taught the lords their brotherly duties.

22. 'In this manner the ways of *K*âu penetrated everywhere, and the interaction of ceremonies and music was established;—is it not right that in the performance of the Wû there should be that gradual and long-continuing action[1]?'

23. A superior man says: 'Ceremonies and music should not for a moment be neglected by any one. When one has mastered completely (the principles of) music, and regulates his heart and mind accordingly, the natural, correct, gentle, and honest heart is easily developed, and with this development of the heart comes joy. This joy goes on to a feeling of repose. This repose is long-continued. The man in this constant repose becomes (a sort of) Heaven. Heaven-like, (his action) is spirit-like. Heaven-like, he is believed without the use of words. Spirit-like, he is regarded with awe, without any display of rage. So it is, when one by his mastering of music regulates his mind and heart.

24. 'When one has mastered completely (the principle of) ceremonies so as to regulate his person accordingly, he becomes grave and reverential. Grave and reverential, he comes to be regarded with awe. If the heart be for a moment without the feeling of harmony and joy, meanness and deceitfulness enter

[1] The preceding seven paragraphs form the ninth chapter, which, like the former, simply bears the name of one of the parties in it, and is called 'The chapter of Pin-mâu *K*iâ.'

it. If the outward demeanour be for a moment without gravity and respectfulness, indifference and rudeness show themselves.

25. 'Therefore the sphere in which music acts is the interior of man, and that of ceremonies is his exterior. The result of music is a perfect harmony, and that of ceremonies a perfect observance (of propriety). When one's inner man is (thus) harmonious, and his outer man thus docile, the people behold his countenance and do not strive with him; they look to his demeanour, and no feeling of indifference or rudeness arises in them. Thus it is that when virtue shines and acts within (a superior), the people are sure to accept (his rule), and hearken to him; and when the principles (of propriety) are displayed in his conduct, the people are sure (in the same way) to accept and obey him. Hence it is said, "Carry out perfectly ceremonies and music, and give them their outward manifestation and application, and under heaven nothing difficult to manage will appear."'

26. Music springs from the inward movements (of the soul); ceremonies appear in the outward movements (of the body). Hence it is the rule to make ceremonies as few and brief as possible, and to give to music its fullest development. This rule for ceremonies leads to the forward exhibition of them, and therein their beauty resides; that for music leads to the introspective consideration of it, and therein its beauty resides. If ceremonies demanding this condensation were not performed with this forward exhibition of them, they would almost disappear altogether; if music, demanding this full development, were not accompanied with this introspection, it would produce a dissipation of the mind. Thus it

is that to every ceremony there is its proper response, and for music there is its introspection. When ceremonies are responded to, there arises pleasure; and when music is accompanied with the right introspection, there arises the (feeling of) repose. The responses of ceremony and the introspection of music spring from one and the same idea, and have one and the same object.

27. Now music produces pleasure;—what the nature of man cannot be without. That pleasure must arise from the modulation of the sounds, and have its embodiment in the movements (of the body);—such is the rule of humanity. These modulations and movements are the changes required by the nature, and they are found complete in music. Thus men will not be without the ministration of pleasure, and pleasure will not be without its embodiment, but if that embodiment be not suitably conducted, it is impossible that disorder should not arise. The ancient kings, feeling that they would feel ashamed (in the event of such disorder arising), appointed the tunes and words of the Yâ and the Sung to guide (in the music), so that its notes should give sufficient pleasure, without any intermixture of what was bad, while the words should afford sufficient material for consideration without causing weariness; and the bends and straight courses, the swell and diminution, the sharp angles, and soft melody throughout all its parts, should be sufficient to stir up in the minds of the hearers what was good in them, without inducing any looseness of thought or depraved air to be suggested. Such was the plan of the ancient kings when they framed their music.

28. Therefore in the ancestral temple, rulers and

ministers, high and low, listen together to the music, and all is harmony and reverence; at the district and village meetings of the heads of clans, old and young listen together to it, and all is harmony and deference. Within the gate of the family, fathers and sons, brothers and cousins, listen together to it, and all is harmony and affection. Thus in music there is a careful discrimination (of the voices) to blend them in unison so as to bring out their harmony; there is a union of the (various) instruments to give ornamental effect to its different parts; and these parts are combined and performed so as to complete its elegance. In this way fathers and sons, rulers and subjects are united in harmony, and the people of the myriad states are associated in love. Such was the method of the ancient kings when they framed their music.

29. In listening to the singing of the Yâ and the Sung, the aims and thoughts receive an expansion. From the manner in which the shields and axes are held and brandished, and from the movements of the body in the practice with them, now turned up, now bent down, now retiring, now stretching forward, the carriage of the person receives gravity. From the way in which (the pantomimes) move to their several places, and adapt themselves to the several parts (of the performance), the arrangement of their ranks is made correct, and their order in advancing and retiring is secured. In this way music becomes the lesson of Heaven and Earth, the regulator of true harmony, and what the nature of man cannot dispense with.

30. It was by music that the ancient kings gave elegant expression to their joy; by their armies and

axes that they gave the same to their anger. Hence their joy and anger always received their appropriate response. When they were joyful, all under heaven were joyful with them; when they were angry, the oppressive and disorderly feared them. In the ways of the ancient kings, ceremonies and music may be said to have attained perfection[1].

31. (Once), when Ȝze-kung had an interview with the music-master Yî, he asked him, saying, 'I have heard that in the music and words belonging to it there is that which is specially appropriate to every man; what songs are specially appropriate to me?' The other replied, 'I am but a poor musician, and am not worthy to be asked what songs are appropriate for particular individuals;—allow me to repeat to you what I have heard, and you can select for yourself (what is appropriate to you). The generous and calm, the mild and correct, should sing the Sung; the magnanimous and calm, and those of wide penetration and sincere, the Tâ Yâ (Major Odes of the Kingdom); the courteous and self-restraining, the lovers of the rules of propriety, the Hsiâo Yâ (Minor Odes of the Kingdom); the correct, upright, and calm, the discriminating and humble, the Făng (Airs of the States); the determinedly upright, but yet gentle and loving, the Shang; and the mild and honest, but yet capable of decision, the *Kh*î. The object of this singing is for one to make himself right, and then to display his virtue. When he has thus put

[1] From paragraph 23 to this forms the tenth chapter of the Book, which has the name of Yo Hwâ (樂化), 'The Transforming Operation of Music,' supplementing and summarising all the previous chapters.

himself in a condition to act, Heaven and Earth respond to him, the four seasons revolve in harmony with him, the stars and constellations observe their proper laws, and all things are nourished and thrive.

32. 'What are called the Shang[1] were the airs and words transmitted from the five Tîs; and having been remembered by the people of Shang, we call them the Shang. What are called the *Kh*î were transmitted from the three dynasties; and having been remembered by the people of *Kh*î, we call them the *Kh*î. He who is versed in the airs of the Shang will generally be found to manifest decision in the conduct of affairs. He who is versed in the airs of the *Kh*î, when he is attracted by the prospect of profit, will yet give place to others. To manifest decision in the conduct of affairs is bravery; to give place to others in the prospect of gain is righteousness. Who, without singing these songs, can assure himself that he will always preserve such bravery and righteousness?

33. 'In singing, the high notes rise as if they were borne aloft; the low descend as if they were falling to the ground; the turns resemble a thing broken off; and the finale resembles (the breaking) of a willow tree; emphatical notes seem made by the

[1] All the other pieces of song mentioned in the preceding paragraph are well known, as the divisions under which the odes of the Shih King are arranged. What are called the Shang and *Kh*î are lost, but some account of them is given in this paragraph. When it is said that the people of Shang remembered the airs and poetry of the five Tîs, we must understand by Shang the duchy of Sung, which was ruled by the representation of the line of the Shang kings. Why the state of *Kh*î should have remembered the airs and songs of 'the three dynasties' more than any other state, I cannot tell.

square; quavers are like the hook (of a spear); and those prolonged on the same key are like pearls strung together. Hence, singing means the prolonged expression of the words; there is the utterance of the words, and when the simple utterance is not sufficient, the prolonged expression of them. When that prolonged expression is not sufficient, there come the sigh and exclamation. When these are insufficient, unconsciously there come the motions of the hands and the stamping of the feet[1].'

(Such was the answer to) 3ze-kung's question about music[2].

[1] On this passage, P. Callery says:—'Quoique, à la rigueur, on puisse comparer des airs à des objets, ou à des accidents matériels, comme nous disons de tel motif musical qu'il est "Large," "Sec," "Dur," etc., il faut avouer que les comparaisons adoptées par l'artiste Chinois sont, en général, fort mauvaises, c'est une amplification gâtée de ce qu'il a dit plus haut.'

[2] This and the two preceding paragraphs form the eleventh chapter of the Book, the last of those of which the text has been preserved. It is called, 'Questions of 3ze-kung about Music.'

BOOK XVIII. ƷÂ *K*Î

OR

MISCELLANEOUS RECORDS[1].

SECTION I. PART I.

1. When a feudal lord was on the march and died in his lodging[2], they called back his soul in the same way as in his state. If he died on the road, (one) got up on the nave of the left wheel of the chariot in which he had been riding, and called it, waving the pennon of his flag.

(For the carriage with the bier) there was a pall, and attached to it a fringe made of black cloth, like a lower garment, serving as a curtain (to the temporary coffin), and the whole was made into a sort of house by a covering of white brocade. With this they travelled (back to his state), and on arriving at the gate of the temple, without removing the (curtain) wall, they entered and went straight to the place where the coffining was to take place. The pall was removed at the outside of the door.

2. When a Great officer or an ordinary officer died on the road, (one) got up on the left end of the nave of his carriage, and called back his soul, waving his pennon. If he died in his lodging, they called the soul back in the same manner as if he had died in his house.

---

[1] See the introductory notice, vol. xxvii, page 34.

[2] The public lodging assigned to him in the state where he was.

In the case of a Great officer they made a pall of cloth, and so proceeded homewards. On arriving at the house, they removed the pall, took the (temporary) coffin on a handbarrow, entered the gate, and proceeding to the eastern steps, there halted and removed the barrow, after which they took the body up the steps, right to the place where it was to be coffined.

3. The pall-house made over the body of an ordinary officer was made of the phragmites rush; and the fringe for a curtain below of the typha.

4. In every announcement of a death to the ruler it was said, 'Your lordship's minister, so and so, has died.' When the announcement was from a parent, a wife, or an eldest son, it was said, 'Your lordship's minister, my ——, has died.' In an announcement of the death of a ruler to the ruler of another state, it was said, 'My unworthy ruler has ceased to receive his emoluments. I venture to announce it to your officers[1].' If the announcement were about the death of his wife, it was said, 'The inferior partner of my poor ruler has ceased to receive her emoluments.' On the death of a ruler's eldest son, the announcement ran, 'The heir-son of my unworthy ruler, so and so, has died.'

5. When an announcement of the death of a Great officer was sent to another of the same grade in the same state, it was said, 'So and so has ceased to receive his emoluments.' The same terms were employed when the announcement was to an ordinary officer. When it was sent to the ruler of another state, it ran, 'Your lordship's outside minister,

[1] Not daring to communicate the evil tidings directly to the ruler.

my poor Great officer, so and so, has died.' If it were to one of equal degree (in the other state), it was said, 'Sir, your outside servant, our poor Great officer, has ceased to receive his emoluments, and I am sent here to inform you.' If it were to an ordinary officer, the announcement was made in the same terms.

6. In the announcement of the death of an ordinary officer to the same parties, it was made in the same style, only that 'So and so has died,' was employed in all the cases.

7. A Great officer had his place in the lodgings about the palace, till the end of the mourning rites (for a ruler), while another officer returned to his home on the completion of a year. An ordinary officer had his place in the same lodgings. A Great officer occupied the mourning shed; another officer, the unplastered apartment[1].

8. In the mourning for a cousin, either paternal or maternal, who had not attained to the rank of a Great officer, a Great officer wore the mourning appropriate

[1] Two places of lodging about the palace are mentioned here:—the mourning shed, and the unplastered apartment. Both these appear to have been in the courtyard, outside the palace itself; the former, a hut, formed by trees and branches of trees, placed against the wall on the east, with the most slender provision for accommodation and comfort; the latter, an apartment in some other place, made of unburnt bricks, and unplastered, more commodious, but nearly as destitute of comfort. In the former, the chief mourners 'afflicted themselves,' while those whose mourning was not so intense occupied the other.

The ordinary officer, who returned home at the end of a year, is supposed to have had his charge in some town at a distance from court, where his presence could no longer be dispensed with; and the other, who occupies the unplastered apartment to the end of the rites, to have been employed at the court.

for an ordinary officer; and an ordinary officer, in mourning similarly for a cousin on either side who had been a Great officer, wore the same mourning.

9. The son of a Great officer by his wife proper wore the mourning appropriate for a Great officer.

10. The son of a Great officer by any other member of his harem, who was himself a Great officer, wore for his father or mother the mourning of a Great officer; but his place was only the same as that of a son by the proper wife who was not a Great officer.

11. When the son of an ordinary officer had become a Great officer, his parents could not preside at his mourning rites. They made his son do so; and if he had no son, they appointed some one to perform that part, and be the representative of the deceased.

12. When they were divining by the tortoise-shell about the grave and the day of interment of a Great officer, the officer superintending (the operation) wore an upper robe of sackcloth, with (strips of) coarser cloth (across the chest), and a girdle of the same and the usual mourning shoes. His cap was of black material, without any fringe. The diviner wore a skin cap.

13. If the stalks were employed, then the manipulator wore a cap of plain silk, and the long robe. The reader of the result wore his court robes.

14. At the mourning rites for a Great officer (preparatory to the interment), the horses were brought out. The man who brought them wailed, stamped, and went out. After this (the son) folded up the offerings, and read the list (of the gifts that had been sent).

15. At the mourning rites for a Great officer, one from the department of the chief superintendent of the ancestral temple assisted (the presiding mourner), and one from that of the assistant superintendent put the question to the tortoise-shell, which was then manipulated in the proper form by the diviner.

16. In calling back (the soul of) a feudal lord, they used the robe which had first been conferred on him, with the cap and corresponding robes, varying according to the order of his nobility.

17. (In calling back the soul of) a friend's wife, they used the black upper robe with a purple border, or that with pheasants embroidered on it in various colours; both of them lined with white crape.

18. (In calling back that of) the wife of a high noble, they used the upper robe of light green, worn on her first appointment to that position, and lined with white crape; (in calling back that of the wife of) a Great officer of the lowest grade, the upper robe of plain white. (The souls of other wives were called back) by parties with the same robe as in the case of an ordinary officer.

19. In the calling back, they stood (with their faces to the north), inclining to the west[1].

20. (To the pall over the coffin of a Great officer) there was not attached the (curtain of) yellow silk with pheasants on it, descending below the (bamboo) catch for water.

21. (The tablet of a grandson who had been) a Great officer was placed (in the shrine of his grandfather who had (only) been an officer; but not if he

[1] Paragraph 18 in the ordinary editions is before 16. The tablets must have been confused, and were, perhaps, defective.

had only been an officer, and the grandfather a Great officer. In that case, the tablet was placed in the shrine of a brother of the grandfather (who had only been an officer). If there were no such brother, (it was placed in the shrine of their high ancestor), according to the regular order of relationship. Even if his grand-parents were alive, it was so.

22. The (tablet of a) wife was placed after that of the wife (of the principal of the shrine), in which her husband's tablet was placed. If there had been no such wife, it was placed in the shrine of the wife of the high ancestor, according to the regular order of relationship. The (tablet of a) concubine was placed in the shrine of her husband's grandmother (concubine). If there had been no such concubine, then (it was placed in that of the concubine of the high ancestor) according to the regular order of relationship.

23. (The tablet of) an unmarried son was placed in the shrine of his grandfather, and was used at sacrifices. That of an unmarried daughter was placed in the shrine of her grandmother, but was not used at sacrifices. The (tablet of) the son of a ruler was placed in the shrine of (one of) the sons (of his grandfather), that grandfather having also been a ruler.

24. When a ruler died, his eldest son was simply styled son (for that year), but he was treated (by other rulers) as the ruler.

25. If one, after wearing for a year the mourning and cap proper to the three years for a parent, met with the death of a relative for whom he had to wear the mourning of nine months, he changed it for the hempen-cloth proper to the nine months; but he did not change the staff and shoes.

26. In mourning for a parent, (after a year) the sackcloth of the nine months' mourning is preferred; but if there occurred the placing in its shrine of the tablet of a brother who had died prematurely, the cap and other mourning worn during that first year was worn in doing so. The youth who had died prematurely was called 'The Bright Lad,' and (the mourner said), 'My so and so,' without naming him. This was treating him with reference to his being in the spirit-state.

27. In the case of brothers living in different houses, when one first heard of the death of another, he might reply to the messenger simply with a wail. His first step then was to put on the sackcloth, and the girdle with dishevelled edges. If, before he had put on the sackcloth, he hurried off to the mourning rites, and the presiding mourner had not yet adjusted his head-band and girdle, in the case of the deceased being one for whom he had to mourn for five months, he completed that term along with the presiding mourner. If nine months were due to the deceased, he included the time that had elapsed since he assumed the sackcloth and girdle.

28. The master, presiding at the mourning rites for a concubine, himself conducted the placing of her tablet (in its proper shrine). At the sacrifices at the end of the first and second years, he employed her son to preside at them. The sacrifice at her offering did not take place in the principal apartment.

29. A ruler did not stroke the corpse of a servant or a concubine.

30. Even after the wife of a ruler was dead, the concubines (of the harem) wore mourning for her

relatives. If one of them took her place (and acted as mistress of the establishment), she did not wear mourning for the relatives[1].

PART II.

1. If one heard of the mourning rites for a cousin for whom he had to wear mourning for nine months or more, when he looked in the direction of the place where those rites were going on, he wailed. If he were going to accompany the funeral to the grave, but did not get to the house in time, though he met the presiding mourner returning, he himself went on to the grave. The president at the mourning rites for a cousin, though the relationship might not have been near, also presented the sacrifice of Repose.

2. On all occasions of mourning, if, before the mourning robes had all been completed, any one arrived to offer condolences, (the president) took the proper place, wailed, bowed to the visitor, and leaped.

3. At the wailing for a Great officer, another of the same rank, wore the conical cap, with a sackcloth band round it. He wore the same also when engaged with the coffining.

If he had on the cap of dolichos-cloth in mourning for his own wife or son, and were called away to the lighter mourning for a distant relative, he put on the conical cap and band.

4. (In wailing for) an eldest son, he carried a staff, but not for that son's son; he went without it

[1] This lady took the deceased wife's place, and performed many of the duties; but she had not the position of wife. Anciently, a feudal ruler could only, in all his life, have one wife, one lady, that is, to be called by that name.

to the place of wailing. (An eldest son), going to wail for his wife, if his parents were alive, did not carry a staff, nor bow so as to lay his forehead on the ground. If (only) his mother were alive, he did not lay his forehead to the ground. Where such a prostration should have taken place, as in the case of one who brought a gift with his condolence, an ordinary bow was made.

5. (An officer) who had left a feudal prince and gone into the service of a Great officer did not on the lord's death return and wear mourning for him; nor did one who had left a Great officer to serve a prince, return to mourn on the death of the former.

6. The strings of the mourning cap served to distinguish it from one used on a festive occasion. The silk cap worn after a year's mourning, and belonging to that for three years, had such strings, and the seam of it was on the right. That worn in the mourning of five months, and a still shorter time, was seamed on the left. The cap of the shortest mourning had a tassel of reddish silk. The ends of the girdle in the mourning of nine months and upward hung loose.

7. Court robes were made with fifteen skeins (1200 threads) in the warp. Half that number made the coarse cloth for the shortest mourning, which then was glazed by being steeped with ashes.

8. In sending presents to one another for the use of the dead, the princes of the states sent their carriages of the second class with caps and robes. They did not send their carriages of the first class, nor the robes which they had themselves received (from the king).

9. The number of (small) carriages sent (to the

grave) was according to that of the parcels of flesh to be conveyed. Each one had a pall of coarse cloth. All round were ornamental figures. These parcels were placed at the four corners of the coffin.

10. (Sometimes) rice was sent, but Yû-ȝze said that such an offering was contrary to rule. The food put down (by the dead) in mourning was only dried meat and pickled.

11. At the sacrifices (after the sacrifice of Repose), the mourner styled himself 'The filial son,' or 'The filial grandson;' at the previous rites, 'The grieving son,' or 'The grieving grandson.'

12. In the square upper garment of the mourner and the sackcloth over it, and in the carriage in which he rode to the grave, there was no difference of degree.

13. The white cap of high (antiquity) and the cap of black cloth were both without any ornamental fringe. The azure-coloured and that of white silk with turned-up rim had such a fringe.

14. A Great officer wore the cap with the square top when assisting at a sacrifice of his ruler; but that of skin when sacrificing at his own shrines. An ordinary officer used the latter in his ruler's temple, and the cap (of dark cloth) in his own. As an officer wore the skin cap, when going in person to meet his bride, he might also use it at his own shrines.

15. The mortar for the fragrant herbs, in making sacrificial spirits, was made of cypress wood, and the pestle of dryandria. The ladle (for lifting out the flesh) was of mulberry wood, three, some say five, cubits long. The scoop used in addition was of mulberry, three cubits long, with its handle and end carved.

16. The girdle over the shroud used for a prince

or a Great officer was of five colours; that used for another officer, only of two.

17. The must (put into the grave) was made from the malt of rice. There were the jars (for it and other liquids), the baskets (for the millet), and the boxes (in which these were placed). These were placed outside the covering of the coffin; and then the tray for the mats was put in.

18. The spirit-tablet (which had been set up over the coffin) was buried after the sacrifice of Repose.

19. (The mourning rites for) all wives were according to the rank of their husbands.

20. (Visitors who had arrived) during the slighter dressing of the corpse, the more complete dressing, or the opening (the enclosure where the coffin was), were all saluted and bowed to (after these operations were finished).

21. At the wailing morning and evening, (the coffin) was not screened from view. When the bier had been removed, the curtain was no more suspended.

22. When the ruler came to condole, after the carriage with its coffin (had reached the gate of the temple), the presiding mourner bowed towards him with his face towards the east, and moving to the right of the gate, leaped there, with his face towards the north. Going outside, he waited till the ruler took his departure and bade him go back, after which he put down (by the bier the gifts which the ruler had brought).

23. When ʒze-kâo was fully dressed after his death, first, there were the upper and lower garments both wadded with floss silk, and over them a suit of black with a purple border below; next, there was a suit of white made square and straight, (the

suit belonging to) the skin cap; next, that belonging to the skin cap like the colour of a sparrow's head; and next, (that belonging to) the dark-coloured cap, with the square top. Ȝăng-ȝze said, 'In such a dressing there should be nothing of woman's dress.'

24. When an officer died on some commission, upon which he had gone for his ruler, if the death took place in a public hotel, they called his soul back; if in a private hotel, they did not do so. By a public hotel was meant a ruler's palace, or some other building erected by him, and by a private hotel, the house of a noble, a Great officer, or an officer below that rank[1].

25. (On the death of) a ruler, there is the leaping for him for seven days in succession; and on that of a Great officer, it lasts for five days. The women take their share in this expression of grief at intervals, between the presiding mourner and his visitors. On the death of an ordinary officer, it lasts for three days; the women taking their part in the same way.

26. In dressing the corpse of a ruler, there is first put on it the upper robe with the dragon; next, a dark-coloured square-cut suit; next, his court-robes; next, the white lower garment with gathers; next, a purple-coloured lower garment; next, a sparrow-head

[1] It is generally supposed that the Ȝze-kâo here was the disciple of Confucius, so styled, and also known as Kâo *Kh*âi; but the dressing here is that of the corpse of a Great officer, and there is no evidence that the disciple ever attained to that rank; and I am inclined to doubt, with *K*iang *K*âo-hsî and others, whether the party in the text may not have been another Ȝze-kâo. The caps of the last three suits are understood to be used for the suits themselves, with which they were generally worn. Ȝăng-ȝze's condemnation of the dressing was grounded on the purple border of one of the articles in the first suit. See Analects X, 4.

skin cap; next, the dark-coloured cap with the square top; next, the robe given on his first investiture; next, a girdle of red and green; over which was laid out the great girdle.

27. At the slight dressing of the corpse the son (or the presiding mourner) wore the band of sackcloth about his head. Rulers, Great officers, and ordinary officers agreed in this.

28. When the ruler came to see the great dressing of the corpse, as he was ascending to the hall, the Shang priest spread the mat (afresh), and proceeded to the dressing.

29. The gifts (for the dead, and to be placed in the grave), contributed by the people of Lû, consisted of three rolls of dark-coloured silk, and two of light red, but they were (only) a cubit in width, and completing the length of (one) roll[1].

30. When one came (from another ruler) with a message of condolence, he took his place outside, on the west of the gate, with his face to the east. The chief officer attending him was on the south-east of him, with his face to the north, inclining to the west, and west from the gate. The orphan mourner, with his face to the west, gave his instructions to the officer waiting on him, who then went to the visitor and said, 'My orphaned master has sent me to ask why you have given yourself this trouble,' to which the visitor replies, 'Our ruler has sent me to ask for your master in his trouble.' With this reply the officer returned to the mourner and reported it,

[1] This paragraph, which it is not easy to construe or interpret, is understood to be condemnatory of a stinginess in the matter spoken of, which had begun in the Lû. The rule had been that such pieces of silk should be twenty-five cubits wide, and eighteen cubits long.

returning and saying, 'My orphaned master is waiting for you.' On this the visitor advanced. The mourning host then went up to the reception hall by the steps on the east, and the visitor by those on the west. The latter, with his face to the east, communicated his message, saying, 'Our ruler has heard of the bereavement you have sustained, and has sent me to ask for you in your sorrows.' The mourning son then bowed to him, kneeling with his forehead to the ground. The messenger then descended the steps, and returned to his place.

31. The attendant charged with the jade for the mouth of the deceased, and holding it in his hand—a flat round piece of jade—communicated his instructions, saying, 'Our ruler has sent me with the gem for the mouth.' The officer in waiting went in and reported the message, then returning and saying, 'Our orphaned master is waiting for you.' The bearer of the gem then advanced, ascended the steps, and communicated his message. The son bowed to him, with his forehead to the ground. The bearer then knelt, and placed the gem on the south-east of the coffin, upon a phragmites mat; but if the interment had taken place, on a typha mat. After this, he descended the steps, and returned to his place. The major-domo, in his court robes, but still wearing his mourning shoes, then ascended the western steps, and kneeling with his face to the west, took up the piece of jade, and descending by the same steps, went towards the east (to deposit it in the proper place).

32. The officer charged with the grave-clothes said, 'Our ruler has sent me with the grave-clothes.' The officer in waiting, having gone in and reported,

returned and said, 'Our orphaned master is waiting for you.' Then the other took up first the cap with the square top and robes, with his left hand holding the neck of the upper garment, and with his right the waist. He advanced, went up to the hall, and communicated his message, saying, 'Our ruler has sent me with the grave-clothes.' The son bowed to him, with his forehead to the ground; and when the bearer laid down the things on the east of the coffin, he then went down, and received the skin cap of the sparrow's-head colour, with the clothes belonging to it inside the gate, under the eaves. These he presented with the same forms; then the skin cap and clothes which he received in the middle of the courtyard; then the court robes; then the dark-coloured, square-cut garments, which he received at the foot of the steps on the west. When all these presentations were made, five men from the department of the major-domo took the things up, and going down the steps on the west, went away with them to the east. They all took them up with their faces towards the west.

33. The chief of the attendants (of the messenger) had charge of the carriage and horses, and with a long symbol of jade in his hand communicated his message, saying, 'Our ruler has sent me to present the carriage and horses.' The officer in waiting went in and informed the presiding mourner, and returned with the message, 'The orphan, so and so, is waiting for you.' The attendant then had the team of yellow horses and the grand carriage exhibited in the central courtyard, with the front to the north; and with the symbol in hand he communicated his message. His grooms were all below, on

the west of the carriage. The son bowed to him, with his forehead to the ground. He then knelt, and placed his symbol in the corner, on the south-east of the coffin. The major-domo then took the symbol up, and proceeded with it to the east.

34. The message was always delivered with the face turned towards the coffin, and the son always bowed to the attendant charged with it, with his forehead down to the ground. The attendant then knelt with his face to the west, and deposited his gift (or its representative). The major-domo and his employés ascended by the steps on the west to take these up, and did so with their faces towards the west, descending (again) by the same steps.

The attendant charged with the carriage and horses went out, and returned to his place outside the gate.

35. The chief visitor then, (wishing) to perform the ceremony of wailing, said, 'My ruler, being engaged in the services of his own ancestral temple, could not come and take part in your rites, and has sent me, so and so, his old servant, to assist in holding the rope.' The officer in waiting (reported his request), and returned with the message, 'The orphan, so and so, is waiting for you.' The messenger then entered and took his place on the right of the gate. His attendants all followed him, and stood on his left, on the east. The superintendent of ceremonies introduced the visitor, and went up on the hall, and received his ruler's instructions, then descending and saying, 'The orphan ventures to decline the honour which you propose, and begs you to return to your place.' The messenger, however, replied, 'My ruler charged me that I should not

demean myself as a visitor or guest, and I venture to decline doing as you request.' The other then reported this reply, and returned, and told the messenger that the orphan firmly declined the honour which he proposed, and repeated the request that he would return to his place. The messenger repeated his reply, saying that he also firmly declined (to return to his place). The same message from the mourner was repeated, and the same reply to it, (after which) the mourner said, 'Since he thus firmly declines what I request, I will venture respectfully to comply with his wish.'

The messenger then stood on the west of the gate, and his attendants on his left, facing the west. The orphaned mourner descended by the steps on the east, and bowed to him, after which they both ascended and wailed, each of them leaping three times in response to each other. The messenger then went out, escorted by the mourner outside of the gate, who then bowed to him, with his forehead down to the ground.

36. When the ruler of a state had mourning rites in hand for a parent, (any officer who was mourning for a parent) did not dare to receive visits of condolence (from another state).

37. The female relatives of the exterior kept in their apartments; the servants spread the mats; the officer of prayer, who used the Shang forms, spread out the girdle, sash, and upper coverings; the officers washed their hands, standing on the north of the vessel; they then removed the corpse to the place where it was to be dressed. When the dressing was finished, the major-domo reported it. The son then leant on the coffin and leaped. The wife with her

face to the east, also leant on it, kneeling; and then she got up and leaped[1].

38. There are three things in the mourning rites for an officer which agree with those used on the death of the son of Heaven:—the torches kept burning all night (when the coffin is to be conveyed to the grave); the employment of men to draw the carriage; and the keeping of the road free from all travellers on it.

---

[1] See the twelfth paragraph in the second section of next Book. It appears here, with some alteration, by mistake.

SECTION II. PART I.

1. When a man was wearing mourning for his father, if his mother died before the period was completed, he put off the mourning for his father (and assumed that proper for his mother). He put on, however, the proper dress when sacrificial services required it; but when they were over[1], he returned to the mourning (for his mother).

2. When occasion occurred for wearing the mourning for uncles or cousins, if it arrived during the period of mourning for a parent, then the previous mourning was not laid aside, save when the sacrificial services in these cases required it to be so; and when they were finished, the mourning for a parent was resumed.

3. If during the three years' mourning (there occurred also another three years' mourning for the eldest son), then after the coarser girdle of the *K*iung hemp had been assumed in the latter case the sacrifices at the end of the first or second year's mourning for a parent might be proceeded with.

4. When a grandfather had died, and his grandson also died before the sacrifices at the end of the first or second year had been performed, (his spirit-tablet) was still placed next to the grandfather's.

5. When a mourner, while the coffin was in the house, heard of the death of another relative at a

[1] That is, the sacrifices regularly presented at the end of the first and second year from the death. The translation here and in the next three paragraphs, if it were from an Aryan or Semitic language, could not be said to be literal; but it correctly represents the ideas of the author.

distance, he went to another apartment and wailed for him. (Next day), he entered where the coffin was, and put down the offerings (to the deceased), after which he went out, changed his clothes, went to the other apartment, and repeated the ceremony of the day before.

6. When a Great officer or another officer was about to take part in a sacrifice at his ruler's, if, after the inspection of the washing of the vessels to be used, his father or mother died, he still went to the sacrifice; but took his place in a different apartment. After the sacrifice he put off his (sacrificial) dress, went outside the gate of the palace, wailed, and returned to his own house. In other respects he acted as he would have done in hurrying to the mourning rites. If the parent's death took place before the inspection of the washing, he sent a messenger to inform the ruler of his position; and when he returned, proceeded to wail (for his deceased parent).

When the death that occurred was that of an uncle, aunt, or cousin, if he had received the previous notice to fast, he went to the sacrifice; and when it was over, he went out at the ruler's gate, put off his (sacrificial) dress, and returned to his own house. In other respects he acted as if he had been hurrying to the mourning rites. If the deceased relative lived under the same roof with him, he took up his residence in other apartments[1].

---

[1] The *Kh*ien-lung editors doubt the genuineness of this last sentence. A commissioned officer, they say, and much more a Great officer, occupied his own residence, and had left the family at home; and they fail to see how the condition supposed could have existed.

7. Ȝăng-ȝze asked, 'When a high minister or Great officer is about to act the part of the personator of the dead at a sacrifice by his ruler, and has received instructions to pass the night previous in solemn vigil, if there occur in his own family occasion for him to wear the robe of hemmed sackcloth, what is he to do?' Confucius said, 'The rule is for him to leave his own house, and lodge in the ruler's palace till the service (for the ruler) is accomplished.'

8. Confucius said, 'When the personator of the dead comes forth in his leathern cap, or that with the square top, ministers, Great officers, and other officers, all should descend from their carriages when he passes. He should bow forward to them, and he should (also) have people going before him (to notify his approach, that people may get out of the way[1]).'

9. During the mourning rites for a parent, when the occasion for one of the sacrifices was at hand, if a death occurred in the family of a brother or cousin, the sacrifice was postponed till the burial of the dead had taken place. If the cousin or brother were an inmate of the same palace with himself, although the death were that of a servant or concubine, the party postponed his sacrifice in this way. At the sacrifice the mourner went up and descended the steps with only one foot on each, all assisting him, doing the same. They did so even for the sacrifice of Repose, and to put the spirit-tablet in its place.

10. From the feudal rulers down to all officers, at the sacrifice at the end of the first year's mourning

[1] See vol. xxvii, page 341, paragraph 26, which is here repeated.

for a parent, when the chief mourner took the cup offered to him by the chief among the visitors, he raised it to his teeth, while the visitors, brothers, and cousins all sipped the cups presented to them. After the sacrifice at the end of the second year, the chief mourner might sip his cup, while all the visitors, brothers, and cousins might drink off their cups.

11. The attendants at the sacrifices during the funeral rites give notice to the visitors to present the offerings, of which, however, they did not afterwards partake.

12. 3ze-kung asked about the rites of mourning (for parents), and the Master said, 'Reverence is the most important thing; grief is next to it; and emaciation is the last. The face should wear the appearance of the inward feeling, and the demeanour and carriage should be in accordance with the dress.'

He begged to ask about the mourning for a brother, and the Master said, 'The rites of mourning for a brother are to be found in the tablets where they are written.'

13. A superior man will not interfere with the mourning of other men to diminish it, nor will he do so with his own mourning[1].

14. Confucius said, 'Shâo-lien and Tâ-lien demeaned themselves skilfully during their mourning (for their parents). During the (first) three days they were alert; for the (first) three months they manifested no weariness; for the (first) year they were full of grief; for the (whole) three years they were

[1] The *Kh*ien-lung editors think paragraph 13 is out of place, and would place it farther on, after paragraph 43.

sorrowful. (And yet) they belonged to one of the rude tribes on the East[1].'

15. During the three years of mourning (for his father), (a son) might speak, but did not discourse; might reply, but did not ask questions. In the shed or the unplastered apartment he sat (alone), nobody with him. While occupying that apartment, unless there were some occasion for him to appear before his mother, he did not enter the door (of the house). On all occasions of wearing the sackcloth with its edges even, he occupied the unplastered apartment, and not the shed. To occupy the shed was the severest form in mourning.

16. (The grief) in mourning for a wife was like that for an uncle or aunt; that for a father's sister or one's own sister was like that for a cousin; that for any of the three classes of minors dying prematurely was as if they had been full-grown.

17. The mourning for parents is taken away (at the end of three years), (but only) its external symbols; the mourning for brothers (at the end of one year), (and also) internally.

18. (The period of mourning) for a ruler's mother or wife is the same as that for brothers. But (beyond) what appears in the countenance is this, that (in the latter case) the mourners do not eat and drink (as usual).

19. After a man has put off the mourning (for his father), if, when walking along the road, he sees one like (his father), his eyes look startled. If he hear one with the same name, his heart is agitated.

---

[1] Shâo-lien; see Analects XVIII, 8, 3, and 'Narratives of the School,' Article 43.

In condoling with mourners on occasion of a death, and inquiring for one who is ill, there will be something in his face and distressed manner different from other men. He who is thus affected is fit to wear the three years' mourning. So far as other mourning is concerned, he may walk right on (without anything) having such an effect on him.

20. The sacrifice at the end of the second[1] year is signalized by the principal mourner putting off his mourning dress. The evening (before), he announces the time for it, and puts on his court robes, which he then wears at the sacrifice.

21. Ȝze-yû said, 'After the sacrifice at the end of the second year, although the mourner should not wear the cap of white silk, (occasions may occur when) he must do so[2]. Afterwards he resumes the proper dress.'

22. (At the mourning rites of an officer), if, when he had bared his breast, a Great officer arrived (on a visit of condolence), although he might be engaged in the leaping, he put a stop to it, and went to salute and bow to him. Returning then, he resumed his leaping and completed it, after which he readjusted his dress and covered his breast.

In the case of a visit from another officer, he went on with his leaping, completed it, readjusted his upper dress, and then went to salute and bow to him, without having occasion to resume and complete the leaping.

23. At the sacrifice of Repose for a Great officer of the highest grade, there were offered a boar and a

---

[1] So, *Kh*ăn Kâo.

[2] Such as receiving the condolences of visitors on account of some other occasion of mourning.

ram; at the conclusion of the wailing, and at the placing of his spirit-tablet, there was, in addition, the bull. On the similar occasions for a Great officer of the lowest grade, there was in the first case a single victim, and in the others the boar and the ram.

24. In consulting the tortoise-shell about the burial and sacrifice of Repose, the style of the petition was as follows:—A son or grandson spoke of himself as 'the sorrowing,' (when divining about his father or grandfather); a husband (divining about his wife) said, 'So and so for so and so;' an elder brother about a younger brother, simply said, 'So and so;' a younger brother about an elder brother said, 'For my elder brother, so and so.'

25. Anciently, noble and mean all carried staffs. (On one occasion) Shû-sun Wû-shû[1], when going to court, saw a wheelwright put his staff through the nave of a wheel, and turn it round. After this (it was made a rule that) only men of rank should carry a staff.

26. (The custom of) making a hole in the napkin (covering the face of the dead) by which to introduce what was put into the mouth, was begun by Kung-yang *K*iâ[2].

27. What were the grave-clothes (contributed to the dead)? The object of them was to cover the body. From the enshrouding to the slighter dressing, they were not put on, and the figure of the body was seen. Therefore the corpse was first enshrouded, and afterwards came the grave-clothes.

28. Some one asked Ȝăng-ȝze, 'After sending

---

[1] A Great officer of Lû, about B.C. 500.

[2] We do not find anything about this man elsewhere.

away to the grave the offerings to the dead, we wrap up what remains;—is this not like a man, after partaking of a meal, wrapping up what is left (to take with him)? Does a gentleman do such a thing?' Ȝăng-ȝze said, 'Have you not seen what is done at a great feast? At a great feast, given by a Great officer, after all have partaken, he rolls up what is left on the stands for the three animals, and sends it to the lodgings of his guests. When a son treats his parents in this way as his (honoured) guests, it is an expression of his grief (for their loss). Have you, Sir, not seen what is done at a great feast?'

29. 'Excepting at men's funeral rites, do they make such inquiries and present such gifts as they then do? At the three years' mourning, the mourner bows to his visitors in the manner appropriate to the occasion; at the mourning of a shorter period, he salutes them in the usual way[1].'

30. During the three years' mourning, if any one sent wine or flesh to the mourner, he received it after declining it thrice; he received it in his sackcloth and band. If it came from the ruler with a message from him, he did not presume to decline it;—he received it and presented it (in his ancestral temple).

One occupied with such mourning did not send any gift, but when men sent gifts to him he received them. When engaged in the mourning rites for an uncle, cousin, or brother, and others of a shorter period, after the wailing was concluded, he might send gifts to others.

31. Hsien-ȝze said, 'The pain occasioned by the

[1] See vol. xxvii, pp. 122–3, paragraph 5. There is probably something wanting at the beginning of this paragraph.

mourning for three years is like that of beheading; that arising from the one year's mourning, is like the stab from a sharp weapon.'

32. During the one year's mourning, in the eleventh month, they put on the dress of silk, which was called lien; in the thirteenth month they offered the hsiang sacrifice, and in the same month that called than;—which concluded the mourning.

During the mourning for three years, even though they had occasion to assume the dress proper for the nine months' mourning, they did not go to condole (with the other mourners). From the feudal lords down to all officers, if they had occasion to dress and go to wail (for a relative newly deceased), they did so in the dress proper to the mourning for him. After putting on the lien silk, they paid visits of condolence.

33. When one was occupied with the nine months' mourning, if the burial had been performed, he might go and condole with another mourner, retiring after he had wailed without waiting for any other part of the mourner's proceedings.

During the mourning for one year, if before the burial one went to condole with another in the same district, he withdrew after he had wailed, without waiting for the rest of the proceedings.

If condoling during the mourning for nine months, he waited to see the other proceedings, but did not take part in them.

During the mourning for five months or three months, he waited to assist at the other proceedings, but did not take part in the (principal) ceremony[1].

---

[1] That is, in putting down the offerings to the deceased.

34. When one (was condoling with) another whom he had been accustomed to pass with a hasty step[1], (at the interment of his dead relative), he retired when the bier had passed out from the gate of the temple. If they had been on bowing terms, he retired when they had reached the station for wailing. If they had been in the habit of exchanging inquiries, he retired after the coffin was let down into the grave. If they had attended court together, he went back to the house with the other, and wailed with him. If they were intimate friends, he did not retire till after the sacrifice of Repose, and the placing of the spirit-tablet of the deceased in the shrine.

35. Condoling friends did not (merely) follow the principal mourner. Those who were forty (or less) held the ropes when the coffin was let down into the grave. Those of the same district who were fifty followed him back to the house and wailed; and those who were forty waited till the grave was filled up.

36. During mourning, though the food might be bad, the mourner was required to satisfy his hunger with it. If for hunger he had to neglect anything, this was contrary to the rules. If he through satiety forgot his sorrow, that also was contrary to the rules. It was a distress to the wise men (who made the rules) to think that a mourner should not see or hear distinctly; should not walk correctly or be unconscious of his occasion for sorrow; and therefore (they enjoined) that a mourner, when ill, should drink wine and eat flesh; that people of fifty should do nothing to bring on emaciation; that at sixty they should not be emaciated; that at seventy they should drink

[1] This was a mark of respect. Compare Analects IX, 9.

liquor and eat flesh:—all these rules were intended as preventives against death.

37. If one, while in mourning, was invited by another to eat with him, he did not go while wearing the nine months' mourning or that of a shorter period; if the burial had taken place, he might go to another party's house. If that other party belonged to his relative circle, and wished him to eat with him, he might do so; if he did not belong to that circle, he did not eat with him.

38. While wearing the mourning of nine months, one might eat vegetables and fruits, and drink water and congee, using no salt or cream. If he could not eat dry provisions, he might use salt or cream with them.

39. Confucius said, 'If a man have a sore on his body, he should bathe. If he have a wound on his head, he should wash it. If he be ill, he should drink liquor and eat flesh. A superior man will not emaciate himself so as to be ill. If one die from such emaciation, a superior man will say of him that he has failed in the duty of a son.'

40. Excepting when following the carriage with the bier to the grave, and returning from it, one was not seen on the road with the mourning cap, which was used instead of the ordinary one.

41. During the course of mourning, from that worn for five months and more, the mourner did not wash his head or bathe, excepting for the sacrifice of Repose, the placing the spirit-tablet in the shrine, the assuming the dress of lien silk, and the sacrifice at the end of a year.

42. During mourning rites, when the sackcloth with the edges even was worn, after the burial, if one asked an interview with the mourner, he saw him, but

he himself did not ask to see any person. He might do so when wearing the mourning of five months. When wearing that for nine months, he did not carry the introductory present in his hand (when seeking an interview). It was only when wearing the mourning for a parent that the mourner did not avoid seeing any one, (even) while the tears were running from him.

43. A man while wearing the mourning for three years might execute any orders of government after the sacrifice at the end of a year. One mourning for a year, might do so when the wailing was ended; one mourning for nine months, after the burial; one mourning for five months or three, after the encoffining and dressing.

44. Ȝăng Shăn asked Ȝăng-ȝze, saying, 'In wailing for a parent, should one do so always in the same voice?' The answer was, 'When a child has lost its mother on the road, is it possible for it to think about the regular and proper voice?'

PART II.

1. After the wailing was ended, there commenced the avoiding of certain names. (An officer) did not use the name of his (paternal) grandfather or grandmother, of his father's brothers or uncles; of his father's aunts or sisters. Father and son agreed in avoiding all these names. The names avoided by his mother the son avoided in the house. Those avoided by his wife he did not use when at her side. If among them there were names which had been borne by his own paternal great-grand-father or great-grand-uncles, he avoided them (in all places).

2. When (the time for) capping (a young man) came during the time of the mourning rites, though they were those for a parent, the ceremony might be performed. After being capped in the proper place, the subject went in, wailed and leaped,—three times each bout, and then came out again.

3. At the end of the nine months' mourning, it was allowable to cap a son or to marry a daughter. A father at the end of the five months' mourning, might cap a son, or marry a daughter, or take a wife (for a son). Although one himself were occupied with the five months' mourning, yet when he had ended the wailing, he might be capped, or take a wife. If it were the five months' mourning for one who had died in the lowest degree of immaturity, he could not do so [1].

4. Whenever one wore the cap of skin with a sackcloth band (in paying a visit of condolence), his upper garment of mourning had the large sleeves.

5. When the father was wearing mourning, a son, who lived in the same house with him, kept away from all music. When the mother was wearing it, the son might listen to music, but not play himself. When a wife was wearing it, the son, (her husband), did not play music by her side. When an occasion for the nine months' mourning was about to occur, the lute and cithern were laid aside. If it were only an occasion for the five months' mourning, music was not stopped.

6. When an aunt or sister died (leaving no son), if her husband (also) were dead, and there were no

[1] This paragraph seems to me, as to many of the Chinese critics, irretrievably corrupt or defective.

brother or cousin in his relative circle, some other of her husband's more distant relatives was employed to preside at her mourning rites. None of a wife's relatives, however near, could preside at them. If no distant relative even of her husband could be found, then a neighbour, on the east or the west, was employed. If no such person (suitable) could be found, then the head man of the neighbourhood presided. Some say, 'One (of her relatives) might preside, but her tablet was placed by that of the (proper) relative of her husband.'

7. The girdle was not used along with the sackcloth band. That band could not be used by one who carried in his hand his jade-token; nor could it be used along with a dress of various colours.

8. On occasions of prohibitions issued by the state (in connexion with the great sacrifices), the wailing ceased; as to the offerings deposited by the coffin, morning and evening, and the repairing to their proper positions, mourners proceeded as usual[1].

9. A lad, when wailing, did not sob or quaver; did not leap; did not carry a staff; did not wear the straw sandals; and did not occupy the mourning shed.

10. Confucius said, 'For grand-aunts the mourning with the edges even is worn, but the feet in leaping are not lifted from the ground. For aunts and sisters the mourning for nine months is worn, but the feet in leaping are lifted from the ground. If a man understands these things, will he not (always) follow the right forms of ceremonies? Will he not do so?'

---

[1] The punctuation and place of this short paragraph vary. Its integrity is also doubted.

11. When the mother of Î Liû died, his assistants in the rites stood on his left; when Î Liû died, they stood on his right. The practice of the assistants (at funeral rites) giving their aid on the right, originated from the case of Î Liû[1].

12. The mouth of the son of Heaven was stuffed after death with nine shells; that of a feudal lord, with seven; that of a Great officer, with five; and that of an ordinary officer, with three[2].

13. An officer was interred after three months, and the same month the wailing was ended. A Great officer was interred (also) after three months, and after five months the wailing was ended. A prince was interred after five months, and after seven the wailing was ended.

For an officer the sacrifice of Repose was offered three times; for a Great officer, five times; and for a feudal prince, seven times.

14. A feudal lord sent a messenger to offer his condolences; and after that, his contributions for the mouth, the grave-clothes, and the carriage. All these things were transacted on the same day, and in the order thus indicated.

15. When a high minister or Great officer was ill, the ruler inquired about him many times. When an ordinary officer was ill, he inquired about him once. When a Great officer or high minister was buried, the ruler did not eat flesh; when the wailing was finished, he did not have music. When an officer was encoffined, he did not have music.

16. After they had gone up, and made the bier

---

[1] A minister of duke Mû of Lû, B.C. 409–377.

[2] This was not the practice in the *K*âu dynasty.

ready, in the case of the burial of a feudal lord, there were 500 men to draw the ropes. At each of the four ropes they were all gagged. The minister of War superintended the clappers; eight men with these walking on each side of the bier. The chief artizan, carrying a shade of feathers, guided the progress (of the procession). At the burial of a Great officer, after they had gone up and made the bier ready, 300 men drew the ropes; four men with their clappers walked on each side of the bier; and its progress was guided (by the chief artizan) with a reed of white grass in his hand.

17. Confucius said, 'Kwan *K*ung had carving on the square vessels for holding the grain of his offerings, and red ornaments for his cap; he set up a screen where he lodged on the way, and had a stand of earth on which the cups he had used, in giving a feast, were replaced; he had hills carved on the capitals of his pillars, and pondweed on the lower pillars supporting the rafters[1]. He was a worthy Great officer, but made it difficult for his superiors (to distinguish themselves from him).

'An Phing-*k*ung[2], in sacrificing to his father and other progenitors, used only the shoulders of a pig, not large enough to cover the dish. He was a worthy Great officer, but made it difficult for his inferiors (to distinguish themselves from him).

'A superior man will not encroach on (the observances of) those above him, nor put difficulties in the way of those below him.'

---

[1] See Confucian Analects III, 22, and V, 17.

[2] A minister of *Kh*î, contemporary with Confucius, distinguished for his simple, and perhaps parsimonious, ways.

18. Excepting on the death of her father or mother, the wife (of a feudal lord) did not cross the boundaries of the state to pay a visit of condolence. On that occasion she did so, and went back to her original home, where she used the ceremonies of condolence proper to a feudal lord, and she was treated as one. When she arrived, she entered by the women's gate, and went up (to the reception hall) by steps at the side (of the principal steps), the ruler receiving her at the top of the steps on the east. The other ceremonies were the same as those of a guest who hastened to attend the funeral rites.

19. A sister-in-law did not lay the soothing hand on the corpse of her brother-in-law; and vice versâ.

20. There are three things that occasion sorrow to a superior man (who is devoted to learning):—If there be any subject of which he has not heard, and he cannot get to hear of it; if he hear of it, and cannot get to learn it; if he have learned it, and cannot get to carry it out in practice. There are five things that occasion shame to a superior man (who is engaged in governmental duties):—If he occupy an office, and have not well described its duties; if he describe its duties well, but do not carry them into practice; if he have got his office, and lost it again; if he be charged with the care of a large territory, and the people be not correspondingly numerous; if another, in a charge like his own, have more merit than he.

21. Confucius said, 'In bad years they used in their carriages their poorest horses, and in their sacrifices the victims lowest (in the classes belonging to them).'

22. At the mourning rites for Hsü Yû, duke Âi

sent *Z*û Pî to Confucius to learn the rites proper at the mourning for the officer. Those rites were thus committed at that time to writing.

23. Ȝze-kung having gone to see the agricultural sacrifice at the end of the year, Confucius said to him, 'Ȝhze, did it give you pleasure?' The answer was, 'The people of the whole state appeared to be mad; I do not know in what I could find pleasure.' The Master said, 'For their hundred days' labour in the field, (the husbandmen) receive this one day's enjoyment (from the state);—this is what you do not understand. (Even) Wăn and Wû could not keep a bow (in good condition), if it were always drawn and never relaxed; nor did they leave it always relaxed and never drawn. To keep it now strung and now unstrung was the way of Wăn and Wû.'

24. Mâng Hsien-ȝze said, 'If in the first month at the (winter) solstice it be allowable to offer the (border) sacrifice to God, in the seventh month, at the summer solstice, we may offer the sacrifice in the temple of the ancestor (of our ruling House).' Accordingly Hsien-ȝze offered that sacrifice to all the progenitors (of the line of Lû) in the seventh month[1].

25. The practice of not obtaining from the son of Heaven the confirmation of her dignity for the wife (of the ruler of Lû) began with duke *K*âo[2].

---

[1] Hsien-ȝze was the honorary title of *K*ung-sun Mieh, a good officer of Lû, under dukes Wăn, Hsüan, *Kh*ăng, and Hsiang. He must understand him as speaking of the sacrifices of the state, and not of his own.

[2] See Confucian Analects VII, 30. Duke *K*âo married a lady of Wû, of the same surname with himself, and therefore had not announced the marriage to the king.

26. The mourning of a ruler and his wife were regulated by the same rules for the ladies of his family married in other states and for those married in his own[1].

27. When the stables of Confucius were burned, and the friends of his district came (to offer their condolences) on account of the fire, he bowed once to the ordinary officers, and twice to the Greater officers;—according to the rule on occasions of mutual condolence.

28. Confucius said, 'Kwan *K*ung selected two men from among (certain) thieves with whom he was dealing, and appointed them to offices in the state, saying, "They were led astray by bad men with whom they had associated, but they are proper men themselves." When he died, duke Hwan made these two wear mourning for him. The practice of old servants of a Great officer wearing mourning for him, thus arose from Kwan *K*ung. But these two men only mourned for him by the duke's orders.'

29. When an officer, in a mistake, used a name to his ruler which should be avoided, he rose to his feet. If he were speaking to any one who had the name that should be avoided with the ruler, he called him by the name given to him on his maturity.

30. (A Great officer) took no part in any seditious movements within his state, and did not try to avoid calamities coming from without.

31. The treatise on the duties of the Chief Internuncius says, 'The length of the long symbol of rank was for a duke, nine inches; for a marquis or

[1] There are differences of opinion as to the meaning of this paragraph, between which it is not easy to decide. It would be tedious to go into an exhibition and discussion of them.

earl, seven; for a count or baron, five. The width in each case was three inches; and the thickness, half an inch. They tapered to the point for one inch and a half. They were all of jade. The mats for them were made with three different colours, (two rows of each,) six in all.'

32. Duke Âi asked Ȝze-kâo, 'When did members of your family first begin to be in office?' The answer was, 'My ancestor held a small office under duke Wăn[1].'

33. When a temple was completed, they proceeded to consecrate it with the following ceremony:—The officer of prayer, the cook, and the butcher, all wore the cap of leather of the colour of a sparrow's head, and the dark-coloured dress with the purple border. The butcher rubbed the sheep clean, the officer of prayer blessed it, and the cook with his face to the north took it to the pillar and placed it on the south-east of it. Then the butcher took it in his arms, went up on the roof at the middle point between the east and west, and with his face to the south stabbed it, so that the blood ran down in front; and then he descended. At the gate of the temple, and of each of the two side apartments, they used a fowl, one at the gate of each (going up as before and stabbing them). The hair and feathers about the ears were first pulled out under the roof (before the victims were killed). When the fowls were cut at the gates of the temple, and the apartments on each side of it, officers stood, opposite to each gate on the north. When the thing was over, the officer of prayer announced that it

[1] This paragraph is supposed to be defective. Duke Wăn was marquis of Lû from B.C. 626 to 609.

was so, and they all retired, after which he announced it to the ruler, saying, 'The blood-consecration has been performed.' This announcement was made at the door of the back apartment of the temple, inside which the ruler stood in his court-robes, looking towards the south. This concluded the ceremony, and all withdrew[1].

When the great apartment (of the palace) was completed, it was inaugurated (by a feast), but there was no shedding of blood. The consecration by blood of the temple building was the method taken to show how intercourse with the spirits was sought. All the more distinguished vessels of the ancestral temple were consecrated, when completed, by the blood of a young boar.

34. When a feudal lord sent his wife away, she proceeded on her journey to her own state, and was received there with the observances due to a lord's wife. The messenger, accompanying her, then discharged his commission, saying, 'My poor ruler, from his want of ability, was not able to follow her, and take part in the services at your altars and in your ancestral temple. He has, therefore, sent me, so and so, and I venture to inform your officer appointed for the purpose of what he has done.' The officer presiding (on the occasion) replied, 'My poor ruler in his former communication did not lay (her defects) before you, and he does not presume to do anything but respectfully receive your lord's message.' The officers in attendance on the commis-

[1] This ceremony is also described in the 'Rites of the greater Tâi,' Book X, with some difference in the details. It is difficult, even from the two accounts, to bring the ceremony fully before the mind's eye.

sioner then set forth the various articles sent with the lady on her marriage, and those on the other side received them.

35. When the wife went away from her husband, she sent a messenger and took leave of him, saying, 'So and so, through her want of ability, is not able to keep on supplying the vessels of grain for your sacrifices, and has sent me, so and so, to presume to announce this to your attendants.' The principal party (on the other side) replied, 'My son, in his inferiority, does not presume to avoid your punishing him, and dares not but respectfully receive your orders.' The messenger then retired, the principal party bowing to him, and escorting him. If the father-in-law were alive, then he named himself; if he were dead, an elder brother of the husband acted for him, and the message was given as from him; if there were no elder brother, then it ran as from the husband himself. The message, as given above, was, 'The son of me, so and so, in his inferiority.' (At the other end of the transaction), if the lady were an aunt, an elder sister, or a younger, she was mentioned as such.

36. Confucius said, 'When I was at a meal at Shâo-shih's, I ate to the full. He entertained me courteously, according to the rules. When I was about to offer some in sacrifice, he got up and wished to stop me, saying, "My poor food is not worth being offered in sacrifice." When I was about to take the concluding portions, he got up and wished to stop me, saying, "I would not injure you with my poor provisions[1]."'

---

[1] See pages 20, 21, paragraph 13.

37. A bundle of silk (in a marriage treaty) contained five double rolls, each double roll being forty cubits in length.

38. At the (first) interview of a wife with her father and mother-in-law, (her husband's) unmarried aunts and sisters all stood below the reception hall, with their faces towards the west, the north being the place of honour. After this interview, she visited all the married uncles of her husband, each in his own apartment.

Although not engaged to be married, the rule was for a young lady to wear the hair-pin;—she was thus treated with the honours of maturity. The (principal) wife managed the ceremony. When she was unoccupied and at ease, she wore her hair without the pin, on each side of her head.

39. The apron (of the full robes) was three cubits long, two cubits wide at bottom, and one at the top. The border at the top extended five inches; and that at the sides was of leather the colour of a sparrow's head, six inches wide, terminating five inches from the bottom. The borders at top and bottom were of white silk, embroidered with the five colours.

BOOK XIX. SANG TÂ *KÎ*

OR

THE GREATER RECORD OF MOURNING RITES[1].

SECTION I.

1. When the illness was extreme, all about the establishment was swept clean, inside and out. In the case of a ruler or Great officer, the stands, with the martial instruments suspended from them, were removed; in that of an officer, his lute and cithern. The sufferer lay with his head to the east, under the window on the north. His couch was removed (and he was laid on the ground). The clothes ordinarily worn at home were removed, and new clothes substituted for them. (In moving the body) one person took hold of each limb. Males and females changed their dress[2]. Some fine floss was put (on the mouth and nostrils), to make sure that the breath was gone. A man was not permitted to die in the hands of the women, or a woman in the hands of the men.

2. A ruler and his wife both died in the Great chamber, a Great officer and his acknowledged wife in the Proper chamber[3]; the not yet acknowledged

---

[1] See introductory notice, vol. xxvii, pages 34, 35.

[2] The clothes of the dying master and friend were changed; it was right that all about them should also change their dress. The court or best robes were put on, moreover, that inquiring visitors might be properly received.

[3] This proper, or 'legitimate' chamber corresponded in the mansion of a Great officer to the Grand chamber in the palace.

wife of a high minister, in an inferior chamber, but the corpse was then removed to the higher chamber. The wives of officers died in their chambers.

3. At (the ceremony of) calling back the soul, if (the deceased were a lord on whose territory) there were forests and copses, the forester arranged the steps (by which to go up on the roof); and if there were no forests, one of the salvage men (employed about the court in menial offices) did so. An officer of low rank performed the ceremony. All who did so employed some of the court robes (of the deceased):—for a ruler, the robe with the descending dragon; for the wife, that with the descending pheasant; for a Great officer, the dark robe and red skirt; for his recognised wife, the robe of fresh yellow; for an officer, that worn with the cap of deep purple leather; and for his wife, the dark dress with the red border. In all cases they ascended from the east wing to the middle of the roof, where the footing was perilous. Facing the north, they gave three loud calls for the deceased, after which they rolled up the garment they had employed, and cast it down in front, where the curator of the robes received it, and then they themselves descended by the wing on the north-west.

If the deceased were a visitor, and in a public lodging, his soul was called back; if the lodging were private, it was not called back. If he were in the open country, one got up on the left end of the nave of the carriage in which he had been riding, and called it back.

Connected with the Grand chamber were two smaller apartments. It is mentioned in the Ȝo *K*wan, under B.C. 627, that duke Hsî of Lû died 'in the small apartment;' which has always been understood as discreditable to him.

4. The garment which had been used in calling the soul back was not employed to cover the corpse, nor in dressing it. In calling back the soul of a wife, the upper robe with the purple border in which she had been married was not employed. In all cases of calling back the soul, a man was called by his name, and a woman by her designation. Nothing but the wailing preceded the calling the soul back. After that calling they did what was requisite on an occasion of death.

5. Immediately after death, the principal mourners sobbed[1]; brothers and cousins (of the deceased) wailed; his female relatives wailed and leaped.

6. When the dead body (of a ruler) had been placed properly (beneath the window with the head to the south), his son sat (or knelt) on the east; his ministers, Great officers, uncles, cousins, their sons and grandsons, stood (also) on the east; the multitude of ordinary officers, who had the charge of the different departments, wailed below the hall, facing the north. His wife knelt on the west; the wives, aunts, sisters, their daughters and grand-daughters, whose husbands were of the same surname as he, stood (behind her) on the west; and the wives, his relatives of the same surname, whose position had been confirmed in their relation to their husbands, at the head of all the others married similarly to husbands of other surnames, wailed above in the hall, facing the north.

7. At the mourning rites (immediately after death) of a Great officer, the (son), presiding, knelt on the east, and the wife, presiding, on the west. The

[1] They were too much affected, it is said, to give loud expression to their grief.

husbands and wives (among the relations) whose positions had been officially confirmed, sat (or knelt); others who had not that confirmation, stood.

At the rites for a deceased officer, the son presiding, uncles, brothers, and cousins, with their sons and grandsons, all sat (or knelt) on the east; the wife presiding, aunts, sisters, and cousins, with their female children and grandchildren, all sat (or knelt) on the west.

Whenever they wailed by the corpse in the apartment, the presiding mourner did so, holding up the shroud with his two hands at the same time.

8. At the mourning rites of a ruler, before the slighter dressing was completed, the principal mourner came out to receive the visit of a refugee ruler, or a visitor from another state.

At those for a Great officer, at the same period, he came out to receive a message from his ruler. At those for an ordinary officer, also at the same period, he came out to receive a Great officer, if he were not engaged in the dressing.

9. Whenever the presiding mourner went forth (to meet visitors), he had his feet bare, his skirt tucked under his girdle, and his hands across his chest over his heart. Having gone down by the steps on the west, if a ruler, he bowed to a refugee ruler, or a minister commissioned from another state, each in his proper place. When a message from his ruler came to a Great officer, he came to the outside of the door of the apartment (where the dead was), to receive the messenger who had ascended to the hall and communicated his instructions. (They then went down together), and the mourner bowed to the messenger below.

When a Great officer came himself to condole with an ordinary officer, the latter wailed along with him, but did not meet him outside the gate.

10. The wife of a ruler went out (of her apartment) on a visit from the wife of a refugee ruler.

The confirmed wife (of a Great officer) went out (in the same way) on the arrival of a message from the ruler's wife.

The wife of an officer, if not engaged in the dressing, (also) went out to receive the confirmed wife (of a Great officer).

11. At the slighter dressing, the presiding mourner took his place inside the door (on the east of it), and the presiding wife had her face to the east. When the dressing was ended, both of them made as if they leant on the body, and leaped. The mourner unbared his breast, took off the tufts of juvenility, and bound up his hair with sackcloth. The wife knotted up her hair, and put on her sackcloth girdle in her room.

12. When the curtain (which screened the body) was removed, the men and women carried it and put it down in the hall, (the eldest son) going down the steps and bowing (to the visitors).

13. The (young) ruler (who was mourning) bowed to refugee lords, and to ministers, commissioners from other states. Great officers and other officers bowed to ministers and Great officers in their respective places. In the case of (the three grades of) officers, they received three side-bows[1], one for each grade. The ruler's wife also bowed to the wife of a refugee

[1] The side-bows were somehow made, without the ruler's turning directly towards the officers.

lord, above in the hall. With regard to the wives of Great officers and of other officers, she bowed specially to each whose position had received the official appointment; to the others she gave a general bow;—all above in the hall.

14. When the mourner had gone to his own place (after bowing to his visitors), he closed the robe which was drawn on one side, covering his breast, put on his girdle and head-band, and leapt. When the mourning was for his mother, he went to his place, and tied up his hair, after which he put down the offerings by the body. The visitors who had come to condole, covered their fur robes, put the roll at the back of their caps, assumed their girdles and head-bands, and leapt in correspondence with the mourner.

15. At the funeral rites for a ruler, the chief forester supplied wood and horns; the chief of the salvage-men supplied the vases for water; the chief of the slaughtering department supplied boilers; and (an officer from the department of) the minister of War (saw to the) hanging of these. Thus they secured the succession of wailers. Some of those in the department took their part in the wailing. If they did not hang up the vases, and the Great officers were sufficient to take the wailing in turns, then they did not use those others[1].

In the hall of the ruler there were two lights above and two below; for that of a Great officer, one above

[1] The object of the arrangements in this obscure paragraph was evidently to maintain the wailing uninterrupted, and to provide, by means of the clepsydra, a regular marking of the time for that purpose. See, in the *K*âu Kwan XXX, 51–52, the duties of the officer of the department of the minister of War who had charge of the vase.

and two below; for that of an ordinary officer, one above and one below[1].

16. When the guests went out, the curtain was removed[2].

17. When they were wailing the corpse above in the hall, the principal mourner was at the east; visitors coming from without, took their place at the west, and the women stood facing the south.

18. The wife (presiding), in receiving guests and escorting them, did not go down from the hall with them. If she did go down (as with the wife of the ruler), she bowed to her, but did not wail.

If the son (presiding), had occasion to go outside the door of the apartment, and saw the guest (whom he so went to meet), he did not wail.

When there was no female to preside, a son did so, and bowed to the female visitors inside the door of the apartment. If there were no son to preside, a daughter did so, and bowed to the male visitors at the foot of the steps on the east.

If the son were a child, then he was carried in his sackcloth in the arms, and his bearer bowed for him.

If the successor of the deceased were not present, and was a man of rank, an apology was made to the guests; if he were not a man of rank, some other one bowed to them for him.

If he were anywhere in the state, they waited for him; if he had gone beyond it, the encoffining and burial might go on. The funeral rites might proceed without the presence of the successor of the deceased, but not without one to preside over them.

---

[1] This must have been towards morning. During the night torches were kept burning.

[2] This should be at the end of paragraph 14.

19. At the mourning rites for a ruler, on the third day his sons and his wife assumed the staff. On the fifth day, when the corpse was put into the coffin, his daughters who had become the wives of Great officers were allowed to use it. His (eldest) son and Great officers used it outside the door of the apartment (where the coffin was); inside the door they carried it in their hands (but did not use it). The wife and his daughters, the wives of Great officers, used the staff in their rooms; when they went to their places (in the apartment where the coffin was), people were employed to hold it for them.

When a message came from the king, (the son presiding) put away his staff; when one came from the ruler of another state, he only held it in his hand. When attending to any consultation of the tortoise-shell about the corpse, he put away his staff.

A Great officer, in the place of the ruler, carried his staff in his hand; at another Great officer's, he used it.

20. At the mourning rites for a Great officer, on the morning of the third day, when the body was put into the coffin, his son presiding, his wife presiding, and the steward of the House, all assumed the staff. On a message from the ruler, the (new) Great officer put away his staff; on a message from another Great officer, he carried it in his hand. His wife, on a message from the wife of the ruler, put her staff away; on a message from the confirmed wife (of another Great officer), she gave it to some one to hold for her.

21. At the mourning rites for an officer, the body on the second day was put into the coffin. On the morning of the third day, the presiding mourner

assumed the staff, and his wife also. The same observances as in the rites for a Great officer were observed on messages arriving from the ruler or his wife, or from a Great officer and his confirmed wife.

22. All the sons assumed the staff, but only the eldest son used it when they were going to their places (in the apartment where the coffin was). Great officers and other officers, when wailing by the coffin, used the staff; when wailing by the bier, they carried it in their hands. When the staff (used in mourning) was thrown away, it was broken and thrown away in secret.

23. As soon as death took place, the corpse was transferred to the couch [1], and covered with a large sheet. The clothes in which the deceased had died were removed. A servant plugged the mouth open with the spoon of horn; and to keep the feet from contracting, an easy stool was employed [2]. These observances were the same for a ruler, a Great officer, and an ordinary officer [3].

24. The servant in charge of the apartments drew the water, and without removing the well-rope from the bucket gathered it up, and carried the whole up to the top of the steps. There, without going on the hall, he gave it to the attendants in waiting on the body. These then went in to wash the corpse, four

[1] When death seemed to be imminent, the body was removed from the couch and laid on the ground;—if, perhaps, contact with 'mother' earth might revive it. When death had taken place, it was replaced on the couch.

[2] I do not quite understand how this stool was applied so as to accomplish its purpose.

[3] This paragraph is the 24th in the *Kh*ien-lung edition. See below, paragraph 26.

lower servants holding up the sheet, and two performing the washing; having put the water in basins, to which they took it with ladles. In washing they used napkins of fine linen, and in drying the body the ordinary bathing clothes. Another servant then pared the nails of the feet, after which they threw away the rest of the water into the pit. At the funeral rites for a mother (or other female), the female attendants in waiting in the inner room held up the sheet and washed the body.

25. The servant in charge of the apartments, having drawn water and given it to the attendants in waiting on the body, these prepared the wash for the head, above in the hall:—for a ruler, made from maize-water; for a Great officer, from that of the glutinous millet; and for an ordinary officer, that from maize-water. After this, some of the forester's department made a sort of furnace at the foot of the wall on the west; and the potter brought out a large boiler, in which the servant in charge of the apartments should boil the water. The servants of the forester's department brought the fuel which he had removed from the crypt in the north-west of the apartment, now converted into a shrine, to use for that purpose. When the water was heated, he gave it to the attendants, who proceeded to wash the head, and poured the water into an earthenware basin, using the napkin as on ordinary occasions to dry the head. Another servant then clipped the nails of the fingers, and wiped the beard. The water was then thrown into the pit.

26. For a ruler they put down a large vessel, full of ice; for a Great officer, a middle-sized one, full of ice; and for an ordinary officer, only one of earthen-

ware, without any ice in it. Over these they placed the couch with a single sheet and pillow on it; another couch on which the jade should be put into the mouth; and another still, where the fuller dressing should be done. Then the corpse was removed to a couch in the hall, on which was a pillow and mat. The same forms were observed for a ruler, a Great officer, and an ordinary officer[1].

27. At the mourning rites for a ruler, his (eldest) son, Great officers, his other sons, and all the (other) officers (employed about the court), ate nothing for three days, but confined themselves to gruel. (Afterwards) for their consumption they received in the morning a handful of rice, and another in the evening; which they ate without any observance of stated times. Officers (at a distance) were restricted to coarse rice and water for their drink, without regard to any stated times. The wife (of the new ruler), the confirmed wives (of the Great officers), and all the members of their harems, had coarse rice and drank water, having no regard in their eating to stated times.

28. At the mourning rites for a Great officer, the presiding mourner, the steward, and grandsons, all were confined to gruel. All the inferior officers were restricted to coarse rice, and water to drink. Wives and concubines took coarse rice, and water to drink. At the rites for an ordinary officer the same rules were observed.

29. After the burial, the presiding mourner had (only) coarse rice and water to drink;—he did not

---

[1] This paragraph is the 23rd in the *Kh*ien-lung edition, confessedly out of place.

eat vegetables or fruits. His wife observed the same rule. So it was in the case of rulers, Great officers, and other officers.

After the change of mourning, towards the end of the year, they ate vegetables and fruit; and after the subsequent sacrifice, they ate flesh.

30. They took their gruel in bowls, and did not wash their hands (before doing so). When they took their rice from the basket, they washed their hands. They ate their vegetables along with pickles and sauces. When they first ate flesh, it was dry flesh; when they first drank liquor, it was that newly made.

31. During the mourning of a year, on three occasions they abstained from eating. When eating coarse rice, with water to drink, they did not eat vegetables or fruits. After the burial, at the end of three months, they ate flesh and drank liquor. When the year's mourning was ended, they did not eat flesh nor drink liquor. When the father was alive, in the mourning of nine months, the rules were the same as in that for a year, on account of the mother or of the wife. Though they ate flesh and drank liquor, they could not take the enjoyment of these things in company with others[1].

32. During the mourning for five months, and that for three months, it was allowable to abstain from eating once or twice. Between the coffining and burial[2], when eating flesh and drinking liquor,

---

[1] The statements in this paragraph, and those in the next, might certainly be stated more distinctly.

[2] Such is the meaning of the text here, as fully defined by a Fang Pâo (方苞):—比葬者自殯後比至于葬也.

they did not take the enjoyment of these things in company with others. While mourning for an aunt, the confirmed wife of an uncle, one's old ruler, or the head of a clan, they ate flesh and drank liquor.

If a mourner could not eat the gruel, he might eat soup of vegetables. If he were ill, he might eat flesh and drink liquor. At fifty, one did not go through all the observances of mourning. At seventy, he simply wore the sackcloth on his person.

33. After the burial, if his ruler feasted a mourner, he partook of the viands; if a Great officer or a friend of his father did so, he partook in the same way. He did not even decline the grain and flesh that might be set before him, but wine and new wine he declined.

SECTION II.

1. The slighter dressing was performed inside the door (of the apartment where the body was); the fuller dressing (at the top of) the steps (leading up to the reception hall) on the east. The body of a ruler was laid on a mat of fine bamboo; of a Great officer, on one of typha grass; and of an ordinary officer, on one of phragmites grass.

2. At the slighter dressing one band of cloth was laid straight, and there were three bands laid cross-wise. The sheet for a ruler's body was embroidered; for a Great officer's, white; for an ordinary officer's, black:—each had one sheet.

There were nineteen suits of clothes[1]; those for

[1] So in all our dictionaries; as in Medhurst, 衣一稱, 'a suit of clothes.' But why nineteen suits? *K*ăng and Ying-tâ say, 'To make up ten, the concluding number of heaven; and nine, that of

the ruler, displayed in the corridor on the east; and those for a Great officer, or a common officer, inside the apartments:—all with their collars towards the west, those in the north being the best. The sash and sheet were not reckoned among them.

3. At the fuller dressing there were three bands of cloth laid straight, and five laid cross-wise. There were (also) strings of cloth, and two sheets:—equally for a ruler, a Great officer, and a common officer. The clothes for a ruler consisted of one hundred suits, displayed in the courtyard, having their collars towards the north, those on the west being the best; those of a Great officer were fifty suits, displayed in the corridor on the east, having the collars towards the west, those on the south being the best; those of a common officer were thirty suits, displayed also in the corridor on the east, with their collars towards the west, the best on the south. The bands and strings were of the same quality as the court robes. One strip of the band-cloth was divided into three, but at the ends was not further divided. The sheets were made of five pieces, without strings or buttons.

4. Among the clothes at the slighter dressing, the sacrificial robes were not placed below the others. For the ruler no clothes were used that were presented. For a Great officer and a common officer, the sacrificial (and other) robes belonging to the principal mourner were all used, and then they used those contributed by their relatives; but these were not displayed along with the others.

earth.' But how shall we account for the hundred, fifty, and thirty suits at the greater dressing, in next paragraph? These suits were set forth, I suppose, for display; they could hardly be for use.

At the slighter dressing, for a ruler, a Great officer, and a common officer, they used wadded upper robes and sheets.

At the greater dressing, the number of sacrificial (and other) robes put on a ruler, a Great officer, or another officer, was not definitely fixed; but the upper robes and sheets for a ruler had only a thin lining, (instead of being wadded); for a Great officer and a common officer, they were as at the slighter dressing.

5. The long robe (worn in private) had a shorter one placed over it;—it was not displayed alone. It was the rule that with the upper garment the lower one should also be shown. So only could they be called a suit.

6. All who set forth the clothes took them from the chests in which they had been deposited; and those who received the clothes brought (as contributions) placed them in (similar) chests. In going up to the hall and descending from it, they did so by the steps on the west. They displayed the clothes without rumpling them. They did not admit any that were not correct; nor any of fine or coarse dolychos fibre, or of coarse flax.

7. All engaged in dressing the corpse had their arms bared; those who moved it into the coffin, had their breasts covered. At the funeral rites for a ruler, the Great officer of prayer performed the dressing, assisted by all the members of his department; at those for a Great officer, the same officer stood by, and saw all the others dress the body; at those of a common officer, the members of that department stood by, while other officers (his friends) performed the dressing.

8. At both the dressings the sacrificial robes were not placed below the others. They were all placed with the lappel to lie on the left side. The bands were tied firmly, and not in a bow-knot.

9. The rule was that the dressers should wail, when they had completed their work. But in the case of an officer, as the dressing was performed by those who had served in office along with him, they, after the work was done, omitted a meal. In all cases the dressers were six.

10. The body cases (used before the dressing) were made :—for a ruler, the upper one embroidered, and the lower one striped black and white, with seven strings on the open side; for a Great officer, the upper one dark blue, and the lower one striped black and white, with five tie-strings on the side; for a common officer, the upper one black, and the lower one red, with three tie-strings at the side. The upper case came down to the end of the hands, and the lower case was three feet long. At the smaller dressing and afterwards, they used coverlets laid on the body (instead of these cases), their size being the same as that of the cases.

11. When the great dressing of a ruler's body was about to commence, his son, with the sackcloth band about his cap, went to his place at the (south) end of the (eastern) corridor, while the ministers and Great officers took theirs at the corner of the hall, with the pillar on their west, their faces to the north, and their row ascending to the east. The uncles, brothers, and cousins were below the hall, with their faces to the north. The (son's) wife, and other wives whose position had been confirmed were on the west of the body, with their faces to

the east. The female relations from other states were in their apartments with their faces to the south. Inferior officers spread the mats. The Shang officers of prayer spread the strings, the coverlet, and clothes. The officers had their hands over the vessels. They then lifted the corpse and removed it to the place for the dressing. When the dressing was finished, the superintendent announced the fact. The son then (seemed to) lean on it, and leaped while his wife did the same, with her face to the east.

12. At the mourning rites of a Great officer, when they were about to proceed to the great dressing, and the tie-strings, coverlets, and clothes had all been spread out, the ruler arrived, and was met by (the son), the principal mourner. The son entered before him, (and stood) at the right of the gate, outside which the exorcist stopped. The ruler having put down the vegetables (as an offering to the spirit of the gate), and the blesser preceding him, entered and went up to the hall. He then repaired to his place at the end of the corridor, while the ministers and Great officers took theirs at the corner of the hall on the west of the pillar, looking to the north, their row ascending to the east. The presiding mourner was outside the apartment (where the corpse was), facing the south. His wife presiding was on the west of the body, facing the east. When they had moved the corpse, and finished the dressing, the steward reported that they had done so, and the presiding mourner went down below the hall, with his face to the north. There the ruler laid on him the soothing hand, and he bowed with his forehead to the ground. The ruler signified to him to go up, and lean on the

body, and also requested his wife, presiding, to lean on it.

13. At the mourning rites for a common officer, when they were about to proceed to the great dressing, the ruler was not present. In other respects the observances were the same as in the case of a Great officer.

14. They also leaped at the spreading out of the ties and strings; of the sheet; of the clothes; at the moving of the corpse; at the putting on of the clothes; of the coverlet; and of the adjusting of the ties and bands.

15. The ruler laid his hand on the body of a Great officer, and on that of the most honourable ladies of his own harem. A Great officer laid his hand on the body of the steward of his house, and on that of his niece and the sister of his wife, who had accompanied her to the harem.

The ruler and a Great officer leant closely with their breasts over the bodies of their parents, wives, and eldest sons, but not over those of their other sons.

A common officer, however, did so also to all his other sons.

If a son by a concubine had a son, the parents did not perform this ceremony over him. When it was performed, the parents did it first, and then the wife and son.

A ruler laid his hand on the body of a minister; parents, while bending over that of a son, also took hold of his hand. A son bent over his parents, bringing his breast near to theirs. A wife seemed as if she would place her two arms beneath the bodies of her parents-in-law; while they (simply) laid their hands on her. A wife made as if she would cling to her husband's body; while the husband held her hand as he did that of a brother or cousin. When others brought the breast near the body of a corpse, they avoided the point at which the ruler had touched it. After every such mark of sorrow, the mourner rose up and leaped.

16. At the mourning rites for a parent, (the son) occupied the slanting shed, unplastered; slept on straw, with a clod of earth for his pillow. He spoke of nothing but what related to the rites. A ruler enclosed this hut; but Great and common officers left it exposed.

After the burial, the inclined posts were set up on lintels, and the hut was plastered, but not on the outside which could be seen. Rulers, Great and common officers, all had it enclosed.

All the other sons, but the eldest by the proper wife, even before the burial had huts made for themselves in out-of-the-way places.

17. After the burial, the son would stand with others. If a ruler, he would speak of the king's affairs, but not of those of his own state. If a Great officer, or a common officer, he would speak of the ruler's affairs, but not of those of his own clan or family.

18. When the ruler was buried, the royal ordinances came into the state. After the wailing was finished, the new ruler engaged in the king's affairs.

When a Great officer or a common officer was buried, the ordinances of the state came to his family. After the wailing was finished, while continuing the sackcloth band round his cap, and the girdle, he might don his armour and go into the field.

19. After the mourning was changed at the end of a year, (the sons) occupied the unplastered apartment, and did not occupy one along with others. Then the ruler consulted about the government of the state; and Great officers and common officers about the affairs of their clan and families. After the sacrifice at the end of two years, the ground of the apartment was made of a dark green, and the walls were whitened. After this, they no longer wailed outside; and after the sacrifice at the end of twenty-seven months, they did not do so inside; for, after it, music began to be heard.

20. After that sacrifice, at the end of twenty-seven months, (the son) attended to all his duties; and after the felicitous sacrifice (of re-arranging the tablets in his ancestral temple), he returned to his (usual) chamber.

At the one year's mourning, he occupied the hut; and when it was completed, the occasions on which he did not seek the nuptial chamber were:—when his father was alive, and he had been wearing the hemmed sackcloth of a year for his mother or his wife, and when he had been wearing the cloth mourning of nine months; on these occasions, for three months he did not seek the intercourse of the inner chamber.

A wife did not occupy the hut, nor sleep on the straw. At the mourning for her father or mother, when she had changed the mourning at the end of a year, she returned to her husband; when the mourning was that of nine months, she returned after the burial.

21. At the mourning rites for a duke (of the royal domain), his Great officers continued till the

change of mourning at the end of a year, and then returned to their own residences. A common officer returned at the conclusion of the wailing.

22. At the mourning rites for their parents, (the other sons who were) Great officers or common officers, returned to their own residences after the change of the mourning at the end of the year; but on the first day of the month and at full moon, and on the return of the death-day, they came back and wailed in the house of him who was now the Head of their family.

At the mourning for uncles and cousins, they returned to their own residences at the conclusion of the wailing.

23. A father did not take up his quarters (during the mourning) at a son's, nor an elder brother at a younger's.

24. At the mourning rites for a Great officer or his acknowledged wife, a ruler (went to see) the greater dressing; but if he wished to show special favour, he attended the slighter dressing.

The ruler, in the case of an acknowledged wife, married to a Great officer of a different surname from his own, arrived after the lid was put on the coffin.

He went to an officer's, when the body was put into the coffin; but if he wanted to show special favour, he attended at the greater dressing.

The ruler's wife, at the mourning for a (Great officer's) acknowledged wife, attended at the greater dressing; but if she wished to show special favour, at the slighter. In the case of his other wives, if she wished to show special favour, she attended at the greater dressing. In the case of a Great officer's acknowledged wife, who was of a different surname from her own, she appeared after the coffining had taken place.

25. When the ruler went to a Great officer's or a common officer's, after the coffining had taken place, he sent word beforehand of his coming. The chief mourner provided all the offerings to be set down for the dead in the fullest measure, and waited outside the gate, till he saw the heads of the horses. He then led the way in by the right side of the gate. The exorcist stopped outside, and the blesser took his place, and preceded the ruler, who put down the offerings of vegetables (for the spirit of the gate) inside it. The blesser then preceded him up the eastern steps, and took his place with his back to the wall, facing the south. The ruler took his place at (the top of) the steps; two men with spears standing before him, and two behind. The officer of reception then advanced. The chief mourner bowed, laying his forehead to the ground. The ruler then said what he had to say; looked towards the blesser and leaped. The chief mourner then (also) leaped.

26. If the visit were paid to a Great officer, the offerings might at this point be put down by the coffin. If it were to a common officer, he went out to wait outside the gate. Being requested to return and put down the offerings, he did so. When this was done, he preceded the ruler, and waited for him outside the gate. When the ruler retired, the chief mourner escorted him outside the gate, and bowed to him, with his forehead to the ground.

27. When a Great officer was ill, the ruler thrice inquired for him; and when his body was coffined, visited (his son) thrice. When a common officer

was ill, he inquired for him once; and when his body was coffined, visited (his son) once.

When the ruler came to condole (after the coffining), the (son) put on again the clothes he had worn at the coffining.

28. When the ruler's wife went to condole at a Great officer's or a common officer's, the chief mourner went out to meet her outside the gate, and, when he saw her horses' heads, went in before her by the right side of the gate. She then entered, went up to the hall, and took her place. The wife presiding went down by the steps on the west, and bowed with her head to the ground below (the hall). The ruler's wife looked towards her eldest son (who had accompanied her), and leaped.

The offerings were put down according to the rules for them on the visit of the ruler. When she retired, the wife presiding went with her to the inside of the door of the apartment, and bowed to her with her head to the ground. The chief mourner escorted her to the outside of the great gate, but did not bow.

29. When a Great officer came to the mourning rites of one of his officers to whom he stood in the relation of ruler, the officer did not meet him outside the gate. He entered and took his place below the hall. The chief mourner (stood on the south of his place), with his face to the north, though the general rule for chief mourners was to face the south. The wife took her place in the room.

If, at this juncture, there came a message from the ruler of the state, or one from a confirmed (Great) officer or his confirmed wife, or visitors from the neighbouring states, the Great officer-ruler, having the chief mourner behind him, performed the bow of ceremony to each visitor.

30. When a ruler, on a visit of condolence, saw the bier for the corpse, he leaped.

If a ruler had not given notice beforehand of his coming to a Great officer or a common officer, and he had not prepared the various offerings to be put down by the coffin on the occasion, when the ruler withdrew, the rule was that they should then be put down.

31. The largest (or outermost) coffin of the ruler of a state was eight inches thick; the next, six inches; and the innermost, four inches. The larger coffin of a Great officer of the highest grade was eight inches thick; and the inner, six inches; for one of the lowest grade, the dimensions were six inches and four. The coffin of a common officer was six inches thick.

32. The (inner) coffin of a ruler was lined with red (silk), fixed in its place with nails of various metals; that of a Great officer with (silk of a) dark blue, fixed with nails of ox-bone; that of a common officer was lined, but had no nails.

33. The lid of a ruler's coffin was varnished, with three double wedges (at the edges) over which were three bands; that of a Great officer's was (also) varnished, with two double wedges and two bands; that of a common officer was not varnished, but it had two double wedges and two bands.

34. The (accumulated) hair and nails of a ruler and Great officer were placed (in bags) at the four corners of the coffin; those of an officer were buried (without being put in the coffin).

35. The coffin of a ruler was placed upon a bier,

which was surrounded with high stakes, inclined over it till, when all was finished and plastered, there was the appearance of a house. That of a Great officer, having been covered with a pall, was placed in the western corridor and staked, but the plastering did not reach all over the coffin. That of a common officer was placed so that the double wedges could be seen; above that it was plastered. All were screened.

36. Of scorched grain there were put by the coffin of a ruler eight baskets, containing four different kinds; by that of a Great officer, six baskets, containing three kinds; by that of a common officer, four baskets, containing two kinds. Besides these, there were (dried) fish and flesh.

37. Ornamenting the coffin (on its way to the grave), there were for a ruler:—the curtains with dragons (figured on them), and over them three gutter-spouts; the fluttering ornaments (with pheasants figured on them and the ends of the curtains); above (on the sloping roof of the catafalque) were figures of axe-heads, of the symbol of discrimination, thrice repeated, and of flames, thrice repeated. These occupied the pall-like roof of white silk, as embroidery, and above it was the false covering attached to it by six purple ties, and rising up with ornaments in five colours and five rows of shells. There were (at the corners) two streamers of feathers, suspended from a frame with the axes on it; two from another, bearing the symbol of discrimination; two from another, variously figured; all the frames on staffs, showing jade-symbols at the top. Fishes were made as if leaping at the ends of the gutters. The whole of the catafalque was kept together by six supports rising from the coffin, and wound round with purple

silk, and six sustaining ropes, also purple, (drawn through the curtains).

For the catafalque of a Great officer there were painted curtains, with two gutter-spouts (above them); there were not the fluttering ornaments; above (on the sloping roof) there were flames painted, thrice repeated; and three symbols of discrimination. These formed the pall-like roof, and there were two purple ties, and two of deep blue. At the very top there were ornaments in three colours, and three rows of shells. There were two feather-streamers from a frame with axes, and two from a painted frame; all the frames on staffs with plumage at the tops. Figures of fishes were made at the ends of the gutters. The front supports of a Great officer's catafalque were purple, and those behind deep blue. So also were the sustaining ropes.

For the catafalque of a common officer, the curtains were of (plain) linen, and there was the sloping roof. There was (but) one gutter-spout. There were the fluttering pheasants on the bands. The purple ties were two, and the black also two. At the very top the ornaments were of three colours, and there was only one row of shells. The streamers of feathers from a painted frame were two, the staffs of which had plumage at their tops. The front supports of the catafalque were purple, and those behind black. The sustaining ropes were purple.

38. In burying the coffin of a ruler, they used a bier, four ropes, and two pillars. Those guiding the course of the coffin carried the shade with pendent feathers.

In burying a Great officer, they used two ropes and two pillars. Those who guided the coffin used a reed of white grass.

In burying a common officer, they used a carriage of the state. They employed two ropes and no post. As soon as they left the residence, those who directed the coffin used the shade of merit.

39. In letting down the coffin into the grave, they removed the ropes from the posts, and pulled at them with their backs to the posts. For a ruler's coffin, they also used levers, and for a Great officer's or a common officer's, ropes attached to the sides of the coffin. Orders were given that they should not cry out in letting down that of the ruler. They let it down as guided by the sound of a drum. In letting down a Great officer's, they were commanded not to wail. In letting down a common officer's, those who began to wail stopped one another.

40. The outer shell of the coffin of a ruler was of pine; of a Great officer, of cypress; of another officer, of various kinds of wood.

41. The surface between the coffin and shell of a ruler was sufficient to contain a music stopper; in the case of the coffin and shell of a Great officer, a vase for water; in that of the coffin and shell of a common officer, a jar of liquor.

42. In the rites of a ruler, the shell was lined, and there were baskets of yü; in those of a Great officer, the shell was not lined; in those of a common officer, there were no baskets of yü[1].

---

[1] We cannot tell what these baskets were. *K*ăng says he did not know, and the *Kh*ien-lung editors think they may have contained the grain mentioned in paragraph 36. Otherwise, the paragraph is obscure.

On the next page there is given a figure of the catafalque over the coffin as borne to the grave, copied from the second volume of

P. Zottoli's work. A larger one, more fully illustrating the details of the text, forms the last plate in the *Kh*ien-lung edition of the Classic; but it is so rough and complicated that the friend who has assisted me with most of the figures that I have ventured to introduce shrank from attempting to reproduce it on a smaller scale.

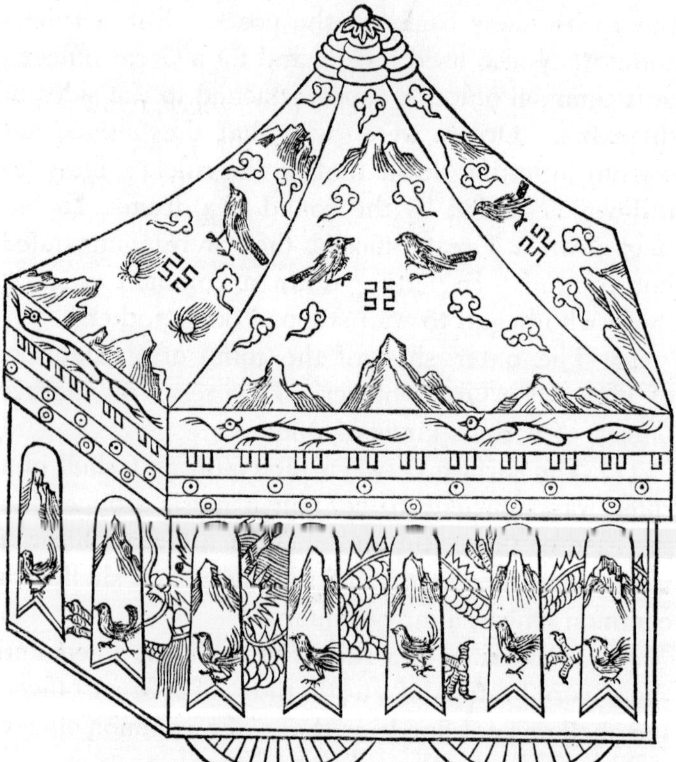

BOOK XX. *K*Î FÂ

OR

THE LAW OF SACRIFICES[1].

1. According to the law of sacrifices, (Shun), the sovereign of the line of Yü, at the great associate sacrifice, gave the place of honour to Hwang Tî, and at the border sacrifice made *Kh*û the correlate of Heaven; he sacrificed (also) to *K*wan-hsü as his ancestor (on the throne), and to Yâo as his honoured predecessor.

---

[1] See the introduction, vol. xxvii, pp. 35, 36. It is there said that in the idea of sacrifices (*k*î), which is here given, there is no indication of deprecation by means of them, and much less of atonement, but that they were merely expressions of gratitude. The character *k*î (祭) is one of those formed by combination of the ideas in its several parts. The Shwo-wăn, the earliest Chinese dictionary, says that it is made up of two ideagrams: 示, the symbol for spiritual beings; and another, composed of 肉 and 又, representing a right hand and a piece of flesh. Offerings of flesh must have been common when the character was formed, which then itself entered, as the phonetic element, into the formation of between twenty and thirty other characters. The explanations of it given by Morrison (Dict., part i), taken mostly from the Khang-hsî dictionary, are:—'To carry human affairs before the gods [i. e. spirits]. That which is the medium between, or brings together men and gods [spirits]. To offer flesh in the rites of worship; to sacrifice with worship.' There is nothing, however, in the Khang-hsî corresponding to this last sentence; and I suppose that Morrison gave it from the analysis of the character in the Shwo-wăn. The general idea symbolised by it is—an offering whereby communication and communion with spiritual beings is effected.

The sovereigns of Hsiâ, at the corresponding sacrifice, gave the place of honour also to Hwang Tî, and made Khwăn the correlate at the border sacrifice; they sacrificed to *K*wan-hsü as their ancestor, and to Yü as their honoured predecessor.

Under Yin, they gave the place of honour to *Kh*û, and made Ming the correlate at the border sacrifice; they sacrificed to Hsieh as their ancestor, and to Thang as their honoured predecessor.

Under *K*âu they gave the place of honour to *Kh*û, and made *K*î the correlate at the border sacrifice; they sacrificed to king Wân as their ancestor, and to king Wû as their honoured predecessor[1].

2. With a blazing pile of wood on the Grand altar they sacrificed to Heaven[2]; by burying (the victim)

[1] This and other portions of the Book are taken mainly from the seventh article in the second section of the 'Narratives of the States,' part i. The statements have much perplexed the commentators, and are held to be of doubtful authority. Some of them, indeed, are said by *Kh*ăn Hâo to be inexplicable. Khwăn, 'the correlate in the sacrifices of Hsiâ, was the father of Yü,' of whom we receive a bad impression from the references to him in the Shû *K*ing; and Ming, who occupied the same position in those of Yin, was the fifth in descent from Hsieh, the ancestor of that dynasty, a minister of Works, who died somehow in his labours on a flood. P. Zottoli thinks that of the four sacrifices here mentioned, the first (禘) was to the Supreme Deity (Supremo Numini), and the second, to the Highest Heaven (Summo Coelo). My own view is different, and agrees with that of the *Kh*ien-lung editors. They discuss the different questions that have been agitated on the subject, and their conclusions may be taken as the orthodoxy of Chinese scholars on the subject; into the exhibition of which it is not necessary to go at greater length.

[2] On the blazing pile were placed the victim and pieces of jade; in the square mound were buried the victim and pieces of silk. For

in the Grand mound, they sacrificed to the Earth. (In both cases) they used a red victim [1].

3. By burying a sheep and a pig at the (altar of) Great brightness, they sacrificed to the seasons. (With similar) victims they sacrificed to (the spirits of) cold and heat, at the pit and the altar, using prayers of deprecation and petition [2]; to the sun, at the (altar called the) royal palace; to the moon, at the (pit called the) light of the night; to the stars at the honoured place of gloom; to (the spirits of) flood and drought at the honoured altar of rain; to the (spirits of the) four quarters at the place of the four pits and altars; mountains, forests, streams, valleys, hills, and mounds, which are able to produce clouds, and occasion winds and rain, were all regarded as (dominated by) spirits.

He by whom all under the sky was held sacrificed to all spirits. The princes of states sacrificed to those which were in their own territories; to those which were not in their territories, they did not sacrifice.

4. Generally speaking, all born between heaven and earth are said to have their allotted times; the death of all creatures is spoken of as their dissolution; but man when dead is said to be in the ghostly

---

泰折, which follow, Zottoli gives solenni angulari, and I have met with 'the great pit' as a translation of them. Of course a 'pit' was formed in the mound to receive the offerings; but in the Khang-hsî dictionary 折 is specially defined with reference to this passage as 'a mound of earth as a place of sacrifice;' though we do not find this account of the character in Morrison, Medhurst, or Williams.

[1] This was specially the colour of the victims under the *K*âu dynasty.

[2] Such is the meaning given by Ying-tâ and others to 相近, which they think should be 禳祈.

state. There was no change in regard to these points in the five[1] dynasties. What the seven[2] dynasties made changes in, were the assessors at the Great associate and the border sacrifices, and the parties sacrificed to in the ancestral temple;—they made no other changes.

5. The sovereigns, coming to the possession of the kingdom, divided the land and established the feudal principalities; they assigned (great) cities (to their nobles), and smaller towns (to their chiefs); they made ancestral temples, and the arrangements for altering the order of the spirit-tablets; they raised altars, and they cleared the ground around them for the performance of their sacrifices. In all these arrangements they made provision for the sacrifices according to the nearer or more remote kinship, and for the assignment of lands of greater or less amount.

Thus the king made for himself seven ancestral temples, with a raised altar and the surrounding area for each. The temples were—his father's; his grandfather's; his great-grandfather's; his great-great-grandfather's; and the temple of his (high) ancestor. At all of these a sacrifice was offered every month. The temples of the more remote ancestors formed the receptacles for the tablets as they were displaced; they were two, and at these only the seasonal sacrifices were offered. For the removed tablet of one more remote, an altar was

---

[1] Those of Yâo, Shun, Hsiâ, Shang or Yin, and *K*âu.

[2] What these 'seven' dynasties were is doubtful. Add to the preceding five, the names of *K*wan-hsü and *Kh*û, and we get the number, all descended from Hwang Tî. The writer must have regarded him as the founder of the Chinese kingdom.

raised and its corresponding area; and on occasions of prayer at this altar and area, a sacrifice was offered, but if there were no prayer, there was no sacrifice. In the case of one still more remote, (there was no sacrifice);—he was left in his ghostly state.

A feudal prince made for himself five ancestral temples, with an altar and a cleared area about it for each. The temples were—his father's; his grandfather's; and his great-grandfather's; in all of which a sacrifice was offered every month. In the temples of the great-great-grandfather, and that of the (high) ancestor only, the seasonal sacrifices were offered. For one beyond the high ancestor a special altar was raised, and for one still more remote, an area was prepared. If there were prayer at these, a sacrifice was offered; but if there were no prayer, there was no sacrifice. In the case of one still more remote, (there was no service);—he was left in his ghostly state.

A Great officer made for himself three ancestral temples and two altars. The temples were—his father's; his grandfather's; and his great-grandfather's. In this only the seasonal sacrifices were offered. To the great-great-grandfather and the (high) ancestor there were no temples. If there were occasion for prayer to them, altars were raised, and sacrifices offered on them. An ancestor still more remote was left in his ghostly state.

An officer of the highest grade had two ancestral temples and one altar;—the temples of his father and grandfather, at which only the seasonal sacrifices were presented. There was no temple for his great-grandfather. If there were occasion to pray to him, an altar was raised, and a sacrifice offered to him.

Ancestors more remote were left in their ghostly state.

An officer in charge merely of one department had one ancestral temple; that, namely, of his father. There was no temple for his grandfather, but he was sacrificed to (in the father's temple.) Ancestors beyond the grandfather were left in their ghostly state.

The mass of ordinary officers and the common people had no ancestral temple. Their dead were left in their ghostly state, (to have offerings presented to them in the back apartment, as occasion required).

6. The king, for all the people, erected an altar to (the spirit of) the ground, called the Grand altar, and one for himself, called the Royal altar.

A feudal prince, for all his people, erected one called the altar of the state, and one for himself called the altar of the prince.

Great officers and all below them in association erected such an altar, called the Appointed altar.

7. The king, for all the people, appointed (seven altars for) the seven sacrifices:—one to the superintendent of the lot; one in the central court, for the admission of light and the rain from the roofs; one at the gates of the city wall; one in the roads leading from the city; one for the discontented ghosts of kings who had died without posterity; one for the guardian of the door; and one for the guardian of the furnace. He also had seven corresponding altars for himself.

A feudal prince, for his state, appointed (five altars for) the five sacrifices:—one for the superintendent of the lot; one in the central court, for the admission of light and rain; one at the gates of the city wall;

one in the roads leading from the city; one for the discontented ghosts of princes who had died without posterity. He also had five corresponding altars for himself.

A Great officer appointed (three altars for) the three sacrifices:—one for the discontented ghosts of his predecessors who had died without posterity; one at the gates of his city; and one on the roads leading from it.

An officer of the first grade appointed (two altars for) the two sacrifices:—one at the gates, and one on the roads (outside the gates).

Other officers and the common people had one (altar and one) sacrifice. Some raised one altar for the guardian of the door; and others, one for the guardian of the furnace.

8. The king, carrying down (his favour), sacrificed to five classes of those who had died prematurely:—namely, to the rightful eldest sons (of former kings); to rightful grandsons; to rightful great-grandsons; to rightful great-great-grandsons; and to the rightful sons of these last.

A feudal prince, carrying down (his favour), sacrificed to three classes; a Great officer similarly to two; another officer of the first grade and the common people sacrificed only to the son who had died prematurely[1].

9. According to the institutes of the sage kings about sacrifices, sacrifice should be offered to him who had given (good) laws to the people; to him

---

[1] From paragraph 1 down to this is absent from the expurgated edition of Fan Ȝze-tăng, which P. Callery translated, so that the book contains in it only the one long paragraph that follows.

who had laboured to the death in the discharge of his duties; to him who had strengthened the state by his laborious toil; to him who had boldly and successfully met great calamities; and to him who had warded off great evils.

Such were the following:—Năng, the son of the lord of Lî-shan[1], who possessed the kingdom, and showed how to cultivate all the cereals; and *Kh*î (the progenitor) of *K*âu, who continued his work after the decay of Hsiâ, and was sacrificed to under the name of *K*î[2]; Hâu-thû, a son of the line of Kung-kung[3], that swayed the nine provinces, who was able to reduce them all to order, and was sacrificed to as the spirit of the ground; the Tî *Kh*û, who could define all the zodiacal stars, and exhibit their times to the people; Yâo, who rewarded (the worthy), made the penal laws impartial, and the end of whose course was distinguished by his righteousness; Shun, who, toiling amid all his affairs, died in the country (far from his capital); Yü, (the son of) Khwăn, who was kept a prisoner till death for trying to dam up the waters of the flood, while Yü completed the work, and atoned for his father's failure; Hwang Tî, who gave everything its right name, thereby showing the people how to avail themselves of its qualities; *K*wan-hsü, who completed this work

[1] Lî-shan is generally mentioned as Lieh-shan, and sometimes Lien-shan. Where the country so-called was, we do not know. Năng, or Shăn Năng, is generally accepted as the first of the line, about B.C. 3072.

[2] This account of *K*î is given confusedly.

[3] It is difficult to find a place in chronology for this Kung-kung. An article in the Ȝo *K*wan (under duke *K*ao's seventeenth year, paragraph 3) places him between Fû-hsî and Shăn Năng.

of Hwang Tî; Hsieh, who was minister of Instruction, and perfected the (condition and manners of the) people; Ming, who, through his attention to the duties of his office, died in the waters; Thang, who ruled the people with a benignant sway and cut off their oppressor; and king Wăn, who by his peaceful rule, and king Wû, who by his martial achievements, delivered the people from their afflictions. All these rendered distinguished services to the people.

As to the sun and moon, the stars and constellations, the people look up to them, while mountains, forests, streams, valleys, hills, and mountains supply them with the materials for use which they require. Only men and things of this character were admitted into the sacrificial canon.

BOOK XXI. *Kî Î*

OR

THE MEANING OF SACRIFICES[1].

Section I.

1. Sacrifices should not be frequently repeated. Such frequency is indicative of importunateness; and importunateness is inconsistent with reverence. Nor should they be at distant intervals. Such infrequency is indicative of indifference; and indifference leads to forgetting them altogether. Therefore the superior man, in harmony with the course of Heaven, offers the sacrifices of spring[2] and autumn. When he treads on the dew which has descended as hoar-frost he cannot help a feeling of sadness, which arises in his mind, and cannot be ascribed to the cold. In spring, when he treads on the ground, wet with the rains and dews that have fallen heavily, he cannot avoid being moved by a feeling as if he were seeing his departed friends. We meet the approach of our friends with music, and escort them away with sadness, and hence at the sacrifice in spring we use music, but not at the sacrifice in autumn.

2. The severest vigil and purification is maintained and carried on inwardly; while a looser vigil

---

[1] See the introduction, vol. xxvii, pages 36, 37.

[2] The spring sacrifice is here called tî (禘), probably by mistake for yo (禴), the proper name for it.

is maintained externally. During the days of such vigil, the mourner thinks of his departed, how and where they sat, how they smiled and spoke, what were their aims and views, what they delighted in, and what things they desired and enjoyed. On the third day of such exercise he will see those for whom it is employed.

3. On the day of sacrifice, when he enters the apartment (of the temple), he will seem to see (the deceased) in the place (where his spirit-tablet is). After he has moved about (and performed his operations), and is leaving at the door, he will seem to be arrested by hearing the sound of his movements, and will sigh as he seems to hear the sound of his sighing.

4. Thus the filial piety taught by the ancient kings required that the eyes of the son should not forget the looks (of his parents), nor his ears their voices; and that he should retain the memory of their aims, likings, and wishes. As he gave full play to his love, they seemed to live again; and to his reverence, they seemed to stand out before him. So seeming to live and stand out, so unforgotten by him, how could his sacrifices be without the accompaniment of reverence?

5. The superior man, while (his parents) are alive, reverently nourishes them; and, when they are dead, he reverently sacrifices to them;—his (chief) thought is how to the end of life not to disgrace them. The saying that the superior man mourns all his life for his parents has reference to the recurrence of the day of their death. That he does not do his ordinary work on that day does not mean that it would be unpropitious to do so; it

means that on that day his thoughts are occupied with them, and he does not dare to occupy himself as on other days with his private and personal affairs.

6. It is only the sage[1] who can sacrifice to God, and (only) the filial son who can sacrifice to his parents. Sacrificing means directing one's self to. The son directs his thoughts (to his parents), and then he can offer his sacrifice (so that they shall enjoy it). Hence the filial son approaches the personator of the departed without having occasion to blush; the ruler leads the victim forward, while his wife puts down the bowls; the ruler presents the offerings to the personator, while his wife sets forth the various dishes; his ministers and Great officers assist the ruler, while their acknowledged wives assist his wife. How well sustained was their reverence! How complete was the expression of their loyal devotion! How earnest was their wish that the departed should enjoy the service!

7. King Wăn, in sacrificing, served the dead as if he were serving the living. He thought of them dead as if he did not wish to live (any longer himself)[2]. On the recurrence of their death-day, he was sad; in calling his father by the name elsewhere forbidden, he looked as if he saw him. So sincere was he in sacrificing that he looked as if he saw the things which his father loved, and the

[1] According to rule, and in fact, only the sovereign sacrifices to God. He may be 'a sage,' but more frequently is not. But the ritual of China should impress on him, as on no other person, the truth in the words 'noblesse oblige.'

[2] *Kh*ăn Hâo says here:—'As if he wished to die himself and follow them.'

pleased expression of his face:—such was king Wăn! The lines of the ode (II, v, ode 2),

'When early dawn unseals my eyes,
Before my mind my parents rise,'

might be applied to king Wăn. On the day after the sacrifice, when the day broke, he did not sleep, but hastened to repeat it; and after it was finished, he still thought of his parents. On the day of sacrifice his joy and sorrow were blended together. He could not but rejoice in the opportunity of offering the sacrifice; and when it was over, he could not but be sad.

8. At the autumnal sacrifice, when *K*ung-nî advanced, bearing the offerings, his general appearance was indicative of simple sincerity, but his steps were short and oft repeated. When the sacrifice was over, 3ze-kung questioned him, saying, 'Your account of sacrificing was that it should be marked by the dignity and intense absorption of all engaged in it; and now how is it that in your sacrificing there has been no such dignity and absorption?'

The Master said, 'That dignity of demeanour should belong to those who are only distantly connected (with him who is sacrificed to), and that absorbed demeanour to one whose thoughts are turned in on himself (lest he should make any mistake). But how should such demeanour consist with communion with the spirits (sacrificed to)? How should such dignity and absorption be seen in my sacrifice? (At the sacrifices of the king and rulers) there is the return of the personator to his apartment, and the offering of food to him there; there are the performances of the music, and the setting forth of the stands with the victims on them; there are the ordering of the various ceremonies and the music; and there is the complete array of the officers for all the services. When they are engaged in the maintenance of that dignity and absorption in their duties, how can they be lost in their abandonment to intercourse with the spiritual presences? Should words be understood only in one way? Each saying has its own appropriate application.'

9. When a filial son is about to sacrifice, he is anxious that all preparations should be made beforehand; and when the time arrives, that everything necessary should be found complete; and then, with a mind free from all pre-occupation, he should address himself to the performance of his sacrifice.

The temple and its apartments having been repaired, the walls and roofs having been put in order, and all the assisting officers having been provided, husband and wife, after vigil and footing, bathe their heads and persons, and array themselves in full dress. In coming in with the things which they carry, how grave and still are they! how absorbed in what they do! as if they were not able to sustain their weight, as if they would let them fall:—Is not theirs the highest filial reverence? He sets forth the stands with the victims on them; arranges all the ceremonies and music; provides the officers for the various ministries. These aid in sustaining and bringing in the things, and thus he declares his mind and wish, and in his lost abstraction of mind seeks to have communion with the dead in their spiritual state, if peradventure they will enjoy his offerings, if peradventure they will do so. Such is the aim of the filial son (in his sacrifices)!

10. The filial son, in sacrificing, seems never able

to exhaust his earnest purpose, his sincerity, and reverence. He observes every rule, without transgression or short-coming. His reverence appears in his movements of advancing and retiring, as if he were hearing the orders (of his parents), or as if they were perhaps directing him.

11. What the sacrifice of a filial son should be can be known. While he is standing (waiting for the service to commence), he should be reverent, with his body somewhat bent; while he is engaged in carrying forward the service, he should be reverent, with an expression of pleasure; when he is presenting the offerings, he should be reverent, with an expression of desire. He should then retire and stand, as if he were about to receive orders; when he has removed the offerings and (finally) retires, the expression of reverent gravity should continue to be worn on his face. Such is the sacrifice of a filial son.

To stand without any inclination of the body would show insensibility; to carry the service forward without an expression of pleasure would show indifference; to present the offerings without an expression of desire (that they may be enjoyed) would show a want of love; to retire and stand without seeming to expect to receive orders would show pride; to retire and stand, after the removal of the offerings, without an expression of reverent gravity would show a forgetfulness of the parent to whom he owes his being. A sacrifice so conducted would be wanting in its proper characteristics.

12. A filial son, cherishing a deep love (for his parents), is sure to have a bland air; having a bland air, he will have a look of pleasure; having a look

of pleasure, his demeanour will be mild and compliant. A filial son will move as if he were carrying a jade symbol, or bearing a full vessel. Still and grave, absorbed in what he is doing, he will seem as if he were unable to sustain the burden, and in danger of letting it fall. A severe gravity and austere manner are not proper to the service of parents;—such is the manner of a full-grown man.

13. There were five things by means of which the ancient kings secured the good government of the whole kingdom:—the honour which they paid to the virtuous; to the noble; and to the old; the reverence which they showed to the aged; and their kindness to the young. It was by these five things that they maintained the stability of the kingdom.

Why did they give honour to the virtuous? Because of their approximation to the course of duty[1]. They did so to the noble because of their approximation to the position of the ruler; and to the old because of their approximation to that of parents. They showed reverence to the aged, because of their approximation to the position of elder brothers; and kindness to the young, because of their approximation to the position of sons.

[1] P. Callery translates this by—'Parce qu'ils sont proche de la vérité,' saying in a note:—'According to the Chinese philosophers, they understand by teh (德) that which man has obtained by his own efforts or the virtue he has acquired, and by tâo (道) that which all men should be striving to reach, what is suitable, what is in order, or virtue in the abstract. Now, as I think, there is nothing but truth which satisfies these conditions, for, according to the Christian philosophy, God Himself is the truth,' &c. Zottoli's translation is, 'Quia hi appropinquant ad perfectionem.'

14. Therefore he who is perfectly filial approximates to be king, and he who is perfectly fraternal approximates to being presiding chieftain. He who is perfectly filial approximates to being king, for even the son of Heaven had the father (whom he must revere); and he who is perfectly fraternal approximates to being presiding chieftain, for even a feudal lord had his elder brothers (or cousins), (whom he must obey). The observance of the lessons of the ancient kings, without admitting any change in them, was the way by which they united and kept together the kingdom with its states and families[1].

15. The Master said, 'The laying the foundation of (all) love in the love of parents teaches people concord. The laying the foundation of (all) reverence in the reverence of elders teaches the people obedience. When taught loving harmony, the people set the (proper) value on their parents; when taught to reverence their superiors, the people set the (proper) value in obeying the orders given to them. Filial piety in the service of parents, and obedience in the discharge of orders can be displayed throughout the kingdom, and they will everywhere take effect.

16. At (the time of) the border sacrifice (to Heaven), those who are engaged in funeral rites do not dare to wail, and those who are wearing mourning do not dare to enter the gate of the capital;—this is the highest expression of reverence.

17. On the day of sacrifice, the ruler led the victim forward, along with and assisted by his son on

[1] The sequence in the writer's mind in this paragraph almost eludes my discovery; it does so still more in the translation of it by Callery and Zottoli.

the opposite side; while the Great officers followed in order. When they had entered the gate of the temple, they fastened the victim to the stone pillar. The ministers and Great officers then bared their arms, and proceeded to inspect the hair, paying particular attention to that of the ears. They then with the knife with the bells attached to it, cut it open, took out the fat about the inwards, and withdrew (for a time[1]). Afterwards they offered some of the flesh boiled, and some raw, then (finally) withdrawing. There was the highest reverence about everything.

18. The sacrifice in the suburb of the capital was the great expression of gratitude to Heaven, and it was specially addressed to the sun, with which the moon was associated[2]. The sovereigns of Hsiâ presented it in the dark. Under the Yin dynasty they did so

[1] They withdrew for a time, 'to offer the hair and blood.'

[2] This sentence is translated by Zottoli:—'Coeli sacrificio summe rependitur coelum sed potissimum intenditur sol, consociatus cum luna.' Callery says:—'Le sacrifice qu'on offre dans la campagne est un acte de grande reconnaissance envers le ciel, et principalement envers le soleil, auquel on associe la lune.'

Here, again, nature-worship seems to crop up. *Kh*ăn Hâo says on the passage:—'Heaven is the great source of tâo (the course of nature and duty), and of all the visible bodies which it hangs out, there are none greater than the sun and moon. Therefore, while the object of the suburban sacrifice was a grateful acknowledgment of Heaven, the sun was chosen as the resting-place for its spirit (or spirits). The idea in the institution of the rite was deep and far-reaching.' It must be borne in mind that the rites described in the text are those of former dynasties, especially of that of *K*âu. I cannot bring to mind any passages in which there is mention made of any sacrifice to the sun or sun-spirit in connexion with the great sacrifice to Heaven, or Shang Tî, at the service on the day of the winter solstice in the southern suburb.

at noon. Under the *K*âu they sacrificed all the day, especially at daybreak, and towards evening.

19. They sacrificed to the sun on the altar, and to the moon in the hollow;—to mark the distinction between (the) gloom (of the one) and (the) brightness (of the other), and to show the difference between the high and the low. They sacrificed to the sun in the east, and to the moon in the west;—to mark the distinction between (the) forthcoming (of the former) and (the) withdrawing (of the latter), and to show the correctness of their (relative) position. The sun comes forth from the east, and the moon appears in the west; the darkness and the light are now long, now short; when the one ends, the other begins, in regular succession:—thus producing the harmony of all under the sky[1].

20. The rites to be observed by all under heaven were intended to promote the return (of the mind) to the beginning (= Creator of all); to promote (the honouring of) spiritual Beings; to promote the harmonious use (of all resources and appliances) of government; to promote righteousness; and to promote humility. They promote the return to the beginning, securing the due consideration of their originator. They promote (the honouring) of spiritual Beings, securing the giving honour to superiors. They promote the (proper) use of all resources, thereby establishing the regulations (for the well-being of) the people. They promote

[1] The sacrifices in this paragraph are those at the equinoxes; that to the sun at the vernal in the eastern suburb, and that to the moon at the autumnal in the western suburb. They are still maintained. See the ritual of the present dynasty (大清通禮), Book VIII, where the former is called 朝日, and the latter 夕月.

righteousness, and thus there are no oppositions and conflictings between high and low. They promote humility, in order to prevent occasions of strife. Let these five things be united through the rites for the regulation of all under heaven, and though there may be some extravagant and perverse who are not kept in order, they will be few.

Section II.

1. Ȝâi Wo said, 'I have heard the names Kwei and Shăn, but I do not know what they mean[1].' The Master said, 'The (intelligent) spirit[2] is of the shăn nature, and shows that in fullest measure; the animal soul is of the kwei nature, and shows that in fullest measure. It is the union of kwei and shăn that forms the highest exhibition of doctrine.

'All the living must die, and dying, return to the ground; this is what is called kwei. The bones and flesh moulder below, and, hidden away, become the earth of the fields. But the spirit issues forth, and is displayed on high in a condition of glorious brightness. The vapours and odours which produce a feeling of sadness, (and arise from the decay of their substance), are the subtle essences of all things, and (also) a manifestation of the shăn nature.

---

[1] I am unable to give a translation of the characters kwei (鬼) and shăn, so as to make the meaning readily intelligible to the English reader. Callery gives for them 'L'âme et l'esprit.' Zottoli, 'Manes Spiritusque.' Evidently the question is about the application of them to the dead and gone, and the component elements of the human constitution.

[2] The character in the text here is *khî* (氣), 'the breath.' Zottoli translates it by 'rationalis vis,' and Callery by 'la respiration de l'homme.'

'On the ground of these subtle essences of things, with an extreme decision and inventiveness, (the sages) framed distinctly (the names of) kwei and shăn, to constitute a pattern for the black-haired race[1]; and all the multitudes were filled with awe, and the myriads of the people constrained to submission.'

2. 'The sages did not consider these (names) to be sufficient, and therefore they built temples with their (different) apartments, and framed their rules for ancestors who were always to be honoured, and those whose tablets should be removed;—thus making a distinction for nearer and more distant kinship, and for ancestors the remote and the recent, and teaching the people to go back to their oldest fathers, and retrace their beginnings, not forgetting those to whom they owed their being. In consequence of this the multitude submitted to their lessons, and listened to them with a quicker readiness.

3. 'These two elements (of the human constitution) having been established (with the two names), two ceremonies were framed in accordance with them. They appointed the service of the morning, when the fat of the inwards was burned so as to bring out its fragrance, and this was mixed with the blaze of dried southern-wood. This served as a tribute to the (intelligent) spirit, and taught all to go back to their originating ancestors. They (also) presented millet and rice, and offered the delicacies of the liver, lungs, head, and heart, along with two bowls (of

[1] It is observed by many of the commentators that the characters here employed for 'black-haired race' were unused in the time of Confucius, and became current under the *Kh*in dynasty.

liquor) and odoriferous spirits. This served as a tribute to the animal soul, and taught the people to love one another, and high and low to cultivate good feeling between them;—such was the effect of those ceremonies.

4. 'The superior man, going back to his ancient fathers, and returning to the authors of his being, does not forget those to whom he owes his life, and therefore he calls forth all his reverence, gives free vent to his feelings, and exhausts his strength in discharging the above service;—as a tribute of gratitude to his parents he dares not but do his utmost[1].'

5. Thus it was that anciently the son of Heaven had his field of a thousand acres, in which he himself held the plough, wearing the square-topped cap with red ties. The feudal princes also had their field of a hundred acres, in which they did the same, wearing the same cap with green ties. They did this in the service of Heaven, Earth, the Spirits of the land and grain, and their ancient fathers, to supply the new wine, cream, and vessels of grain. In this way did they procure these things;—it was a great expression of their reverence.

6. Anciently, the son of Heaven and the feudal lords had their officers who attended to their animals; and at the proper seasons, after vigil and fasting, they washed their heads, bathed, and visited them in person[2], taking from them for victims those which

[1] The above conversation with Ȝâi Wo is found in the 'Narratives of the School,' Article 17, headed 'Duke Âi's Questions about Government;' and the reply of Confucius ends here. I hesitate, therefore, to continue the points of quotation in what follows.

[2] The first day, probably, of the last month of spring. If it were not bright, perhaps another was chosen.

were spotless and perfect;—it was a great expression of their reverence.

The ruler ordered the oxen to be brought before him, and inspected them; he chose them by their hair, divined whether it would be fortunate to use them, and if the response were favourable, he had them cared for. In his skin cap, and the white skirt gathered up at the waist, on the first day and at the middle of the month, he inspected them. Thus did he do his utmost;—it was the height of filial piety.

7. Anciently, the son of Heaven and the feudal lords had their own mulberry trees and silkworms' house; the latter built near a river, ten cubits in height, the surrounding walls being topped with thorns, and the gates closed on the outside. In the early morning of a very bright day, the ruler, in his skin cap and the white skirt, divined for the most auspicious of the honourable ladies in the three palaces of his wife[1], who were then employed to take the silkworms into the house. They washed the seeds in the stream, gathered the leaves from the mulberry trees, and dried them in the wind to feed the worms.

When the (silkworm) year was ended, the honourable ladies had finished their work with the insects, and carried the cocoons to show them to the ruler. They then presented them to his wife, who said, 'Will not these supply the materials for the ruler's robes?' She forthwith received them, wearing her head-dress and the robe with pheasants on it, and afterwards caused a sheep and a pig to be killed and

[1] The queen had six palaces; the wife of a prince, three. The writer confines his account here to the latter.

cooked to treat (the ladies). This probably was the ancient custom at the presentation of the cocoons.

Afterwards, on a good day, the wife rinsed some of them thrice in a vessel, beginning to unwind them, and then distributed them to the auspicious and honourable ladies of her three palaces to (complete) the unwinding. They then dyed the thread red and green, azure and yellow, to make the variously-coloured figures on robes. When the robes were finished, the ruler wore them in sacrificing to the former kings and dukes;—all displayed the greatest reverence.

8. The superior man says, 'Ceremonies and music should not for a moment be neglected by any one. When one has mastered (the principles of) music, and regulates his heart and mind accordingly, the natural, correct, gentle, and honest heart is easily developed, and with this development of the heart comes joy. This joy goes on to a feeling of repose. This repose is long continued. The man in this constant repose becomes (a sort of) heaven. Heaven-like, his action is spirit-like. Heaven-like, he is believed, though he do not speak. Spirit-like, he is regarded with awe, though he display no rage. So it is when one by his mastering of music regulates his mind and heart.

'When one has mastered (the principle of) ceremonies, and regulates his person accordingly, he becomes grave and reverential. Grave and reverential, he is regarded with awe. If the heart be for a moment without the feeling of harmony and joy, meanness and deceitfulness enter it. If the outward demeanour be for a moment without gravity and reverentialness, indifference and rudeness show themselves.

'Therefore the sphere in which music acts is the interior of man, and that of ceremonies is his exterior. The result of music is a perfect harmony, and that of ceremonies is a perfect observance (of propriety). When one's inner man is thus harmonious, and his outer man thus docile, the people behold his countenance and do not strive with him; they look to his demeanour, and no feeling of indifference or rudeness arises in them. Thus it is that when virtue shines and moves within (a superior), the people are sure to accept (his rule) and hearken to him; and when the principles (of propriety) are displayed in his conduct, the people are all sure to accept (his rule) and obey him. Therefore it is said, 'Let ceremonies and music have their course till all under heaven is filled with them; then give them their manifestation and application, and nothing difficult to manage will appear.'

Music affects the inward movements (of the soul); ceremonies appear in the outward movements (of the body). Hence it is the rule to make ceremonies as few and brief as possible, and to give to music its fullest development. This leads to the forward exhibition of ceremonies, and therein their beauty resides; and to the introspective consideration of music, and therein its beauty resides. If ceremonies, demanding this condensation, did not receive this forward exhibition of them, they would almost disappear altogether; if music, demanding this full development, were not accompanied with the introspection, it would produce a dissipation of the mind. Thus it is that to every ceremony there is its proper response, and for music there is this introspection. When ceremonies are responded to, there arises pleasure, and when music is accompanied with the right introspection, there arises repose. The response of ceremony and the introspection of music spring from one and the same idea, and have one and the same object.

9. 3ăng-ȝze said, 'There are three degrees of filial piety. The highest is the honouring of our parents; the second is the not disgracing them; and the lowest is the being able to support them.'

10. (His disciple), Kung-ming Î, said, 'Can you, master, be considered (an example of a) filial son?' 3ăng-ȝze replied, 'What words are these? What words are these? What the superior man calls filial piety requires the anticipation of our parents' wishes, the carrying out of their aims and their instruction in the path (of duty). I am simply one who supports his parents;—how can I be considered filial?'

11. 3ăng-ȝze said, 'The body is that which has been transmitted to us by our parents; dare any one allow himself to be irreverent in the employment of their legacy? If a man in his own house and privacy be not grave, he is not filial; if in serving his ruler, he be not loyal, he is not filial; if in discharging the duties of office, he be not reverent, he is not filial; if with friends he be not sincere, he is not filial; if on the field of battle he be not brave, he is not filial. If he fail in these five things, the evil (of the disgrace) will reach his parents;—dare he but reverently attend to them?'

To prepare the fragrant flesh and grain which he has cooked, tasting and then presenting them before his parents, is not filial piety; it is only nourishing them. He whom the superior man pronounces filial is he whom (all) the people of (his) state praise, saying with admiration, 'Happy are the parents who have such a son as this!'—that indeed is what can be called being filial. The fundamental lesson for all is filial piety. The practice of it is seen in the support (of parents). One may be able to support them; the difficulty is in doing so with the proper reverence. One may attain to that reverence;—the difficulty is to do so without self-constraint. That freedom from constraint may be realised;—the difficulty is to maintain it to the end. When his parents are dead, and the son carefully watches over his actions, so that a bad name, (involving) his parents, shall not be handed down, he may be said to be able to maintain his piety to the end. True love is the love of this; true propriety is the doing of this; true righteousness is the rightness of this; true sincerity is being sincere in this; true strength is being strong in this. Joy springs from conformity to this; punishments spring from the violation of this.

12. Ȝăng-ȝze said, 'Set up filial piety, and it will fill the space from earth to heaven; spread it out, and it will extend over all the ground to the four seas; hand it down to future ages, and from morning to evening it will be observed; push it on to the eastern sea, the western sea, the southern sea, and the northern sea, and it will be (everywhere) the law for men, and their obedience to it will be uniform. There will be a fulfilment of the words of the ode (III, i, ode 10, 6),

"From west to east, from south to north,
There was no unsubmissive thought."'

13. Ȝăng-ȝze said, 'Trees are felled and animals killed, (only) at the proper seasons. The Master said[1],

[1] The master here is Confucius. The record of his saying is found only here.

"To fell a single tree, or kill a single animal, not at the proper season, is contrary to filial piety."'

There are three degrees of filial piety:—the least, seen in the employment of one's strength (in the service of parents); the second, seen in the endurance of toil (for them); and the greatest, seen in its never failing. Thinking of the gentleness and love (of parents) and forgetting our toils (for them) may be called the employment of strength. Honouring benevolences and resting with the feeling of repose in righteousness may be called the endurance of toil; the wide dispensation of benefits and the providing of all things (necessary for the people) may be called the piety that does not fail.

When his parents love him, to rejoice, and not allow himself to forget them; when they hate him, to fear and yet feel no resentment; when they have faults, to remonstrate with them, and yet not withstand them; when they are dead, to ask (the help only of) the good to obtain the grain with which to sacrifice to them;—this is what is called the completion (by a son) of his proper services.

14. The disciple Yo-*k*ăng *Kh*un[1] injured his foot in descending from his hall, and for some months was not able to go out. Even after this he still wore a look of sorrow, and (one of the) disciples of the school said to him, 'Your foot, master, is better; and though for some months you could not go out, why should you still wear a look of sorrow?' Yo-*k*ăng *Kh*un replied, 'It is a good question which

[1] Yo-*k*ăng *Kh*un evidently was a disciple of Ȝăng-ȝze. Mencius had a disciple of the same surname, Yo-*k*ăng Kho (I, ii, 16). Another is mentioned by him (V, ii, 3). Lieh-ȝze mentions a fourth. The Yo-*k*ăngs are said to have sprung from the ducal stock of Sung.

you ask! It is a good question which you ask! I heard from 3ăng-ȝze what he had heard the Master say, that of all that Heaven produces and Earth nourishes, there is none so great as man. His parents give birth to his person all complete, and to return it to them all complete may be called filial duty. When no member has been mutilated and no disgrace done to any part of the person, it may be called complete; and hence a superior man does not dare to take the slightest step in forgetfulness of his filial duty. But now I forgot the way of that, and therefore I wear the look of sorrow. (A son) should not forget his parents in a single lifting up of his feet, nor in the utterance of a single word. He should not forget his parents in a single lifting up of his feet, and therefore he will walk in the highway and not take a by-path, he will use a boat and not attempt to wade through a stream;—not daring, with the body left him by his parents, to go in the way of peril. He should not forget his parents in the utterance of a single word, and therefore an evil word will not issue from his mouth, and an angry word will not come back to his person. Not to disgrace his person and not to cause shame to his parents may be called filial duty.'

15. Anciently, the sovereigns of the line of Yü honoured virtue, and highly esteemed age; the sovereigns of Hsiâ honoured rank, and highly esteemed age; under Yin they honoured riches, and highly esteemed age; under *K*âu, they honoured kinship, and highly esteemed age. Yü, Hsiâ, Yin, and *K*âu produced the greatest kings that have appeared under Heaven, and there was not one of them who neglected age. For long has honour been paid

to years under the sky; to pay it is next to the service of parents.

16. Therefore, at court among parties of the same rank, the highest place was given to the oldest. Men of seventy years carried their staffs at the court. When the ruler questioned one of them, he made him sit on a mat. One of eighty years did not wait out the audience, and when the ruler would question him he went to his house. Thus the submission of a younger brother (and juniors generally) was recognised at the court.

17. A junior walking with one older (than himself), if they were walking shoulder to shoulder, yet it was not on the same line. If he did not keep transversely (a little behind), he followed the other[1]. When they saw an old man, people in carriages or walking got out of his way. Men, where the white were mingling with their black hairs, did not carry burdens on the roads. Thus the submission of juniors was recognised on the public ways.

Residents in the country took their places according to their age, and the old and poor were not neglected, nor did the strong come into collision with the weak, or members of a numerous clan do violence to those of a smaller. Thus the submission of juniors was recognised in the country districts and hamlets[2].

18. According to the ancient rule, men of fifty years were not required to serve in hunting expeditions[3]; and in the distribution of the game, a larger

[1] If the elder were a brother or cousin, the junior kept a little behind, and apart. If he were an uncle, the other followed in a line.

[2] Five *K*âu, translated 'districts,' made a 'hsiang,' here translated 'the country districts.'

[3] Literally, 'men of the tien' (甸). The tien was a tract of

share was given to the more aged. Thus the submission of juniors was recognised in the arrangements for the hunts. In the tens and fives of the army and its detachments, where the rank was the same, places were given according to age. Thus the submission of juniors was recognised in the army.

19. The display of filial and fraternal duty in the court; the practice of them on the road; their reaching to the districts and hamlets; their extension to the huntings; and the cultivation of them in the army, (have thus been described). All would have died for them under the constraint of righteousness, and not dared to violate them.

20. The sacrifice in the Hall of Distinction served to inculcate filial duty on the feudal lords; the feasting of the three classes of the old and five classes of the experienced in the Great college served to inculcate brotherly submission on those princes; the sacrifices to the worthies of former times in the western school served to inculcate virtue on them; the (king's) ploughing in the field set apart for him, served to teach them the duty of nourishing (the people); their appearances at court in spring and autumn served to inculcate on them their duty as subjects or ministers. Those five institutions were the great lessons for the kingdom.

21. When feasting the three classes of the old and five classes of the experienced, the son of Heaven bared his arm, cut up the bodies of the victims, and handed round the condiments; he also presented

considerable size; contributing to the army a chariot, three mailed men, and seventy-two foot-men. There was a levy on it also of men to serve in the hunting expeditions.

the cup with which they rinsed their mouths, wearing the square-topped cap, and carrying a shield. It was thus he inculcated brotherly submission on the princes. It was thus that in the country and villages regard was paid to age, that the old and poor were not neglected, and that the members of a numerous clan did not oppress those of a smaller;—these things came from the Great college.

The son of Heaven appointed the four schools; and when his eldest son entered one of them, he took his place according to his age.

22. When the son of Heaven was on a tour of inspection, the princes (of each quarter) met him on their borders. The son of Heaven first visited those who were a hundred years old. If there were those of eighty or ninety, on the way to the east, he, though going to the west, did not dare to pass by (without seeing them); and so, if their route was to the west, and his to the west. If he wished to speak of matters of government, he, though ruler, might go to them.

23. Those who had received the first degree of office took places according to age (at meetings) in the country and villages; those who had received the second, took places in the same way (at meetings) of all the members of their relatives. Those who had received the third degree did not pay the same regard to age. But at meetings of all the members of a clan no one dared to take precedence of one who was seventy years old.

Those who were seventy, did not go to court unless for some great cause. When they did so for such a cause, the ruler would bow and give place to them, afterwards going on to the parties possessed of rank.

24. Whatever good was possessed by the son of Heaven, he humbly ascribed the merit of it to Heaven; whatever good was possessed by a feudal lord, he ascribed it to the son of Heaven; whatever good was possessed by a minister or Great officer, he attributed it to the prince of his state; whatever good was possessed by an officer or a common man, he assigned the ground of it to his parents, and the preservation of it to his elders. Emolument, rank, felicitations, and rewards were (all) transacted in the ancestral temple; and it was thus that they showed (the spirit of) submissive deference.

25. Anciently, the sages, having determined the phenomena of heaven and earth in their states of rest and activity, made them the basis of the Yî (and divining by it). The diviner held the tortoise-shell in his arms, with his face towards the south, while the son of Heaven, in his dragon-robe and square-topped cap, stood with his face to the north. The latter, however intelligent might be his mind, felt it necessary to set forth and obtain a decision on what his object was;—showing that he did not dare to take his own way, and giving honour to Heaven (as the supreme Decider)[1]. What was good in him (or in his views) he ascribed to others; what was wrong, to himself; thus teaching not to boast, and giving honour to men of talents and virtue.

26. When a filial son was about to sacrifice, the

[1] Who does not see that, from the writer's point of view, divination was originally had recourse to in the search for an 'infallible' director in matters to be done? The Decider was held to be 'Heaven;' the error was in thinking that the will of Heaven could be known through any manipulation of the tortoise-shell, or the stalks.

rule was that he should have his mind well adjusted and grave, to fit him for giving to all matters their full consideration, for providing the robes and other things, for repairing the temple and its fanes, and for regulating everything. When the day of sacrifice arrived, the rule was that his countenance should be mild, and his movements show an anxious dread, as if he feared his love were not sufficient. When he put down his offerings, it was required that his demeanour should be mild, and his body bent, as if (his parents) would speak (to him) and had not yet done so; when the officers assisting had all gone out[1], he stood lowly and still, though correct and straight, as if he were about to lose the sight (of his parents).

After the sacrifice, he looked pleased and expectant, as if they would again enter[2].

In this way his ingenuousness and goodness were never absent from his person; his ears and eyes were never withdrawn from what was in his heart; the exercises of his thoughts never left his parents. What was bound up in his heart was manifested in his countenance; and he was continually examining himself;—such was the mind of the filial son.

---

[1] The text here is difficult. I have followed *K*ăng, as has Zottoli;—the interpretation of 宿者 as 'assisting officers,' can otherwise be defended. Callery gives for the clause:—'Toutes les pensées étrangères (au sacrifice) il les chasse au dehors,' which it would be difficult to justify.

[2] Here again translation is difficult. Zottoli gives:—'Cumque sacrificium transiverit, intendet animo, prosequetur ore, quasi mox iterum ingressuri essent.' Callery:—'Après le sacrifice il s'en va lentement, comme (s'il suivait quelqu'un pas à pas, et avait envie) de rentrer (avec lui dans le temple).'

27. The sites for the altars to the spirits of the land and grain were on the right; that for the ancestral temple on the left[1].

---

[1] That is, with reference to the palace. As you looked out from it to the south, the altars were on the right hand and the temple on the left.

BOOK XXII. *KÎ* THUNG

OR

A SUMMARY ACCOUNT OF SACRIFICES[1].

1. Of all the methods for the good ordering of men, there is none more urgent than the use of ceremonies. Ceremonies are of five kinds[2], and there is none of them more important than sacrifices.

Sacrifice is not a thing coming to a man from without; it issues from within him, and has its birth in his heart. When the heart is deeply moved, expression is given to it by ceremonies; and hence, only men of ability and virtue can give complete exhibition to the idea of sacrifice.

2. The sacrifices of such men have their own blessing;—not indeed what the world calls blessing[3]. Blessing here means perfection;—it is the name given to the complete and natural discharge of all duties. When nothing is left incomplete or improperly discharged;—this is what we call perfection, implying the doing everything that should be done in one's internal self, and externally the performance of everything according to the proper method. There is a fundamental agreement between a loyal subject in his service of his ruler and a filial son in

---

[1] See the introduction, vol. xxvii, pp. 37, 38.

[2] The five kinds of ceremonies are the Auspicious (吉 including all acts of religious worship); the Mourning (凶); those of Hospitality (賓); the Military (軍); and the Festive (嘉).

[3] Success, longevity, the protection of spiritual Beings.

his service of his parents. In the supernal sphere there is a compliance with (what is due to) the repose and expansion of the energies of nature[1]; in the external sphere, a compliance with (what is due) to rulers and elders; in the internal sphere, the filial service of parents;—all this constitutes what is called perfection.

It is only the able and virtuous man who can attain to this perfection; and can sacrifice when he has attained to it. Hence in the sacrifices of such a man he brings into exercise all sincerity and good faith, with all right-heartedness and reverence; he offers the (proper) things; accompanies them with the (proper) rites; employs the soothing of music; does everything suitably to the season. Thus intelligently does he offer his sacrifices, without seeking for anything to be gained by them:—such is the heart and mind of a filial son.

3. It is by sacrifice that the nourishment of parents is followed up and filial duty to them perpetuated. The filial heart is a storehouse (of all filial duties). Compliance with everything that can mark his course, and be no violation of the relation (between parent and child):—the keeping of this is why we call it a storehouse. Therefore in three ways is a filial son's service of his parents shown:—while they are alive, by nourishing them; when they are dead, by

[1] Callery gives for these:—'Conformité avec les Esprits et les Dieux.' Zottoli:—'Ordo erga Genios Spiritusque.' Medhurst:—'Being obedient to the Kwei Shins.' If they had observed the 'three spheres' of the writer, I think they would have translated differently. I believe the idea is—'Compliance with the will of Heaven or God, as seen in the course of Nature and Providence.'

all the rites of mourning; and when the mourning is over by sacrificing to them. In his nourishing them we see his natural obedience; in his funeral rites we see his sorrow; in his sacrifices we see his reverence and observance of the (proper) seasons. In these three ways we see the practice of a filial son.

4. When a son had done everything (for his sacrifices) that he could do himself, he proceeded to seek assistance from abroad; and this came through the rites of marriage. Hence the language of a ruler, when about to marry a wife, was:—'I beg you, O ruler, to give me your elegant daughter, to share this small state with my poor self, to do service in the ancestral temple, and at the altars to (the spirits of) the land and grain.' This underlay his seeking for that assistance (from abroad).

In sacrificing, husband and wife had their several duties which they personally attended to; and on this account there was the array of officials belonging to the exterior and interior departments (of the palace). When these officers were complete, all things necessary (for the service) were made ready:—small things, such as the sourcrout of water plants and pickles from the produce of dry grounds; and fine things, such as the stands for the bodies of the three victims, and the supplies for the eight dishes. Strange insects and the fruits of plants and trees, produced under the best influences of light and shade, were all made ready. Whatever heaven produces, whatever earth developes in its growth;—all were then exhibited in the greatest abundance. Everything was there from without, and internally there was the utmost effort of the will:—such was the spirit in sacrificing.

5. For this reason, also, the son of Heaven himself guided the plough in the southern suburb, to provide the grain for the sacrificial vessels; and the queen looked after her silkworms in the northern suburb, to provide the cap and robes of silk. The princes of the states guided the plough in their eastern suburb, also to provide the grain for the sacrificial vessels, and their wives looked after their silkworms in the northern suburb, to provide the cap and robes of silk. This was not because the son of Heaven and the princes had not men to plough for them, or because the queen and the princes' wives had not women to tend the silkworms for them; it was to give the exhibition of their personal sincerity. Such sincerity was what is called doing their utmost; and such doing of their utmost was what is called reverence. When they had reverently done their utmost, they could serve the spiritual Intelligences—such was the way of sacrificing.

6. When the time came for offering a sacrifice, the man wisely gave himself to the work of purification. That purification meant the production of uniformity (in all the thoughts);—it was the giving uniformity to all that was not uniform, till a uniform direction of the thoughts was realised. Hence a superior man, unless for a great occasion, and unless he were animated by a great reverence, did not attempt this purification. While it was not attained, he did not take precautions against the influence of (outward) things, nor did he cease from all (internal) desires. But when he was about to attempt it, he guarded against all things of an evil nature, and suppressed all his desires. His ears did not listen to music;—as it is said in the Record, 'People occupied with purification

have no music,' meaning that they did not venture to allow its dissipation of their minds. He allowed no vain thoughts in his heart, but kept them in a strict adherence to what was right. He allowed no reckless movement of his hands or feet, but kept them firmly in the way of propriety. Thus the superior man, in his purification, devotes himself to carrying to its utmost extent his refined and intelligent virtue.

Therefore there was the looser ordering of the mind for seven days, to bring it to a state of fixed determination; and the complete ordering of it for three days, to effect the uniformity of all the thoughts. That determination is what is called purification; the final attainment is when the highest degree of refined intelligence is reached. After this it was possible to enter into communion with the spiritual Intelligences.

7. Moreover, on the eleventh day, before that appointed for the sacrifice, the governor of the palace gave warning notice to the wife of the ruler, and she also conducted that looser ordering of her thoughts for seven days, and that more complete ordering of them for three. The ruler accomplished his purification in the outer apartment, and the wife her purification in the inner. After this they met in the grand temple.

The ruler, in the dark-coloured square-topped cap, stood at the top of the steps on the east; his wife in her head-dress and pheasant-embroidered robe stood in the eastern chamber. The ruler from his mace-handled libation-cup poured out the fragrant spirit before the personator of the dead; and the great minister in charge of the temple with his halfmacehandled cup poured the second libation (for the wife). When the victim was introduced, the ruler held it by the rope; the ministers and Great officers followed; other officers carried the dried grass (to lay on the ground when it should be killed); the wives of the ruler's surname followed the wife with the basins; she presented the purified liquid; the ruler held in his hand the knife with bells; he prepared the lungs (to be offered to the personator); and his wife put them on the dishes and presented them. All this shows what is meant in saying that husband and wife had their parts which they personally performed.

8. When they went in for the dance, the ruler, holding his shield and axe, went to the place for the performance. He took his station at the head of those on the east, and in his square-topped cap, carrying his shield, he led on all his officers, to give pleasure to the august personator of the dead. Hence the son of Heaven in his sacrifices (gave expression to) the joy of all in the kingdom. (In the same way) the feudal princes at their sacrifices (gave expression to) the joy of all within their territories. In their square-topped caps, and carrying their shields, they led on all their officers, to give joy to the august personators:—with the idea of showing the joy of all within their territories.

9. At a sacrifice there were three things specially important. Of the offerings there was none more important than the libation; of the music there was none more important than the singing in the hall above; of the pantomimic evolutions there was none more important than that representing (king) Wû's (army) on the night (before his battle). Such was

the practice of the *K*âu dynasty. All the three things were designed to increase the aim of the superior man by the use of these external representations. Hence their movements in advancing and retreating were regulated by (the degree of) that aim. If it were less intense, they were lighter; if it were more intense, they were more vehement. If the aim were less intense, and they sought to make the outward representation more vehement, even a sage could not have accomplished this.

Therefore the superior man, in sacrificing, exerted himself to the utmost in order to give clear expression to these more important things. He conducted everything according to the rules of ceremony, thereby giving prominent exhibition to them, and displaying them to the august personator:—such was the method of the sages.

10. At sacrifices there are the provisions that are left. The dealing with these is the least important thing in sacrifices, but it is necessary to take knowledge of it. Hence there is the saying of antiquity, 'The end must be attended to even as the beginning:'—there is an illustration of it in these leavings. Hence it was the remark of a superior man of antiquity, that 'The personator also eats what the spirits have left;—it is a device of kindness, in which may be seen (the method of) government.'

Hence, when the personator rose, the ruler and his three ministers partook of what he had left. When the ruler had risen, the six Great officers partook;—the officers partook of what the ruler had left. When the Great officers rose, the eight officers partook:—the lower in rank ate what the higher had left. When these officers rose, each one took what was before him and went out, and placed it (in the court) below the hall, when all the inferior attendants entered and removed it:—the inferior class ate what the superior had left.

11. Every change in the disposal of these relics was marked by an increase in the number (of those who partook of them); and thus there was marked the distinction between the degrees of the noble and the mean, and a representation given of the dispensation of benefits (by the sovereign). Hence by means of the four vessels of millet there is shown the cultivation of this in the ancestral temple, which becomes thereby a representation of all comprised within the confines (of the state).

What is done at sacrifices afforded the greatest example of the dispensation of favours[1]. Hence when the superior possessed the greatest blessing, acts of favour were sure to descend from him to those below him, the only difference being that he enjoyed the blessing first, and those below him afterwards;—there was no such thing as the superior's accumulating a great amount for himself, while the people below him might be suffering from cold and want. Therefore when the superior enjoyed his great blessing, even private individuals waited till the stream should flow down, knowing that his favours would surely come to them. This was shown by what was done with the relics at sacrifices, and hence came the saying that 'By the dealing with these was seen (the method of) government.'

[1] It is difficult to detect the mind of the writer here, and make out the train of his reasoning. Zottoli:—'Sacrificium, beneficiorum maximum est.' Callery:—'Dans les sacrifices, les bien-

12. Sacrifice is the greatest of all things. Its apparatus of things employed in it is complete, but that completeness springs from all being in accordance with the requirements (of nature and reason):—is it not this which enables us to find in it the basis of all the lessons of the sages? Therefore those lessons, in the external sphere, inculcated the honouring of the ruler and of elders, and, in the internal sphere, filial piety towards parents. Hence, when there was an intelligent ruler above, all his ministers submitted to and followed him. When he reverently sacrificed in his ancestral temple, and at the altars to the (spirits of the) land and grain, his sons and grandsons were filially obedient. He did all his duty in his own walk, and was correct in his righteousness; and thence grew up the lessons (of all duty).

Therefore a superior man, in the service of his ruler, should find (guidance for) all his personal conduct. What does not satisfy him in (the behaviour of) his superiors, he will not show in his employment of those below himself; and what he dislikes in the behaviour of those below him, he will not show in the service of his superiors. To disapprove of anything in another, and do the same himself, is contrary to the rule of instruction. Therefore the superior in the inculcation of his lessons, ought to proceed from the foundation (of all duty). This will show him pursuing the greatest method of what is natural and right in the highest degree; and is not this what is seen in sacrifice? Hence we have the saying that

---

faits sont la plus grande chose.' Wylie:—'Sacrifice is the greatest of the virtuous influences.' But is not the writer simply referring to what he has said about the admission of all classes to participate in the relics of a sacrifice?

'The first and greatest teaching is to be found in sacrifice.'

13. In sacrifice there is a recognition of what belongs to ten relationships[1]. There are seen in it the method of serving spiritual Beings; the righteousness between ruler and subject; the relation between father and son; the degrees of the noble and mean; the distance gradually increasing between relatives; the bestowment of rank and reward; the separate duties of husband and wife; impartiality in government affairs; the order to be observed between old and young; and the boundaries of high and low. These are what are called the (different duties in the) ten relationships.

14. The spreading of the mat and placing on it a stool to serve for two, was intended as a resting-place for the united spirits (of husband and wife)[2]. The instruction to the blesser in the apartment and the going out to the inside of the gate[3], was the method pursued in (seeking) communion with the spirits.

15. The ruler went to meet the victim, but not to meet the representative of the dead;—to avoid misconstruction[4]. While the representative was outside

[1] Zottoli:—'Sacrificium habet decem sensus.' Callery:—'Les sacrifices renferment dix ordres d'idées.'

[2] The reason given for this practice is peculiar. 'While alive,' says *Kh*ăn Hâo, 'every individual has his or her own body, and hence in the relation of husband and wife, there are the separate duties to be discharged by each; but when they are dead, there is no difference or separation between their spiritual essences (精氣無間), and one common stool for support is put down for them both.' Is there any truth that these Chinese speculators are groping after?

[3] See vol. xxvii, page 444, paragraph 18.

[4] It was not for the ruler to go to meet one who was still a

the gate of the temple, he was to be regarded only as a subject; inside the temple, he had the full character of a ruler. While the ruler was outside the gate of the temple, he was there the ruler; when he entered that gate (on the occasion of the sacrifice), he had the full character of a subject, or a son. Hence his not going forth (to meet the representative) made clear the right distinction between the ruler and subject.

16. According to the rule in sacrifices, a grandson acted as the representative of his grandfather. Though employed to act the part of representative, yet he was only the son of the sacrificer. When his father, with his face to the north, served him, he made clear how it is the way of a son to serve his father. Thus (sacrifice) illustrated the relation of father and son.

17. When the representative had drunk the fifth cup, the ruler washed the cup of jade, and presented it to the ministers. When he had drunk the seventh cup, that of green jasper was presented to the Great officers. When he had drunk the ninth cup, the plain one varnished was presented to the ordinary officers, and all who were taking part in the service. In all the classes the cup passed from one to another, according to age; and thus were shown the degrees of rank as more honourable and lower.

18. At the sacrifice the parties taking part in it were arranged on the left and right, according to their order of descent from the common ancestor, and thus the distinction was maintained between the order of fathers and sons, the near and the

---

subject, and had not yet entered on the function, which placed him in a position of superiority for the time and occasion.

distant, the older and the younger, the more nearly related and the more distantly, and there was no confusion. Therefore at the services in the grand ancestral temple, all in the two lines of descent were present, and no one failed to receive his proper place in their common relationship. This was what was called (showing) the distance gradually increasing between relatives.

19. Anciently the intelligent rulers conferred rank on the virtuous, and emoluments on the meritorious; and the rule was that this should take place in the Grand temple, to show that they did not dare to do it on their own private motion. Therefore, on the day of sacrifice, after the first presenting (of the cup to the representative), the ruler descended and stood on the south of the steps on the east, with his face to the south, while those who were to receive their appointments stood facing the north. The recorder was on the right of the ruler, holding the tablets on which the appointments were written. He read these, and (each man) bowed twice, with his head to the ground, received the writing, returned (home), and presented it in his (own) ancestral temple:—such was the way in which rank and reward were given.

20. The ruler, in the dragon robe and square-topped cap, stood at the top of the steps on the east, while his wife in her head-dress and pheasant-embroidered robe, stood in the chamber on the east. When the wife presented and put down the dishes on stands, she held them by the foot; (the officer) who held the vessels with new wine, presented them to her, holding them by the bottom; when the representative of the dead was handing the cup to the wife, he held it by the handle, and she gave it to him by

the foot; when husband and wife were giving and receiving, the one did not touch the place where the other had held the article; in passing the pledge cup, they changed the cups:—so was the distinction to be maintained between husband and wife shown.

21. In all arrangements with the stands, the chief attention was given to the bones. Some bones were considered nobler, and some meaner. Under the Yin they preferred the thigh bone; and under the *K*âu, the shoulder bone. Generally, the bones in front were thought nobler than those behind. The stands served to illustrate the rule in sacrifices of showing favours. Hence the nobler guests received the nobler bones, and the lower, the less noble; the nobler did not receive very much, and the lower were not left without any:—impartiality was thus shown. With impartiality of favours, government proceeded freely; with the free proceeding of government, undertakings were accomplished; with the accomplishment of undertakings, merit was established. It is necessary that the way in which merit is established should be known. The stands served to show the rule for the impartial bestowment of favours. So did the skilful administrators of government proceed, and hence it is said that (sacrifices showed the principle of) impartiality in the business of government.

22. Whenever they came to the (general) circulation of the cup, those whose place was on the left stood in one row, and also those whose place was on the right. The members of each row had places according to their age; and in the same way were arranged all the assistants at the service. This was what was called (exhibiting) the order of the old and young.

23. At sacrifices there were portions given to the skinners, cooks, assistants, feather-wavers, and door-keepers,—showing how favours should descend to the lowest. Only a virtuous ruler, however, could do this; having intelligence sufficient to perceive (the wisdom of) it, and benevolence equal to the bestowment of it. Apportioning means bestowing; they were able to bestow what was left on those below them.

Skinners were the meanest of those who looked after the buff-coats; cooks' assistants, the meanest of those who looked after the flesh; feather-wavers, the meanest of those who had to do with the music; door-keepers, those who looked after the doors; for anciently they did not employ men who had suffered dismemberment to keep the doors. These four classes of keepers were the meanest of the servants; and the representative of the dead was the most honoured of all. When the most honoured, at the close of the sacrifice, did not forget those who were the most mean, but took what was left and bestowed it on them, (it may be seen how) with an intelligent ruler above, there would not be any of the people within his territory who suffered from cold and want. This is what was meant by saying that sacrifices show the relation between high and low.

24. For the sacrifices (in the ancestral temple) there were the four seasons. That in spring was called yo[1]; that in summer, tî; that in autumn, *kh*ang; and that in winter, *kh*ăng. The yo and tî expressed the idea in the bright and expanding (course of nature); the *kh*ang and *kh*ăng, that in

[1] Meaning, it is said, 'meagre;' the things offered being few in the spring season; but such explanations are far-fetched.

the sombre and contracting (course). The tî showed the former in its fullest development, and the *kh*ang showed the latter in the same. Hence it is said, 'There is nothing more important than the tî and *kh*ang.' Anciently, at the tî sacrifice, they conferred rank, and bestowed robes;—acting according to the idea in the bright and expanding (course); and at the *kh*ang they gave out fields and homesteads, and issued the rules of autumn-work;—acting according to the idea in the sombre and contracting (course). Hence it is said in the Record, 'On the day of the *kh*ang sacrifice they gave forth (the stores of) the ruler's house;' showing how rewards (were then given). When the plants were cut down, the punishment of branding might be inflicted. Before the rules of autumn-work were issued, the people did not dare to cut down the grass.

25. Hence it is said that 'the ideas in the tî and *kh*ang are great, and lie at the foundation of the government of a state; and should by all means be known.' It is for the ruler to know clearly those ideas, and for the minister to be able to execute (what they require). The ruler who does not know the ideas is not complete, and the minister who cannot carry them into execution is not complete.

Now the idea serves to direct and help the aim, and leads to the manifestation of all virtue. Hence he whose virtue is the completest, has the largest aims; and he whose aims are the largest, has the clearest idea. He whose idea is the clearest, will be most reverent in his sacrifices. When the sacrifices (of a state) are reverent, none of the sons and grandsons within its borders will dare to be irreverent. Then the superior man, when he has a sacrifice, will feel it necessary to preside at it in person. If there be a (sufficient) reason for it, he may commit the performance of it to another. But when committing the performance to another, the ruler will not fail (to think) of its meaning, because he understands the ideas in it. He whose virtue is slight, has but a small aim. He who is in doubts as to the idea in it, and will yet seek to be reverent in his sacrifice, will find it impossible to be so; and how can he, who sacrifices without reverence, be the parent of his people?

26. The tripods (at the sacrifices) had inscriptions on them. The maker of an inscription named himself, and took occasion to praise and set forth the excellent qualities of his ancestors, and clearly exhibit them to future generations. Those ancestors must have had good qualities and also bad. But the idea of an inscription is to make mention of the good qualities and not of the bad:—such is the heart of a filial descendant; and it is only the man of ability and virtue who can attain to it.

The inscriber discourses about and panegyrises the virtues and goodness of his ancestors, their merits and zeal, their services and toils, the congratulations and rewards (given to them), their fame recognised by all under heaven; and in the discussion of these things on his spiritual vessels, he makes himself famous; and thus he sacrifices to his ancestors. In the celebration of his ancestors he exalts his filial piety. That he himself appears after them is natural. And in the clear showing (of all this) to future generations, he is giving instruction.

27. By the one panegyric of an inscription benefit accrues to the ancestors, to their descendant and to

others after them. Hence when a superior man looks at an inscription, while he admires those whom it praises, he also admires him who made it. That maker had intelligence to see (the excellences of his ancestors), virtue to associate himself with them, and wisdom to take advantage (of his position);—he may be pronounced a man of ability and virtue. Such worth without boasting may be pronounced courteous respect.

28. Thus the inscription on the tripod of Khung Khwei of Wei was:—'In the sixth month, on the day ting-hâi, the duke went to the Grand Temple, and said, "My young uncle, your ancestor *K*wang Shû assisted duke *Kh*ăng, who ordered him to follow him in his difficulties on the south of the Han, and afterwards to come to him in his palace (of imprisonment) in the honoured capital of *K*âu; and all these hurried journeyings he endured without wearying of them. From him came the helper of duke Hsien, who charged your (later) ancestor *Kh*ăng Shuh to continue the service of his ancestor. Your deceased father Wăn Shû cherished and stimulated in himself the old desires and aims, roused and led on the admirable officers, and showed his own great personal interest in the state of Wei. His labours for our ducal house never wearied early or late, so that the people all testified how good he was." The duke further said, "My young uncle, I give you (this tripod with) its inscription. Carry on and out the services of your father." Khwei bowed with his head to the ground, and said, "In response to the distinction (you have conferred upon me) I will take your great and important charge, and I will put it on the vases and tripods of my winter sacrifice."' Such

was the inscription on the tripod of Khung Khwei of Wei[1].

In this way the superior men of antiquity panegyrised the excellent qualities of their ancestors, and clearly exhibited them to future generations, thereby having the opportunity to introduce their own personality and magnify their states. If descendants who maintain their ancestral temples and the altars to the spirits of the land and grain, praised their ancestors for good qualities which they did not possess, that was falsehood; if they did not take knowledge of the good qualities which they did possess, that showed their want of intelligence; if they knew them and did not transmit them (by their inscriptions), that showed a want of virtue:—these are three things of which a superior man should have been ashamed.

29. Anciently, Tan, duke of *K*âu, did most meritorious service for the kingdom. After his death the kings *Kh*ăng and Khang, bearing in mind all his admirable work, and wishing to honour Lû, granted to its lords the right of offering the greatest sacrifices;—those in the borders of their capital to Heaven and Earth, in the wider sphere of sacrifice; and the great summer and autumnal sacrifices in the ancestral temple of the state. At those great summer and autumnal sacrifices, on the hall above, they sang the *Kh*ing Miâo, and in the courtyard below it they danced the Hsiang to the flute; they

[1] In the year that Confucius died, B.C. 479, this Khung Khwei was obliged to flee from Wei to Sung. The duke *K*ăng, who is mentioned in connexion with his ancestor known as *K*wang Shû, was marquis of Wei from B.C. 635 to 600. Duke Hsien ruled from B.C. 577 to 559.

carried red shields and axes adorned with jade in performing the Tâ Wû dance; and this was the music employed by the son of Heaven. (Those kings) in acknowledgment of the great merit of the duke of *K*âu, allowed (the use of those sacrifices and this music) to the (marquis of) Lû. His descendants have continued it, and down to the present day it is not abolished, thereby showing clearly the virtue of the lords of *K*âu and magnifying their state [1].

[1] This distinction, said to have been thus conferred on the princes of Lû, is contrary to the views of the ablest commentators on the subject.

BOOK XXIII. *K*ING *K*IEH

OR

THE DIFFERENT TEACHING OF THE DIFFERENT *K*INGS[1].

1. Confucius said, 'When you enter any state you can know what subjects (its people) have been taught. If they show themselves men who are mild and gentle, sincere and good, they have been taught from the Book of Poetry. If they have a wide comprehension (of things), and know what is remote and old, they have been taught from the Book of History. If they be large-hearted and generous, bland and honest, they have been taught from the Book of Music. If they be pure and still, refined and subtile, they have been taught from the Yî. If they be courteous and modest, grave and respectful, they have been taught from the Book of Rites and Ceremonies. If they suitably adapt their language to the things of which they speak, they have been taught from the *Kh*un *Kh*iû.

'Hence the failing that may arise in connexion with the study of the Poems is a stupid simplicity; that in connexion with the History is duplicity; that in connexion with Music is extravagance; that in connexion with the Yî is the violation (of reason)[1]; that in connexion with the practice of Rites and Ceremonies is fussiness; and that in connexion with the *Kh*un *Kh*iû is insubordination[2].

---

[1] See the introductory notice, vol. xxvii, p. 38.

[2] Callery translates the character in the text by 'l'hérésie.' I have met with 'robbery' for it.

2. 'If they show themselves men who are mild and gentle, sincere and good, and yet free from that simple stupidity, their comprehension of the Book of Poetry is deep. If they have a wide comprehension (of things), and know what is remote and old, and yet are free from duplicity, their understanding of the Book of History is deep. If they are large-hearted and generous, bland and honest, and yet have no tendency to extravagance, their knowledge of Music is deep. If they are pure and still, refined and subtle, and yet do not violate (reason), they have made great attainments in the Yî. If they are courteous and modest, grave and reverent, and yet not fussy, their acquaintance with the Book of Rites and Ceremonies is deep. If they suitably adapt their language to the things of which they speak, and yet have no disposition to be insubordinate, their knowledge of the *Kh*un *Kh*iû is deep.'

3. The son of Heaven forms a ternion with heaven and earth. Hence, in power of his goodness he is their correlate, and his benefits extend at once to all things[1]. His brilliancy is equal to that of the sun and moon, and enlightens all within the four seas, not excepting anything, however minute and small. In the audiences at his court everything is done according to the orderly procedure of benevolence, wisdom, propriety, and righteousness. At his entertainments he listens to the singing of the Odes of the Kingdom and the Odes of the Temple and Altar. When he walks, there are the notes from his girdle pendant. When he rides in his chariot, there are the harmonious sounds of the bells attached to

[1] Compare vol. xxvii, pp. 377, 378.

his horses. When he is in private at ease, there is the observance of the rules of propriety. When he advances or retires, he does so according to rule and measure. All the officers fulfil their duties rightly, and all affairs are carried on with order. It is as described in the Book of Poetry (I, xiv, 3),

'That virtuous man, the princely one,
Has nothing wrong in his deportment;
He has nothing wrong in his deportment,
And thus he rectifies the four quarters of the state.'

4. When (a ruler) issues his notices and gives forth his orders, and the people are pleased, we have what may be called the condition of harmony. When superiors and inferiors love one another, we have the condition of benevolence. When the people get what they desire without seeking for it, we have the condition of confidence. When all things in the operations of heaven and earth that might be injurious are taken out of the way, we have the condition of rightness. Rightness and confidence, harmony and benevolence are the instruments of the presiding chieftain and the king. If any one wishes to govern the people, and does not employ these instruments, he will not be successful.

5. In the right government of a state, the Rules of Propriety serve the same purpose as the steel-yard in determining what is light and what is heavy; or as the carpenter's line in determining what is crooked and what is straight; or as the circle and square in determining what is square and what is round. Hence, if the weights of the steel-yard be true, there can be no imposition in the matter of weight; if the line be truly applied, there can be no

imposition in the evenness of a surface; if the square and compass be truly employed, there can be no imposition in the shape of a figure. When a superior man (conducts the government of his state) with a discriminating attention to these rules, he cannot be imposed on by traitors and impostors.

6. Hence he who has an exalted idea of the rules, and guides his conduct by them, is called by us a mannerly gentleman, and he who has no such exalted idea and does not guide his conduct by the rules, is called by us one of the unmannerly people. These rules (set forth) the way of reverence and courtesy; and therefore when the services in the ancestral temple are performed according to them, there is reverence; when they are observed in the court, the noble and the mean have their proper positions; when the family is regulated by them, there is affection between father and son, and harmony among brothers; and when they are honoured in the country districts and villages, there is the proper order between old and young. There is the verification of what was said by Confucius, 'For giving security to superiors and good government of the people, there is nothing more excellent than the Rules of Propriety[1].'

7. The ceremonies at the court audiences of the different seasons were intended to illustrate the righteous relations between ruler and subject; those of friendly messages and inquiries, to secure mutual honour and respect between the feudal princes; those of mourning and sacrifice, to illustrate the kindly feelings of ministers and sons; those of social

[1] See vol. iii, page 482 (The Hsiâo King).

meetings in the country districts, to show the order that should prevail between young and old; and those of marriage, to exhibit the separation that should be maintained between males and females. Those ceremonies prevent the rise of disorder and confusion, and are like the embankments which prevent the overflow of water. He who thinks the old embankments useless and destroys them is sure to suffer from the desolation caused by overflowing water; and he who should consider the old rules of propriety useless and abolish them would be sure to suffer from the calamities of disorder.

8. Thus if the ceremonies of marriage were discontinued, the path of husband and wife would be embittered, and there would be many offences of licentiousness and depravity. If the drinking ceremonies at country feasts were discontinued, the order between old and young would be neglected, and quarrelsome litigations would be numerous. If the ceremonies of mourning and sacrifice were discontinued, the kindly feeling of officers and sons would become small; there would be numerous cases in which there was a revolt from the observances due to the dead, and an oblivion of (those due) to the living. If the ceremonies of friendly messages and court attendances were discontinued, the positions of ruler and subject would fall into disuse, the conduct of the feudal princes would be evil, and the ruin wrought by rebellion, encroachment, and oppression would ensue.

9. Therefore the instructive and transforming power of ceremonies is subtile; they stop depravity before it has taken form, causing men daily to move towards what is good, and keep themselves farther

apart from guilt, without being themselves conscious of it. It was on this account that the ancient kings set so high a value upon them. This sentiment is found in the words of the Yî, 'The superior man is careful at the commencement; a mistake, then, of a hair's breadth, will lead to an error of a thousand lî[1].'

[1] But these words, common enough in later Chinese writings, are not found in the Yî King. Khung Ying-tâ says they are from the 'Great Appendix.' It is more likely that he was in error, than that they existed there in his time.

BOOK XXIV. ÂI KUNG WĂN

OR

QUESTIONS OF DUKE ÂI[1].

1. Duke Âi[2] asked Confucius, saying, 'What do you say about the great rites? How is it that superior men, in speaking about them, ascribe so much honour to them?' Confucius said, 'I, *Kh*iû, am a small man, and unequal to a knowledge of the rites.' 'By no means,' said the ruler. 'Tell me what you think, my Master.' Then Confucius replied, 'According to what I have heard, of all things by which the people live the rites are the greatest. Without them they would have no means of regulating the services paid to the spirits of heaven and earth; without them they would have no means of distinguishing the positions proper to father and son, to high and low, to old and young; without them they would have no means of maintaining the separate character of the intimate relations between male and female, father and son, elder brother and younger, and conducting the intercourse between the contracting families in a marriage, and the frequency or infrequency (of the reciprocities between friends). These

---

[1] See the introduction, vol. xxvii, pp. 39, 40.

[2] Âi ('The Courteous, Benevolent, and Short-lived') was the posthumous title of the marquis 3iang (蔣) of Lû (B.C. 494–468), in whose sixteenth year Confucius died. He seems to have often consulted the sage on important questions, but was too weak to follow his counsels.

are the grounds on which superior men have honoured andr everenced (the rites) as they did.

2. 'Thereafter, (having this view of the rites), they taught them to the people, on the ground of their ability (to practise them), not disregarding their general principles or the limitations (that circumstances impose in particular cases).

3. 'When their object had been accomplished (so far), they proceeded to give rules for the engraving (of the ceremonial vessels), and the embroidering in various colours (of the robes), in order to secure the transmission (of the rites).

4. 'Having obtained the concurrence (of the people in these things), they proceeded to tell them the different periods of mourning; to provide the full amount of tripods and stands; to lay down the (offerings of) pork and dried meats; to maintain in good order their ancestral temples; and then at the different seasons of the year reverently to present their sacrifices; and to arrange thereat, in order, the different branches and members of their kindred. Meanwhile (they themselves) were content to live economically, to have nothing fine about their dress; to have their houses low and poor; to eschew much carving about their carriages; to use their vessels without carving or graving; and to have the plainest diet, in order to share all their advantages in common with the people. In this manner did the superior men of antiquity practise the rites.'

5. The duke said, 'How is it that the superior men of the present day do not practise them (in this way).' Confucius said, 'The superior men of the present day are never satisfied in their fondness for wealth, and never wearied in the extravagance of

their conduct. They are wild, idle, arrogant, and insolent. They determinedly exhaust the (resources of the) people, put themselves in opposition to the multitude, and seek to overthrow those who are pursuing the right way. They seek to get whatever they desire, without reference to right or reason. The former using of the people was according to the ancient rules; the using of them now-a-days is according to later rules. The superior men of the present day do not practise the rites (as they ought to be practised).'

6. Confucius was sitting beside duke Âi, when the latter said, 'I venture to ask, according to the nature of men, which is the greatest thing (to be attended to in dealing with them).' Confucius looked startled, changed countenance, and replied, 'That your lordship should put this question is a good thing for the people. How should your servant dare but express his opinion on it?' Accordingly he proceeded, and said, 'According to the nature of men, government is the greatest thing for them.'

7. The duke said, 'I venture to ask what is meant by the practice of government.' Confucius replied, 'Government is rectification. When the ruler is correct himself, all the people will follow his government. What the ruler does is what the people follow. How should they follow what he does not do?'

8. The duke said, 'I venture to ask how this practice of government is to be effected?' Confucius replied, 'Husband and wife have their separate functions; between father and son there should be affection; between ruler and minister there should be a strict adherence to their several parts. If

these three relations be correctly discharged, all other things will follow.'

9. The duke said, 'Although I cannot, in my unworthiness, count myself as having attained, I should like to hear how these three things which you have mentioned can be rightly secured. May I hear it from you?' Confucius replied, 'With the ancients in their practice of government the love of men was the great point; in their regulation of this love of men, the rules of ceremony was the great point; in their regulation of those rules, reverence was the great point. For of the extreme manifestation of reverence we find the greatest illustration in the great (rite of) marriage. Yes, in the great (rite of) marriage there is the extreme manifestation of respect; and when one took place, the bridegroom in his square-topped cap went in person to meet the bride;—thus showing his affection for her. It was his doing this himself that was the demonstration of his affection. Thus it is that the superior man commences with respect as the basis of love. To neglect respect is to leave affection unprovided for. Without loving there can be no (real) union; and without respect the love will not be correct. Yes, love and respect lie at the foundation of government.'

10. The duke said, 'I wish that I could say I agree with you, but for the bridegroom in his square-topped cap to go in person to meet the bride,—is it not making too much (of the ceremony)?' Confucius looked startled, changed countenance, and said, '(Such a marriage) is the union of (the representatives of) two different surnames in friendship and love, in order to continue the posterity of the

former sages[1], and to furnish those who shall preside at the sacrifices to heaven and earth, at those in the ancestral temple, and at those at the altars to the spirits of the land and grain;—how can your lordship say that the ceremony is made too great?'

11. The duke said, 'I am stupid. But if I were not stupid, how should I have heard what you have just said? I wish to question you, but cannot find the proper words (to do so); I beg you to go on a little further.' Confucius said, 'If there were not the united action of heaven and earth, the world of things would not grow. By means of the grand rite of marriage, the generations of men are continued through myriads of ages. How can your lordship say that the ceremony in question is too great?' He immediately added, 'In their own peculiar sphere, (this marriage) serves for the regulation of the ceremonies of the ancestral temple, and is sufficient to supply the correlates to the spiritual Intelligences of heaven and earth; in the (wider) sphere abroad, it serves for the regulation of the ceremonies of the court[2], and is sufficient to establish the respect of those below him to him who is

[1] *K*ǎng takes this in the singular, 'the former sage,' meaning the duke of *K*âu, so that Confucius should say that the ceremony in question was a continuation of that instituted by the duke of *K*âu. I cannot construe or interpret the text so.

[2] The text here seems to be corrupt. Translating it as it stands—治直言之禮—we should have to say, 'the regulation of straightforward speech.' *Kh*ǎn Hâo says that he does not understand the 直言, and mentions the conjecture of 'some one' that they should be 朝廷. I have followed this conjecture, which also is followed in Callery's expurgated edition.

above them all. If there be ground for shame on account of (a deficiency of) resources, this is sufficient to stimulate and secure them; if there be ground for shame on account of the condition of the states, this is sufficient to revive and renew them. Ceremonies are the first thing to be attended to in the practice of government. Yes, (this) ceremony (of marriage) lies at the foundation of government!'

12. Confucius continued, 'Anciently, under the government of the intelligent kings of the three dynasties, it was required of a man to show respect to his wife and son. When the path (of right government) was pursued, the wife was the hostess of the (deceased) parents;—could any husband dare not to show her respect? And the son was the descendant of those parents;—could any father dare not to show him respect? The superior man's respect is universal. Wherein it appears the greatest is in his respect for himself. He is in his person a branch from his parents;—can any son but have this self-respect? If he is not able to respect his own person, he is wounding his parents. If he wound his parents, he is wounding his own root; and when the root is wounded, the branches will follow it in its dying. These three things are an image of what is true with the whole people (in the body politic). One's own person reaches to the persons of others; one's own son to the sons of others; one's own wife to the wives of others. If a ruler do these things, the spirit of his conduct will reach to all under the sky. If the course of the great king be thus, all the states and families will be docilely obedient.'

13. The duke said, 'I venture to ask what is meant by "respecting one's self."' Confucius replied,

'When a man who is over others[1] transgresses in his words, the people will fashion their speech accordingly; when he transgresses in his actions, the people will make him their model. If in his words he do not go beyond what should be said, nor in his actions what should be a model, then the people, without being commanded, will reverence and honour him. When this obtains, he can be said to have respected his person. Having succeeded in respecting his person, he will (at the same time) be able to do all that can be done for his parents.'

14. The duke said, 'I venture to ask what is meant by doing all that can be done for one's parents?' Confucius replied, '*K*ün-ȝze is the completest name for a man; when the people apply the name to him, they say (in effect) that he is the son of a *k*ün-ȝze; and thus he makes his parents (? father) to be a *k*ün-ȝze. This is what I intend by saying that he does all that can be done for his parents[2].'

Confucius forthwith added, 'In the practice of

---

[1] The phrase in the text for 'a man who is high in rank' is *K*ün-ȝze (君子, Keun-ȝze, in Southern mandarin, and as it is transliterated by Morrison and our older scholars), meaning 'ruler's son,' 'a princely man,' 'a superior man,' 'a wise man,' 'a sage.' In all these ways it has been translated by Chinese scholars, and I have heard it proposed to render it by 'a gentleman.' Here all the commentators say it is to be understood of a man of rank and position (君子以位言), which is a not unfrequent application of it.

[2] What I translate by 'doing all that can be done for his parents' is in the text 'completing his parents.' Callery renders it:—'Assurant (un nom honorable) à ses père et mère.' Wylie:—'Completing his duty to his parents.' It certainly is not easy to catch the mind of Confucius here and in the context.

government in antiquity, the love of men was the great point. If (a ruler) be not able to love men he cannot possess[1] his own person; unable to possess his own person, he cannot enjoy in quiet his land; unable to enjoy in quiet his land, he cannot rejoice in Heaven; unable to rejoice in Heaven, he cannot do all that can be done for his person.'

15. The duke said, 'I venture to ask what is meant by "doing all that could be done for one's person."' Confucius replied, 'It is keeping from all transgression of what is due in all the sphere beyond one's self[2].'

16. The duke said, 'I venture to ask what it is that the superior man values in the way of Heaven.' Confucius replied, 'He values its unceasingness. There is, for instance, the succession and sequence of the sun and moon from the east and west:—that is the way of Heaven. There is the long continuance of its progress without interruption:—that is the way of Heaven. There is its making (all) things complete without doing anything:—that is the way of Heaven. There is their brilliancy when they have been completed:—that is the way of Heaven.'

17. The duke said, 'I am very stupid, unintelligent also, and occupied with many things; do you, Sir, help me that I may keep this lesson in my mind.'

18. Confucius looked grave, moved a little from his mat, and replied, 'A man of all-comprehensive

---

[1] *K*ăng says that 'to possess' is equivalent to 'to preserve' (有猶保也), adding 'men will injure him.' So all the other commentators.

[2] Callery gives for this:—'Ce n'est autre chose que de se maintenir dans le devoir.' Wylie:—'It is not to transgress the natural order of things.' The reply of Confucius appears more fully in the 'Narratives of the School.'

virtue[1] does not transgress what is due from him in all the sphere beyond himself, and it is the same with a filial son. Therefore a son of all-comprehensive virtue serves his parents as he serves Heaven, and serves Heaven as he serves his parents. Hence a filial son does all that can be done for his person[2].'

19. The duke said, 'I have heard your (excellent) words;—how is it that I shall hereafter not be able to keep from the guilt (of transgressing)?' Confucius answered, 'That your lordship gives expression to such words is a happiness to me.'

---

[1] 'A man of all-comprehensive virtue' is in the text simply 'the benevolent man (仁人).' But that name must be to be taken in the sense of Mencius, who says that 'Benevolence is man (仁也者人也)' (vii, 11, 16); as Julien translates it, 'Humanitas homo est.' There 仁, 'benevolence,' is a name denoting the complex of human virtues, with the implication that it is itself man's distinguishing characteristic. So 'humanity' may be used in English to denote 'the peculiar nature of man as distinguished from other beings.'

[2] Callery has a note on this paragraph:—'Ces axiômes de Confucius ne sont pas d'une grande clarté; on y entrevoit, cependant, que le philosophe veut établir l'identité entre le devoir chez l'homme et la vérité éternelle, ou la vertu dans le sens abstrait.' But perhaps the sayings of the Master seem to be wanting in 'clearness' because it is difficult to catch his mind and spirit in them. Nor do I think that the latter part of what the French sinologue says is abundantly clear or appropriate. I have often said that Confucius and his school try to make a religion out of filial virtue. That appears here with a qualification; for the text makes out 'the service of Heaven,' which would be religion, to be identical with the full discharge of all filial duty, equivalent, in the Chinese system, to all morality.

BOOK XXV. *K*UNG-NÎ YEN *K*Ü

OR

*K*UNG-NÎ AT HOME AT EASE[1].

1. *K*ung-nî 'being at home at ease[1],' with 3ze-*k*ang, 3ze-kung, and Yen Yû by him, their conversation went on from general matters to the subject of ceremonies.

2. The Master said, 'Sit down[2], you three, and I will discourse to you about ceremonies, so that you may rightly employ them everywhere and in all circumstances.'

3. 3ze-kung crossed over (3ze-*k*ang's) mat[3], and replied, 'Allow me to ask what you mean.' The Master said, 'Respect shown without observing the rules of propriety is called vulgarity; courtesy without observing those rules is called forwardness; and boldness without observing them is called violence.' The Master added, 'Forwardness takes away from gentleness and benevolence.'

4. The Master said, 'Sze, you err by excess, and Shang by defect.' 3ze-*kh*ân might be regarded as a

---

[1] See the introductory notice of this Book, vol. xxvii, page 40. The Yen (燕) in Yen *K*ü is said by *K*ăng to denote that the party had been to court, and was now at his ease in his own residence.

[2] The three disciples must have risen from their mats on the introduction of a new topic, according to vol. xxvii, page 76, paragraph 21.

[3] Substantially a violation of vol. xxvii, page 71, paragraph 26.

mother of the people. He could feed them, but he could not teach them[1].

5. 3ze-kung (again) crossed the mat, and replied, 'Allow me to ask by what means it is possible to secure this due mean.' The Master said, 'By means of the ceremonial rules; by the rules. Yes, it is those rules which define and determine the due mean.'

6. 3ze-kung having retired, Yen Yû advanced, and said, 'May I be allowed to ask whether the rules of ceremony do not serve to control what is bad, and to complete what is good?' The Master said, 'They do.' 'Very well, and how do they do it?' The Master said, 'The idea in the border sacrifices to Heaven and Earth is that they should give expression to the loving feeling towards the spirits; the ceremonies of the autumnal and summer services in the ancestral temple give expression to the loving feeling towards all in the circle of the kindred; the ceremony of putting down food (by the deceased) serves to express the loving feeling towards those who are dead and for whom they are mourning; the ceremonies of the archery fêtes and the drinking at them express the loving feeling towards all in the district and neighbourhood; the ceremonies of festal entertainments express the loving feeling towards visitors and guests.'

---

[1] The *Kh*ien-lung editors say that in this paragraph, the part from '3ze-*kh*ân' has been introduced by an error in manipulating the tablets. It is found, and more fully, also in the Narratives of the School, article 41 (正論解). The previous sentence of it also appears to me to be out of place. Why should Confucius address himself to Sze?—that was not the name of 3ze-kung. What is said to him is found in the Analects, VI, 15, and also more fully.

7. The Master said, 'An intelligent understanding of the idea in the border sacrifices to Heaven and Earth, and of the ceremonies of the autumnal and summer services, would make the government of a state as easy as to point to one's palm. Therefore let the ceremonial rules be observed:—in the ordinary life at home, and there will be the (right) distinction between young and old; inside the door of the female apartments, and there will be harmony among the three branches of kin; at court, and there will be the right ordering of office and rank; in the different hunting expeditions, and skill in war will be acquired; in the army and its battalions, and military operations will be successful.

'In this way, houses and their apartments will be made of the proper dimensions; measures and tripods will have their proper figure; food will have the flavour proper to its season; music will be according to the rules for it; carriages will have their proper form; spirits will receive their proper offerings; the different periods of mourning will have their proper expression of sorrow; discussions will be conducted by those who from their position should take part in them; officers will have their proper business and functions; the business of government will be properly distributed and applied. (The duty) laid on (each) person being discharged in the matter before him (according to these rules), all his movements, and every movement will be what they ought to be.'

8. The Master said, 'What is (the object of) the ceremonial rules? It is just the ordering of affairs. The wise man who has affairs to attend to must have the right method of ordering them. (He who

should attempt) to regulate a state without those rules would be like a blind man with no one to lead him;—groping about, how could he find his way? Or he would be like one searching all night in a dark room without a light;—how could he see anything?

'If one have not the ceremonial rules, he would not (know how to) dispose of his hands and feet, or how to apply his ears and eyes; and his advancing and retiring, his bowings and giving place would be without any definite rules. Hence, when the rules are thus neglected:—in the ordinary life at home, then the right distinction between old and young will be lost; in the female apartments, then the harmony among the three branches of kin will be lost; in the court, then the order of office and rank will be lost; in the different hunting expeditions, then the prescribed methods of military tactics will be lost; in the army and its battalions, then the arrangements that secure success in war will be lost. (Also), houses and apartments will want their proper dimensions; measures and tripods will want their proper figure; food will want its seasonal flavour; music will want its proper parts; Spirits will want their proper offerings; the different periods of mourning will want their proper expression of sorrow; discussions will not be conducted by the proper men for them; officers will not have their proper business; the affairs of government will fail to be properly distributed and applied; and (in the duties) laid on (each) person to be discharged in the matters before him, all his movements, every movement, will fail to be what they ought to be. In this condition of things it will be impossible to put one's self at the head of the multitudes, and secure harmony among them.'

9. The Master said, 'Listen attentively, you three, while I discourse to you about the ceremonial rules. There are still nine things (to be described), and four of them belong to the Grand festive entertainments. When you know these, though your lot may lie among the channeled fields, if you carry them into practice, you will become wise as sages.

'When one ruler is visiting another, they bow to each other, each courteously declining to take the precedence, and then enter the gate. As soon as they have done so, the instruments of music, suspended from their frames, strike up. They then bow and give place to each other again, and ascend to the hall; and when they have gone up, the music stops. In the court below, the dances Hsiang and Wû are performed to the music of the flute, and that of Hsiâ proceeds in due order with (the brandishing of feathers and) fifes. (After this), the stands with their offerings are set out, the various ceremonies and musical performances go on in regular order, and the array of officers provided discharge their functions. In this way the superior man perceives the loving regard (which directs the entertainment). They move forward in perfect circles; they return and form again the squares. The bells of the equipages are tuned to the *Kh*âi-*kh*î; when the guest goes out they sing the Yung; when the things are being taken away, they sing the *Kh*ăn-yü; and thus the superior man (sees that) there is not a single thing for which there is not its proper ceremonial usage. The striking up of the instruments of metal, when they enter the gate, serves to indicate their good feeling; the singing of the *Kh*ing Miâo, when they have gone up to the hall, shows the virtue (they should cultivate); the performance of the Hsiang to the flute in the court below, reminds them of the events (of history). Thus the superior men of antiquity did not need to set forth their views to one another in words; it was enough for them to show them in their music and ceremonies.'

10. The Master said, 'Ceremonial usages are (the prescriptions of) reason; music is the definite limitation (of harmony). The superior man makes no movement without (a ground of) reason, and does nothing without its definite limitation. He who is not versed in the odes will err in his employment of the usages, and he who is not versed in music will be but an indifferent employer of them. He whose virtue is slender will vainly perform the usages.'

11. The Master said, 'The determinate measures are according to the rules; and the embellishments of them are also so; but the carrying them into practice depends on the men.'

12. 3ze-kung crossed over the mat and replied, 'Allow me to ask whether even Khwei was ignorant (of the ceremonial usages)[1]?'

13. The Master said, 'Was he not one of the ancients? Yes, he was one of them. To be versed in the ceremonial usages, and not versed in music, we call being poorly furnished. To be versed in the usages and not versed in music, we call being one-sided. Now Khwei was noted for his acquaintance with music, and not for his acquaintance with cere-

[1] Khwei was Shun's Director of Music. See the Shû, II, i, 24.

monies, and therefore his name has been transmitted with that account of him (which your question implies). But he was one of the men of antiquity.'

14. Ʒze-*k*ang asked about government. The Master said, 'Sze, did I not instruct you on that subject before? The superior man who is well acquainted with ceremonial usages and music has only to take and apply them (in order to practise government).'

15. Ʒze-*k*ang again put the question, and the Master said, 'Sze, do you think that the stools and mats must be set forth, the hall ascended and descended, the cups filled and offered, the pledge-cup presented and returned, before we can speak of ceremonial usages? Do you think that there must be the movements of the performers in taking up their positions, the brandishing of the plumes and fifes, the sounding of the bells and drums before we can speak of music? To speak and to carry into execution what you have spoken is ceremony; to act and to give and receive pleasure from what you do is music. The ruler who vigorously pursues these two things may well stand with his face to the south, for thus will great peace and order be secured all under heaven; the feudal lords will come to his court; all things will obtain their proper development and character; and no single officer will dare to shrink from the discharge of his functions. Where such ceremony prevails, all government is well ordered; where it is neglected, all falls into disorder and confusion. A house made by a good (though unassisted) eye will yet have the corner of honour, and the steps on the east for the host to ascend by; every mat have its upper and lower end; every chariot have

its right side and left; walkers follow one another, and those who stand observe a certain order:—such were the right rules of antiquity. If an apartment were made without the corner of honour and the steps on the east, there would be confusion in the hall and apartment. If mats had not their upper and lower ends, there would be confusion among the occupants of them; if carriages were made without their left side and right, there would be confusion in their seats; if people did not follow one another in walking, there would be confusion on the roads; if people observed no order in standing, there would be disorder in the places they occupy. Anciently the sage Tîs and intelligent kings and the feudal lords, in making a distinction between noble and mean, old and young, remote and near, male and female, outside and inside, did not presume to allow any to transgress the regular rule they had to observe, but all proceeded in the path which has been indicated.'

16. When the three disciples had heard these words from the Master, they saw clearly as if a film had been removed from their eyes.

BOOK XXVI. KHUNG-ȜZE HSIEN *KÜ*

OR

CONFUCIUS AT HOME AT LEISURE[1].

1. Confucius being at home at leisure, with Ȝze-hsiâ by his side, the latter said, 'With reference to the lines in the Book of Poetry (III, ii, ode 8, 1),

"The happy and courteous sovereign
Is the father and mother of the people;"

I beg to ask what the sovereign must be, who can be called "the parent of the people."' Confucius said, 'Ah! the parent of the people! He must have penetrated to the fundamental principles of ceremonies and music, till he has reached the five extreme points to which they conduct, and the three that have no positive existence, and be able to exhibit these all under heaven; and when evil is impending in any part of the kingdom, he must have a foreknowledge of it:—such an one is he whom we denominate 'the parent of the people.'

2. Ȝze-hsiâ said, 'I have thus heard (your explanation) of the name "parent of the people;" allow me to ask what "the five extreme points" (that you mention) mean.' Confucius said, 'The furthest aim of the mind has also its furthest expression in the Book of Poetry. The furthest expression of the Book of Poetry has also its furthest embodiment in the ceremonial usages. The furthest embodiment

[1] See the introductory notice, vol. xxvii, page 41.

in the ceremonial usages has also its furthest indication in music. The furthest indication of music has also its furthest indication in the voice of sorrow. Sorrow and joy produce, each the other; and thus it is that when we look with the directest vision of the eyes at (these extreme points) we cannot see them, and when we have bent our ears with the utmost tension we cannot hear them. The mind and spirit must embrace all within heaven and earth:—these are what we denominate "the five extreme points."'

3. Ȝze-hsiâ said, 'I have heard your explanation of "the five extreme points;" allow me to ask what "the three points that have no positive existence" mean.' Confucius said, 'The music that has no sound; ceremonial usages that have no embodiment; the mourning that has no garb:—these are what we denominate "the three points that have no positive existence." Ȝze-hsiâ said, 'I have heard what you have said on those three negations; allow me to ask in which of the odes we find the nearest expression of them.' Confucius said, 'There is that (IV, ii, ode 1, 6),

"Night and day he enlarged its foundations by his deep and silent virtue:"—

there is music without sound. And that (I, iii, ode 1, 3),

"My deportment has been dignified and good,
Without anything wrong that can be pointed out:"—

there is the ceremony that has no embodiment. And that (I, iii, ode 10, 4),

"When among any of the people there was a death,
I crawled on my knees to help them:"—

there is the mourning that has no garb.'

4. 3ze-hsiâ said, 'Your words are great, admirable, and complete. Do they exhaust all that can be said on the subject? Is there nothing more?' Confucius said, 'How should it be so? When a superior man practises these things, there still arise five other points.'

5. 3ze-hsiâ said, 'How is that?' Confucius said, 'When there is that music without sound, there is no movement of the spirit or will in opposition to it. When there is that ceremony without embodiment, all the demeanour is calm and gentle. When there is that mourning without garb, there is an inward reciprocity, and great pitifulness.

'When there is that music without sound, the spirit and will are mastered. When there is that ceremony without embodiment, all the demeanour is marked by courtesy. When there is that mourning without garb, it reaches to all in all quarters.

'When there is that music without sound, the spirit and will are followed. When there is that ceremony without embodiment, high and low are harmonious and united. When there is that mourning without garb, it goes on to nourish all regions.

'When there is that music without sound, it is daily heard in all the four quarters of the kingdom. When there is that ceremony without embodiment, there is a daily progress and a monthly advance. When there is that mourning without garb, the virtue (of him who shows it) becomes pure and very bright.

'When there is that music without sound, all spirits and wills are roused by it. When there is that ceremony without embodiment, its influence extends to all within the four seas. When there is that mourning without garb, it extends to future generations.'

6. Ȝze-hsiâ said, '(It is said that) the virtue of the kings (who founded the) three dynasties was equal to that of heaven and earth; allow me to ask of what nature that virtue was which could be said to put its possessors on an equality with heaven and earth.' Confucius said, 'They reverently displayed the Three Impartialities, while they comforted all beneath the sky under the toils which they imposed.' Ȝze-hsiâ said, 'Allow me to ask what you call the "Three Impartialities."' Confucius said, 'Heaven overspreads all without partiality; Earth sustains and contains all without partiality; the Sun and Moon shine on all without partiality. Reverently displaying these three characteristics and thereby comforting all under heaven under the toils which they imposed, is what is called "the Three Impartialities." It is said in the Book of Poetry (IV, iii, ode 4, 3),

"God in His favour Thang's House would not leave,
And then Thang rose that favour to receive.
Thang's birth was not from Hsieh too far removed,
His sagely reverence daily greater proved;
For long to Heaven his brilliant influence rose,
And while his acts the fear of God disclose,
God Thang as model fit for the nine regions chose:"—

such was the virtue of Thang.

7. 'To Heaven belong the four seasons, spring autumn, winter, summer, with wind, rain, hoar-frost, and dew;—(in the action) of all and each of these there is a lesson.

'Earth contains the mysterious energy (of nature). That mysterious energy (produces) the wind and thunder-clap. By the wind and thunder-clap the (seeds of) forms are carried abroad, and the various things show the appearance of life:—in all and each of these things there is a lesson.

8. 'When the personal character is pure and bright, the spirit and mind are like those of a spiritual being. When what such an one desires is about to come, there are sure to be premonitions of it in advance, (as when) Heaven sends down the seasonable rains, and the hills produce the clouds. As it is said in the Book of Poetry (III, iii, ode 5, 1),

"How grand and high, with hugest bulk, arise
Those southern hills whose summits touch the skies!
Down from them came a Spirit to the earth,
And to the sires of Fû and Shăn gave birth.
In those two states our *K*âu a bulwark has,
O'er which the southern foemen dare not pass,
And all its states they screen, and through them spread
Lessons of virtue, by themselves displayed:"—

such was the virtue of (kings) Wăn and Wû.

9. 'As to the kings (who founded) the three dynasties, it was necessary that they should be preceded by the fame of their forefathers. As it is said in the Book of Poetry (III, iii, ode 8, 6),

"Very intelligent were the sons of Heaven,
Their good fame was without end:"—

such was the virtue of (the founders) of the three dynasties.

'(And again),

"He displayed his civil virtues,

And they permeated all parts of the kingdom:"—

such was the virtue of king Thâi.'

10. Ȝze-hsiâ rose up with a sudden joy, and, standing with his back to the wall, said, 'Your disciple dares not but receive (your instructions) with reverence.'

BOOK XXVII. FANG *K*Î

OR

RECORD OF THE DYKES[1].

1. According to what the Masters said, the ways laid down by the superior men may be compared to dykes, the object of which is to conserve that in which the people may be deficient; and though they may be on a great scale, the people will yet pass over them. Therefore the superior men framed rules of ceremony for the conservation of virtue; punishments to serve as a barrier against licentiousness; and declared the allotments (of Heaven), as a barrier against evil desires[2].

2. The Master said, 'The small man, when poor, feels the pinch of his straitened circumstances; and when rich, is liable to become proud. Under the pinch of that poverty he may proceed to steal; and when proud, he may proceed to deeds of disorder. The rules of propriety recognise these feelings of men, and lay down definite regulations for them, to serve as dykes for the people. Hence the sages dealt with riches and honours, so that riches should

---

[1] See the introductory notice, vol. xxvii, pp. 41, 42.

[2] Any reader acquainted with Chinese will see that the character fang (坊) is used substantively and meaning 'a dyke,' and as a verb, 'to serve as a dyke.' But a dyke has two uses:—to conserve what is inside it, preventing its flowing away; and to ward off what is without, barring its entrance and encroachment. So the character is here used in both ways. The *Kh*ien-lung editors insist on this twofold application of it, tersely and convincingly.

not have power to make men proud; that poverty should not induce that feeling of being pinched; and that men in positions of honour should not be intractable to those above them. In this way the causes of disorder would more and more disappear.'

3. The Master said, 'Under heaven the cases are few in which the poor yet find enjoyment[1], the rich yet love the rules of propriety, and a family that is numerous (and strong) yet remains quiet and at peace. As it is said in the Book of Poetry (III, iii, ode 3, 11),

"The people desire disorder,
And find enjoyment in bitter, poisonous ways."

Hence it was made the rule that no state should have more than 1000 chariots, no chief city's wall more than 100 embrasures, no family, however rich, more than 100 chariots. These regulations were intended for the protection of the people, and yet some of the lords of states rebelled against them.'

4. The Master said, 'It is by the rules of ceremony that what is doubtful is displayed, and what is minute is distinguished, that they may serve as dykes for the people. Thus it is that there are the grades of the noble and the mean, the distinctions of dress, the different places at court; and so the people (are taught to) give place to one another.'

5. The Master said, 'There are not two suns in the sky, nor two kings in a territory, nor two masters in a family, nor two superiors of equal honour; and the people are shown how the distinction between ruler and subject should be maintained.

[1] Literally, 'the poor are fond of (enjoyment);' but the 'fond of' is acknowledged to be an addition to the text.

The *Kh*un *Kh*iû does not mention the funeral rites for the kings of *Kh*û and Yüeh. According to the rules, the ruler of a state is not spoken of as "Heaven's," and a Great officer is not spoken of as "a ruler;"—lest the people should be led astray. It is said in the ode,

> "Look at (that bird) which in the night calls out for
> the morning[1]."

Even this is still occasion for being dissatisfied with it.'

6. The Master said, 'A ruler does not ride in the same carriage with those of the same surname with himself; and when riding with those of a different surname, he wears a different dress;—to show the people that they should avoid what may give rise to suspicion. This was intended to guard the people (from incurring suspicion), and yet they found that there were those of the same surname who murdered their ruler[2].'

7. The Master said, 'The superior man will decline a position of high honour, but not one that is mean; and riches, but not poverty. In this way confusion and disorder will more and more disappear. Hence the superior man, rather than have his emoluments superior to his worth, will have his worth superior to his emoluments.'

8. The Master said, 'In the matter of a cup of liquor and a dish of meat, one may forego his claim and receive that which is less than his due;

[1] This is from one of the old pieces, which have been forgotten and lost. Is the bird alluded to the cock? and where is the point of the reference?

[2] The *Kh*ien-lung editors labour in vain to make this paragraph clear, and say that it is 'an error of errors' to ascribe it to Confucius.

and yet the people will try to obtain more than is due to their years. When one's mat has been spread for him in a high place, he may move and take his seat on a lower; and yet the people will try to occupy the place due to rank. From the high place due to him at court one may in his humility move to a meaner place; and yet the people shall be intrusive even in the presence of the ruler. As it is said in the Book of Poetry (II, vii, ode 9, 4),

"When men in disputations fine
To hear their consciences refuse,
Then 'gainst each other they repine,
And each maintains his special views.
If one a place of rank obtain,
And scorn humility to show,
The others view him with disdain,
And, wrangling, all to ruin go."'

9. The Master said, 'The superior man exalts others and abases himself; he gives the first place to others and takes the last himself;—and thus the people are taught to be humble and yielding. Thus when he is speaking of the ruler of another state, he calls him "The Ruler;" but when mentioning his own ruler, he calls him "Our ruler of little virtue."'

10. The Master said, 'When advantages and rewards are given to the dead first[1], and to the living afterwards, the people will not act contrarily to the (character of) the dead. When (the ruler) places those who are exiles (from and for their state) first, and those who remain in it last, the people may be

[1] The memory of the dead would be honoured, and titles given to them, while those they left behind would be supported.

trusted with (the most arduous duties). It is said in the Book of Poetry (I, iii, ode 3, 4),

"In thinking of our deceased lord,
She stimulated worthless me."

When this dyke is set up for the people, will they still act contrarily to the dead and have to bewail their lot, with none to whom to appeal?'

11. The Master said, 'When the ruler of a state, with its clans, thinks much of the men and little of the emoluments (which he bestows on them), the people give place readily (to those men). When he thinks much of their ability, and little of the chariots (with which he rewards them), the people address themselves to elegant arts. Hence a superior man keeps his speech under control, while the small man is forward to speak.'

12. The Master said, 'If superiors consider and are guided by the words of the people, the people receive their gifts or commands as if they were from Heaven. If superiors pay no regard to the words of the people, the people put themselves in opposition to them. When inferiors do not receive the gifts of their superiors as if they were from Heaven, there ensues violent disorder. Hence, when the superior exhibits his confidence and courtesy in the government of the people, then the usages of the people in response to him are very great. It is said in the Book of Poetry (III, ii, ode 10, 3),

"Remember what in days of old they spake,
With grass and fuel-gatherers counsel take."'

13. The Master said, 'If (the ruler) ascribe what is good to others, and what is wrong to himself, the

people will not contend (among themselves). If he ascribe what is good to others, and what is wrong to himself, dissatisfactions will more and more disappear. It is said in the Book of Poetry (I, v, ode 4, 2),

"You had consulted the tortoise-shell; you had consulted the stalks;
In their responses there was nothing unfavourable."'

14. The Master said, 'If (the ruler) ascribe what is good to others and what is wrong to himself, the people will yield to others (the credit of) what is good in them. It is said in the Book of Poetry (III, i, ode 10, 7),

"He examined and divined, did the king,
About settling in the capital of Hâo.
The tortoise-shell decided the site,
And king Wû completed the city."'

15. The Master said, 'If (ministers) ascribe what is good to their ruler and what is wrong to themselves, the people will become loyal. It is said in the Book of History (V, xxi, 6),

'"When you have any good plans or counsels, enter and lay them before your ruler in the court; and thereafter, when you are acting abroad in accordance with them, say, 'This plan, or this view, is all due to the virtue of our ruler!' Oh! in this way how good and distinguished will you be!"'

16. The Master said, 'If (a ruler, being a son,) ascribe what is good to his father, and what is wrong to himself, the people will become filial. It is said in "The Great Declaration," "If I subdue *K*âu, it will not be my prowess, but the faultless virtue of

my deceased father Wăn. If *K*âu subdues me, it will not be from any fault of my deceased father Wăn, but because I, who am as a little child, am not good"' (Shû, V, i, sect. 3, 6).

17. The Master said, 'A superior man will forget and not make much of the errors of his father, and will show his reverence for his excellence. It is said in the Lun Yü (I, xi), "He who for three years does not change from the way of his father, may be pronounced filial;" and in the Kâo Ʒung (Shû, III, viii, 1) it is said, "For three years he kept without speaking; when he did speak, they were delighted."'

18. The Master said, 'To obey (his parents') commands without angry (complaint); to remonstrate with them gently without being weary; and not to murmur against them, though they punish him, may be pronounced filial piety. It is said in the Book of Poetry (III, ii, ode 3, 5),

"Your filial son was unceasing in his service."'

19. The Master said, 'To cultivate harmony with all the kindred of parents may be pronounced filial! It is said in the Book of Poetry (II, vii, ode 9, 3),

"Brethren whose virtue stands the test,
By bad example still unchanged,
Their generous feelings manifest,
Nor grow among themselves estranged.
But if their virtue weakly fails
The evil influence to withstand,
Then selfishness o'er love prevails,
And troubles rise on every hand."'

20. The Master said, '(A son) may ride in the chariot of an intimate friend of his father, but he

should not wear his robes. By this (rule) the superior man widens (the sphere of) his filial duty.'

21. The Master said, 'Small men are all able to support their parents. If the superior man do not also reverence them, how is his supporting to be distinguished (from theirs)?'

22. The Master said, 'Father and son should not be in the same (official) position;—to magnify the reverence (due to the father). It is said in the Book of History (Shû, III, v, sect. 1, 3), "If the sovereign do not show himself the sovereign, he disgraces his ancestors."'

23. The Master said, 'Before his parents (a son) should not speak of himself as old; he may speak of the duty due to parents, but not of the gentle kindness due from them; inside the female apartments he may sport, but should not sigh. By these (rules) the superior man would protect the people (from evil), and still they are found slight in their acknowledgment of filial duty, and prompt in their appreciation of gentle kindness.'

24. The Master said, 'When they who are over the people show at their courts their respect for the old, the people become filial.'

25. The Master said, 'The (use of) the representatives of the deceased at sacrifices, and of one who presides (at the services) in the ancestral temple, was intended to show the people that they had still those whom they should serve. The repairing of the ancestral temple and the reverential performance of the sacrifices were intended to teach the people to follow their dead with their filial duty. These things should guard the people (from evil), and still they are prone to forget their parents.'

26. The Master said, 'When (it is wished to) show respect (to guests), the vessels of sacrifice are used[1]. Thus it is that the superior man will not in the poverty of his viands neglect the rules of ceremony, nor in their abundance and excellence make those rules disappear. Hence, according to the rules of feasting, when the host gives in person anything to a guest, the guest offers a portion in sacrifice, but he does not do so with what the host does not himself give him. Therefore, when there is no ceremony in the gift, however admirable it may be, the superior man does not partake of it. It is said in the Yî, "The ox slain in sacrifice by the neighbour on the east is not equal to the spare spring sacrifice of the neighbour on the west, (whose sincerity) receives the blessing[2]." It is said in the Book of Poetry (III, ii, ode 3, 1),

"You have made us drink to the full of your spirits,
You have satiated us with your virtue."

But though in this way the people are admonished, they will still keep striving after profit, and forget righteousness.'

27. The Master said, 'There are the seven days of fasting, and the three days of vigil and adjustment of the thoughts; there is the appointment of the one man to act as the personator of the dead, in passing whom it is required to adopt a hurried pace:—all to teach reverence (for the departed).'

---

[1] This would be in the entertainment, at the close of the sacrifices, given to the relatives and others who had taken part in them.

[2] This is the symbolism of the fifth line of the 63rd Hexagram (*Kî 3î*). See vol. xvi, pp. 206–208.

The sweet liquor is in the apartment (where the personator is); the reddish in the hall; and the clear in the court below:—all to teach the people not to go to excess in being greedy[1].

The personator drinks three cups, and all the guests drink one:—teaching the people that there must be the distinction of high and low.

The ruler takes the opportunity of the spirits and flesh of his sacrifice to assemble all the members of his kindred:—teaching the people to cultivate harmony.

Thus it is that on the hall above they look at what is done in the apartment, and in the court below at what is done by those in the hall (for their pattern); as it is said in the Book of Poetry (II, vi, ode 5, 3),

'Every form is according to rule;
Every smile and word is as it should be.'

28. The Master said, 'The giving place to a visitor at every stage of his advancing (from the entrance gate), according to the rules for visitors; and the repetition of the ceremonies, according to the mourning rites, in an ever-increasing distance from the apartment of the corpse; the washing of the corpse over the pit in the centre of the open court; the putting the rice into the mouth under the window; the slighter dressing of the corpse inside the door of the apartment; the greater dressing at the top of the steps on the east; the coffining in the place for guests; the sacrifice on taking the road (with the coffin) in the courtyard; and the interment in the grave:—these were intended to teach the people how the element of distance enters into the

[1] The best liquor was in the lowest place.

usages. Under the Yin dynasty they condoled with the mourners at the grave; they do so under *K*âu in the house:—showing the people that they should not neglect the custom.'

The Master said, '(These services in connexion with) death are the last duties which the people have to pay (to their departed). I follow *K*âu in them. They were intended to serve as guards to the people (to keep them from error). Among the princes, however, there still were those who did not attend the burials of other princes, and take part in them[1].'

29. The Master said, 'The going up to the hall by the steps for the guests, and receiving the condolences sent to him in the guests' place, are designed to teach the filial to continue their filial duty even to the dead.

'Until the mourning rites are finished, a son is not styled "Ruler:"—showing the people that there ought to be no contention (between father and son). Hence in the *Kh*un *Kh*iû of Lû, recording deaths in Ʒin, it is said, "(Lî Kho) killed Hsî-*kh*î, the son of his ruler, and his ruler *Kh*o[2]:"—a barrier was thus raised to prevent the people (from doing such deeds). And yet there were sons who still murdered their fathers.'

30. The Master said, 'Filial duty may be transferred to the service of the ruler, and brotherly sub-

---

[1] It is not easy to determine the meaning of the text in this sentence. Chinese writers differ about it among themselves. The whole paragraph, indeed, is confused; and the second 'The Master said' should probably form a paragraph by itself.

[2] This forms two entries in the *Kh*un *Kh*iû, under the ninth and tenth years of duke Hsî. The first notice is according to the rule about a son of a feudal prince being still only called 'Son' till the mourning for his father was completed, and the second is contrary to it. The concluding remark is also away from the point.

mission to the service of elders:—showing the people that they ought not to be double-minded. Hence a superior man, while his ruler is alive, should not take counsel about taking office (in another state). It is only on the day of his consulting the tortoise-shell (about such a thing) that he will mention two rulers[1].'

'The mourning for a father lasts for three years, and that for a ruler the same time:—showing the people that they must not doubt (about the duty which they owe to their ruler).

'While his parents are alive, a son should not dare to consider his wealth as his own, nor to hold any of it as for his own private use:—showing the people how they should look on the relation between high and low. Hence the son of Heaven cannot be received with the ceremonies of a guest anywhere within the four seas, and no one can presume to be his host. Hence, also, when a ruler goes to a minister's (mansion) he goes up to the hall by the (host's) steps on the east and proceeds to the place (of honour) in the hall: showing the people that they should not dare to consider their houses their own.

'While his parents are alive, the gifts presented to a son should not extend to a carriage and its team:—showing the people that they should not dare to monopolise (any honours).

'All these usages were intended to keep the people from transgressing their proper bounds; and yet there are those who forget their parents, and are double-minded to their ruler.'

31. The Master said, 'The ceremony takes place before the silks (offered in connexion with it) are

[1] The translation here is according to a view appended by the *Kh*ien-lung editors to the usual notes on the sentence.

presented :—this is intended to teach the people to make the doing of their duties the first thing, and their salaries an after consideration. If money be sought first and the usages of propriety last, then the people will be set on gain: if the mere feeling be acted on, without any expressions (of courtesy and deference), there will be contentions among the people. Hence the superior man, when presents are brought to him, if he cannot see him who offers them, does not look at the presents. It is said in the Yî, "He reaps without having ploughed that he may reap; he gathers the produce of the third year's field without having cultivated them the first year;—there will be evil[1]." In this way it is sought to guard the people, and yet there are of them who value their emoluments and set little store by their practice.'

32. The Master said, 'The superior man does not take all the profit that he might do, but leaves some for the people. It is said in the Book of Poetry (II, vi, ode 8, 3),

"There shall be handfuls left on the ground,
And ears here and there left untouched;—
For the benefit of the widow."

'Hence, when a superior man is in office (and enjoys its emoluments), he does not go in for farming; if he hunts, he does not (also) fish; he eats the (fruits of the) season, and is not eager for delicacies; if a Great officer, he does not sit on sheepskins; if a lower officer, he does not sit on dogskins. It is said in the Book of Poetry (I, iii, ode 10, 1),

[1] See the symbolism of line 2, of the 25th Hexagram, vol. xvi, pp. 110, 111. The last character here is not in the Yî, and a different moral seems to be drawn from the whole.

"When we gather the mustard-plant and earth-
melons,
We do not reject them because of their roots.
While I do nothing contrary to my good name,
I should live with you till our death."

In this way it was intended to guard the people against loving wrong; and still some forget righteousness and struggle for gain, even to their own ruin.'

33. The Master said, 'The ceremonial usages serve as dykes to the people against bad excesses (to which they are prone). They display the separation which should be maintained (between the sexes), that there may be no occasion for suspicion, and the relations of the people be well defined. It is said in the Book of Poetry (I, viii, ode vi, 3, 4),

"How do we proceed in hewing an axe-handle?
Without another axe it cannot be done.
How do we proceed in taking a wife?
Without a go-between it cannot be done.
How do we proceed in planting hemp?
The acres must be dressed length-wise and cross-
wise.
How do we proceed in taking a wife?
Announcement must first be made to our parents."

In this way it was intended to guard the people (against doing wrong), and still there are some (women) among them, who offer themselves (to the male).'

34. The Master said, 'A man in taking a wife does not take one of the same surname with himself:—to show broadly the distinction (to be maintained between man and wife). Hence, when a man is buying a concubine, if he do not know her surname,

he consults the tortoise-shell about it. In this way it was intended to preserve the people (from going wrong in the matter); and yet the *Kh*un *Kh*iû of Lû still suppresses the surname of duke *K*âo's wife, simply saying "Wû," and the record of her death is "Măng (the elder) 3ze died[1]."'

35. The Master said, 'According to the rules, male and female do not give the cup to one another, excepting at sacrifice. This was intended to guard the people against (undue freedom of intercourse); and yet the marquis of Yang killed the marquis of Mû, and stole away his wife[2]. Therefore the presence of the wife at the grand entertainments was disallowed.'

36. The Master said, 'With the son of a widow one does not have interviews:—this would seem to be an obstacle to friendship, but a superior man will keep apart from intercourse in such a case, in order to avoid (suspicion). Hence, in the intercourse of friends, if the master of the house be not in, a visitor, unless there is some great cause, does not enter the door. This was intended to preserve the people (from all appearance of evil); and yet there are of them who pay more regard to beauty than to virtue.'

37. The Master said, 'The love of virtue should be like the love of beauty (from an inward constraint). Princes of states should not be like fishers for beauty

---

[1] The latter entry is found in the *Kh*un *Kh*iû, under the twelfth year of duke Âi. The lady's surname is not found in that *K*ing at all; and Confucius himself probably suppressed it. Compare what is said in the Analects, VII, 30, where the sage, on the same subject, does not appear to more advantage than he does here.

[2] Who these princes were, or what were the circumstances of the case, is not known.

(in the families) below them. Hence the superior man keeps aloof from beauty, in order to constitute a rule for the people. Thus male and female, in giving and receiving, do not allow their hands to touch; in driving his wife in a carriage, a husband advances his left hand; when a young aunt, a sister, or a daughter has been married, and returns (to her father's house), no male can sit on the same mat with her; a widow should not wail at night; when a wife is ill, in asking for her, the nature of her illness should not be mentioned:—in this way it was sought to keep the people (from irregular connexions); and yet there are those who become licentious, and introduce disorder and confusion among their kindred.'

38. The Master said, 'According to the rules of marriage, the son-in-law should go in person to meet the bride. When he is introduced to her father and mother, they bring her forward, and give her to him[1]:—being afraid things should go contrary to what is right. In this way a dyke is raised in the interest of the people; and yet there are cases in which the wife will not go (to her husband's)[2].'

---

[1] 'Warning her, at the same time, to see that she reverenced her husband.'

[2] We should rather say here—'in which the bride will not go to the bridegroom's.' The commentators do not give instances in point from the records of Chinese history. Perhaps the Master merely meant to say that there were cases in which the bride did not go to her new home in the spirit of reverence and obedience enjoined upon her.

BOOK XXVIII. *K*UNG YUNG

OR

THE STATE OF EQUILIBRIUM AND HARMONY[1].

SECTION I.

1. What Heaven has conferred is called the Nature. An accordance with this nature is called the Path of Duty; the regulation of this path is called the System of Instruction.

2. The path should not be left for an instant; if it could be left, it would not be the path.

3. On this account the superior man does not wait till he sees things to be cautious, nor till he hears things to be apprehensive.

4. There is nothing more visible than what is secret, and nothing more manifest than what is minute. Therefore the superior man is watchful over himself when he is alone.

5. When there are no stirrings of pleasure, anger, sorrow, or joy, we call it the State of Equilibrium. When those feelings have been stirred, and all in their due measure and degree, we call it the State of Harmony. This Equilibrium is the great root (from which grow all the human actings) in the world; and this Harmony is the universal path (in which they should all proceed).

6. Let the State of Equilibrium and Harmony exist in perfection, and heaven and earth

---

[1] See the introductory notice, vol. xxvii, pp. 42, 43.

would have their (right) places, (and do their proper work), and all things would be nourished (and flourish)[1].

7. *K*ung-nî[2] said, 'The superior man (exhibits) the state of equilibrium and harmony[3]; the small

---

[1] These six short paragraphs may be considered a summary of the Confucian doctrine, and a sort of text to the sermon which follows in the rest of the Treatise;—the first chapter of it. The commencing term, Heaven, gives us, vaguely, the idea of a supreme, righteous, and benevolent Power; while 'heaven and earth,' in paragraph 6, bring before us the material heaven and earth with inherent powers and capabilities, by the interaction of which all the phenomena of production, growth, and decay are produced. Midway between these is Man; and nothing is wanting to make a perfectly happy world but his moral perfection, evidenced by his perfect conformity to the right path, the path of duty. 'The superior man,' in paragraph 3, has evidently the moral signification of the name in its highest degree. He is the man 'who embodies the path (體道之人).' The description of him in paragraph 4, that 'he is watchful over himself when alone,' is, literally, that 'he is watchful over his solitariness,—his aloneness,' that 'solitariness' being, I conceive, the ideal of his own nature to which every man in his best and highest moments is capable of attaining.

[2] See the introductory notice of Book XXV.

[3] Formerly I translated this by 'The superior man (embodies) the course of the mean.' Zottoli gives for it, 'Sapiens vir tenet medium;' Rémusat, 'Le sage tient invariablement le milieu,' and 'Sapiens medio constat.' The two characters *K*ung yung (中庸), however, are evidently brought on from the preceding chapter, yung (庸) being used instead of the ho (和) in paragraphs 5 and 6. In the Khang-hsî dictionary, we find that yung is defined by ho, among other terms, with a reference to a remark of *K*ăng Hsüan, preserved by Lû Teh-ming, that 'the Book is named the *K*ung Yung, because it records the practice of the *K*ung Ho.' *K*ăng was obliged to express himself so, having defined the yung of the title by another yung (用), meaning 'use' or 'practice.' But both *k*ung and yung are adjectival terms used substantively.

man presents the opposite of those states. The superior man exhibits them, because he is the superior man, and maintains himself in them; the small man presents the opposite of them, because he is the small man, and exercises no apprehensive caution.'

8. The Master said, 'Perfect is the state of equilibrium and harmony! Rare have they long been among the people who could attain to it!'

9. The Master said, 'I know how it is that the Path is not walked in. The knowing go beyond it, and the stupid do not come up to it. The worthy go beyond it, and the unworthy do not come up to it. There is nobody but eats and drinks; but they are few who can distinguish the flavours (of what they eat and drink)[1].'

10. The Master said, 'Ah! how is the path untrodden!'

11. The Master said, 'Was not Shun grandly wise? Shun loved to question others, and to study their words though they might be shallow. He concealed what was bad (in them), and displayed what was good. He laid hold of their two extremes, determined the mean[2] between them, and used it in (his government of) the people. It was this that made him Shun!'

12. The Master said, 'Men all say, "We are wise;" but being driven forward and taken in a net, a trap, or a pitfall, not one of them knows how to escape. Men all say, "We are wise;" but when they have chosen the state of equilibrium and harmony, they are not able to keep in it for a round month.'

---

[1] Men eat and drink without knowing why or what.

[2] Here *K*ung has the signification of 'the mean,' the just medium between two extremes.

13. The Master said, 'This was the character of Hui:—Having chosen the state of equilibrium and harmony, when he found any one thing that was good, he grasped it firmly, wore it on his breast, and did not let it go[1].'

14. The Master said, 'The kingdom, its states, and clans may be perfectly ruled; dignities and emoluments may be declined; but the state of equilibrium and harmony cannot be attained to.'

15. Ȝze-lû[2] asked about fortitude. 16. The Master said, 'Do you mean the fortitude of the South, the fortitude of the North, or your fortitude?' 17. To show forbearance and gentleness in teaching others; and not to return conduct towards one's self which is contrary to the right path:—this is the fortitude of the South, and the good man makes it his study. 18. To lie under arms, and to die without regret:—this is the bravery of the North, and the bold make it their study. 19. Therefore, the superior man cultivates a (friendly) harmony, and is not weak;—how firm is he in his fortitude! He stands erect in the middle, and does not incline to either side;—how firm is he in his fortitude! If right ways prevail in (the government of his state), he does not change from what he was in retirement;—how firm is he in his fortitude! If bad ways prevail, he will die sooner than change;—how firm is he in his fortitude!'

20. The Master said, 'To search for what is

---

[1] Ȝze-hui was Yen Yüan, Confucius' favourite disciple.

[2] Ȝze-lû was *K*ung Yû, another celebrated disciple, famous for his bravery. 'Your fortitude,' in paragraph 16, is probably the fortitude which you ought to cultivate, that described in paragraph 19.

mysterious[1], and practise marvellous (arts), in order to be mentioned with honour in future ages:—this is what I do not do. 21. The good man tries to proceed according to the (right) path, but when he has gone half-way, he abandons it;—I am not able (so) to stop. 22. The superior man, acting in accordance with the state of equilibrium and harmony, may be all unknown and unregarded by the world, but he feels no regret:—it is only the sage who is able for this[2].

23. 'The way of the superior man reaches far and wide, and yet is secret. 24. Common men and women, however ignorant, may intermeddle with the knowledge of it; but in its utmost reaches there is that which even the sage does not know. Common men and women, however much below the ordinary standard of character, can carry it into practice; but in its utmost reaches, there is that which even the sage cannot attain to. 25. Great as heaven and earth are, men still find things in their action with which to be dissatisfied[3].

26. 'Therefore, if the superior man were to speak (of this way) in its greatness, nothing in the world would be able to contain it; and if he were to speak of it in its smallness, nothing in the world would be

---

[1] This is translated from a reading of the text, as old as the second Han dynasty.

[2] With this ends the second chapter of the Treatise, in which the words of Confucius are so often quoted; specially it would appear, to illustrate what is meant by 'the state of equilibrium and harmony.' Yet there is a great want of definiteness and practical guidance about the utterances.

[3] Who does not grumble occasionally at the weather, and disturbances apparently of regular order in the seasons?

found able to divide it. 27. It is said in the Book of Poetry (III, i, ode 5),

"Up to heaven flies the hawk;
Fishes spring in the deep,"

telling how (the way) is seen above and below. 28. The way of the superior man may be found in its simple elements among common men and women, but in its utmost reaches it is displayed in (the operations of) heaven and earth [1].'

29. The Master said, 'The path is not far from man. When men try to pursue a path which is far from what their nature suggests, it should not be considered the Path. 30. It is said in the Book of Poetry (I, xv, ode 5),

"In hewing an axe-shaft, in hewing an axe-shaft,
The pattern is not far off."

We grasp one axe-handle to hew the other; but if we look askance at it, we still consider it far off. 31. Therefore the superior man governs men according to their humanity; and when they change (what is wrong), he stops. 32. Fidelity to one's self and the corresponding reciprocity are not far from the path. What you do not like when done to yourself, do not do to others. 33. In the way of the superior man there are four things, to not one of which have I, *Kh*iû [2], as yet attained.—To

[1] With this chapter commences, it is commonly and correctly held, the third part of the Treatise, intended to illustrate what is said in the second paragraph of it, that 'the path cannot be left for an instant.' The author proceeds to quote sayings of Confucius to make his meaning clear, but he does so 'in a miscellaneous way,' and so as to embrace some of the widest and most difficult exercises of Chinese thought.

[2] The name first given to Confucius by his parents.

serve my father as I would require my son to serve me, I am not yet able; to serve my ruler as I would require my minister to serve me, I am not yet able; to serve my elder brother as I would require a younger brother to serve me, I am not yet able; to set the example in behaving to a friend as I would require him to behave to me, I am not yet able. 34. In the practice of the ordinary virtues, and attention to his ordinary words, if (the practice) be in anything defective, (the superior man) dares not but exert himself; if (his words) be in any way excessive, he dares not allow himself in such license. His words have respect to his practice, and his practice has respect to his words. 35. Is not the superior man characterised by a perfect sincerity?

36. 'The superior man does what is proper to the position in which he is; he does not wish to go beyond it. In a position of wealth and honour, he does what is proper to a position of wealth and honour. In a position of poverty and meanness, he does what is proper to a position of poverty and meanness. Situated among barbarous tribes, he does what is proper in such a situation. In a position of sorrow and difficulty, he does what is proper in such a position. The superior man can find himself in no position in which he is not himself. 37. In a high situation, he does not insult or oppress those who are below him; in a low situation, he does not cling to or depend on those who are above him.

38. 'He rectifies himself, and seeks for nothing from others; and thus none feel dissatisfied with him. Above, he does not murmur against Heaven; below, he does not find fault with men. 39. Therefore the superior man lives quietly and calmly, waiting for the

appointments (of Heaven); while the mean man does what is full of risk, looking out for the turns of luck.' 40. The Master said, 'In archery we have something like (the way of) the superior man. When the archer misses the centre of the target, he turns round and seeks for the cause of his failure in himself.

41. 'The way of the superior man may be compared to what takes place in travelling, when to go far we must traverse the space that is near, and in ascending a height we must begin from the lower ground. 42. It is said in the Book of Poetry (II, i, ode 4, 7, 8),

"Children and wife we love;
Union with them is sweet,
As lute's soft strain, that soothes our pain.
How joyous do we meet!
But brothers more than they
Can satisfy the heart.
'Tis their accord does peace afford,
And lasting joy impart.
For ordering of your homes,
For joy with child and wife,
Consider well the truth I tell;—
This is the charm of life!"'

43. The Master said, 'How complacent are parents (in such a state of things)!'

44. The Master said, 'How abundant and rich are the powers possessed and exercised by Spiritual Beings! We look for them, but do not see them; we listen for, but do not hear them; they enter into all things, and nothing is without them[1]. 45. They

[1] We hardly see the relevancy of pars. 44–47 as illustrating the

cause all under Heaven to fast and purify themselves, and to array themselves in their richest dresses in order to attend at their sacrifices. Then, like overflowing water, they seem to be over the heads, and on the left and right (of their worshippers). 46. It is said in the Book of Poetry (III, iii, ode 2, 7),

"The Spirits come, but when and where,
No one beforehand can declare.
The more should we not Spirits slight,
But ever feel as in their sight."

47. 'Such is the manifestness of what is minute. Such is the impossibility of repressing the outgoings of sincerity!'

48. The Master said, 'How greatly filial was Shun! His virtue was that of a sage; his dignity was that of the son of Heaven; his riches were all within the four seas; his ancestral temple enjoyed his offerings; his descendants preserved (those to) himself. 49. Thus it was that with his great virtue he could not but obtain his position, his riches, his fame, and his long life. 50. Therefore Heaven, in

---

statement that 'the path cannot be left.' They bear rather on the next statement of the first chapter, the manifestness of that which is most minute, and serve to introduce the subject of 'sincerity,' which is dwelt upon so much in the last part of the Treatise. But what are the Spirits or Spiritual Beings that are spoken of? In paragraphs 45, 46, they are evidently the spirits sacrificed to in the ancestral temple and spirits generally, according to our meaning of the term. The difficulty is with the name in paragraph 44, the Kwei Shăn there. Rémusat renders the phrase simply by 'les esprits,' and in his Latin version by 'spiritus geniique,' as also does Zottoli. Wylie gives for it 'the Spiritual Powers.' Of course *K*âu Hsî and all the Sung scholars take it, according to their philosophy, as meaning the phenomena of expansion and contraction, the displays of the Power or Powers, working under Heaven, in nature.

producing things, is sure to be bountiful to them according to their qualities. 51. Thus it nourishes the tree that stands flourishing, and that which is ready to fall it overthrows. 52. It is said in the Book of Poetry (III, ii, ode 5, 1),

"What brilliant virtue does our king,
Whom all admire and love, display!
People and officers all sing
The praise of his impartial sway.

Heaven to his sires the kingdom gave,
And him with equal favour views,
Heaven's strength and aid will ever save
The throne whose grant it oft renews."

Hence (we may say that) he who is greatly virtuous is sure to receive the appointment (of Heaven).'

53. The Master said, 'It is only king Wăn of whom it can be said that he had no cause for grief! His father was king *K*î, and his son was king Wû. His father laid the foundations of his dignity, and his son transmitted it. 54. King Wû continued the line and enterprise of kings Thâi, *K*î, and Wăn. Once for all he buckled on his armour, and got possession of all under heaven; and all his life he did not lose the illustrious name of being that possessor. His dignity was that of the son of Heaven; his riches were all within the four seas; his ancestral temple enjoyed his offerings; and his descendants preserved those to himself. 55. It was in his old age that king Wû received the appointment (to the throne), and the duke of *K*âu completed the virtuous achievements of Wăn and Wû. He carried back the title of king to Thâi and *K*î, sacrificing also to all the dukes before them with the ceremonies of the son

of Heaven. And the practice was extended as a rule to all the feudal princes, the Great officers, all other officers, and the common people. If the father were a Great officer, and the son an inferior officer, the former was buried with the ceremonies due to a Great officer, and sacrificed to with those due by an inferior officer. If the father were an ordinary officer, and the son a Great officer, the burial was that of an ordinary officer, and the sacrifices those of a Great officer. The one year's mourning extended up to Great officers; the three years' mourning extended to the son of Heaven (himself). In the mourning for a father or mother no difference was made between the noble and the mean;—it was one and the same for all.'

56. The Master said, 'How far-extending was the filial piety of king Wû and the duke of *K*âu! Now filial piety is the skilful carrying out of the wishes of our forefathers, and the skilful carrying on of their undertakings. In spring and autumn[1] they repaired and beautified the temple-halls of their ancestors, set forth their ancestral vessels, displayed their dresses, and presented the offerings of the several seasons. 57. By means of the ceremonies of the ancestral temple, they maintained the order of their ancestors sacrificed to, here on the left, there on the right, according as they were father or son; by arranging the parties present according to their rank, they distinguished between the more noble and the less; by the arrangement of the various services, they made a distinction of the talents and virtue of

[1] Two seasons, instead of the four, as in the title of the *Kh*un *Kh*iû.

those discharging them; in the ceremony of general pledging, the inferiors presented the cup to the superiors, and thus something was given to the lowest to do; at the (concluding) feast, places were given according to the hair, and thus was made the distinction of years. 58. They occupied the places (of their forefathers); practised their ceremonies; performed their music; showed their respect for those whom they honoured; and loved those whom they regarded with affection. Thus they served the dead as they served them when alive, and served the departed as they would have served them if they had been continued among them:—all this was the perfection of filial duty.

59. 'By the ceremonies of the border sacrifices (to Heaven and Earth) they served God, and by those of the ancestral temple they sacrificed to their forefathers[1]. 60. If one understood the ceremonies of the border sacrifices and the meaning of the sacrifices of the ancestral temple, it would be as easy for him to rule a state as to look into his palm[2].'

---

[1] The phraseology of this paragraph and the next is to be taken in accordance with the usage of terms in the chapters on Sacrifices.

[2] With this ends, according to the old division of the Treatise, followed by the *Kh*ien-lung editors, the first section of it; and with it, we may say, ends also the special quotation by the author of the words of Confucius to illustrate what is said in the first chapter about the path being never to be left. The relevancy of much of what we read from paragraph 24 downwards to the purpose which it is said to serve, it is not easy for us to appreciate. All that the Master says from paragraph 48 seems rather to belong to a Treatise on Filial Piety than to one on the States of Equilibrium and Harmony.

Section II.

1. Duke Âi asked about government[1]. The Master said, 'The government of Wăn and Wû is exhibited in (the Records),—the tablets of wood and bamboo. Let there be the men, and their government would (again) flourish; but without the men, their government must cease. 2. With the (right) men the growth of government is rapid, (just as) in the earth the growth of vegetation is rapid. 3. Government is (like) an easily-growing rush[2]. 4. Therefore the exercise of government depends on (getting) the proper men. 5. (Such) men are to be got by (the ruler's) own character. That character is to be cultivated by his pursuing the right course. That course is to be cultivated by benevolence. 6. Benevolence is (the chief element in) humanity[3], and the greatest exercise of it is in the love of relatives. Righteousness is (the accordance of actions with) what is right, and the greatest exercise of it is in the honour paid to the worthy. The decreasing

[1] A considerable portion of this chapter, with variations and additions, is found in the Narratives of the School, forming the 17th article of that compilation. It may very well stand by itself; but the author of the *K*ung Yung adopted it, and made it fit into his own way of thinking.

[2] Literally, 'a typha or a phragmites.' Such is *K*û Hsî's view of the text. The old commentators took a different view, which appears to me, and would appear to my readers, very absurd.

[3] Literally, 'Benevolence is Man (仁者人也);' a remarkable saying, found elsewhere in the Lî *K*î, and also in Mencius. The value of it is somewhat marred by what follows about 'righteousness' and 'propriety.'

measures in the love of relatives, and the steps in the honour paid to the worthy, are produced by (the principle of) propriety. 7. When those in inferior situations do not obtain (the confidence of) their superiors, the people cannot be governed successfully[1]. 8. Therefore the wise ruler should not neglect the cultivation of his character. Desiring to cultivate his character, he should not neglect to serve his parents. Desiring to serve his parents, he should not neglect to know men. Desiring to know men, he should not neglect to know Heaven. 9. The universal path for all under heaven is five-fold, and the (virtues) by means of which it is trodden are three. There are ruler and minister; father and son; husband and wife; elder brother and younger; and the intercourse of friend and friend:—(the duties belonging to) these five (relationships) constitute the universal path for all. Wisdom, benevolence, and fortitude:—these three are the universal virtues of all. That whereby these are carried into exercise is one thing[2]. 10. Some are born with the knowledge of these (duties); some know them by study; and some know them as the result of painful experience. But the knowledge being possessed, it comes to one and the same thing. 11. Some practise them with the ease of nature; some for the sake of their advantage; and some by

[1] This short sentence is evidently out of place. It is found again farther on in its proper place. It has slipped in here by mistake. There is a consent of opinion, ancient and modern, on this point.

[2] 'One thing;' literally 'one,' which might be translated 'singleness,' meaning, probably, the 'solitariness' of chapter i, or the 'sincerity' of which we read so often in the sequel.

dint of strong effort. But when the work of them is done, it comes to one and the same thing[1].'

12. The Master said, 'To be fond of learning is near to wisdom; to practise with vigour is near to benevolence; to know to be ashamed is near to fortitude. He who knows these three things, knows how to cultivate his own character. Knowing how to cultivate his own character, he knows how to govern other men. Knowing how to govern other men, he knows how to govern the kingdom with its states and families.

13. 'All who have the government of the kingdom with its states and families have nine standard rules to follow:—the cultivation of themselves; the honouring of the worthy; affection towards their relatives; respect towards their great ministers; kind and sympathetic treatment of the whole body of officers; dealing with the mass of the people as their children; encouraging the resort of all classes of artisans; indulgent treatment of men from a distance; and the kindly cherishing of the princes of the states.

14. 'By (the ruler's) cultivation of himself there is set up (the example of) the course (which all should pursue); by his honouring of the worthy, he will be preserved from errors of judgment; by his showing affection towards his relatives, there will be no dissatisfaction among his uncles and brethren; by respecting the great ministers he will be kept from mistakes; by kindly treatment of the whole body of officers, they will be led to make the most

[1] After this, it follows in the 'Narratives:'—The duke said, 'Your words are admirable, are perfect; but I am really stupid and unable to fulfil them.'

grateful return for his courtesies; by dealing with the mass of the people as his children, they will be drawn to exhort one another (to what is good); by encouraging the resort of artisans, his wealth for expenditure will be rendered sufficient; by indulgent treatment of men from a distance, they will come to him from all quarters; by his kindly cherishing of the princes of the states, all under heaven will revere him.

15. 'The adjustment of all his thoughts, purification, arraying himself in his richest dresses, and the avoiding of every movement contrary to the rules of propriety;—this is the way in which (the ruler) must cultivate his own character. Discarding slanderers, keeping himself from (the seductions of) beauty, making light of riches and honouring virtue:—this is the way by which he will encourage the worthy. Giving his relatives places of honour, and large emolument, and entering into sympathy with them in their likes and dislikes:—this is the way by which he can stimulate affection towards relatives. Giving them numerous officers to discharge their functions and execute their orders:—this is the way by which he will stimulate his Great ministers. According to them a generous confidence, and making their emoluments large:—this is the way by which he will stimulate (the body of) his officers. Employing them (only) at the regular times and making the imposts light:—this is the way by which he will stimulate the people. Daily examinations and monthly trials, and rations and allowances in proportion to the work done:—this is the way in which he will stimulate the artisans. Escorting them on their departure, and meeting them on their coming, commending the good among them and showing pity to the incom-

petent;—this is the way in which he will manifest his indulgent treatment of men from a distance. Continuing families whose line of succession has been broken, reviving states that have ceased to exist, reducing confusion to order, supporting where there is peril; having fixed times for receiving the princes themselves and their envoys; sending them away after liberal treatment and with liberal gifts, and requiring from them small offerings on their coming:—this is the way in which he will cherish with kindness the princes of the states.

16. 'All who have the government of the kingdom with its states and families have these nine standard rules to attend to. That whereby they are carried into exercise is one thing. In all things success depends on previous preparation; without such preparation there is failure. If what is to be spoken be determined beforehand, there will be no stumbling in the utterance. If the things to be done be determined beforehand, there will be no difficulty with them. If actions to be performed be determined beforehand, there will be no difficulty with them. If actions to be performed be determined beforehand, there will be no sorrow or distress in connexion with them. If the courses to be pursued be determined beforehand, the pursuit of them will be inexhaustible[1].

17. 'When those in inferior situations do not

[1] The 'one thing' in this paragraph carries us back to the same phrase in paragraph 9. If we confine our attention to this paragraph alone, we shall say, with *K*ăng and Ying-tâ, 'the one thing' is the 'preparation beforehand,' of which it goes on to speak; and it seems to be better not to grope here for a more mysterious meaning.

obtain (the confidence of) their superiors, the people cannot be governed successfully.

18. 'There is a way to obtain (the confidence of) the superior;—if one is not believed in by his friends, he will not obtain the confidence of his superior. There is a way to secure being believed in by his friends;—if he be not in submissive accord with his parents, he will not be believed in by his friends. There is a way to secure submissive accord with parents;—if one, on turning his thoughts in on himself, finds that he has not attained to the perfection of his nature[1], he will not be in submissive accord with his parents. There is a way to secure the perfection of the nature;—if a man have not a clear understanding of what is good, he will not attain to that perfection.

19. 'Perfection of nature is characteristic of Heaven. To attain to that perfection belongs to man. He who possesses that perfection hits what is right without any effort, and apprehends without any exercise of thought;—he is the sage[2] who

[1] Literally, 'that he is not sincere,' which is Mr. Wylie's rendering; or, as I rendered it in 1861, 'finds a want of sincerity.' But in the frequent occurrence of 誠 in the 'Sequel of the Treatise,' 'sincerity' is felt to be an inadequate rendering of it. Zottoli renders the clause by 'Si careat veritate, integritate,' and says in a note, '誠 est naturalis entis perfectio, quae rei convenit juxta genuinum Creatoris protypon, quaeque a creatore infunditur; proindeque est rei veritas, seu rei juxta veritatem perfectio.' It seems to me that this ideal perfection, as belonging to all things, which God made 'good,' is expressed by 善 in the last clause; and that the realisation of that perfection by man, as belonging to his own nature, is the work of 誠, and may be spoken of as actually and fully accomplished, or in the process of being accomplished. It is difficult with our antecedent knowledge and opinions to place ourselves exactly in the author's point of view.

[2] 聖人,—Rémusat, Zottoli, and many give for this name

naturally and easily embodies the right way. He who attains to perfection is he who chooses what is good, and firmly holds it fast.

20. 'He extensively studies what is good; inquires accurately about it; thinks carefully over it; clearly discriminates it; and vigorously practises it. While there is anything he has not studied, or in what he has studied there is anything he cannot (understand), he will not intermit his labour. While there is anything he has not asked about, or anything in what he has asked about that he does not know, he will not intermit his labour. While there is anything he has not thought over, or anything in what he has thought about that he does not know, he will not intermit his labour. While there is anything which he has not tried to discriminate, or anything in his discrimination that is not clear, he will not intermit his labour. While there is anything which he has not practised, or any want of vigour so far as he has practised, he will not intermit his labour.

'If another man succeed by one effort, he will use a hundred efforts; if another succeed by ten, he will use a thousand. Let a man proceed in this way, and though stupid, he is sure to become intelligent; though weak, he is sure to become strong.'

21. The understanding (of what is good), springing from moral perfection, is to be ascribed to the nature; moral perfection springing from the under-

'sanctus vir,' 'un saint,' 'the holy man.' I prefer, after all, to adhere to the rendering, 'le sage,' 'the sage.' The sage is the ideal man; the saint is the man sanctified by the Spirit of God. Humanity predominates in the former concept; Divinity in the latter. The ideas of morality and goodness belong to both names. See Mencius, VII, ix, 25, for his graduation of the appellations of good men.

standing (of what is good) is to be ascribed to instruction. But given the perfection, and there shall be the understanding; given the understanding, and there shall be the perfection[1].

22. It is only he of all under heaven who is entirely perfect that can give its full development to his nature. Able to give its full development to his own nature, he can also give the same to the nature of other men. Able to give its full development to the nature of other men, he can also give the same to the natures of animals and things[2]. Able to give their full development to these, he can assist the transforming and nourishing operations of heaven and earth. Capable of assisting those transforming and nourishing operations, he can form a ternion with heaven and earth.

23. Next to the above is he who cultivates to the utmost the shoots (of goodness in his nature)[3], till he becomes morally perfect. This perfection will then obtain embodiment; embodied, it will be manifested; manifested, it will become brilliant; brilliant,

---

[1] With this paragraph there commences the last chapter of the Treatise. 3ze-sze, it is said, takes up in it the commencing utterances in paragraph 19, and variously illustrates and prosecutes them. From the words 'nature and instruction' it is evident how he had the commencing chapter of the Treatise in his mind.

[2] The text is simply 'the nature of things;' but the word 'things (物)' comprehends all beings besides man. Zottoli's 'rerum natura' seems quite inadequate. Rémusat's Latin version is the same; his French is 'la nature des choses.' Wylie says, 'the nature of other objects.' This chapter has profoundly affected all subsequent philosophical speculation in China. The ternion of 'Heaven, Earth, and Man' is commonly called San 3hâi (三才), 'the Three Powers.'

[3] The character in the text here is a difficult one:—*khû* (曲),

it will go forth in action; going forth in action, it will produce changes; producing changes, it will effect transformations. It is only he of all under heaven who is entirely perfect that can transform.

24. It is characteristic of him who is entirely perfect that he can foreknow. When a state or family is about to flourish, there are sure to be lucky omens, and when it is about to perish, there are sure to be unlucky omens. They will be seen in the tortoise-shell and stalks[1]; they will affect the movements of the four limbs. When calamity or happiness is about to come, the good is sure to be foreknown by him, and the evil also. Hence, he who is entirely perfect is like a Spirit[2].

---

meaning 'crooked,' often used as the antithesis of 'straight;' but the title of the first Book in this collection shows that it need not be used only of what is bad. In that case, the phrase 致曲 would mean—'carries to the utmost what is bad.' Zottoli's rendering of it by 'promovere declinatam naturam' is inadmissible. Nor can we accept Rémusat's 'diriger efforts vers une seule vertu,' which Wylie follows, merely substituting 'object' for 'vertu.' See the introduction on the title of the first Book. Very much to the point is an illustration by the scholar Pâi Lü:—'Put on stone on a bamboo shoot, or where it would show itself, and it will travel round the stone and come out crookedly at its side.' So it is with the good nature, whose free and full development is repressed.

[1] These were the two principal methods of divination practised from very ancient times. The stalks were those of the Ptarmica Sibirica; of which I possess a bundle brought from the tomb of Confucius in 1873. It is difficult to say anything about 'the four limbs,' which were to *K*ăng 'the four feet of the tortoise.'

[2] 'The Spirit-man' is, according to Mencius' graduation, an advance on the Sage or Holy man, one whose action is mysterious and invisible, like the power of Heaven and Earth working in nature. Chinese predicates about him could not go farther.

25. Perfection is seen in (its possessor's) self-completion; and the path (which is its embodiment), in its self-direction.

26. Perfection is (seen in) the beginning and end of (all) creatures and things. Without this perfection there would be no creature or thing.

27. Therefore the superior man considers perfection as the noblest of all attainments.

28. He who is perfect does not only complete himself; his perfection enables him to complete all other beings also. The completion of himself shows the complete virtue of his nature; the completion of other beings shows his wisdom. (The two) show his nature in good operation, and the way in which the union of the external and internal is effected.

29. Hence, whenever he exercises it, (the operation) is right.

30. Thus it is that entire perfection is unresting; unresting, it continues long; continuing long, it evidences itself; evidencing itself, it reaches far; reaching far, it becomes large and substantial; large and substantial, it becomes high and brilliant.

31. By being large and substantial it contains (all) things. By being high and brilliant, it overspreads (all) things. By reaching far and continuing long, it completes (all) things. By its being so large and substantial, it makes (its possessor) the co-equal of earth; by its height and brilliancy, it makes him the co-equal of heaven; by its reaching far and continuing long, it makes him infinite.

32. Such being his characteristics, without any manifestation he becomes displayed; without any movement he effects changes; without any exertion

he completes. The way of heaven and earth may be completely described in one sentence:—

33. They are without any second thought, and so their production of things is inexhaustible.

34. The characteristics of heaven and earth are to be large; to be substantial; to be high; to be brilliant; to be far-reaching; to be long-continuing.

35. There now is this heaven; it is only this bright shining spot, but when viewed in its inexhaustible extent, the sun, moon, stars, and constellations of the zodiac are suspended in it, and all things are overspread by it. There is this earth; it is only a handful of soil, but when regarded in its breadth and thickness, it sustains mountains like the Hwâ and the Yo, without feeling the weight, and contains the rivers and seas without their leaking away. There is this mountain; it looks only the size of a stone, but when contemplated in all its altitude the grass and trees are produced on it, birds and beasts dwell on it, and the precious things which men treasure up are found in it. There is this water; it appears only a ladleful, but, when we think of its unfathomable depths, the largest tortoises, iguanas, iguanadons, dragons, fishes, and turtles are produced in them, and articles of value and sources of wealth abound in them.

36. It is said in the Book of Poetry (IV, i, sect. 1, ode 2),

'The ordinances of Heaven,
How profound are they and unceasing!'

intimating that it is thus that Heaven is Heaven. (And again):—

'Oh! how illustrious
Was the singleness of the virtue of king Wăn!'

intimating that it was thus that king Wăn was the accomplished (king), by his singleness unceasing.

37. How great is the course of the sage! Like an overflowing flood it sends forth and nourishes all things! It rises up to the height of heaven.

38. How complete is its greatness! It embraces the three hundred usages of ceremony, and the three thousand modes of demeanour. It waits for the right man, and then it is trodden. Hence it is said, 'If there be not perfect virtue, the perfect path cannot be exemplified.'

39. Therefore the superior man honours the virtuous nature, and pursues the path of inquiry and study (regarding it); seeking to carry it out in its breadth and greatness, so as to omit none of the exquisite and minute points (which it embraces); raising it to its greatest height and brilliancy, so as to be found in the way of equilibrium and harmony. He cherishes his old knowledge so as (continually) to be acquiring new, and thus manifests an honest, generous, earnestness in the esteem and practice of all propriety

40. Therefore, when occupying a high situation he is not proud, and in a low situation he is not insubordinate. If the state is well-governed, his words are able to promote its prosperity; and if it be ill-governed, his silence is sufficient to secure forbearance (for himself).

41. Is not this what is said in the Book of Poetry (III, iii, ode 6, 4),

> 'Intelligent is he and wise,
> Protecting his own person?'

42. The Master said, 'Let a man who is ignorant be fond of using his own judgment; let one who is

in a low situation be fond of arrogating a directing power; let one who is living in the present age go back to the ways of antiquity;—on all who act thus calamity is sure to come.'

43. To no one but the son of Heaven does it belong to discuss the subject of ceremonial usages; to fix the measures; and to determine (the names of) the written characters.

44. Now, throughout the whole kingdom, carriages have all wheels of the same breadth of rim; all writing is with the same characters; and for conduct there are the same rules.

45. One may occupy the throne, but if he have not the proper virtue, he should not presume to make ceremonies or music. One may have the virtue, but if he have not the throne, he in the same way should not presume to make ceremonies or music.

46. The Master said, 'I might speak of the ceremonies of Hsiâ, but *Kh*î could not sufficiently attest (my words). I have learned the ceremonies of Yin, and they are preserved in Sung. I have learned the ceremonies of *K*âu, and they are now used. I follow *K*âu.'

47. If he who attains to the sovereignty of all the kingdom attach the due importance to (those) three points[1], there are likely to be few errors (among the people).

48. However excellent may have been (the regulations of) those of former times, they cannot be attested. Not being attested, they cannot command credence. Not commanding credence, the people

[1] What are those three points? The old interpretations said,—'The ceremonies of the three kings;' *K*û Hsî thought they were the three things in paragraph 43;—which is more likely.

would not follow them. However excellent might be those of one in an inferior station, they would not be honoured. Not honoured, they would not command credence. Not commanding credence, the people would not follow them.

49. Therefore the course of the superior man is rooted in his own character and conduct, and attested by the multitudes of the people. He examines (his institutions) by comparison with those of the founders of the three dynasties, and finds them without mistake. He sets them up before heaven and earth, and there is nothing in them contrary to (their mode of operation). He presents himself with them before Spiritual Beings, and no doubts about them arise. He is prepared to wait for the rise of a sage a hundred ages hence, and has no misgivings. That he can present himself with them before Spiritual Beings, without any doubts about them arising, shows that he knows Heaven; that he is prepared to wait for the rise of a sage a hundred ages hence, without any misgivings, shows that he knows men.

50. Therefore the movements of the superior man mark out for ages the path for all under heaven; his actions are the law for ages for all under heaven; and his words are for ages the pattern for all under heaven. Those who are far from him look longingly for him, and those who are near are never weary of him.

51. It is said in the Book of Poetry (IV, i, sect. 2, ode 3),

'There in their own states are they loved,
Nor tired of are they here;
Their fame through lapse of time shall grow,
Both day and night, more clear.'

Never has a superior man obtained an early renown throughout the kingdom who did not correspond to this description.

52. *K*ung-nî handed down (the views of) Yâo and Shun as if they had been his ancestors, and elegantly displayed (the ways) of Wăn and Wû, taking them as his model. Above, he adopted as his law the seasons of heaven; and below, he conformed to the water and land.

53. He may be compared to heaven and earth in their supporting and containing, their overshadowing and curtaining all things. He may be compared to the four seasons in their alternating progress, and to the sun and moon in their successive shining. All things are nourished together without their injuring one another; the courses (of the seasons and of the sun and moon) proceed without any collision among them. The smaller energies are like river-currents; the greater energies are seen in mighty transformations. It is this which makes heaven and earth so great.

54. It is only he possessed of all sagely qualities that can exist under heaven, who shows himself quick in apprehension, clear in discernment, of far-reaching intelligence and all-embracing knowledge, fitted to exercise rule; magnanimous, generous, benign, and mild, fitted to exercise forbearance; impulsive, energetic, firm, and enduring, fitted to maintain a strong hold; self-adjusted, grave, never swerving from the mean, and correct, fitted to command respect; accomplished, distinctive, concentrative, and searching, fitted to exercise discrimination.

55. All-embracing is he and vast, deep and active as a fountain, sending forth in their due seasons these (qualities).

56. All-embracing is he and vast, like heaven. Deep and active as a fountain, he is like an abyss. He shows himself, and the people all revere him; he speaks, and the people all believe him; he acts, and the people all are pleased with him. In this way his fame overspreads the Middle kingdom, and extends to all barbarous tribes. Wherever ships and carriages reach; wherever the strength of man penetrates; wherever the heavens overshadow and the earth sustains; wherever the sun and moon shine; wherever frosts and dews fall; all who have blood and breath unfeignedly honour and love him. Hence it is said, 'He is the equal of Heaven[1].'

57. It is only he among all under heaven who is entirely perfect that can adjust and blend together the great standard duties of all under heaven, establish the great fundamental principles of all, and know the transforming and nourishing operations of heaven and earth.

58. How shall this individual have any one beyond himself on whom he depends? Call him man in his ideal, how earnest is he! Call him an abyss, how deep is he! Call him Heaven, how vast is he!

59. Who can know him but he who is indeed quick in apprehension and clear in discernment, of sagely wisdom, and all-embracing knowledge, possessing heavenly virtue?

60. It is said in the Book of Poetry (I, v, ode 3, 1),

---

[1] It was the old opinion that in this part of the Treatise we have his grandson's eloquent eulogium of Confucius, and I agree with that opinion. Yet I have not ventured to translate the different parts of it in the past tense. Let it be read as the description of the ideal sage who found his realisation in the Master.

'Over her embroidered robe she wears a (plain)
garment;'

expressing how the wearer disliked the display of the beauty (of the robe). Just so, it is the way of the superior man to prefer the concealment (of his virtue), while it daily becomes more illustrious, and it is the way of the small man to seek notoriety, while he daily goes more and more to ruin.

61. It is characteristic of the superior man, appearing insipid, yet not to produce satiety; preferring a simple negligence, yet to have his accomplishments recognised; seeming mild and simple, yet to be discriminating. He knows how what is distant lies in what is near. He knows where the wind proceeds from. He knows how what is minute becomes manifested[1]. He, we may be assured, will enter (the innermost recesses of) virtue.

62. It is said in the Book of Poetry (II, iv, ode 8, 11),

'Though they dive to the bottom, and lie there,
They are very clearly seen.'

Therefore the superior man internally examines his heart, that there may be nothing wrong there, and no occasion for dissatisfaction with himself.

63. That wherein the superior man cannot be equalled is simply this,—his (work) which other men do not see. It is said in the Book of Poetry (III, iii, ode 2, 7),

'When in your chamber, 'neath its light,
Maintain your conscience pure and bright.'

[1] That is how the ruler's character acts on the people as the wind on grass and plants.

64. Therefore the superior man, even when he is not acting, has the feeling of reverence; and when he does not speak, he has the feeling of truthfulness. It is said in the Book of Poetry (IV, iii, ode 2),

'These offerings we set forth without a word,
Without contention, and with one accord,
To beg the presence of the honoured lord.'

65. Therefore the superior man does not use rewards, and the people are stimulated (to virtue); he does not show anger, and the people are awed more than by hatchets and battle-axes. It is said in the Book of Poetry (IV, i, sect. 1, ode 4),

'What is most distinguished is the being virtuous;
It will secure the imitation of all the princes.'

66. Therefore the superior man being sincerely reverential, the whole kingdom is made tranquil. It is said in the Book of Poetry (III, i, ode 7, 7),

'I am pleased with your intelligent virtue,
Not loudly proclaimed, nor pourtrayed.'

67. The Master said, 'Among the appliances to transform the people, sounds and appearances (may seem to) have a trivial effect. But it is said in another ode (III, iii, ode 6, 6),

"Virtue is light as a hair."

68. 'But a hair will still admit of comparison (as to its size). In what is said in another ode (III, i, ode 1, 7),

"The doings of high Heaven
Have neither sound nor odour,"

we have the highest description (of transforming virtue).'

BOOK XXIX. PIÂO *KÎ*

OR

THE RECORD ON EXAMPLE[1].

1. These were the words of the Master:—'Let us return[2].' The superior man, in obscurity, yet makes himself manifest; without giving himself any airs, his gravity is acknowledged; without the exercise of severity, he inspires awe; without using words, he is believed.

2. The Master said, 'The superior man takes no erroneous step before men, nor errs in the expression of his countenance, nor in the language of his speech. Therefore his demeanour induces awe, his countenance induces fear, and his words produce confidence. It is said in The Punishments of Fû (The Shû, V, xxvii, 11): "They were all reverence and caution. They had no occasion to make choice of words in reference to their conduct."'

3. The Master said, 'The dress and the one worn over it do not take the place, the one of the other, it being intimated to the people thereby that they should not trouble or interfere with one another.'

4. The Master said, 'When a sacrifice has come to the point of greatest reverence, it should not be immediately followed by music. When the dis-

---

[1] See the introductory notice, vol. xxvii, pp. 44, 45.

[2] Compare Analects, V, 22. When Confucius thus spoke, he was accepting his failure in the different states, and saying in effect that his principles and example would ultimately win their way, without his being immediately successful.

cussion of affairs at court has reached its utmost nicety, it should not be immediately followed by an idle indifference.'

5. The Master said, 'The superior man is careful (in small things), and thereby escapes calamity. His generous largeness cannot be kept in obscurity. His courtesy keeps shame at a distance.'

6. The Master said, 'The superior man, by his gravity and reverence, becomes every day stronger (for good); while indifference and want of restraint lead to a daily deterioration. The superior man does not allow any irregularity in his person, even for a single day;—how should he be like (a small man) who will not end his days (in honour)?'

7. The Master said, 'Vigil and fasting are required (as a preparation) for serving the spirits (in sacrifice); the day and month in which to appear before the ruler are chosen beforehand:—these observances were appointed lest the people should look on these things without reverence.'

8. The Master said, '(The small man) is familiar and insolent. He may bring death on himself (by being so), and yet he stands in no fear[1].'

9. The Master said, 'Without the interchange of the formal messages, there can be no reception of one party by another; without the presenting of the ceremonial (gifts), there can be no interview (with a superior):—these rules were made that the people might not take troublesome liberties with one another! It is said in the Yî, "When he shows (the sincerity that marks) the first recourse to divination, I instruct him. If he apply a second and third time,

[1] The text of this short paragraph is supposed to be defective.

that is troublesome, and I do not instruct the troublesome[1].'"

10. These were the words of the Master:—'(Humanity, of which the characteristic is) Benevolence, is the Pattern for all under Heaven; Righteousness is the Law for all under Heaven; and the Reciprocations (of ceremony) are for the Profit of all under Heaven.'

11. The Master said, 'When kindness is returned for kindness, the people are stimulated (to be kind). When injury is returned for injury, the people are warned (to refrain from wrong-doing). It is said in the Book of Poetry (III, iii, ode 26):—

"Answers to every word will leap,
Good deeds their recompense shall reap."

'It is said in the Thâi *K*iâ (Shû, IV, v, sect. 2, 2), "Without the sovereign, the people cannot enjoy repose with one another; without the people, the sovereign would have none to rule over in the four quarters (of the kingdom)."'

12. The Master said, 'They who return kindness for injury are such as have a regard for their own persons. They who return injury for kindness are men to be punished and put to death[2].'

13. The Master said, 'Under heaven there is only a man (here and there) who loves what is proper to humanity without some personal object in the

[1] See the explanation of the 4th Hexagram, Măng, vol. xvi, pp. 64, 65,—with this paragraph ends the first section of the Treatise. It seems to be extended to exhibit the necessity of reverence in the superior man, who is to be an example to others.

[2] Comparing this utterance with the decision of Confucius in the Analects, XIV, 36, *Kh*ăn Hâo thinks it doubtful that we have here the sentiment or words of the sage.

matter, or who hates what is contrary to humanity without being apprehensive (of some evil). Therefore the superior man reasons about the path to be trodden from the standpoint of himself, and lays down his laws from the (capabilities of the) people.'

14. The Master said, '(The virtues of) humanity appear in three ways. (In some cases) the work of humanity is done, but under the influence of different feelings. In these, the (true character of the) humanity cannot be known; but where there is some abnormal manifestation of it, in those the true character can be known[1]. Those to whom it really belongs practise it easily and naturally; the wise practise it for the sake of the advantage which it brings; and those who fear the guilt of transgression practise it by constraint.

15. Humanity is the right hand; pursuing the right path is the left[2]. Humanity comprehends the (whole) man; the path pursued is the exhibition of righteousness. Those whose humanity is large, while their exhibition of righteousness is slight, are loved and not honoured. Those whose righteousness is large and their humanity slight are honoured and not loved.

16. There is the perfect path, the righteous path, and the calculated path. The perfect path conducts to sovereignty; the righteous path, to chieftaincy; and the calculated path, to freedom from error and failure[3].

---

[1] In illustration of this point there is always adduced the case of the duke of *K*âu, who erred, under the influence of his brotherly love, in the promotion of his brothers that afterwards joined in rebellion.

[2] The right hand is used most readily and with greatest effect.

[3] With this paragraph ends the second section of the Treatise. It

17. These were the words of the Master:—'Of humanity there are various degrees; righteousness is now long, now short, now great, now small. Where there is a deep and compassionate sympathy in the heart, we have humanity evidenced in the love of others; where there is the following of (old) examples, and vigorous endeavour, we have the employment of humanity for the occasion. It is said in the Book of Poetry (III, i, ode 10, 6),

"Where the Făng-water flows,
Is the white millet grown.
So his men Wû employed,
And his merit was shown!
To his sons he would leave
His wise plans and his throne
And our Wû was a sovereign true."

'That was a humanity extending to many generations. In the Lessons from the States it is said (I, iii, ode 10, 3),

"Person slighted, life all blighted,
What can the future prove?"

'That was a humanity extending (only) to the end of the speaker's life.'

18. The Master said, 'Humanity is like a heavy vessel, and like a long road. He who tries to lift the vessel cannot sustain its weight; he who travels the road cannot accomplish all its distance. There is nothing that has so many different degrees as (the course of) humanity; and thus he who tries to nerve himself to it finds it a difficult task. Therefore when

---

is occupied with the subject of humanity, or the whole nature of man, of which benevolence is the chief element and characteristic, as the most powerful form of example.

the superior man measures men with the scale of righteousness, he finds it difficult to discover the men (whom he seeks); when he looks at men and compares them with one another, he knows who among them are the more worthy.'

19. The Master said, 'It is only one man (here and there) under heaven, who with his heart of hearts naturally rests in humanity. It is said in the Tâ Yâ, or Major Odes of the Kingdom (III, iii, ode 6, 6),

"Virtue is very light,—
Light as a hair, yet few can bear
The burden of its weight.
'Tis so; but *K*ung Shan, as I think,
Needs not from virtue's weight to shrink
That other men defies.
Aid from my love his strength rejects.
(If the king's measures have defects,
What's needed he supplies)."

'In the Hsiâo Yâ, or Minor Odes of the Kingdom, it is said (II, vii, ode 4, 5),

"To the high hills I looked;
The great way I pursued."'

The Master said, 'So did the poets love (the exhibition of) humanity. (They teach us how) one should pursue the path of it, not giving over in the way, forgetting his age, taking no thought that the years before him will not be sufficient (for his task), urging on his course with earnestness from day to day, and only giving up when he sinks in death.'

20. The Master said, 'Long has the attainment of a perfect humanity been difficult among men! all men err in what they love;—and hence it is easy to

apologise for the errors of those who are seeking this humanity[1].'

21. The Master said, 'Courtesy is near to propriety; economy is near to humanity; good faith is near to the truth of things. When one with respect and humility practises these (virtues), though he may fall into errors, they will not be very great. Where there is courtesy, the errors are few; where there is truth, there can be good faith; where there is economy, the exercise of forbearance is easy:—will not failure be rare in the case of those who practise these things? It is said in the Book of Poetry (III, iii, ode 2, 9),

"Mildness and reverence base supply
For virtue's structure, broad and high."'

22. The Master said, 'Long has the attainment of perfect humanity been difficult among men; it is only the superior man who is able to reach it. Therefore the superior man does not distress men by requiring from them that which (only) he himself can do, nor put them to shame because of what they cannot do. Hence the sage, in laying down rules for conduct, does not make himself the rule, but gives them his instructions so that they shall be able to stimulate themselves to endeavour, and have the feeling of shame if they do not put them in practice. (He enjoins) the rules of ceremony to regulate the conduct; good faith to bind it on them; right demeanour to set it off; costume to distinguish it; and friendship to perfect it:—he desires in this way to produce a uniformity of the people. It is said in the Hsiâo Yâ (V, ode 5, 3),

[1] This seems to be the meaning, about which there are various opinions.

"Shall they unblushing break man's law?
Shall they not stand of Heaven in awe?"

23. 'Therefore, when a superior man puts on the dress (of his rank), he sets it off by the demeanour of a superior man. That demeanour he sets off with the language of a superior man; and that language he makes good by the virtues of a superior man. Hence the superior man is ashamed to wear the robes, and not have the demeanour; ashamed to have the demeanour, and not the style of speech; ashamed to have the style of speech, and not the virtues; ashamed to have the virtues, and not the conduct proper to them. Thus it is that when the superior man has on his sackcloth and other mourning, his countenance wears an air of sorrow; when he wears the square-cut dress and square-topped cap, his countenance wears an air of respect; and when he wears his mail-coat and helmet, his countenance says that he is not to be meddled with. It is said in the Book of Poetry (I, xiv, ode 2, 2),

"Like pelicans, upon the dam
Which stand, and there their pouches cram,
Unwet the while their wings,
Are those who their rich dress display,
But no befitting service pay,
Intent on meanest things[1]."'

[1] With this paragraph ends the 3rd section of the Book. 'It speaks,' say the *Kh*ien-lung editors, 'of the perfect humanity, showing that to rest naturally in this is very difficult, yet it is possible by self-government to advance from the practice of it, with a view to one's advantage, to that natural resting in it; and by means of instruction to advance from the practice of it by constraint to the doing so for its advantages.'

24. These were the words of the Master:—'What the superior man calls righteousness is, that noble and mean all have the services which they discharge throughout the kingdom. The son of Heaven himself ploughs the ground for the rice with which to fill the vessels, and the black millet from which to distil the spirit to be mixed with fragrant herbs, for the services of God, and in the same way the feudal lords are diligent in discharging their services to the son of Heaven.'

25. The Master said, 'In serving (the ruler) his superior, (an officer) from his position has great opportunity to protect the people; but when he does not allow himself to have any thought of acting as the ruler of them, this shows a high degree of humanity. Therefore, the superior man is courteous and economical, seeking to exercise his benevolence, and sincere and humble in order to practise his sense of propriety. He does not himself set a high value on his services; he does not himself assert the honour due to his person. He is not ambitious of (high) position, and is very moderate in his desires. He gives place willingly to men of ability and virtue. He abases himself and gives honour to others. He is careful and in fear of doing what is not right. His desire in all this is to serve his ruler. If he succeed in doing so (and obtaining his ruler's approbation), he feels that he has done right; if he do not so succeed, he still feels that he has done right:—prepared to accept the will of Heaven concerning himself. It is said in the Book of Poetry (III, i, ode 5, 6),

"How the creepers close twine
Round the branches and stems!

Self-possession and ease
  Robed our prince as with gems.
Happiness increased unsought,
  Nor by crooked ways was bought."

Might not this have been said of Shun, Yü, king Wăn, or the duke of *K*âu, who had the great virtues (necessary) to govern the people, and yet were (only) careful to serve their rulers? It is said again in the same Book of Poetry (III, i, ode 2, 3),

"This our king Wăn in all his way
Did watchful reverence display,
With clearest wisdom serving God,
Who, pleased to see the course he trod,
  Him with great favour crowned.
His virtue no deflection knew,
But always to the right was true.
The states beheld, and all approved.
With loyal ardour stirred and moved,
  Wăn as their head they owned."'

26. The Master said, 'The practice of the ancient kings in conferring honorary posthumous names was to do honour to the fame (of the individuals); but they limited themselves to one excellence (in the character);—they would have been ashamed if the name had been beyond the actions (of the life). In accordance with this the superior man does not himself magnify his doings, nor himself exalt his merit, seeking to be within the truth; actions of an extraordinary character he does not aim at, but seeks to occupy himself only with what is substantial and good. He displays prominently the good qualities of others, and celebrates their merits, seeking to place himself below them in the scale of worth. There-

fore, although the superior man abases himself, yet the people respect and honour him.'

27. The Master said, 'The meritorious services of Hâu *K*î were the greatest of all under Heaven; could his hands and feet be described as those of an ordinary man? But all which he desired was that his doings should be superior to his name, and therefore he said of himself that he was simply "a man useful to others[1]."'

28. These were the words of the Master:—'Difficult is it to attain to what is called the perfect humanity of the superior man! It is said in the Book of Poetry[2],

"The happy and courteous prince
Is the father and mother of his people."

Happy, he (yet) vigorously teaches them; courteous, he makes them pleased and restful. With all their happiness, there is no wild extravagance; with all their observance of ceremonial usages, there is the feeling of affection. Notwithstanding his awing gravity, they are restful; notwithstanding his son-like gentleness, they are respectful. Thus he causes

[1] With this ends the 4th section of the Book, 'On the service of his ruler by an inferior, showing the righteousness between them, and how that righteousness completes the humanity.'

[2] The ode here quoted from can hardly be any other than III, ii, 7. The first character in the former of the two lines in that ode, however, is only the phonetic part of that in the text here, and the meaning of 'force or vigour' which the writer employs seems incongruous with that belonging to it in the Shih, where it occurs several times, in combination with the character that follows it, used as a binomial adjective. I need not say more on the difficulty. The meaning of the paragraph as a whole is plain:—'The superior man,' the competent ruler, must possess, blended together, the strength of the father and the gentleness of the mother.

them to honour him as their father, and love him as their mother. There must be all this before he is the father and mother of his people. Could any one who was not possessed of perfect virtue be able to accomplish this?

29. 'Here now is the affection of a father for his sons;—he loves the worthy among them, and places on a lower level those who do not show ability; but that of a mother for them is such, that while she loves the worthy, she pities those who do not show ability:—the mother deals with them on the ground of affection and not of showing them honour; the father, on the ground of showing them honour and not of affection. (So we may say of) water and the people, that it manifests affection to them, but does not give them honour; of fire, that it gives them honour, but does not manifest affection; of the ground, that it manifests affection, but does not give honour; of Heaven, that it gives them honour, but does not manifest affection; of the nature conferred on them, that it manifests affection, but does not give them honour; and of the manes of their departed, that they give honour, but do not manifest affection[1].'

30. 'Under the Hsiâ dynasty it was the way to give honour to the nature conferred on men; they served the manes of the departed, and respected Spiritual Beings, keeping them at a distance, while they brought the people near, and made them loyal; they put first the (attraction) of emolument, and last the terrors of power; first rewards, and then punishments; showing their affection (for the people), but

[1] The ruler-father of the previous paragraph is here contrasted with the ordinary parent; but the second half of the text is not easily translated, and is difficult to comprehend.

not giving them honour. The bad effect on the people was, that they became stupid and ignorant, proud and clownish, and uncultivated, without any accomplishments.

'Under the Yin dynasty, they honoured Spiritual Beings, and led the people on to serve them; they put first the service of their manes, and last the usages of ceremony; first punishments, and then rewards; giving honour (to the people), but not showing affection for them. The bad effect on the people was, that they became turbulent and were restless, striving to surpass one another without any sense of shame.

'Under the *K*âu dynasty, they honoured the ceremonial usages, and set a high value on bestowing (favours); they served the manes and respected Spiritual Beings, yet keeping them at a distance; they brought the people near, and made them loyal; in rewarding and punishing they used the various distinctions and arrangements of rank; showing affection (for the people), but not giving them honour. The bad effects on the people were, that they became fond of gain and crafty; were all for accomplishments, and shameless; injured one another, and had their moral sense obscured.'

31. The Master said, 'It was the method of the Hsiâ dynasty not to trouble (the people) with many notices; it did not require everything from the people, nor (indeed) look to them for great things; and they did not weary of the affection (between them and their rulers).

'Under the Yin dynasty, they did not trouble (the people) with ceremonies, and yet they required everything from them.

'Under the *K*âu dynasty, they were rigorous with

the people, and not troublesome in the services to the spirits; but they did all that could be done in the way of awards, conferring rank, punishments, and penalties.'

32. The Master said, 'Under the methods of (the dynasties of the line of) Yü[1] and Hsiâ, there were few dissatisfactions among the people. The methods of Yin and *K*âu were not equal to the correction of their errors.'

33. The Master said, 'The plain and simple ways of (the dynasties of the line of) Yü and Hsiâ, and the multiplied forms of Yin and *K*âu were both extreme. The forms of Yü and Hsiâ did not neutralise their simplicity, nor was there sufficient simplicity under Yin and *K*âu to neutralise their forms.'

34. These were the words of the Master:—'Although in subsequent ages there arose (distinguished sovereigns), yet none of them succeeded in equalling the Tî of (the line of) Yü. He ruled over all under heaven, but, while he lived, he had not a selfish thought, and when he died, he did not make his son great (with the inheritance). He treated the people as his sons, as if he had been their father and mother. He had a deep and compassionate sympathy for them (like their mother); he instructed them in loyalty and what was profitable (like their father). While he showed his affection for them, he also gave them honour; in his natural restfulness, he was reverent; in the terrors of his majesty, he yet was loving; with all his riches, he was yet observant

[1] 'The line of Yü' was Shun, who succeeded to Yâo. He did not found a dynasty; but he is often spoken of as if he had done so.

of the rules of propriety; and his kindness was yet (rightly) distributed. The superior men who stood in connexion with him gave honour to benevolence, and stood in awe of righteousness; were ashamed of lavish expenditure, and set little store by their accumulation of substance; loyal, but not coming into collision with their sovereign; righteous, and yet deferential to him; accomplished, and yet restful; generous, and yet discriminating. It is said in Fû on Punishments, "He sought to awe the people by his virtue, and all were filled with dread; he proceeded to enlighten them by his virtue, and all were enlightened." Who but the Tî of (the line of) Yü could have been able to do this[1]?' (Shû, V, xxvii, 7.)

35. These were the words of the Master:—'(A minister) in the service of his ruler will first offer his words of counsel, and (when they are accepted), he will bow and voluntarily offer his person to make good his sincerity. Hence, whatever service a ruler requires from his minister, the minister will die in support of his words. In this way the salary which he receives is not obtained on false pretences, and the

[1] With this paragraph it is understood that the 5th section of the Book ends, 'illustrating the perfect humanity of the superior man in the government of the people.' Every fresh section thus far, however, has commenced with a—'These were the words of the Master,' and in no case ended with that phraseology. Paragraph 35 rightly begins with it. It is out of place, or rather misplaced, in this; and belongs, I believe, to another place, as we shall see. We should read here, instead of it, 'The Master said.' With regard to the greater part of the section, its genuineness is liable to suspicion, and is indeed denied by the majority of commentators, including the *Kh*ien-lung editors. The sentiments are more Tâoistic than Confucian. See the introductory notice of the Book.

things for which he can be blamed will be more and more few.'

36. The Master said, 'In the service of a ruler, when great words are spoken to (and accepted by) him, great advantages (to the state) may be expected from them; and when words of small importance are presented to him, only small advantages are to be looked for. Therefore a superior man will not for words of small importance receive great emolument, nor for words of great importance small emolument. It is said in the Yî, "He does not enjoy his revenues in his own family, (but at court); there will be good fortune[1]."'

37. The Master said, 'In the service of a ruler, (a minister) should not descend to subjects beneath him, nor set a high value on speeches, nor accept an introduction from improper individuals. It is said in the Hsiâo Yâ (II, vi, ode 3, 4),

"Your duties quietly fulfil,
And hold the upright in esteem,
With friendship fast;
So shall the Spirits hear your cry,
You virtuous make, and good supply
In measure vast."'

38. The Master said, 'In the service of a ruler, for (a minister) whose place is remote from (the court), to remonstrate is an act of sycophancy; for one whose place is near the ruler, not to remonstrate is to hold his office idly for the sake of gain.'

39. The Master said, 'Ministers near (the ruler) should (seek to) preserve the harmony (of his

[1] See the Thwan, or first of the appendixes of the Yî, on Hexagram 26, vol. xvi, page 234.

virtues). The chief minister should maintain correctness in all the departments. Great ministers should be concerned about all parts (of the kingdom).'

40. The Master said, 'In the service of a ruler there should be the wish to remonstrate, but no wish to set forth (his faults). It is said in the Book of Poetry (II, viii, ode 4, 4),

"I cherish those men in my heart;—
Might not my words my love impart?
No;—if the words were once but spoken,
The charm of love might then be broken.
The men shall dwell within my heart,
Nor thence with lapse of time depart."'

41. The Master said, 'In the service of a ruler, when it is difficult to advance and easy to retire, there is a proper order maintained in the occupancy of places (according to the character of their holders). If it were easy to advance and difficult to retire, there would be confusion. Hence a superior (visitor) advances (only) after he has been thrice bowed to, while he retires after one salutation on taking leave; and thus confusion is prevented.'

42. The Master said, 'In the service of a ruler, if (an officer), after thrice leaving the court (on his advice being rejected), do not cross the borders (of the state), he is remaining for the sake of the profit and emolument. Although men say that he is not trying to force (his ruler), I will not believe them.'

43. The Master said, 'In the service of a ruler, (an officer) should be careful at the beginning, and respectful to the end.'

44. The Master said, 'In the service of a ruler, one may be in a high position or a low, rich or poor, to live or to die (according to the will of the ruler),

but he should not allow himself to be led to do anything contrary to order or right.'

45. The Master said, 'In the service of a ruler, if it be in the army, (an officer) should not (try to) avoid labour and danger; if it be at court, he should not refuse a mean office. To occupy a post and not perform its business is contrary to order and right. Hence, when a ruler employs him on any duty, if it suit his own mind, he thinks carefully of what it requires, and does it; if it do not suit his own mind, he thinks the more carefully of what it requires, and does it. When his work is done, he retires from office:—such is an officer who well discharges his duty. It is said in the Yî (vol. xvi, p. 96), "He does not serve either king or feudal lord, but in a lofty spirit prefers (to attend to) his own affairs."'

46. The Master said, 'It is only the son of Heaven who receives his appointment from Heaven; officers receive their appointments from the ruler. Therefore if the ruler's orders be conformed (to the mind of Heaven), his orders to his ministers are also conformed to it; but if his orders be contrary (to that mind), his orders to them are also contrary to it. It is said in the Book of Poetry (I, iv, ode 5, 2),

"How strong the magpies, battling fierce,
  Each one to keep his mate!
How bold the quails together rush,
  Upon the same debate!
This woman, with no trait that's good,
  Is stained by vicious crime,
Yet her I hail as marchioness;—
  Alas! woe worth the time!"'

47. The Master said, 'The superior man does not consider that his words (alone) show fully what a

man is. Hence when right ways prevail in the kingdom, the branches and leaves (from the stem) of right conduct appear; but when there are not right ways in the kingdom, the branches and leaves of (mere) words appear.

'In accordance with this, when a superior man is by the side of one occupied with the mourning rites, and cannot contribute to assist him in his expenditure, he does not ask him what it is; when he is by the side of one who is ill, and cannot supply him with food, he does not ask what he would like; when he has a visitor for whom he cannot provide a lodging, he does not ask where he is staying. Hence the intercourse of a superior man may be compared to water, and that of a small man, to sweet wine. The superior man seems insipid, but he helps to perfection; the small man seems sweet, but he leads to ruin. It is said in the Hsiâo Yâ (II, v, ode 4, 3),

"He trusts the rogues that lie and sneak,
And make things worse;
Their duties shirked, their words so meek
Prove but a curse."'

48. The Master said[1], 'The superior man does not confine himself to praising men with his words; and so the people prove loyal to him. Thus, when he asks about men who are suffering from cold, he clothes them; or men who are suffering from want, he feeds them; and when he praises a man's good qualities, he (goes on to) confer rank on him. It

[1] With this commences the 7th section of the Book, but it commences irregularly with 'the Master said,' instead of 'The words of the Master were;' see note above, on page 344.

is said in the Lessons from the States (I, xiv, ode 1, 3),

"I grieve; would they but lodge with me!"'

49. The Master said, 'Dissatisfaction and calamity will come to him whose lip-kindness is not followed by the corresponding deeds. Therefore the superior man will rather incur the resentment arising from his refusal than the charge of promising (and then not fulfilling). It is said in the Lessons from the States (V, ode 4, 6),

"I wildly go; I'll never know
Its smiles and chat again,
To me you clearly swore the faith,
Which now to break you're fain.
Could I foresee so false you'd be?
And now regrets are vain."'

50. The Master said, 'The superior man is not affectionate to others with his countenance (merely) as if, while cold in feeling, he could assume the appearance of affection. That belongs to the small man, and stamps him as no better than the thief who makes a hole in the wall.'

51. The Master said, 'What is required in feeling is sincerity; in words, that they be susceptible of proof[1].'

52. These were the words of the Master:—'The ancient and intelligent kings of the three dynasties all served the Spiritual Intelligences of heaven and earth, but invariably used the tortoise-shell and divining stalks. They did not presume to employ their own private judgment in the service of God.

[1] Here ends the 7th section, showing how the superior man strives to be sincere in his words and looks.

In this way they did not transgress in the matter of the day or month, for they did not act contrary to the result of the divination. The tortoise and the shell were not consulted in succession on the same point.

53. 'For the great (sacrificial) services there were (fixed) seasons and days; for the smaller services these were not fixed. They fixed them by divination (near the time). (In divining) about external affairs they used the odd days; and for internal affairs, the even. They did not go against the (intimations of the) tortoise-shell and stalks.'

54. The Master said, 'With the victims perfect, the proper ceremonies and music, and the vessels of grain, (they sacrificed); and thus no injury was received from the Spiritual Powers, and the people had no occasion for dissatisfaction.'

55. The Master said, 'The sacrifices of Hâu *K*î were easily provided. His language was reverential; his desires were restricted; and the blessings received extended down to his descendants. It is said in the Book of Poetry (III, ii, ode 1, 8),

> "Hâu *K*î founded the sacrifice;
> No one has failed in it,
> Down to the present day."'

56. The Master said, 'The shell and stalks employed by the great men[1] must be held in awe and reverence. But the son of Heaven does not divine by the stalks. While the princes are keeping guard in their states, they divine by the stalks. When the son of Heaven is on the road (travelling), he (also) divines by the stalks. In any other state but their

[1] The king and feudal lords.

own they do not divine by the stalks. They consult the tortoise-shell about the chambers and apartments of the houses (where they lodge). The son of Heaven does not so consult the tortoise-shell; he stays always in the grand ancestral temples.'

57. The Master said, 'The men of rank, on occasions of special respect, use their sacrificial vessels. On this account they do not fail to observe the set seasons and days, and do not act contrary to the intimations of the shell and stalks; thus seeking to serve with reverence the ruler and their superiors. In this way superiors are not troublesome to the people, and the people do not take liberties with their superiors [1].'

---

[1] Paragraphs 52 to 57 from the last section of the Book. They are not so interesting as the previous sections, nor do they hang closely together. 'The section,' say the *Kh*ien-lung editors, 'treats of the two methods of divination, and also of reverence. Reverence is the subject of the first section, and here again it occurs in the end of the Treatise. Reverence is the beginning and end of the learning of the superior man.'

BOOK XXX. 3ZE Î

OR

THE BLACK ROBES[1].

1. These were the words of the Master[2]:—'When the superior is easily served, his inferiors are easily known[3], and in this case punishments are not numerous (in the state).'

2. The Master said, 'When (the superior) loves the worthy as (the people of old loved him of) the black robes (Shih, I, vii, ode 1), and hates the bad as Hsiang-po (hated them;—II, v, ode 6), then without the frequent conferring of rank the people are stimulated to be good, and without the use of punishments they are all obedient to his orders. It is said in the Tâ Yâ (III, i, ode 1, 7),

"From Wăn your pattern you must draw,
And all the states will own your law."'

3. The Master said, 'If the people be taught by lessons of virtue, and uniformity sought to be given to them by the rules of ceremony, their minds will go on to be good. If they be taught by the laws, and uniformity be sought to be given to them by punishments, their minds will be thinking of how

---

[1] See the introductory notice, vol. xxvii, pp. 45, 46.

[2] Thus the Book begins as if it were another section of the preceding Treatise.

[3] They are 'easily known,' there being nothing in the ruler's method to make them deceitful.

they can escape (the punishment;—Analects, II, iii). Hence, when the ruler of the people loves them as his sons, they feel to him as a parent; when he binds them to himself by his good faith, they do not turn away from him; when he presides over them with courtesy, their hearts are docile to him. It is said in the Punishments of Fû (Shû, V, xxvii, 3), "Among the people of Miâo they did not use orders simply, but the restraints of punishment. They made the five punishments engines of oppression, calling them the laws." In this way their people became bad, and (their rulers) were cut off for ever (from the land).'

4. The Master said, 'Inferiors, in serving their superiors, do not follow what they command, but what they do. When a ruler loves anything, those below him are sure to do so much more. Therefore the superior should by all means be careful in what he likes and dislikes. This will make him an example to the people[1].'

5. The Master said, 'When Yü had been on the throne three years, the humanity of the common people was in accordance with his;—was it necessary that all (at court) should be perfectly virtuous? It is said in the Book of Poetry (II, v, ode 7, 1),

"Awe-inspiring are you, O (Grand-)Master Yin,
And the people all look up to you."

It is said in the Punishments of Fû (V, xxvii, 13), "I, the One man, will have felicity, and the millions of the people will look to you as their sure dependence." It is said in the Tâ Yâ (III, i, ode 9, 3),

[1] This again looks very much as if this Treatise were a continuation of the last.

"King Wû secured the people's faith,
And gave to all the law."'

6. The Master said, 'When superiors are fond of showing their humanity, inferiors strive to outstrip one another in their practice of it. Therefore those who preside over the people should cherish the clearest aims and give the most correct lessons, honouring the requirement of their humanity by loving the people as their sons; then the people will use their utmost efforts with themselves to please their superiors. It is said in the Book of Poetry (III, iii, ode 2, 2),

"Where from true virtue actions spring,
All their obedient homage bring."'

7. The Master said, 'The king's words are (at first) as threads of silk; but when given forth, they become as cords. Or they are (at first) as cords; but when given forth, they become as ropes. Therefore the great man does not take the lead in idle speaking. The superior does not speak words which may be spoken indeed but should not be embodied in deeds; nor does he do actions which may be done in deed but should not be expressed in words. When this is the case, the words of the people can be carried into action without risk, and their actions can be spoken of without risk. It is said in the Book of Poetry (III, iii, ode 2, 8),

"Keep on your acts a watchful eye,
That you may scrutiny defy."'

8. The Master said, 'The superior man leads men on (to good) by his words, and keeps them (from evil) by (the example of) his conduct. Hence, in speaking, he must reflect on what may be the end of his words, and examine whether there may not be

some error in his conduct; and then the people will be attentive to their words, and circumspect in their conduct. It is said in the Book of Poetry (III, iii, ode 2, 5),

"Be circumspect in all you say,
And reverent bearing still display."

It is said in the Tâ Yâ (III, i, ode 1, 4),

"Deep were Wăn's thoughts, unstained his ways;
His reverence lit its trembling rays."'

9. The Master said, 'When the heads of the people use no (improper) variations in their dress, and their manners are always easy and unconstrained, and they seek thus to give uniformity to the people, the virtue of the people does become uniform. It is said in the Book of Poetry (II, viii, ode 1, 1),

"In the old capital they stood,
With yellow fox-furs plain;
Their manners all correct and good,
Speech free from vulgar stain.
Could we go back to *K*âu's old days,
All would look up to them with praise."'

10. The Master said, 'When (the ruler) above can be known by men looking at him, and (his ministers) below can have their doings related and remembered, then the ruler has no occasion to doubt his ministers, and the ministers are not led astray by their ruler. The Announcement of Yin says (Shû, IV, vi, 3), "There were I, Yin, and Thang; both possessed the same pure virtue." It is said in the Book of Poetry (I, xiv, ode 3, 3),

"In soul so steadfast is that princely man,
Whose course for fault or flaw we vainly scan."'

11. The Master said, 'When the holders of states

and clans give distinction to the righteous and make it painful for the bad, thus showing the people the excellence (they should cultivate), then the feelings of the people do not swerve (to what is evil). It is said in the Book of Poetry (II, vi, ode 3, 5),

"Your duties quietly fulfil,
And hold the upright in esteem,
With earnest love."'

12. The Master said, 'When the highest among men has doubts and perplexities, the common people go astray. When (the ministers) below him are difficult to be understood, the toil of the ruler is prolonged. Therefore when the ruler exhibits clearly what he loves, and thus shows the people the style of manners (they should aim at), and is watchful against what he dislikes, and thereby guards the people against the excesses (of which they are in danger), then they do not go astray.

'When the ministers are exemplary in their conduct, and do not set a value on (fine) speeches; when they do not try to lead (the ruler) to what is unattainable, and do not trouble him with what cannot be (fully) known, then he is not toiled. It is said in the Book of Poetry (III, ii, ode 10, 1),

"Reversed is now the providence of God;
The lower people groan beneath their load."

It is said in the Hsiâo Yâ (II, v, ode 4, 4),

"They do not discharge their duties,
But only cause distress to the king."'

13. The Master said, 'When (the measures of) government do not take effect, and the lessons of the ruler do not accomplish their object, (it is because) the giving of rank and emoluments is

unfit to stimulate the people to good, and (the infliction of) punishments and penalties is unfit to make them ashamed (of evil). Therefore (the ruler) above must not be careless in punishing, nor lightly confer rank. It is said in the Announcement to the Prince of Khang (Shû, V, ix, 8), "Deal reverently and understandingly in your infliction of punishments;" and in the Punishments of Fû (Shû, V, xxvii, 12), "He spreads abroad his lessons to avert punishments."'

14. The Master said, 'When the great ministers are not on terms of friendly intimacy (with the ruler), and the common people consequently are not restful, this is because the loyalty (of the ministers) and the respect (of the ruler) are not sufficient, and the riches and rank conferred (on the former) are excessive. (The consequence is, that) the great ministers do not discharge their functions of government, and the ministers closer (to the ruler) form parties against them. Therefore the great ministers should by all means be treated with respect; they are examples to the people; and ministers nearer (to the ruler) should by all means be careful;—they direct the way of the people. Let not the ruler consult with inferior officers about greater, nor with those who are from a distance about those who are near to him, nor with those who are beyond the court about those who belong to it. If he act thus, the great ministers will not be dissatisfied; the ministers closer to him will not be indignant; and those who are more remote will not be kept in obscurity. The duke of Sheh in his dying charge said, "Do not by little counsels ruin great enterprises; do not for the sake of a favourite concubine

provoke queen *K*wang; do not for the sake of a favourite officer provoke your grave officers,—the Great officers or high ministers[1].'"

15. The Master said, 'If the great man be not in affectionate sympathy with (his officers) whom he considers worthy, but give his confidence to others whom he despises, the people in consequence will not feel attached to him, and the lessons which he gives them will be troublesome (and ineffective). It is said in the Book of Poetry (II, ii, ode 8),

"As if I were hidden they sought me at first,
At court for a pattern to shine;
'Tis with hatred intense they now bend their scowls,
And my services curtly decline."

It is said in the *K*ün-*kh*ăn (Shû, V, xxiv, 4), "While they have not seen a sage, (they are full of desire) as if they could not get a sight of him; but after they have seen him, they are still unable to follow him."'

16. The Master said, 'A small man is drowned in the water; a superior man is drowned or ruined by his mouth; the great man suffers his ruin from the people;—all suffer from what they have played and taken liberties with. Water is near to men, and yet it drowns them. Its nature makes it easy to play with, but dangerous to approach;—men are easily drowned in it. The mouth is loquacious and

---

[1] This is an error. The dying counsels referred to were not given by any duke of Sheh (a dependency of *Kh*û), but by Wân-fû, duke of Ʒâi, to king Mû of *K*âu. They are found with some slight alterations in the Apocryphal Books of *K*âu (逸周書), Book VIII, article 1. Confucius would not have fallen into such a mistake.

troublesome; for words once uttered there is hardly a place of repentance;—men are easily ruined by it. The people, restricted in their humanity, have vulgar and rude minds; they should be respected, and should not be treated with contempt;—men are easily ruined by them. Therefore the superior man should by all means be careful in his dealings with them. It is said in the Thâi *K*iâ (Shû, III, v, sect. 1, 5, 7), "Do not frustrate the charge to me, and bring on yourself your own overthrow. Be like the forester, who, when he has adjusted the string, goes to examine the end of the arrow, whether it be placed according to rule, and then lets go." It is said in the Charge to Yüeh (III, viii, sect. 2, 4), "It is the mouth which gives occasion to shame; they are the coat of mail and helmet which give occasion to war. The upper robes and lower garments (for reward) should not be taken (lightly from) their chests; before spear and shield are used, one should examine himself." It is said in the Thâi *K*iâ (Shu, III, v, sect. 2, 3), "Calamities sent by Heaven may be avoided; but from those brought on by one's self there is no escape." It is said in the Announcement of Yin (Shû, III, v, sect. 1, 3), "I have seen it myself in Hsiâ with its western capital, that when its sovereigns went through a prosperous course to the end, their ministers also did the same."'

17. The Master said, 'To the people the ruler is as their heart; to the ruler the people are as his body. When the heart is composed, the body is at ease; when the heart is reverent, the body is respectful; when the heart loves anything, the body is sure to rest in it. (So), when the ruler loves anything, the people are sure to desire it. The

body is the complement of the heart, and a wound in it makes the heart also suffer. So the ruler is preserved by the people, and perishes also through the people. It is said in an ode,

"Once we had that former premier,
His words were wise and pure;
The states and clans by him were at rest,
The chief cities and towns by him were well regulated,
All the people by him enjoyed their life.
Who (now) holds the ordering of the kingdom?
Not himself attending to the government,
The issue is toil and pain to the people[1]."

It is said in the *K*ün-yâ (Shû, V, xxv, 5), "In the heat and rain of summer days the inferior people may be described as murmuring and sighing. And so it may be said of them in the great cold of winter."'

18. The Master said, 'In the service by an inferior of his superior, if his personal character be not correct, his words will not be believed; and in this case their views will not be the same, and the conduct (of the superior) will not correspond (to the advice given to him)[2].'

19. The Master said, 'Words should be capable of proof by instances, and conduct should be conformed to rule; when the case is so, a man's aim cannot be taken from him while he is alive, nor can his good name be taken away when he is dead. Therefore the superior man, having heard much, verifies it by

---

[1] This is from an ode not in the Shih, and only preserved, so far, here. The three concluding lines, however, are also found in the Shih, II, iv, ode 7, 6.

[2] The meaning of this latter part is matter of dispute.

inquiry, and firmly holds fast (what is proved); he remembers much, verifies it by inquiry, and makes it his own; when he knows it exactly, he carries the substance of it into practice. It is said in the *K*ün-*kh*ăn (Shû, V, xxi, 5), "Going out and coming in, seek the judgment of the people about things, till you find a general agreement upon them." It is said in the Book of Poetry (I, xiv, ode 3, 1),

"The virtuous man, the princely one,
Is uniformly correct in his deportment."'

20. The Master said, 'It is only the superior man who can love what is correct, while to the small man what is correct is as poison. Therefore the friends of the superior man have the definite aims which they pursue, and the definite courses which they hate. In consequence, those who are near at hand have no perplexities of thought about him, and those who are far off, no doubts. It is said in the Book of Poetry (I, i, ode 1, 1),

"For our prince a good mate."'

21. The Master said, 'When a man on light grounds breaks off his friendship with the poor and mean, and only on great grounds with the rich and noble, his love of worth cannot be great, nor does his hatred of evil clearly appear. Though men may say that he is not influenced by (the love of) gain, I do not believe them. It is said in the Book of Poetry (III, ii, ode 3, 4),

"And all the friends assisting you
Behave with reverent mien."'

22. The Master said, 'The superior man will not voluntarily remain to share in private acts of kind-

ness not offered on grounds of virtue. In the Book of Poetry it is said (II, i, ode 1, 1),

"They love me, and my mind will teach
How duty's highest aim to reach."'

23. The Master said, 'If there be a carriage (before you), you are sure (by-and-by) to see the cross-board (in front); if there be a garment, you are sure (in the same way) to see (the traces of) its being worn; if one speaks, you are sure to hear his voice; if one does anything, you are sure to see the result. It is said in the Book of Poetry (I, i, ode 2, 2),

"I will wear them without being weary of them."'

24. The Master said, 'When one says anything, and immediately proceeds to act it out, his words cannot embellish it; and when one does anything, and immediately proceeds to describe it, the action cannot be embellished. Hence the superior man saying little, and acting to prove the sincerity of his words, the people cannot make the excellence of their deeds greater than it is, nor diminish the amount of their badness[1]. It is said in the Book of Poetry (III, iii, ode 2, 5),

"A flaw in mace of white jade may
By patient toil be ground away;
But for a flaw we make in speech,
What can be done? 'Tis past our reach."

[1] The excellence and the badness would seem, in the text, to belong to the conduct of the superior man; but to predicate badness of him would be too daring. To justify the view which appears in my translation, the *Kh*ien-lung editors, in their expansion of the meaning, after 'the people,' interpolate 'who come under the transforming influence of his example.'

It is said in the Hsiâo Yâ (II, iii, ode 5, 8),

"Well does our lord become his place,
And high the deeds his reign have crowned."

It is said to the Prince Shih (Shû, V, xvi, 11), "Aforetime, when God beheld the virtue of king Wăn in the fields of *K*âu, he made the great decree light on his person."'

25. The Master said, 'The people of the south have a saying that "A man without constancy cannot be a diviner either with the tortoise-shell or the stalks." This was probably a saying handed down from antiquity. If such a man cannot know the tortoise-shell and stalks, how much less can he know other men[1]? It is said in the Book of Poetry (II, v, ode 1, 3),

"Our tortoise-shells are wearied out,
And will not tell us anything about the plans."

The Charge to Yüeh says (Shû, IV, viii, sect. 2, 5, 11), "Dignities should not be conferred on men of evil practices. (If they be), how can the people set themselves to correct their ways? If this be sought merely by sacrifices, it will be disrespectful (to the spirits). When affairs come to be troublesome, there ensues disorder; when the spirits are served so, difficulties ensue[2]."

'It is said in the Yî, "When one does not conti-

---

[1] I cannot make anything but this of this sentence, though Khung Ying-tâ takes it differently. The whole paragraph is evidently very corrupt, and even the *Kh*ien-lung editors have put forth all their strength upon it in vain.

[2] We have here a quotation from the Shû, IV, viii, sect. 2; but it is very different from the textus receptus. All the commentators and critics are at fault upon it; see vol. iii, pp. 115, 116.

nuously maintain his virtue, some will impute it to him as a disgrace[1];—(in the position indicated in the Hexagram.) When one does maintain his virtue continuously (in the other position indicated), this will be fortunate in a wife, but in a husband evil.'"

[1] See the symbolism of the 3rd and 5th lines of the Hăng or 32nd Hexagram, vol. xvi, pp. 125-128.

BOOK XXXI. PĂN SANG

OR

RULES ON HURRYING TO MOURNING RITES[1].

1. According to the rules for hurrying to attend the mourning rites, when one first heard that the mourning rites for a relative were going on, he wailed as he answered the messenger[2], and gave full vent to his sorrow. Having asked all the particulars, he wailed again, with a similar burst of grief, and immediately arranged to go (to the place). He went 100 lî a day, not travelling in the night.

2. Only when the rites were those for a father or a mother did he travel while he could yet see the stars, and rested when he (again) saw them[3]. If it was impossible for him to go (at once)[4], he assumed the mourning dress, and then went (as soon as he could). When he had passed through the state (where he was), and reached its frontier, he stopped and wailed, giving full vent to his sorrow. He avoided wailing in the market-place and when near the court. He looked towards the frontier of his own state when he wailed.

---

[1] See the introductory notice, vol. xxvii, pp. 46, 47.

[2] The mourner is absent from his state, and a messenger has been sent to tell him of the death. The relative, it is argued, may have been any one within the 'five degrees' of consanguinity.

[3] That is, from peep of dawn till the stars came out again after sunset.

[4] Being restrained by the duties of the commission, with which he was charged by the ruler.

3. When he came to the house, he entered the gate at the left side of it, (passed through the court), and ascended to the hall by the steps on the west. He knelt on the east of the coffin, with his face to the west, and wailed, giving full vent to his grief. He (then) tied up his hair in a knot, bared his arms, and went down from the hall, proceeding to his place on the east, where he wailed towards the west. Having completed the leaping, he covered his arms and put on his sash of sackcloth in the corridor on the east; and after tucking up the ends of his sash, he returned to his place. He bowed to the visitors, leaping with them, and escorted them (to the gate), returning (afterwards) to his place. When other visitors arrived, he bowed to them, leaped with them, and escorted them;—all in the same way.

4. (After this), all the principal mourners[1], with their cousins, went out at the gate, stopping there while they wailed. The gate was then closed, and the director told them to go to the mourning shed[2].

5. At the next wailing, the day after, they tied up their hair, bared their arms, and went through the leaping. At the third wailing next day, they again tied up their hair, bared their arms, and went through the leaping. On these three days, the finishing the mourning dress, bowing to and escorting the visitors, took place as in the first case.

6. If he who has hurried to be present at the

[1] This seems to mean 'all the sons of the departed.' Of course there was really but one 'chief or host-man,' as in par. 6.

[2] This takes us by surprise. Did all go to the shed? Were there many sheds?

rites were not the presiding mourner on the occasion[1], then that presiding mourner, instead of him, bowed to the visitors and escorted them.

7. When one hurried to the rites, even where they were less than those for a mother or father, which required the wearing of sackcloth, with even edge or frayed, he entered the gate at the left side of it, and stood in the middle of the court-yard with his face to the north, wailing and giving full vent to his sorrow. He put on the cincture for the head and the sackcloth girdle in the corridor on the east, and repaired to his place, where he bared his arms. Then he wailed along with the presiding mourner, and went through the leaping. For the wailing on the second day and the third, they wore the cincture and bared the arms. If there were visitors, the presiding mourner bowed to them on their arrival, and escorted them.

The husbands and wives (of the family) waited for him at the wailing-places for every morning and evening, without making any change.

8. When one hurries to the mourning rites for a mother, he wails with his face to the west, giving full vent to his sorrow. He then ties up his hair, bares his arms, descends from the hall, and goes to his station on the east, where, with his face to the west, he wails and goes through the leaping. After that, he covers his arms and puts on the cincture and sash in the corridor on the east. He bows to the visitors, and escorts them (to the gate) in the same way as if he had hurried to the rites for his

[1] This seems to imply that, in the preceding paragraphs, he had been the principal mourner.

father. At the wailing on the day after, he does not tie up his hair.

9. When a wife[1] hurried to the mourning rites, she went up to the hall by the (side) steps on the east, and knelt on the east of the coffin with her face to the west. There she wailed, giving full vent to her grief. Having put on the lower cincture on the east[2], she went to the station (for wailing), and there leaped alternately with the presiding mourner.

10. When one, hurrying to the mourning rites, did not arrive while the coffin with the body was still in the house, he first went to the grave; and there kneeling with his face to the north, he wailed, giving full vent to his sorrow. The principal mourners have been waiting for him (at the grave), and have taken their stations,—the men on the left of it, and the wives on the right. Having gone through the leaping, and given full expression to his sorrow, he tied up his hair, and went to the station of the principal mourners on the east. In his headband of sackcloth, and sash with the ends tucked up, he wailed and went through the leaping. He then bowed to the visitors, and returned to his station, going (again) through the leaping, after which the director announced that the business was over[3].

11. He then put on the cap, and returned to the

[1] An aunt, sister, or daughter of the family, who was married, and hurried to the family home from her husband's.

[2] I suppose this was in the corridor on the east. The rule was for the women to dress in an apartment; but a distinction was made between those residing in the house, and those who returned to it for the occasion.

[3] It is understood that this mourner was the eldest and rightful son of the deceased.

house. There he entered at the left side of the door, and, with his face to the north, wailed and gave full vent to his sorrow. He then tied up his hair, bared his arms, and went through the leaping. Going to his station on the east, he bowed to the visitors, and went through the leaping. When the visitors went out, the presiding mourner bowed to them, and escorted them. When other visitors afterwards arrived, he bowed to them, went through the leaping, and escorted them in the same way. All the principal mourners and their cousins went out at the gate, wailed there and stopped, when the directors instructed them to go to the shed. At the wailing next day, he bound up his hair and went through the leaping. At the third wailing, he did the same. On the third day he completed his mourning dress (as was required). After the fifth wailing, the director announced that the business was over.

12. Wherein the usages at the rites for a mother differed from those at the rites for a father, was that there was but one tying up of the hair. After that the cincture was worn to the end of the business. In other respects the usages were the same as at the rites for a father.

13. At the rites for other relations, after those for the mother or father, the mourner who did not arrive while the coffin was in the house, first went to the grave, and there wailed with his face to the west, giving full vent to his sorrow. He then put on the cincture and hempen sash, and went to his station on the east, where he wailed with the presiding mourner, and went through the leaping. After this he covered his arms; and if there were visitors, the presiding mourner bowed to them and escorted them away.

If any other visitors afterwards came, he bowed to them, as in the former case, and the director announced that the business was over.

Immediately after he put on the cap, and returned to the house. Entering at the left side of the door, he wailed with his face to the north, giving full vent to his sorrow. He then put on the cincture, bared his arms, and went through the leaping. Going then to the station on the east, he bowed to the visitors, and went through the leaping again. When the visitors went out, the presiding mourner bowed to them and escorted them.

At the wailing next day, he wore the cincture, bared his arms, and went through the leaping. At the third wailing he did the same. On the third day, he put on his mourning-garb; and at the fifth wailing, the director announced that the business was over.

14. When one heard of the mourning rites, and it was impossible (in his circumstances) to hurry to be present at them, he wailed and gave full vent to his grief. He then asked the particulars, and (on hearing them) wailed again, and gave full vent to his grief. He then made a place (for his mourning) where he was, tied up his hair, bared his arms, and went through the leaping. Having covered his arms, and put on the higher cincture and his sash with the ends tucked up, he went (back) to his place. After bowing to (any visitors that arrived), he returned to the place, and went through the leaping. When the visitors went out, he, as the presiding mourner, bowed to them, and escorted them outside the gate, returning then to his station. If any other visitors came afterwards, he bowed to them and went through the leaping, then escorting them as before.

At the wailing next day, he tied up his hair, bared his arms, and went through the leaping. At the third wailing he did the same. On the third day, he put on his mourning-garb, wailed, bowed to his visitors, and escorted them as before.

15. If one returned home after the mourning rites had been completed, he went to the grave, and there wailed and went through the leaping. On the east of it, he tied up his hair, bared his arms, put on the cincture for the head, bowed to the visitors, and went (again) through the leaping. Having escorted the visitors, he returned to his place, and again wailed, giving full vent to his grief. With this he put off his mourning. In the house he did not wail. The principal mourner, in his treatment of him, made no change in his dress; and though he wailed with him (at the grave), he did not leap.

16. Wherein at other observances than those for the death of a mother or father, the usages (of such a mourner) differed from the above, were in the cincture for the head and the hempen sash.

17. In all cases where one made a place for his mourning (away from home), if it were not on occasion of the death of a parent, but for some relative of the classes not so nearly related, he went to the station, and wailed, giving full vent to his sorrow. Having put on the cincture for the head and the girdle on the east, he came back to the station, bared his arms, and went through the leaping. He then covered his arms, bowed to the visitors, went back to the station, wailed, and went through the leaping. (After this), he escorted the guests away, and came back to the station, when the director told him to go to the shed. When the fifth wailing

was ended, on the third day, the presiding mourner came forth and escorted the visitors away. All the principal mourners and their cousins went out at the gate, wailed, and stopped there. The director announced to them that the business was ended. He put on his full mourning-garb, and bowed to the visitors [1].

18. If the home were far distant from the place which an absent mourner has selected (for his wailing), they completed all their arrangements about dress before they went to it.

19. One hurrying to mourning rites, if they were for a parent, wailed when he looked towards the district (where they had lived); if they were for a relation for whom nine months' mourning was due, he wailed when he could see the gate of his house; if for one to whom five months' mourning was due, he wailed when he got to the door; if for one to whom but three months' mourning was due, he wailed when he took his station.

20. For one of his father's relations (for whom he did not need to go into mourning) a man wailed in the ancestral temple; for one of his mother or wife's relatives, in the back chamber of the temple; for his teacher, outside the gate of the temple; for a friend, outside the door of the back-chamber; for an acquaintance, in the open country, having pitched a tent for the occasion. Some say the wailing for a mother's relation was in the temple.

---

[1] The *Kh*ien-lung editors think that this last sentence is an erroneous addition to the paragraph. But with other parts of it there are great difficulties, insoluble difficulties, as some of the commentators allow.

21. In all cases where a station was selected, away from the house of mourning, for paying funeral rites, no offerings were put down (for the departed).

22. For the son of Heaven they wailed nine days; for a feudal prince, seven; for a high minister and Great officer, five; for another officer, three.

23. A Great officer, in wailing for the ruler of his state, did not presume to bow to the visitors.

24. Ministers in other states, when they selected a station (for their wailing), did not presume to bow to the visitors.

25. Officers, of the same surname with a feudal prince, (but who were serving in other states), also made a place at which to wail for him (on his death).

26. In all cases where one made a place (at a distance) at which to wail, he bared his arms (only) once.

27. In condoling with (the relations of) an acquaintance (after he has been buried), one first wailed in his house, and afterwards went to the grave; in both cases accompanying the wailing with the leaping. He alternated his leaping with that of the presiding mourner, keeping his face towards the north.

28. At all mourning rites (in a household), if the father were alive, he acted as presiding mourner; if he were dead, and brothers lived together in the house, each presided at the mourning for one of his own family-circle. If two brothers were equally related to the deceased for whom rites were necessary, the eldest presided at those rites; if they were not equally related, the one most nearly so presided.

29. When one heard of the death of a brother or cousin at a distance, but the news did not arrive till the time which his own mourning for him would have taken had expired[1], he (notwithstanding) put on the mourning cincture, bared his arms, and went through the leaping. He bowed to his visitors, however, with the left hand uppermost[2].

30. The only case in which a place was chosen in which to wail for one for whom mourning was not worn, was the death of a sister-in-law, the wife of an elder brother. For a female member of the family who had married, and for whom therefore mourning was not worn, the hempen sash was assumed.

31. When one had hurried to the mourning rites, and a Great officer came (to condole with him), he bared his arms, and bowed to him. When he had gone through the leaping, he covered his arms. In the case of a similar visit from an ordinary officer, he covered his arms, and then bowed to him.

---

[1] The deceased would have been only in the degree of relationship, to which five months' mourning was assigned.

[2] The left hand uppermost made the bow one more appropriate to a festive occasion.

BOOK XXXII. WĂN SANG

OR

QUESTIONS ABOUT MOURNING RITES[1].

1. Immediately after his father's death, (the son put off his cap, and) kept his hair, with the pin in it, in the bag (of silk); went barefoot, with the skirt of his dress tucked up under his girdle; and wailed with his hands across his breast. In the bitterness of his grief, and the distress and pain of his thoughts, his kidneys were injured, his liver dried up, and his lungs scorched, while water or other liquid did not enter his mouth, and for three days fire was not kindled (to cook anything for him). On this account the neighbours prepared for him gruel and rice-water, which were his (only) meat and drink. The internal grief and sorrow produced a change in his outward appearance; and with the severe pain in his heart, his mouth could not relish any savoury food, nor his body find ease in anything pleasant.

2. On the third day there was the (slighter) dressing (of the corpse). While the body was on the couch it was called the corpse; when it was put into the coffin, it was called *k*iû. At the moving of the corpse, and lifting up of the coffin, (the son) wailed and leaped, times without number. Such was the bitterness of his heart, and the pain of his thoughts, so did his grief and sorrow fill his mind and

[1] See the introductory notice, vol. xxvii, pp. 47, 48.

agitate his spirit, that he bared his arms and leaped, seeking by the movement of his limbs to obtain some comfort to his heart and relief to his spirit.

The women could not bare their arms, and therefore they (merely) pushed out the breast, and smote upon their hearts, moving their feet with a sliding, hopping motion, and with a constant, heavy sound, like the crumbling away of a wall. The expression of grief, sorrow, and deep-seated pain was extreme; hence it is said, 'With beating of the breast and movement of the feet, did they sorrowfully accompany the body; so they escorted it away, and so did they come back to meet its essential part.'

When (the mourners) went, accompanying the coffin (to the grave), they looked forward, with an expression of eagerness, as if they were following some one, and unable to get up to him. When returning to wail, they looked disconcerted, as if they were seeking some one whom they could not find. Hence, when escorting (the coffin), they appeared full of affectionate desire; when returning, they appeared full of perplexity. They had sought the (deceased), and could not find him; they entered the gate, and did not see him; they went up to the hall, and still did not see him; they entered his chamber, and still did not see him; he was gone; he was dead; they should see him again nevermore. Therefore they wailed, wept, beat their breasts, and leaped, giving full vent to their sorrow, before they ceased. Their minds were disappointed, pained, fluttered, and indignant. They could do nothing more with their wills; they could do nothing but continue sad.

3. In presenting the sacrifice (of repose) in the

ancestral temple[1], (the son) offered it (to his parent) in his disembodied state, hoping that his shade would peradventure return (and enjoy it). When he came back to the house from completing the grave, he did not venture to occupy his chamber, but dwelt in the mourning shed, lamenting that his parent was now outside. He slept on the rushes, with a clod for his pillow, lamenting that his parent was in the ground. Therefore he wailed and wept, without regard to time; he endured the toil and grief for three years. His heart of loving thoughts showed the mind of the filial son, and was the real expression of his human feelings.

4. Some one may ask, 'Why does the dressing not commence till three days after death?' and the answer is:—When his parent is dead, the filial son is sad and sorrowful, and his mind is full of trouble. He crawls about and bewails his loss, as if the dead might come back to life;—how can he hurriedly take (the corpse) and proceed to dress it? Therefore, when it is said that the dressing does not begin till after three days, the meaning is, that (the son) is waiting that time to see if (his father) will come to life. When after three days there is no such return, the father is not alive, and the heart of the filial son is still more downcast. (During this space, moreover), the means of the family can be calculated, and the clothes that are necessary can be provided and made accordingly; the relations and connexions who live at a distance can also arrive. Therefore the sages decided in the case

[1] 'Not the structure so called,' says Khung Ying-tâ, 'but the apartment where the coffin had been;'—now serving for the occasion as a temple.

that three days should be allowed, and the rule was made accordingly.

5. Some one may ask, 'How is it that one with the cap on does not bare his arms, and show the naked body?' and the answer is:—The cap is the most honourable article of dress, and cannot be worn where the body is bared, and the flesh exposed. Therefore the cincture for the head is worn instead of the cap, (when the arms are bared).

6. And so, when a bald man does not wear the cincture, and a hunchback does not bare his arms, and a lame man does not leap, it is not that they do not feel sad, but they have an infirmity which prevents them from fully discharging the usages. Hence it is said that in the rites of mourning it is the sorrow that is the principal thing. When a daughter wails, weeps, and is sad, beats her breast, and wounds her heart; and when a son wails, weeps, is sad, and bows down till his forehead touches the ground, without regard to elegance of demeanour, this may be accepted as the highest expression of sorrow.

7. Some one may ask, 'What is the idea in the cincture?' and the reply is:—The cincture is what is worn while uncapped. The Rule says, 'Boys do not wear (even) the three months' mourning; it is only when the family has devolved on one that he does so.' The cincture, we may suppose, was what was worn in the three months' mourning (by a boy). If he had come to be the representative of the family, he wore the cincture, and carried the staff.

8. Some one may ask, 'What is meant by (using) the staff?' and the answer is:—The staff of bamboo

and that of elaeococcus wood have the same meaning. Hence, for a father they used the black staff of bamboo; and for a mother, the square-cut staff, an elaeococcus branch[1].

9. Some one may say, 'What is meant by (using) the staff?' and the answer is:—When a filial son mourns for a parent, he wails and weeps without regard to the number of times; his endurances are hard for three years; his body becomes ill and his limbs emaciated; and so he uses a staff to support his infirmity.

10. Thus, while his father is alive he does not dare to use a staff, because his honoured father is still living. Walking in the hall, he does not use the staff;—refraining from doing so in the place where his honoured father is. Nor does he walk hastily in the hall,—to show that he is not hurried. Such is the mind of the filial son, the real expression of human feeling, the proper method of propriety and righteousness. It does not come down from heaven, it does not come forth from the earth; it is simply the expression of the human feelings.

---

[1] On Book XIII, i, 3 the *Kh*ien-lung editors say, that the staff of old men was carried with the root up, and the other end down; but the opposite was the case with the mourner's staff. In breaking off a branch from the elaeococcus, the part which has been torn from the stem is cut square and smooth with a knife. The round stem of the bamboo cane is said by *Kh*ăn Hâo to symbolise heaven, and so is carried for a father; and the square cut end of the dryandria branch, to symbolise earth, and so is used for a mother. But this fanciful explanation seems to be contrary to what is said in the conclusion of the next paragraph.

BOOK XXXIII. FÛ WĂN

OR

SUBJECTS FOR QUESTIONING ABOUT THE MOURNING DRESS[1].

1. The Directory for Mourning says, 'There are cases in which parties wear deep mourning, while those, in consequence of their connexion with whom they assume it, wear only light.' Such is the mourning for her husband's mother by the wife of the son of a ruler (by a concubine)[2].

2. 'There are cases in which parties wear light mourning, while those, in consequence of their connexion with whom they assume it, wear deep mourning.' Such is the mourning of a husband for the father or mother of his wife[3].

3. 'There are cases in which parties wear mourning, while those, in consequence of their connexion with whom they have a relation with the deceased, wear none.' Such is the case of the wife of a ruler's

---

[1] See the introductory notice, vol. xxvii, page 48.

[2] Such a son of a ruler could wear for his mother only the nine months' mourning, as she was but a concubine with an inferior position in the family; but his wife wore mourning for her for a whole year. She was her husband's mother, and the general rule for mourning in such a relation was observed by the wife, without regard to the deceased being only a concubine, and whether the ruler were alive or dead.

[3] The wife, of course, observed the three years' mourning for her father or mother; the husband only the three months.

son with the cousins of her husband on the female side [1].

4. 'There are cases in which parties wear no mourning, while those, in consequence of their connexion with whom they have a relation with the deceased, do wear mourning.' Such is the case of a ruler's son with regard to the father and mother of his wife.

5. The Directory of Mourning says, 'When his mother has been divorced, the son wears mourning for the relatives of the wife whom his father has taken in his mother's place.' When his mother has died [2] (without being divorced), a son wears mourning for her relatives. Wearing mourning for his own mother's relatives, he does not do so for those of the step-mother, whom his father may have taken in her place.

6. After the sacrifice at the end of the first year, during the three years' rites, and after the interment has taken place, during those of one year (occurring at the same time), the mourner puts on the old sash of dolychos cloth, and the headband of the one year's mourning, wearing (at the same time) the sackcloth of the mourning for nine months.

7. The same thing is done (after the interment) during the nine months' mourning.

8. No change is made (after the interment) during the five months' mourning.

---

[1] There is no satisfactory account of this case.

[2] *Kh*ăn Hâo supposed that this mother 'dying' is the wife whom his father has taken in the place of the son's divorced mother. The *Kh*ien-lung editors rightly point out his error; but it shows how these notices are perplexing, not only to foreigners, but also to native scholars.

9. Where they wore the sash with the roots of hemp wrought into the cloth [1], they changed it for the dolychos cloth of the three years' mourning [2].

10. After the sacrifice at the end of a year, if there occurred an occasion for using the hempen sash with the roots cut off, (the mourner) put on the proper band along with the higher cincture. When the cincture was no longer worn, he put off the band. When it was proper to use the band, the rule was to wear it; and when the occasion for it was over, it was put off [3].

11. In the mourning for five months they did not change the cap worn for the sacrifice at the end of a year. If there were occasion to wear the cincture, then they employed the band proper for the mourning of three months or five months; still keeping on the first dolychos sash. The linen of the three months' mourning did not make it necessary to change the dolychos cloth of the five months; nor the linen of the five months to change the dolychos cloth of the nine months. Where the roots were woven with the cloth, they made a change.

12. On occasion of mourning for a minor, if he were of the highest grade or the middle, they changed the dolychos cloth of the three years' mourning, assuming it when they had completed the months of these intervening rites. This was done not because of the value set on the linen, but because no change was made at the conclusion of

[1] This was done in the mourning for nine months and for one year; not in that for five months and for three.

[2] That is, after the sacrifice at the end of the first year.

[3] This is supplementary, say the *Kh*ien-lung editors, to paragraph 8.

the wailing. They did not observe this rule on the death of a minor of the third or lowest grade.

13. The ruler of a state mourned for the son of Heaven for the three years. His wife observed the rule of a lady of her husband's house who had gone to her own married home in mourning for the ruler[1].

14. The heir-son of a ruler did not wear mourning for the son of Heaven[2].

15. A ruler acted as presiding mourner at the mourning rites for his wife, his eldest son, and that son's wife.

16. The eldest son of a Great officer, by his proper wife, wore the mourning of an ordinary officer for the ruler, and for the ruler's wife and eldest son.

17. When the mother of a ruler had not been the wife (of the former ruler)[3], the body of the ministers did not wear mourning (on her death). Only the officers of the harem, the charioteer and the man-at-arms who sat on the left, followed the example of the ruler, wearing the same mourning as he did.

18. For a high minister or Great officer, (during the mourning rites for him), the ruler wore in his place the coarse glazed linen, and also when he went out (on business not connected with the rites). If it were on business connected with them, he wore also the skin-cap and the band round it. Great officers dressed in the same way for one another. At the mourning rites for their wives, they wore the same dress, when they were going to be present at

---

[1] That is, for a year.

[2] To avoid suspicion, say the commentators. I do not see it.

[3] She must have been a concubine, or some inferior member of the harem. Various circumstances might have concurred to lead to her son's succession to the state.

those rites; if they went out (on other business), they did not wear it.

19. In all cases of going to see others, the visitor (being in mourning for his parents) did not put off his headband. Even when he was going to the ruler's court, he did not put it off; it was only at the ruler's gate that (in certain circumstances) he put off his sackcloth. The Directory of Mourning says, 'A superior man will not take away from others their mourning rites;' and so it was deemed wrong to put off this mourning.

20. The Directory of Mourning says, 'Crimes are many, but the punishments are only five. The occasions for mourning are many, but there are only five varieties of the mourning dress. The occasions must be arranged, according as they are classed in the upper grade or in the lower.'

BOOK XXXIV. *K*IEN *K*WÂN

OR

TREATISE ON SUBSIDIARY POINTS IN MOURNING USAGES[1].

1. What is the reason that the headband worn with the frayed sackcloth, for a father, must be made of the fibres of the female plant?

Those fibres have an unpleasant appearance, and serve to show outwardly the internal distress. The appearance of (the mourners), wearing the sackcloth for a father with its jagged edges, corresponds to those fibres. That of one wearing the sackcloth for a mother with its even edges, corresponds to the fibres of the male plant. That of one wearing the mourning of nine months looks as if (the ebullitions of sorrow) had ceased. For one wearing the mourning of five months or of three, his (ordinary) appearance is suitable.

These are the manifestations of sorrow in the bodily appearance[2].

2. The wailing of one wearing the sackcloth for his father seems to go forth in one unbroken strain;

---

[1] See the introductory notice, vol. xxvii, pp. 48, 49.

[2] The 3sü (苴) is commonly understood to be the female plant of hemp, and the hsî (枲) the male plant; though some writers reverse the application of the names. The fibres of both are dark coloured, those of the female plant being the darker. The cloth woven of them was also of a coarser texture. All admit that the subject here is the mourning band for the head; the staffs borne in the two cases corresponded in colour to the band.

that of one wearing the sackcloth for a mother is now and then broken; in the mourning of nine months, after the first burst there are three quavers in it, and then it seems to die away; in the mourning of five and three months, an ordinary wailing is sufficient.

These are the manifestations of sorrow in the modulations of the voice[1].

3. When wearing the sackcloth for a father, one indicates that he hears what is said to him, but does not reply in words; when wearing that for a mother, he replies, but does not speak of anything else. During the nine months' mourning, he may speak of other things, but not discuss them; during that for five months or three months, he may discuss other things, but does not show pleasure in doing so.

These are the manifestations of sorrow in speech.

4. When a mourner has assumed the sackcloth for a father, for three days he abstains from food; for a mother, for two days. When he has commenced the nine months' mourning, he abstains from three meals; in that of five months or of three, for two. When an ordinary officer takes part in the dressing (of a friend's corpse), he abstains from one meal. Hence at the mourning rites for a father or mother, when the coffining takes place, (the children) take gruel made of a handful of rice in the morning, and the same quantity in the evening. During all the rites for a mother, they eat coarse rice and drink only water, not touching vegetables or fruits. During the nine months' mourning (the mourners) do not eat pickles or sauces; during that of five months or three, they do not drink prepared liquor, either new or old.

[1] I have read something of the same kind as this account of the 'wailing' in descriptions of the 'keening' at an Irish wake.

These are the manifestations of sorrow in drinking and eating.

5. In the mourning rites for a parent, when the sacrifice of repose has been presented, and the wailing is at an end, (the mourners) eat coarse rice and drink water, but do not take vegetables or fruits. At the end of a year, when the smaller felicitous sacrifice has been offered, they eat vegetables and fruits. After another year, when the greater sacrifice has been offered, they take pickles and sauces. In the month after, the final mourning sacrifice is offered, after which they drink the must and spirits. When they begin to drink these, they first use the must; when they begin to eat flesh, they first take that which has been dried.

6. During the mourning rites for a parent, (the son) occupied the mourning shed, and slept on straw with a clod for his pillow, without taking off the headband or girdle. If they were for a mother (only, and the father were still alive), he occupied the unplastered chamber, (sleeping on) typha rushes with their tops cut off, but not woven together. During the mourning for nine months, there was a mat to sleep on. In that for five months or for three, it was allowed to use a bedstead.

These were the manifestations of sorrow given in the dwelling-places.

7. At the mourning rites for a parent, after the sacrifice of repose, and when the wailing was concluded, the (inclined) posts of the shed were set up on lintels, and the screen (of grass) was clipped, while typha rushes, with the tops cut off, but not woven together, (were laid down for a mat). At the end of a year, and when the smaller felicitous sacrifice had

been offered, (the son) occupied the unplastered chamber, and had a mat to sleep on. After another year, and when the greater felicitous sacrifice had been offered, he returned to his old sleeping apartment. Then, when the final mourning sacrifice was offered, he used a bedstead.

8. The mourning with jagged edges was made with 3 shăng of hempen threads, each shăng containing 81 threads; that with even edge, with 4, 5, or 6 shăng; that for the nine months' mourning with 7, 8, or 9 shăng; that for the five months, with 10, 11, or 12 shăng; that for the three months, with 15 shăng less the half[1]. When the thread was manipulated and boiled, no such operation was performed on the woven cloth, and it was called sze (or the material for the mourning of three months).

These were the manifestations of sorrow shown in the fabrics of the different mournings.

9. The sackcloth with jagged edges (worn at first) was made with 3 shăng, but after the sacrifice of repose when the wailing was over, this was exchanged for a different fabric made with 6 shăng, while the material for the cap was made with 7 shăng. The coarse sackcloth for a mother was made with 4 shăng, exchanged for a material made with 7 shăng, while the cap was made with one of 8 shăng.

When the hempen dress is put away (after the burial), grass-cloth is worn, the sash of it being made of triple twist. At the end of the year, and when the first felicitous sacrifice has been offered, (the son) puts on the cap of dyed silk proper to that

---

[1] *K*û Hsî says, 'Inexplicable!'

sacrifice, and the red collar, still retaining the sash and headband. A son begins at the head, and a woman with the girdle, in putting off their mourning. What is the reason? Because a man considers the head the most important to him, and a woman the waist. In laying aside the mourning, they began with the most important; in changing it, with what was least.

At the end of the second year, and when the greater felicitous sacrifice had been offered, the cap and dress of plain hempen cloth was assumed. After the concluding sacrifice of mourning, in the next month, the black cap and silk of black and white were put on, and all the appendages of the girdle were assumed.

10. Why is it that in changing the mourning they (first) changed what was the lightest? During the wearing of the sackcloth with jagged edges for a father, if when, after the sacrifice of repose and the end of the wailing, there came occasion to wear the even-edged sackcloth for a mother, that, as lighter, was considered to be embraced in the other, and that which was most important was retained.

After the sacrifice at the end of the year, when there occurred occasion for the mourning rites of nine months, both the sackcloth and grass-cloth bands were worn.

During the wearing of the sackcloth for a mother, when, after the sacrifice of repose and the end of the wailing, there came occasion to wear the mourning for nine months, the sackcloth and grass-cloth bands were worn together.

The grass-cloth band with the jagged-edged sack-cloth and the hempen band with the even-edged sackcloth were of the same value. The grass-cloth with the even-edged sackcloth and the hempen band of the nine months' mourning were of the same value. The grass-cloth with the nine months' mourning and the hempen band with that of five months were of the same value. The grass-cloth with the five months' mourning and the hempen with that of three months were of the same value. So they wore them together. When they did so, that which was the lighter was changed first.

BOOK XXXV. SAN NIEN WĂN

OR

QUESTIONS ABOUT THE MOURNING FOR THREE YEARS[1].

1. What purposes do the mourning rites for three years serve?

The different rules for the mourning rites were established in harmony with (men's) feelings. By means of them the differences in the social relations are set forth, and the distinctions shown of kindred as nearer or more distant, and of ranks as more noble or less. They do not admit of being diminished or added to; and are therefore called 'The unchanging rules.'

2. The greater a wound is, the longer it remains; and the more pain it gives, the more slowly is it healed. The mourning of three years, being appointed with its various forms in harmony with the feelings (produced by the occasion of it), was intended to mark the greatest degree of grief. The sackcloth with jagged edges, the dark colour of the sackcloth and the staff, the shed reared against the wall, the gruel, the sleeping on straw, and the clod of earth for a pillow:—these all were intended to set forth the extremity of the grief.

3. The mourning of the three years came really to an end with (the close of) the twenty-fifth month. The sorrow and pain were not yet ended, and the

---

[1] See the introductory notice, vol. xxvii, pp. 49, 50.

longing loving thoughts were not yet forgotten; but in the termination of the mourning dress in this way, was it not shown that there should be an end to the duties rendered to the dead, and that the time was come for the resumption of their duties to the living?

4. All living creatures between heaven and earth, being endowed with blood and breath, have a certain amount of knowledge. Possessing that amount of knowledge, there is not one of them but knows to love its species. Take the larger birds and beasts:—when one of them has lost its mate, after a month or a season, it is sure to return and go about their old haunts. It turns round and round, utters its cries, now moves, now stops, and looks quite embarrassed and uncertain in its movements, before it can leave the place. Even the smaller birds, such as swallows and sparrows, chatter and cry for a little before they can leave the place. But among all creatures that have blood and breath, there is none which has intelligence equal to man; and hence the feeling of man on the death of his kindred remains unexhausted even till death.

5. Will any one follow the example of those men who are under the influence of their depraved lusts? In that case, when a kinsman dies in the morning, he will forget him by the evening. But if we follow the course of such men, we shall find that they are not equal to the birds and beasts. How can they live with their kindred, and not fall into all disorders?

6. Will he rather follow the example of the superior man who attends to all the methods by which the feeling of grief is set forth? In that case, the

twenty-five months, after which the mourning of three years comes to an end, will seem to pass as quickly as a carriage drawn by four horses is whirled past a crevice. And if we continue to indulge the feeling, it will prove to be inexhaustible.

7. Therefore the ancient kings determined the proper medium for mourning, and appointed its definite terms. As soon as it was sufficient for the elegant expression of the varied feeling, it was to be laid aside.

8. This being the case, how is it that (in certain cases the mourning lasts) only for a year? The answer is, that in the case of the nearest kindred, there is a break in it at the end of a year.

9. How is that? The answer is:—The interaction of heaven and earth has run its round; and the four seasons have gone through their changes. All things between heaven and earth begin their processes anew. The rules of mourning are intended to resemble this.

10. Then how is it that there are three years' mourning (for a parent)? The answer is:—From the wish to make it greater and more impressive, the time is doubled, and so embraces two round years.

11. What about the mourning for nine months' and the shorter periods? The answer is:—It is to prevent such mourning from reaching (the longer periods).

12. Therefore the three years should be considered as the highest expression of grief in mourning; the three months and five months, as the lowest; while the year and the nine months are between them. Heaven above gives an example; earth beneath, a law; and man between, a pattern. The

harmony and unity that should characterise men living in their kinships are hereby completely shown.

13. Thus it is that in the mourning of three years the highest forms that vary and adorn the ways of men are displayed. Yes, this is what is called the richest exhibition (of human feelings).

14. In this the hundred kings (of all the dynasties) agree, and ancient and modern customs are one and the same. But whence it came is not known.

15. Confucius said, 'A son, three years after his birth, ceases to be carried in the arms of his parents. The mourning of three years is the universal rule of all under heaven.'

BOOK XXXVI. SHĂN Î

OR

THE LONG DRESS IN ONE PIECE[1].

1. Anciently the long dress had definite measurements, so as to satisfy the requirements of the compass and square, the line, the balance, and the steelyard. It was not made so short as to show any of the skin, nor so long as to touch the ground. The outside pieces of the skirt joined, and were hooked together at the side; (the width of) the seam at the waist was half that at the bottom (of the skirt).

2. The sleeve was joined to the body of the dress at the arm-pit, so as to allow the freest movement of the elbow-joint; the length of the lower part admitted of the cuffs being turned back to the elbow. The sash was put on where there were no bones, so as not to interfere with the action of the thighs below or of the ribs above.

3. In the making (of the garment) twelve strips (of the cloth) were used, to correspond to the twelve months. The sleeve was made round, as if fashioned by a disk. The opening at the neck was square, as if made by means of that instrument so named. The cord-like (seam) at the back descended to the ankles, as if it had been a straight line. The edge at the bottom was like the steelyard of a balance, made perfectly even.

4. In this way through the rounded sleeves the arms could be lifted up in walking (for the purpose of salutation) in the most elegant form. The

[1] See the introductory notice, vol. xxvii, p. 50.

cord-like seam of the back and the square-shaped collar about the neck in front, served to admonish (the wearer) how his government should be correct and his righteousness on the square. It is said in the Yî, 'The movement indicated by the second line in Khwăn, divided, is "from the straight (line) to the square[1]."' The even edge at the bottom, like the steelyard and balance, admonished him to keep his will at rest, and his heart even and calm.

5. These five rules being observed in the making (of the dress), the sages wore it. In its squareness and roundness they saw its warning against selfishness; in its line-like straightness they saw its admonition to be correct, and in its balance-like evenness they saw its lesson of impartiality. Therefore the ancient kings attached a high value to it; it could be worn in the discharge of both their civil and military duties; in it they could receive visitors and regulate the cohorts of their armies. It was complete, but not extravagant; it ranked in the second class of good dresses[2].

6. For ornament, while his parents and grand-parents were alive, (a son) wore the dress with its border embroidered. If (only) his parents were alive, the ornamental border was blue. In the case of an orphan son[3], the border was white. The border round the mouth of the sleeves and all the edges of the dress was an inch and a half wide.

[1] See the symbolism of the second line of the 2nd Hexagram, and especially the lesser symbolism in the 2nd Appendix, from which the quotation is made;—vol. xvi, pages 60 and 268.

[2] That is, next after the court and sacrificial robes.

[3] *Kăng* says that a son whose father was dead was called 'an orphan son' up to thirty.

BOOK XXXVII. THÂU HÛ

OR

THE GAME OF PITCH-POT[1].

1. According to the rules for Pitch-pot, the host carries the arrows in both his hands put together; the superintendent of the archery carries in the same way the stand[2] on which the tallies were placed; and an attendant holds in his hand the pot.

2. The host entreats (one of the guests), saying, 'I have here these crooked[3] arrows, and this pot with its wry[3] mouth; but we beg you to amuse yourself with them.' The guest says, 'I have partaken, Sir, of your excellent drink and admirable viands; allow me to decline this further proposal for my pleasure. The host rejoins, 'It is not worth the while for you to decline these poor arrows and pot; let me earnestly beg you to try them.' The guest repeats his refusal, saying, 'I have partaken (of your entertainment), and you would still further have me enjoy myself;—I venture firmly to decline.' The host again addresses his request in the same words, and then the guest says, 'I have firmly declined what you request, but you will not allow me to refuse;—I venture respectfully to obey you.'

---

[1] See the introductory notice, vol. xxvii, pp. 50, 51.

[2] This was a small stand or tray, with the figure of a stag (or some other animal, according to the rank of the party) carved in wood and put down on it, with a tube by its side in which the tallies were to be placed.

[3] These are merely the customary terms of depreciation in which a Chinese speaks of his own things.

The guest then bows twice, and signifies that he will receive (the arrows). The host wheels round, saying, 'Let me get out of the way;' and then at the top of the steps on the east, he bows to the guest and gives him the arrows. The guest wheels round, and says, 'Let me get out of the way[1].'

3. (The host) having bowed, and received the arrows (for himself), advances to the space between the two pillars. He then retires, and returns to his station, motioning also to the guest to go to his mat (for pitching from).

4. The superintendent of the archery comes forward, and measures the distance of the pot (from the mats), which should be a space of the length of two and a half arrows. He then returns to his station, sets forth the stand for the tallies, and with his face to the east, takes eight counters and stands up. He asks the guest to pitch, saying, 'When the arrow goes straight in, it is reckoned an entry. If you throw a second (without waiting for your opponent to pitch), it is not reckoned.' The victor gives the vanquished a cup to drink; and when the cups of decision have been dispatched, the superintendent begs to set up what he calls 'a horse' for the victor. If he set up one horse, then a second, and finally a third, he begs to congratulate the thrower on the number of his horses. He asks the host to pitch in the same way, and with the same words.

5. He orders the cithern-players to strike up

[1] From this point to the end of the paragraph, it is very difficult to make out from the text the sequence of proceedings between the host and guest.

'The pitching,' say the *Kh*ien-lung editors, 'has been agreed on.'

'The Fox's Head,' with the same interval between (each repetition of the tune), and the director of the music answers, 'Yes.'

6. When the superintendent announces to them on the left and right that the arrows are all used up, he requests them to pitch again. When an arrow enters, he kneels, and puts down a counter. The partners of the guest are on the right, and those of the host on the left.

7. When they have done pitching, he takes up the counters, and says, 'They have done pitching, both on the left and right; allow me to take the numbers.' He then takes the numbers two by two, and leaves the single counters. After this he takes the single counters, and gives the announcement, saying, 'Such and such a side has the better by so many doubles, or naming the number of the singles.' If they are equal, he says, 'Left and right are equal.'

8. He then orders the cups to be filled, saying, 'Let the cup go round,' and the cup-bearer (of the successful side) replies, 'Yes.' Those who have to drink all kneel, and raising their cups with both hands, say, 'We receive what you give us to drink.' The victors (also) kneel and say, 'We beg respectfully to refresh you.'

9. When this cup has gone round, according to rule, (the superintendent) asks leave to exhibit the 'horses' (of the victorious side). Each 'horse' stands for so many counters. (He who has only) one 'horse' gives it to him who has two, to congratulate him (on his superiority). The usage in congratulating (the most successful) is to say, 'Your three "horses" are all here; allow me to congratulate you on their number.' The guests and host all express their

assent. The customary cup goes round, and the superintendent asks leave to remove the 'horses.'

10. The number of the counters varies according to the place in which they kneel (when playing the game). (Each round is with 4 arrows.) (If the game be in) the chamber, there are 5 sets of these; if in the hall, 7; if in the courtyard, 9. The counters are 1 cubit 2 inches long. The neck of the pot is 7 inches long; its belly, 5; and its mouth is 2½ inches in diameter. It contains a peck and 5 pints. It is filled with small beans, to prevent the arrows from leaping out. It is distant from the mats of the players, the length of 2½ arrows. The arrows are made of mulberry wood, or from the zizyphus, without the bark being removed.

11. In Lû, the young people (taking part in the game) were admonished in these words, 'Do not be rude; do not be haughty; do not stand awry; do not talk about irrelevant matters; for those who stand awry, or speak about irrelevant matters, there is the regular (penal) cup.' A similar admonition in Hsieh was to this effect:—'Do not be rude; do not be haughty; do not stand awry; do not speak about irrelevant matters. Those who do any of these things must pay the penalty.'

12. The superintendent of the archery, the overseer of the courtyard, and the capped officers who stood by, all belonged to the party of the guest. The musicians and the boys who acted as attendants, all belonged to the party of the host.

---

13. There follows after this what appears to be a representation of the progress of a game by means of small circles and squares. The circles indicating blows on a small drum

called phî, and the squares, blows on the larger drum (kû);—according, we may suppose, to certain events in the game. The 'drum' marks are followed by what are called 'halves' or semis. The representation is:—

Semis.	Drums.
○ ○ □ ○	○ ○ ○ ○
□ □ ○ □	□ □ □ □
○ □ ○ ○	○ □ ○

Then follows the representation of a game in Lû:—

Semis.	Lû drums.
○ ○	○ □ □ ○ ○
□ □	□ ○ ○ □ □
□ ○	□ □ ○ □ ○
○ ○	○ ○ □ ○ ○

There is then a remark that in the Hsieh drums the semi marks were used for the game of pitch-pot, and all the marks for the archery game; and then we have:—

Semis.	Hsieh drums.	Semis.	Lû drums.
○ ○	○ ○ □ ○ ○	○ ○ ○	□ ○
○ □	□ ○ □ □	□ ○ □	○ □
○ ○	○ ○ ○ ○	○ ○ ○	○ ○
□ □	○ ○ □ ○	○ ○	○
○ ○	□ □ ○ ○	□ □	□

BOOK XXXVIII. *ZÛ* HSING

OR

THE CONDUCT OF THE SCHOLAR[1].

1. Duke Âi of Lû asked Confucius, saying, 'Is not the dress, Master, which you wear that of the scholar[2]?' Confucius replied, 'When I was little, I lived in Lû, and wore the garment with large sleeves; when I was grown up, I lived in Sung, and was then capped with the *k*ang-fû cap[3]. I have heard that the studies of the scholar are extensive, but his dress is that of the state from which he sprang. I do not know any dress of the scholar.'

2. The duke said, 'Allow me to ask what is the conduct of the scholar.' Confucius replied, 'If I were to enumerate the points in it summarily, I could not touch upon them all; if I were to go into details on each, it would take a long time. You would have changed all your attendants-in-waiting before I had concluded[4].' The duke ordered a mat

---

[1] See the introductory notice, vol. xxvii, pp. 51, 52.

[2] Callery renders *Z*û here by 'le Philosophe.' Evidently there was in Confucius' time a class of men, thus denominated, distinguished by their learning and conduct. The name first occurs in the *K*âu Lî. It is now used for the literati of China, the followers of Confucius, in distinction from Tâoists and Buddhists.

[3] See vol. xxvii, page 438, paragraph 3. Confucius' ancestors belonged to the state of Sung, the representative of the ancient Yin.

[4] It was the custom for a ruler to change his attendants-in-waiting, so as not to overtire any.

to be placed for him, and Confucius took his place by his side.

3. He then said, 'The scholar has a precious gem placed upon its mat, with which he is waiting to receive an invitation (from some ruler)[1]; early and late he studies with energy, waiting to be questioned. He carries in his bosom leal-heartedness and good faith, waiting to be raised (to office); he is vigorous in all his doings, waiting to be chosen (to employment):—so does he establish his character and prepare himself (for the future).

4. 'The scholar's garments and cap are all fitting and becoming; he is careful in his undertakings and doings: in declining great compliments he might seem to be rude, and in regard to small compliments, hypocritical; in great matters he has an air of dignity, and in small matters, of modesty; he seems to have a difficulty in advancing, but retires with ease and readiness; and he has a shrinking appearance, as if wanting in power:—such is he in his external appearance.

5. 'The scholar, wherever he resides, ordinarily or only for a time, is grave as if he were apprehensive of difficulties; when seated or on foot, he is courteous and respectful; in speaking, his object is, first of all, to be sincere; in acting, he wishes to be exact and correct; on the road, he does not strive about the most difficult or easiest places; in winter and summer, he does not strive about the temperature, the light and shade; he guards against death that he may be in waiting (for whatever he may be called to); he attends well to his person that he may be

[1] Compare Analects IX, 12. The gem is the scholar's virtue,—his character and capacities.

ready for action:—such are his preparations and precautions for the future.

6. 'The scholar does not consider gold and jade to be precious treasures, but leal-heartedness and good faith; he does not desire lands and territory, but considers the establishment of righteousness as his domain; he does not desire a great accumulation of wealth, but looks on many accomplishments as his riches; it is difficult to win him, but easy to pay him; it is easy to pay him, but difficult to retain him. As he will not show himself when the time is not proper for him to do so, is it not difficult to win him? As he will have no fellowship with what is not righteous, is it not difficult to retain him? As he must first do the work, and then take the pay, is it not easy to pay him?—such are the conditions of his close association with others.

7. 'Though there may be offered to the scholar valuable articles and wealth, and though it be tried to enervate him with delights and pleasures, he sees those advantages without doing anything contrary to his sense of righteousness; though a multitude may attempt to force him (from his standpoint), and his way be stopped by force of arms, he will look death in the face without changing the principles (which) he maintains; (he would face) birds and beasts of prey with their talons and wings, without regard to their fierceness; he would undertake to raise the heaviest tripod, without regard to his strength; he has no occasion to regret what he has done in the past, nor to make preparations for what may come to him in the future; he does not repeat any error of speech; any rumours against him he does not pursue up to their source; he does not allow his

dignity to be interrupted; he does not dread to practise (beforehand) the counsels (which he gives):—such are the things in which he stands out and apart from other men.

8. 'With the scholar friendly relations may be cultivated, but no attempt must be made to constrain him; near association with him can be sought, but cannot be forced on him; he may be killed, but he cannot be disgraced; in his dwelling he will not be extravagant; in his eating and drinking he will not be luxurious; he may be gently admonished of his errors and failings, but he should not have them enumerated to him to his face:—such is his boldness and determination.

9. 'The scholar considers leal-heartedness and good faith to be his coat-of-mail and helmet; propriety and righteousness to be his shield and buckler; he walks along, bearing aloft over his head benevolence; he dwells, holding righteousness in his arms before him; the government may be violently oppressive, but he does not change his course:—such is the way in which he maintains himself.

10. 'The scholar may have a house in (only) a mâu of ground,—a (poor) dwelling each of whose (surrounding) walls is (only) ten paces long, with an outer door of thorns and bamboos, and openings in the wall, long and pointed; within, the inner door stopped up by brushwood, and little round windows like the mouth of a jar[1]; the inmates may have to

[1] This is a picture of squalid poverty, in which it is not easy to understand all the details without a discussion of the force of the Chinese characters, on which it is impossible to enter here. With all the discussion which they have received from the critics, there are still difficulties in interpreting the paragraph.

exchange garments when they go out; they may have to make one day's food serve for two days; if the ruler respond to him, he does not dare to have any hesitation (in accepting office); if he do not respond, he does not have recourse to flattery:—such is he in the matter of taking office, (however small).

11. 'The scholar lives and has his associations with men of the present day, but the men of antiquity are the subjects of his study. Following their (principles and example) in the present age, he will become a pattern in future ages. If it should be that his own age does not understand and encourage him, that those above him do not bring him, and those below him do not push him, forward, or even that calumniators and flatterers band together to put him in danger, his person may be placed in peril, but his aim cannot be taken from him. Though danger may threaten him in his undertakings and wherever he is, he will still pursue his aim, and never forget the afflictions of the people, (which he would relieve):—such is the anxiety which he cherishes.

12. 'The scholar learns extensively, but never allows his researches to come to an end; he does what he does with all his might, but is never weary; he may be living unnoticed, but does not give way to licentiousness; he may be having free course in his acknowledged position, but is not hampered (by it); in his practice of ceremonial usages he shows the value which he sets on a natural ease; in the excellence of his leal-heartedness and good faith, he acts under the law of a benignant playfulness; he shows his fond regard for men of virtue and ability, and yet

is forbearing and kind to all; he (is like a potter who) breaks his square (mould), and his tiles are found to fit together:—such is the largeness and generosity of his spirit.

13. 'The scholar recommends members of his own family (to public employment), without shrinking from doing so, because of their kinship, and proposes others beyond it, without regard to their being at enmity with him; he estimates men's merits, and takes into consideration all their services, selecting those of virtue and ability, and putting them forward, without expecting any recompense from them; the ruler thus gets what he wishes, and if benefit results to the state, the scholar does not seek riches or honours for himself:—such is he in promoting the employment of the worthy and bringing forward the able.

14. 'The scholar when he hears what is good, tells it to (his friends), and when he sees what is good, shows it to them; in the view of rank and position, he gives the precedence to them over himself; if they encounter calamities and hardships, he is prepared to die with them; if they are long (in getting advancement), he waits for them; if they are far off, he brings them together with himself:—such is he in the employment and promotion of his friends.

15. 'The scholar keeps his person free from stain, and continually bathes (and refreshes) his virtue; he sets forth what he has to say (to his superior by way of admonition), but remains himself in the back-ground, trying thus quietly to correct him; if his superior do not acknowledge (his advice), he more proudly and clearly makes his views known, but still does

not press them urgently; he does not go among those who are low to make himself out to be high, nor place himself among those who have little (wisdom) to make himself out to have much; in a time of good government, he does not think little (of what he himself can do); in a time of disorder, he does not allow his course to be obstructed; he does not (hastily) agree with those who think like himself, nor condemn those who think differently:—so does he stand out alone among others and take his own solitary course.

16. 'The scholar sometimes will not take the high office of being a minister of the son of Heaven, nor the lower office of serving the prince of a state; he is watchful over himself in his retirement, and values a generous enlargement of mind, while at the same time he is bold and resolute in his intercourse with others; he learns extensively that he may know whatever should be done; he makes himself acquainted with elegant accomplishments, and thus smoothes and polishes all his corners and angles; although the offer were made to share a state with him, it would be no more to him than the small weights of a balance; he will not take a ministry, he will not take an office:—such are the rules and conduct he prescribes to himself.

17. 'The scholar has those with whom he agrees in aim, and pursues the same objects, with whom he cultivates the same course, and that by the same methods; when they stand on the same level with him, he rejoices in them; if their standing be below his, he does not tire of them; if for long he has not seen them, and hears rumours to their prejudice, he does not believe them; his actions are rooted in

correctness, and his standing is in what is right[1]; if they proceed in the same direction with him, he goes forward with them, if not in the same direction, he withdraws from them:—so is he in his intercourse with his friends.

18. 'Gentleness and goodness are the roots of humanity; respect and attention are the ground on which it stands; generosity and large-mindedness are the manifestation of it; humility and courtesy are the ability of it; the rules of ceremony are the demonstration of it; speech is the ornament of it; singing and music are the harmony of it; sharing and distribution are the giving of it. The scholar possesses all these qualities in union and has them, and still he will not venture to claim a perfect humanity on account of them:—such is the honour (he feels for its ideal), and the humility (with which) he declines it (for himself).

19. 'The scholar is not cast down, or cut from his root, by poverty and mean condition; he is not elated or exhausted by riches and noble condition; he feels no disgrace that rulers and kings (may try to inflict); he is above the bonds that elders and superiors (may try to impose); and superior officers cannot distress him. Hence he is styled a scholar. Those to whom the multitude now-a-days give that name have no title to it, and they constantly employ it to one another as a term of reproach.'

When Confucius came (from his wanderings to Lû) to his own house, duke Âi gave him a (public) lodging. When the duke heard these words, he became more sincere in his speech, and more

[1] I suspect there is here some error in the text.

righteous in his conduct. He said, 'To the end of my days I will not presume to make a jest of the name of scholar[1].'

[1] It is doubtful whether any of this paragraph should be ascribed to Confucius, even in the sense in which we receive the preceding paragraphs as from him. Evidently the latter half of it is a note by the compiler to show the effect which the long discourse had on duke Âi.

BOOK XXXIX. TÂ HSIO

OR

THE GREAT LEARNING[1].

1. What the Great Learning teaches, is to illustrate illustrious virtue; to love the people[2]; and to rest in the highest excellence.

The point where to rest being known, the object of pursuit is then determined; and, that being determined, a calm unperturbedness may be attained to. To that calmness there will succeed a tranquil repose. In that repose there will be careful deliberation, and that deliberation will be followed by the attainment (of the desired end).

Things have their root and their branches; affairs have their end and their beginning. To know what is first and what is last will lead near to what is taught (in the Great Learning).

2. The ancients who wished to illustrate illustrious virtue throughout the kingdom, first ordered well their states. Wishing to order well their states, they first regulated their families. Wishing to regulate their families, they first cultivated their persons. Wishing to cultivate their persons, they

---

[1] See the introductory notice, vol. xxvii, pp. 53, 54.

[2] The text of the Tâ Hsio, since the labours of *K*û Hsî upon it, reads here—'to renovate,' instead of 'to love,' the people. *K*û adopted the alteration from Po-shun, called also Ming-tâo, one of his 'masters,' the two brothers *Kh*ăng; but there is really no authority for it.

first rectified their hearts. Wishing to rectify their hearts, they first sought to be sincere in their thoughts. Wishing to be sincere in their thoughts, they first extended to the utmost their knowledge.

3. The extension of knowledge is by the investigation of things[1].

4. Things being investigated, their knowledge became complete. Their knowledge being complete, their thoughts were sincere. Their thoughts being sincere, their hearts were then rectified. Their hearts being rectified, their persons were cultivated. Their persons being cultivated, their families were regulated. Their families being regulated, their states were rightly governed. Their states being rightly governed, the whole kingdom was made tranquil and happy.

From the son of Heaven down to the multitudes of the people, all considered the cultivation of the person to be the root (of everything besides). It cannot be, when the root is neglected, that what should spring from it will be well ordered. It never has been the case that what was of great importance has been slightly cared for, and at the same time what was of slight importance has been greatly cared for[2].

---

[1] There is great difficulty in determining the meaning of this short sentence. What *K*ăng and Khung Ying-tâ say on it is unsatisfactory. *K*û introduces a long paragraph explaining it from his master *Kh*ăng;—see Chinese Classics, vol. i, pp. 229, 239.

[2] Here ends the first chapter of the Book according to the arrangement of *K*û Hsî. He says that it is 'the words of Confucius, handed down by Ȝăng-ȝze,' all the rest being the commentary of Ȝăng-ȝze, recorded by his disciples. The sentiments in this chapter are not unworthy of Confucius; but there is no

This is called 'knowing the root,' this is called 'the perfection of knowledge.'

5. What is called 'making the thoughts sincere' is the allowing no self-deception;—as when we hate a bad smell and love what is beautiful, naturally and without constraint. Therefore the superior man must be watchful over himself when he is alone. There is no evil to which the small man, dwelling retired, will not proceed; but when he sees a superior man, he tries to disguise himself, concealing his evil, and displaying what is good. The other beholds him as if he saw his heart and reins;—of what use (is his disguise)? This is an instance of the saying, 'What truly is within will be manifested without.' Therefore the superior man must be watchful over himself when he is alone.

6. Ȝăng-ȝze said, 'What ten eyes behold, what ten hands point to, is to be regarded with reverence[1]. (As) riches adorn a house, so virtue adorns the person. When the mind becomes enlarged, the body appears at ease. Therefore the superior man is sure to make his thoughts sincere.

7. It is said in the Book of Poetry (I, v, ode 1, 1),

> 'How rich the clumps of green bamboo,
> Around each cove of *Kh*î!

---

evidence that they really proceeded from him, nor of the other assertions of *K*û. See what is said on the subject in the introductory notice.

[1] This saying is from Ȝăng-ȝze; but standing as it does alone and apart, it gives no sanction to the view that the first chapter was handed down by him, or the rest of the Book compiled by his disciples. Rather, the contrary. 'The ten eyes and ten hands,' says Lo *K*ung-fân, 'indicate all the spirits who know men's inmost solitary thoughts.'

They lead my thoughts to our duke Wû;—
Of winning grace is he!
As knife and file make smooth the bone,
As jade by chisel wrought and stone,
Is stamp upon him set.
Grave and of dignity serene;
With force of will as plainly seen;
Accomplished, elegant in mien;
Him we can ne'er forget.'

(That expression), 'as knife and file make smooth the bone,' indicates the effect of learning. 'Like jade by chisel wrought and stone' indicates that of self-culture. 'Grave and of dignity serene' indicates the feeling of cautious reverence. 'With force of will as plainly seen' indicates an awe-inspiring deportment. (The lines),

'Accomplished, elegant in mien,
Him can we ne'er forget,'

indicate how when virtue is complete, and excellence extreme, the people cannot forget them.

8. It is said in the Book of Poetry (IV, i, ode 4),

'The former kings in mind still bear,
What glory can with theirs compare?'

Superior men deem worthy whom they deemed worthy, and love whom they loved. The inferior people delight in what they delighted in, and are benefited by their beneficial arrangements. It is on this account that the former kings, after they have quitted the world, are not forgotten.

9. It is said in the Announcement to the Prince of Khang (Shû, V, ix, 3),

'He was able to make his virtue illustrious.'

It is said in the Thâi *K*iâ, 'He kept his eye

continually on the bright requirements of Heaven' (Shû, III, v, sect. 1, 2).

It is said in the Canon of the Tî (Yâo), 'He was able to make illustrious his lofty virtue' (Shû, I, 2).

These (passages) all show how (those sovereigns) made themselves illustrious.

10. On the bathing-tub of Thang[1], the following words were engraved, 'If you can one day renovate yourself, do so from day to day. Yea, daily renovate yourself.'

In the Announcement to the Prince of Khang it is said, 'Stir up the new people' (Shû, V, ix, 7).

In the Book of Poetry it is said (III, i, 1, 1),

> 'The state of *K*âu had long been known;
> Heaven's will as new at last was shown.'

Therefore the superior man in everything uses his utmost endeavours[2].

11. It is said in the Book of Poetry (IV, iii, 3),

> 'A thousand lî extends the king's domain,
> And there the people to repose are fain.'

And in another place (II, viii, 1),

> 'Twitters fast the oriole
> Where yonder bends the mound,
> The happy little creature
> Its resting-place has found.'

The Master said, 'Yes, it rests; it knows where

---

[1] A fact not elsewhere noted. But such inscriptions are still common in China.

[2] The repeated use of 'new,' 'renovated,' in this paragraph, is thought to justify the change of 'loving the people,' in paragraph 1, to 'renovating the people;' but the object of the renovating here is not the people.

to rest. Can one be a man, and yet not equal (in this respect) to this bird?'

12. It is said in the Book of Poetry (III, i, 1, 4),

'Deep were Wăn's thoughts, sustained his ways;
And reverent in each resting-place.'

As a ruler, he rested in benevolence; as a minister, he rested in respect; as a son, he rested in filial piety; as a father, he rested in kindness; in intercourse with his subjects, he rested in good faith.

13. The Master said, 'In hearing litigations, I am like any other body.' What is necessary is to cause the people to have no litigations, so that those who are devoid of truth shall find it impossible to carry out their speeches, and a great awe be struck into the minds of the people.

14. This is called 'knowing the root[1].'

15. What is meant by 'The cultivation of the person depends on the rectifying of the mind' (may be thus illustrated):—If a man be under the influence of anger, his conduct will not be correct. The same will be the case, if he be under the influence of terror, or of fond regard, or of sorrow and distress. When the mind is not present, we look and do not see; we hear and do not understand; we eat and do not know the taste of what we eat. This is what is meant by saying that 'the cultivation of the person depends on the rectifying of the mind.'

16. What is meant by 'The regulation of the family depends on the cultivation of the person'

---

[1] It is certainly difficult to see how paragraphs 13, 14 stand where they do. Lo *K*ung-fân omits them.

is this:—Men are partial where they feel affection and love; partial where they despise and dislike; partial where they stand in awe and with a feeling of respect; partial where they feel sorrow and compassion; partial where they are arrogant and rude. Thus it is that there are few men in the world who love and at the same time know the bad qualities (of the object of their love), or who hate and yet know the good qualities (of the object of their hatred). Hence it is said, in the common adage, 'A man does not know the badness of his son; he does not know the richness of his growing corn.' This is what is meant by saying, that 'if his person be not cultivated, a man cannot regulate his family.'

17. What is meant by 'In order to govern well his state, it is necessary first to regulate his family' is this:—It is not possible for one to teach others while he cannot teach his own family. Therefore the superior man (who governs a state), without going beyond his family, completes the lessons for his state. There is filial piety;—it has its application in the service of the ruler. There is brotherly obedience;—it has its application in the service of elders. There is kindly gentleness;—it has its application in the employment of the multitudes. It is said in the Announcement to the Prince of Khang (Shû, V, ix, 9), '(Deal with the people), as if you were watching over an infant.' If (a mother) be really anxious about it, though she may not hit (exactly the wants of her infant), she will not be far from doing so. There never has been (a girl) who learned (first) to bring up an infant that she might afterwards be married.

18. From the loving (example) of one family,

a whole state may become loving, and from its courtesies, courteous, while from the ambition and perverseness of the One man, the whole state may be thrown into rebellious disorder;—such is the nature of the influence. This is in accordance with the saying, 'Affairs may be ruined by a single sentence; a state may be settled by its One man.'

19. Yâo and Shun presided over the kingdom with benevolence, and the people followed them. *K*ieh and *K*âu did so with violence, and the people followed them. When the orders of a ruler are contrary to what he himself loves to practise the people do not follow him.

20. Therefore the ruler must have in himself the (good) qualities, and then he may require them in others; if they are not in himself, he cannot require them in others. Never has there been a man who, not having reference to his own character and wishes in dealing with others, was able effectually to instruct them. Thus we see how 'the government of the state depends on the regulation of the family.'

21. In the Book of Poetry it is said (I, i, 6, 3),

'Graceful and young the peach-tree stands,
  Its foliage clustering green and full.
This bride to her new home repairs;
  Her household will attest her rule.'

Let the household be rightly ordered, and then the people of the state may be taught.

In another ode it is said (II, ii, 9, 3),

'In concord with their brothers may they dwell!'

Let rulers dwell in concord with all their brethren, and then they may teach the people of their states.

In a third ode it is said (I, xiv, 3, 3),

'His movements without fault or flaw beget
Good order for his rule throughout the state.'

When the ruler as a father, a son, an elder brother or a younger, is a model for imitation, then the people imitate him. These (passages) show how 'the government of a state depends on the regulation of the family.'

22. What is meant by 'The making the whole kingdom peaceful and happy depends on the government of its states' is this:—When the superiors behave to their aged as the aged should be behaved to, the people become filial; when they behave to their elders as elders should be behaved to, the people learn brotherly submission; when they treat compassionately the young and helpless, the people do the same. Thus the superior man has a principle with which, as with a measuring square, to regulate his course.

23. What a man dislikes in his superiors, let him not display in his treatment of his inferiors; and what he dislikes in his inferiors, let him not display in his service of his superiors: what he dislikes in those who are before him, let him not therewith precede those who are behind him; and what he dislikes in those who are behind him, let him not therewith follow those who are before him: what he dislikes to receive on the right, let him not bestow on the left; and what he dislikes to receive on the left, let him not bestow on the right:—this is what is called 'The Principle with which, as with a measuring square, to regulate one's course.'

24. In the Book of Poetry it is said (II, ii, 7, 3),

'To be rejoiced in are these noble men,
The parents of the people!'

When (a ruler) loves what the people love, and hates what the people hate, then is he what is called 'The Parent of the People.'

25. In the Book of Poetry it is said (II, iv, 7, 1),

'That southern hill, sublime, uprears its craggy
height;
Such thou, Grand-master Yin, before the nation's
sight!'

Rulers of states should not neglect to be careful. If they deviate (to a selfish regard only for themselves), they will be counted a disgrace throughout the kingdom.

26. In the Book of Poetry it is said (III, i, 1, 6),

'Ere Shang had lost the nation's heart,
Its monarchs all with God had part
In sacrifice. From them we see
'Tis hard to keep High Heaven's decree.'

This shows that by gaining the people, the state is gained; and by losing the people, the state is lost.

Therefore the ruler should first be careful about his (own) virtue. Possessing virtue will give him the people. Possessing the people will give him the territory. Possessing the territory will give him its wealth. Possessing the wealth, he will have resources for expenditure.

Virtue is the root; wealth is the branches. If he make the root his secondary object, and the branches his primary object, he will only quarrel with the people, and teach them rapine. Hence the accumulation of wealth is the way to scatter the people, and the distribution of his wealth is the way to collect the people. Hence (also), when his words go forth contrary to right, they will come back to him in the same way, and wealth got by improper ways will take its departure by the same.

27. It is said in the Announcement to the Prince of Khang (Shû, V, ix, 2, 3), 'The decree (of Heaven) is not necessarily perpetual.' That is, goodness obtains the decree, and the want of goodness loses it.

28. In a Book of *Kh*û it is said[1], 'The state of *Kh*û does not consider (such a toy) to be precious. Its good men are what it considers to be precious.'

29. Fan, the maternal uncle (of duke Wăn of Ȝin), said, 'A fugitive (like you) should not account (that) to be precious. What he should consider precious is the affection due (even) to his (deceased) parent[2].'

30. It is said in the Speech of (duke Mû of) *Kh*in (Shû, V, xxx, 6, 7), 'Let me have but one minister, plain and sincere, not possessed of other abilities, but with a simple, upright, and at the same time a generous, mind, regarding the talents of others as if they were his own; and when he finds accomplished and perspicacious men, loving them in his heart more than his mouth expresses, and really showing himself able to bear them (and employ them),—such a minister will be able to preserve my sons and grandsons, and other benefits (to the state) may well be expected from him. But if (it be his character), when he finds men of ability, to be

[1] The narratives about *Kh*û, Section II, Article 5, in the 'Narratives of the States.' The exact characters of the text are not found in the article, but they might easily arise from what we do find. An officer of Ȝin is asking Wang-sun Wei, an envoy from *Kh*û, about a famous girdle of that state. The envoy calls it a toy, and gives this answer.

[2] See vol. xxvii, page 165, paragraph 19.

jealous of them and hate them; and, when he finds accomplished and perspicacious men, to oppose them, and not allow their advancement, showing himself really not able to bear them,—such a man will not be able to protect my sons and grandsons, and black-haired people; and may he not also be pronounced dangerous (to the state)?'

31. It is only the truly virtuous man that can send away such a man and banish him, driving him out among the barbarous tribes around, determined not to dwell with him in the Middle states. This is in accordance with the saying, 'It is only the truly virtuous man who can love others or can hate others.'

32. To see men of worth, and not be able to raise them to office; to raise them to office, but not to do so quickly:—this is treating them with disrespect. To see bad men, and not to be able to remove them; to remove them, but not to do so to a distance:—this is weakness.

33. To love those whom men hate, and to hate those whom men love:—this is to outrage the natural feeling of men. Calamities are sure to come on him who does so.

34. Thus we see that the ruler has a great course to pursue. He must show entire self-devotion and sincerity to succeed, and by pride and extravagance he will fail.

35. There is a great course (also) for the production of wealth. Let the producers be many, and the consumers few. Let there be activity in the production, and economy in the expenditure. Then the wealth will always be sufficient.

36. The virtuous (ruler) uses his wealth so as to

make himself more distinguished. The vicious ruler will accumulate wealth, even though it cost him his life.

37. Never has there been a case of the superior loving benevolence, and his inferiors not loving righteousness. Never has there been a case where (his inferiors) loved righteousness, and the business (of the superior) has not reached a happy issue. Never has there been a case where the wealth accumulated in the treasuries and arsenals (of such a ruler and people) did not continue to be his.

38. Mang Hsien-ȝze[1] said, 'He who keeps his team of horses[2] does not look after fowls and pigs. The family which has its stores of ice[3] does not keep cattle or sheep. The house which possesses a hundred chariots[4] should not keep a grasping minister to gather up all the taxes for it. Than have such a minister, it would be better to have one who would rob it of its revenues.' This is in accordance with the saying, 'In a state gain should not be considered prosperity; its prosperity lies in righteousness.'

39. When he who presides over a state or a family makes his revenues his chief business, he must be under the influence of some small man. He may consider him to be good; but when such a person is employed in the administration of a state

[1] The worthy minister of Lû, mentioned in vol. xxvii, p. 154, et al. His name was *K*ung-sun Mieh. Hsien was his posthumous title.

[2] An officer who has just attained to be a Great officer, and received from the ruler the carriage of distinction.

[3] To be used in sacrificing; but, we may suppose, for other uses as well.

[4] A dignitary, possessing an appanage.

or family, calamities and injuries will befal it together; and though a good man (may take his place), he will not be able to remedy the evil. This illustrates (again) the saying, 'In a state gain should not be considered prosperity; its prosperity should be sought in righteousness.'

BOOK XL. KWAN Î

OR

THE MEANING OF THE CEREMONY OF CAPPING[1].

1. Generally speaking, that which makes man man is the meaning of his ceremonial usages. The first indications of that meaning appear in the correct arrangement of the bodily carriage, the harmonious adjustment of the countenance, and in the natural ordering of the speech. When the bodily carriage is well arranged, the countenance harmoniously adjusted, and speech naturally ordered, the meaning of the ceremonial usages becomes complete, and serves to render correct the relation between ruler and subject, to give expression to the affection between father and son, and to establish harmony between seniors and juniors. When the relation between ruler and subject is made correct, affection secured between father and son, and harmony shown between seniors and juniors, then the meaning of those usages is established. Hence after the capping has taken place, provision is made for every other article of dress. With the complete provision of the dress, the bodily carriage becomes (fully) correct, the harmonious expression of the countenance is made perfect, and the speech is all conformed to its purposes. Hence it is said that in capping we have the first indications of (the meaning of the) ceremonial usages. It was on this account that the sage

[1] See the introductory notice, vol. xxvii, pp. 54, 55.

kings of antiquity made so much as they did of the capping.

2. Anciently, when about to proceed to the ceremony of capping, they divined for the day by the stalks, and also for the guests (who should be present). In this way did they manifest the value which they attached to capping. Attaching such a value to it, they made the ceremony very important. They made the ceremony so important, showing how they considered it to lie at the foundation of the state's (prosperity).

3. Hence (also) the capping took place at the top of the eastern steps, (appropriate to the use of the Master);—to show that the son would (in due time) take his place. (The father) handed him a (special) cup in the guests' place. Three caps were used in the ceremony, each successive one more honourable, and giving the more importance to his coming of age. When the capping was over, he received the name of his maturity. So was it shown that he was now a full-grown man[1].

4. He presented himself before his mother, and his mother bowed to him; he did the same before his brothers and cousins, and they bowed to him:—he was a man grown, and so they exchanged courtesies with him. In the dark-coloured cap, and the dark-coloured square-cut robes, he put down his gift of introduction before the ruler, and then proceeded with the proper gifts to present himself to the high ministers and Great officers, and to the old gentlemen of the country:—appearing before them as a man grown.

---

[1] Compare paragraph 2 on pages 437, 438, vol. xxvii.

5. Treating him (now) as a grown-up man, they would require from him all the observances of a full-grown man. Doing so, they would require from him the performance of all the duties of a son, a younger brother, a subject, and a junior. But when these four duties or services were required from him, was it not right that the ceremony by which he was placed in such a position should be considered important?

6. Thus when the discharge of filial and fraternal duties, of loyal service, and of deferential submission was established, he could indeed be regarded as a (full-grown) man. When he could be regarded as such, he could be employed to govern other men. It was on this account that the sage kings attached such an importance to the ceremony, and therefore it was said, that in capping we have the introduction to all the ceremonial usages, and that it is the most important of the festive services.

Therefore the ancients considered the capping as so important. Considering it so important, they performed it in the ancestral temple. They did so, to do honour to so important a service. Feeling that it was to be honoured so, they did not dare to take the responsibility of its performance on themselves. Not daring themselves to take the responsibility of it, they therefore humbled themselves, and gave honour in doing so to their forefathers.

BOOK XLI. HWĂN Î

OR

THE MEANING OF THE MARRIAGE CEREMONY[1].

1. The ceremony of marriage was intended to be a bond of love between two (families of different) surnames, with a view, in its retrospective character, to secure the services in the ancestral temple, and in its prospective character, to secure the continuance of the family line. Therefore the superior men, (the ancient rulers), set a great value upon it. Hence, in regard to the various (introductory) ceremonies,—the proposal with its accompanying gift[2]; the inquiries about the (lady's) name; the intimation of the approving divination[3]; the receiving the special offerings[4]; and the request to fix the day[5]:—these all were received by the principal party (on the lady's side), as he rested on his mat or leaning stool in the ancestral temple. (When they arrived), he met the messenger, and greeted him outside the gate, giving place to him as he entered, after which they ascended to the hall. Thus were the instruc-

[1] See the introductory notice, vol. xxvii, page 55.

[2] This gift was always a goose; into the reasons for which it is not necessary to enter.

[3] The gentleman's family had divined on the proposal.

[4] These were various.

[5] The lady's family fixed this. The first proposal was made, and perhaps those which followed also, by that important functionary in Chinese life, 'the go-between,' or a friend acting in that capacity.

tions received in the ancestral temple[1], and in this way was the ceremony respected, and watched over, while its importance was exhibited and care taken that all its details should be correct.

2. The father gave himself the special cup[2] to his son, and ordered him to go and meet the bride; it being proper that the male should take the first step (in all the arrangements). The son, having received the order, proceeded to meet his bride. Her father, who had been resting on his mat and leaning-stool in the temple, met him outside the gate and received him with a bow, and then the son-in-law entered, carrying a wild goose. After the (customary) bows and yieldings of precedence, they went up to the hall, when the bridegroom bowed twice and put down the wild goose. Then and in this way he received the bride from her parents.

After this they went down, and he went out and took the reins of the horses of her carriage, which he drove for three revolutions of the wheels, having handed the strap to assist her in mounting. He then went before, and waited outside his gate. When she arrived, he bowed to her as she entered. They ate together of the same animal, and joined in sipping from the cups made of the same melon[3];

---

[1] Thus a religious sanction entered into the idea of marriage.

[2] The same cup that is mentioned in the last chapter, paragraph 3; the son received it and gave no cup to the father in return. This was its speciality. In the capping ceremonies it was given 'in the guests' place;' in those of marriage, in the son's chamber.

[3] Once when I was permitted to witness this part of a marriage ceremony, the bridegroom raised his half of the melon, with the spirit in it, to the bride's lips, and she raised her half to his. Each sipped a little of the spirit.

thus showing that they now formed one body, were of equal rank, and pledged to mutual affection.

3. The respect, the caution, the importance, the attention to secure correctness in all the details, and then (the pledge of) mutual affection,—these were the great points in the ceremony, and served to establish the distinction to be observed between man and woman, and the righteousness to be maintained between husband and wife. From the distinction between man and woman came the righteousness between husband and wife. From that righteousness came the affection between father and son; and from that affection, the rectitude between ruler and minister. Whence it is said, 'The ceremony of marriage is the root of the other ceremonial observances.'

4. Ceremonies (might be said to) commence with the capping; to have their root in marriage; to be most important in the rites of mourning and sacrifice; to confer the greatest honour in audiences at the royal court and in the interchange of visits at the feudal courts; and to be most promotive of harmony in the country festivals and celebrations of archery. These were the greatest occasions of ceremony, and the principal points in them.

5. Rising early (the morning after marriage), the young wife washed her head and bathed her person, and waited to be presented (to her husband's parents), which was done by the directrix, as soon as it was bright day. She appeared before them, bearing a basket with dates, chestnuts, and slices of dried spiced meat. The directrix set before her a cup of sweet liquor, and she offered in sacrifice some of the dried meat and also of the liquor, thus

performing the ceremony which declared her their son's wife[1].

6. The father and mother-in-law then entered their apartment, where she set before them a single dressed pig,—thus showing the obedient duty of (their son's) wife[1].

7. Next day, the parents united in entertaining the young wife, and when the ceremonies of their severally pledging her in a single cup, and her pledging them in return, had been performed, they descended by the steps on the west, and she by those on the east,—thus showing that she would take the mother's place in the family[1].

8. Thus the ceremony establishing the young wife in her position; (followed by) that showing her obedient service (of her husband's parents); and both succeeded by that showing how she now occupied the position of continuing the family line:—all served to impress her with a sense of the deferential duty proper to her. When she was thus deferential, she was obedient to her parents-in-law, and harmonious with all the occupants of the women's apartments; she was the fitting partner of her husband, and could carry on all the work in silk and linen, making cloth and silken fabrics, and maintaining a watchful care over the various stores and depositories (of the household).

9. In this way when the deferential obedience of the wife was complete, the internal harmony was

[1] The details of the various usages briefly described in these paragraphs are to be found in the 4th Book of the Î Lî, the 2nd of those on the scholar's marriage ceremonies: paragraphs 1–10; 11–17; 18–20. There were differences in the ceremonies according to the rank of the parties; but all agreed in their general character.

secured; and when the internal harmony was secured, the long continuance of the family could be calculated on. Therefore the ancient kings attached such importance (to the marriage ceremonies).

10. Therefore, anciently, for three months before the marriage of a young lady, if the temple of the high ancestor (of her surname) were still standing (and she had admission to it), she was taught in it, as the public hall (of the members of her surname); if it were no longer standing (for her), she was taught in the public hall of the Head of that branch of the surname to which she belonged;—she was taught there the virtue, the speech, the carriage, and the work of a wife. When the teaching was accomplished, she offered a sacrifice (to the ancestor), using fish for the victim, and soups made of duckweed and pondweed. So was she trained to the obedience of a wife[1].

11. Anciently, the queen of the son of Heaven divided the harem into six palace-halls, (occupied) by the 3 ladies called fû-zăn, the 9 pin, the 27 shih-fû, and the 81 yü-*kh*î. These were instructed in the domestic and private rule which should prevail throughout the kingdom, and how the deferential obedience of the wife should be illustrated; and thus internal harmony was everywhere secured, and families were regulated. (In the same way) the son of Heaven established six official departments, in

---

[1] There is supposed to be an allusion to this custom in the Shih, I, ii, 4, beginning,

'She gathers fast the large duckweed,
From valley stream that southward flows;
And for the pondweed to the pools
Left on the plains by floods she goes.'

which were distributed the 3 kung, the 9 *kh*ing, the 27 tâ fû, and the 81 sze of the highest grade. These were instructed in all that concerned the public and external government of the kingdom, and how the lessons for the man should be illustrated; and thus harmony was secured in all external affairs, and the states were properly governed.

It is therefore said, 'From the son of Heaven there were learned the lessons for men; and from the queen, the obedience proper to women.' The son of Heaven directed the course to be pursued by the masculine energies, and the queen regulated the virtues to be cultivated by the feminine receptivities. The son of Heaven guided in all that affected the external administration (of affairs); and the queen, in all that concerned the internal regulation (of the family). The teachings (of the one) and the obedience (inculcated by the other) perfected the manners and ways (of the people); abroad and at home harmony and natural order prevailed; the states and the families were ruled according to their requirements:—this was what is called 'the condition of complete virtue.'

12. Therefore when the lessons for men are not cultivated, the masculine phenomena in nature do not proceed regularly;—as seen in the heavens, we have the sun eclipsed. When the obedience proper to women is not cultivated, the feminine phenomena in nature do not proceed regularly;—as seen in the heavens, we have the moon eclipsed. Hence on an eclipse of the sun, the son of Heaven put on plain white robes, and proceeded to repair what was wrong in the duties of the six official departments, purifying everything that belonged to the masculine

sphere throughout the kingdom; and on an eclipse of the moon, the queen dressed herself in plain white robes, and proceeded to repair what was wrong in the duties of the six palace-halls, purifying everything that belonged to the feminine sphere throughout the kingdom. The son of Heaven is to the queen what the sun is to the moon, or the masculine energy of nature to the feminine. They are necessary to each other, and by their interdependence they fulfil their functions.

13. The son of Heaven attends to the lessons for men;—that is the function of the father. The queen attends to the obedience proper to women;—that is the function of the mother. Therefore it is said, 'The son of Heaven and the queen are (to the people) what father and mother are.' Hence for him who is the Heaven(-appointed) king they wear the sackcloth with the jagged edges,—as for a father; and for the queen they wear the sackcloth with the even edges,—as for a mother.

BOOK XLII. HSIANG YIN *K*IÛ Î

OR

THE MEANING OF THE DRINKING FESTIVITY IN THE DISTRICTS[1].

1. The meaning of the drinking in the country districts may be thus described:—The president on the occasion bows to the (coming) guest as he receives him outside the college gate. They enter and thrice salute each other till they come to the steps. There each thrice yields the precedence to the other, and then they ascend. In this way they carry to the utmost their mutual demonstrations of honour and humility. (The host) washes his hands, rinses the cup, and raises it,—to give the highest idea of purity. They bow on the guest's arrival; they bow as (the cup) is washed; they bow when the cup is received, and when it is presented (in return); they bow when the drinking it is over:—in this way carrying to the utmost their mutual respect.

2. Such giving of honour, such humility, such purity, and such respect belonged to the intercourse of superior men with others. When they gave honour and showed humility, no contentions arose. When they maintained purity and respect, no indifference or rudeness arose. When there was no rudeness or contention, quarrels and disputations were kept at a distance. When men did not quarrel

[1] See the introductory notice, vol. xxvii, page 56.

nor dispute, there came no evils of violence or disorder. It was thus that superior men escaped suffering calamity from other men; and therefore the sages instituted the observances in this ceremony to secure such a result.

3. The chief of the district with the accomplished and virtuous men belonging to it had the vessel of liquor placed between the room (on the east), and the door (leading to the apartments on the west), host and guests sharing it between them. The vessel contained the dark-coloured liquor (of pure water);—showing the value they attached to its simplicity. The viands came forth from the room on the east;—being supplied by the host. All washing took place (in the courtyard) opposite the eastern wing;—showing how the host purified himself and made himself ready to serve the guests.

4. The (principal) guest and the host represented heaven and earth; the attendants of the guest and host respectively represented the forces inherent in nature in their contracting and expanding operations; the three (heads of the) guests (in their threefold division) represented the three (great) luminaries; the precedence thrice yielded (to the guest) represented the three days when the moon is invisible till it begins to reappear; the seating of the parties present (all round or) on the four sides represented the four seasons [1].

[1] P. Callery says:—'There were at this ceremony, 1. the chief and his assistant; 2. the principal guest who was supposed to represent all the other guests, and who also had his assistant; 3. three guests who formed a second category; 4. finally, the crowd of guests, a number not fixed, to whom no honour was paid directly, since they were held to receive all the honours rendered to

5. The snell and icy wind (that blows between) heaven and earth begins in the south-west and is strongest in the north-west. This is the wind that represents the most commanding severity of heaven and earth;—the wind of their righteous justice. The warm and genial wind (that blows between) heaven and earth begins in the north-east and is strongest in the south-east. This is the wind that represents the abundant virtue of heaven and earth;—the wind of their benevolence. The host, wishing to do honour to his guest, assigns him his seat on the north-west, and that of his attendant on the south-west, that he may there (most conveniently) assist him. The guest (represents) the treatment of others according to justice, and therefore his seat is

---

the principal guest.' *Kh*ăn Hâo quotes an opinion that the principal guest was made to represent heaven, to do him the greater honour; and the host to represent the earth, because he was the entertainer and nourisher; and that their assistants represented the yin and yang, because they assisted their principals as these energies in nature assist heaven and earth.

On 'the three Luminaries,' Callery says:—'Ordinarily the name of "the three Luminaries" belongs to the sun, the moon, and the stars, but par. 16 below does not allow us to take it so here. The commentators say that we are to understand the three most brilliant constellations in the firmament, which they call Hsin, Fâ, and Po-*kh*ăn, corresponding, I believe, in part to Orion, Scorpio, and Argo or the Ship.' So also *Kh*ăn Hâo's authority. Hsin is generally understood to be Scorpio (Antares, σ, τ, and two c. 3584 and 3587); Fâ to be υ Orion; and Po-*kh*ăn to be the north polar star.

On the 'thrice-yielded precedence to the guest,' Callery says:—'The comparison is far-fetched; it is intended to say that as the moon would not receive light if the sun did not accord it, so the guest would not receive such honours if the host did not render them.' So the commentators certainly try to explain it.

on the north-west; the host (represents) the treatment of others according to benevolence and a genial kindness, and therefore his seat is on the south-east, and his attendant is seated on the north-east, that he may there (most conveniently) assist him[1].

6. That intercourse according to benevolence and righteousness being established, so as to show the respective duties of host and guest, and the number of stands and dishes being properly fixed;—all this must be the result of sage intelligence. That intelligence established the arrangements, and each one being carried through with respect, it became a ceremonial usage. That usage proceeding to mark and embody the distinction between old and young, it became a virtue. Virtue is that which is the characteristic of the person. Therefore we have the saying, 'In the learning of antiquity, the methods by which they pursued the course adopted were intended to put men in possession of their proper virtue.' On this account the sages employed their powers (on its lessons)[2].

---

[1] P. Callery observes on this paragraph:—'The meteorological observations on which these statements rest must have been made very long ago in the interior of the country, there where the winds come under the influence of the icy plains of Tartary and the high mountains which separate China from Thibet; for on the sea-coasts of China, exactly the contrary has place. During the winter the north-east monsoon prevails, varying sometimes to the north and sometimes to the east, rarely to the north-west; while during the heats of summer the wind blows from the south-west, bending a little towards the south or towards the east, according as the monsoon is in the period of its increase or decline. It is generally in the course of this monsoon that there takes place the terrible storms known by the name of typhoons.'

[2] The *Kh*ien-lung editors do their best to elucidate this

7. When (the guest) offers in sacrifice some of the things that have been set before him, and some of the liquor, he showed how he respected (the host) for his courtesy; when he proceeded to take some of the lungs in his teeth, he thereby tasted (the host's) courtesy; when he then sipped some of the liquor, that was his last step in acknowledgment thereof. This last act was done at the end of his mat, showing that the mat was spread straight before him, not only for the purpose of eating and drinking, but also for the performance of the (proper) rites. In this was shown how it was the ceremony that was valued, while the wealth was made little account of. Finally, when the host filled their cups from the horn, they drained them at the top of the western steps;—showing how the mat was set not (merely) for the purpose of eating and drinking, and how the idea was that of giving to the ceremony the first place, and to wealth the last. But when the ceremony has the first place, and wealth the last, the people become respectful and yielding, and are not contentious with one another.

8. At the ceremony of drinking in the country districts, those who were sixty years old sat, and those who were (only fifty) stood, and were in waiting to receive any orders and perform any services;—thus illustrating the honour which should be paid to elders.

Before those who were sixty, three dishes were placed; before those of seventy, four; before those of eighty, five; before those of ninety, six:—

difficult and obscure paragraph; but are obliged to quote in the end the judgment of *K*û Hsî that 'it is vague and intractable, and not worth taking much trouble about.'

thus illustrating how the aged should be cherished and nourished.

When the people knew to honour their elders and nourish their aged, then at home they could practise filial piety and fraternal duty. Filial and fraternal at home and abroad, honouring elders and nourishing the aged, then their education was complete, and this led to the peace and tranquillity of the state. What the superior man calls filial piety, does not require that (every) family should be visited and its members daily taught; if (the people) be assembled at the archery meetings in the districts, and taught the usages at the district-drinkings, their conduct is brought to be filial and fraternal.

9. Confucius said, 'When I look on at the festivity in the country districts, I know how easily the Royal way may obtain free course.

10. 'The host in person invites the principal guest and his attendant, and all the other guests follow them of themselves. When they arrive outside the gate, he bows (and welcomes) the chief guest and his attendant, and all the others enter of themselves. In this way the distinction between the noble and the mean is exhibited.

11. 'With the interchange of three bows (the host and guest) arrive at the steps; and after precedence has been thrice yielded to him, the guest ascends. In bowing to him (on the hall), (the host) presents to him the cup, and receives the cup from him in return. The usages between them, now declining, now yielding, the one to the other, are numerous; but the attention paid to the assistant is less. As to the crowd of guests, they ascend, and receive the cup. Kneeling down they offer some of it in sacri-

fice; they rise and drink it; and without pledging the host in the return-cup, they descend. In this way the proper distinction is made between the different parties by the multitude or paucity of the observances paid to them.

12. 'The musicians enter, ascend the hall, and sing the three pieces which complete their performance, after which the host offers to them the cup. The organists enter, and (below the hall) play three tunes, which complete their part of the performance, after which the host offers to them (also) the cup. Then they sing and play alternately other three pieces and tunes; and also thrice again they sing and play in concert. When this is finished, the musicians announce that the music is over, and go out.

'At the same time a person (as instructed by the host) takes up the horn, and one is appointed to superintend the drinking, and see that it proceeds correctly. From this we know how they could be harmonious and joyful, without being disorderly.

13. 'The (principal) guest pledges the host, the host pledges the attendants, the attendants pledge all the guests. Young and old pledge one another according to their age, and the cup circulates on to the keepers of the vases and the cup-washers. From this we know how they could practise brotherly deference to their elders without omitting any one.

14. 'Descending (after this), they take off their shoes; ascending again, and taking their seats, they take their cups without any limit as to number. But the regulations of the drinking do not allow them to neglect the duties either of the morning or evening. When the guests go out, the host bows to each as he escorts him away. The regulations and

forms are observed to the end; and from this we know how they could enjoy the feast without turbulence or confusion.

15. 'The distinction between the noble and mean thus exhibited; the discrimination in the multitude or paucity of the observances to different parties; the harmony and joy without disorder; the brotherly deference to elders without omitting any; the happy feasting without turbulence or confusion;—the observance of these five things is sufficient to secure the rectification of the person, and the tranquillity of the state. When that one state is tranquil, all under heaven will be the same. Therefore I say that when I look on at the festivity in the country districts, I know how easily the Royal Way may obtain free course[1].'

16. According to the meaning attached to the festivity of drinking in the country districts, the principal guest was made to represent heaven; the host, to represent earth; their attendants respectively to represent the sun and moon; and the three head guests (according to the threefold division of them) to represent the three (great) luminaries. This was the form which the festivity received on its institution in antiquity: the presiding idea was found in heaven and earth; the regulation of that was found in the sun and moon; and the three luminaries were introduced as a third feature. (The

[1] I have supposed that all from paragraph 9 to this is the language of Confucius, and translated in the present tense as he would speak. Possibly, however, after par. 9 the compiler of the Book may be giving his own views of the different parts of the festivity (which would in that case have to be translated in the past tense), and then winds up with therefore 'He—Confucius—said,' &c.

whole represented) the fundamental principles in the conduct of government and instruction.

17. The dogs were boiled on the eastern side (of the courtyard[1]);—in reverential acknowledgment of the fact that the vivifying and expanding power in nature issues from the east.

The washings took place at the eastern steps, and the water was kept on the east of the washing-place;—in reverential acknowledgment of the fact that heaven and earth have placed the sea on the left.

The vessel contained the dark-coloured liquid;—teaching the people not to forget the original practice (at ceremonies).

18. The rule was that the (principal) guest should face the south. The quarter of the east suggests the idea of the spring, the name of which (also) denotes the appearance of insects beginning to move:—(there is then at work that mysterious) intelligence which gives birth to all things. The quarter of the south suggests the idea of the summer, the name of which (also) denotes what is great:—what nourishes things, encourages their growth, and makes them great is benevolence. The quarter of the west suggests the idea of the autumn, the name of which also denotes gathering or collecting:—the fruits of the earth are gathered at this season, suggesting the idea of justice in discrimi-

[1] Compare the statement in paragraph 3, that 'the viands come forth from the room on the east.' *Kh*ăn Hsiang-tâo says:—'The dog is a creature that keeps watch, and is skilful in its selection of men;—it will keep away from any one who is not what he should be. On this account the ancients at all their festive occasions of eating and drinking employed it.'

nating and guarding. The quarter of the north suggests the idea of winter, the name of which denotes also what is kept within:—and the being within leads us to think of being stored up. On this account, when the son of Heaven stands up, he keeps (the quarter of the life-giving) intelligence on his left hand, faces (the quarter of) benevolence, has that of justice on his right hand, and that of depositing behind him[1].

19. It was the rule that his attendants should face the east; thus (making) the principal guest to be the chief (party) at the festivity.

---

[1] The *Kh*ien-lung editors say that portions of this paragraph have been lost, and that other parts are out of their proper place; and they suggest the additions and alterations necessary to make it right. It is not worth while, however, to consider their views. No alterations will remedy its incurable defects or reverse the severe judgment passed on it by P. Callery:—'The method,' he says, 'by which the author proceeds is exceedingly eccentric, and partakes at once of the nature of the pun, of allegory, and of mysticism. He begins by basing his comparisons on the resemblance of certain sounds, or the homophony of certain words. Then he seeks to find in the sense, proper to those words that are homophonous or nearly so, connexions with the principal word in the text; and as those connexions are far from being natural or simply plausible, he puts his spirit to the torture, and goes to seek in the mysterious action of nature points of contact of which no one would think. Thus in the sound *kh*un (春, 蠢) he finds a natural analogy between the slow and gradual movement of a worm without eyes, and the march, equally slow and gradual, of vegetation in spring; in the sounds hsiâ and *k*iâ (夏, 假) he finds a direct connexion between greatness and the action which makes plants become great in summer. So in the same way with the other sounds which he deals with. To many Chinese this fashion of reasoning appears to be very profound; but, as I think, it is nothing but a childish play on words and hollow ideas.'

It was the rule that the host should be in the eastern quarter. The eastern quarter suggests the idea of spring, the name of which (also) denotes the appearance of insects beginning to move, and (it is spring) which produces all things. The host makes the festivity; that is, he produces all things.

20. The moon, after three days, completes the period of its dark disk. Three months complete a season. Therefore in this ceremony precedence is thrice yielded to the guest, and in establishing a state three high ministers must be appointed. That the guests are in three divisions, each with its head or leader, indicated the fundamental principles in the administration of government and instruction, and was the third great feature of the ceremony.

BOOK XLIII. SHÊ Î

OR

THE MEANING OF THE CEREMONY OF ARCHERY[1].

1. Anciently it was the rule for the feudal lords, when they would practise archery, first to celebrate the ceremony of the Banquet, and for the Great officers and ordinary officers, when they would shoot, first to celebrate the ceremony of the Drinking in the country districts. The ceremony of the Banquet served to illustrate the relation between ruler and subject; that of the District-drinking, to illustrate the distinction between seniors and juniors.

2. The archers, in advancing, retiring, and all their movements, were required to observe the rules. With minds correct, and straight carriage of the body, they were to hold their bows and arrows skilfully and firmly; and when they did so, they might be expected to hit the mark. In this way (from their archery) their characters could be seen [1].

3. To regulate (the discharging of the arrows), there was,—in the case of the son of Heaven, the playing of the Ʒâu-yü; in the case of the feudal lords, that of the Lî-shâu; in the case of the dignitaries, the Great officers, that of the Ʒhâi-pin; and in the case of officers, that of the Ʒhâi-fân[2].

---

[1] See introductory notice, vol. xxvii, pages 56, 57.

[2] Each archer discharged four arrows at the target. According to the account of the duties of the superintendent of archery in

The 3âu-yü[1] is expressive of joy that every office is (rightly) filled; the Lî-shâu is expressive of the joy at audiences of the court; the 3hâi-pin is expressive of the joy in observing the laws (which have been learned); and the 3hâi-fân is expressive of the joy in being free from all failures in duty. Therefore the son of Heaven regulated his shooting by keeping in his mind the right feeling of all officers; a feudal prince, by keeping in his mind the times of his appearing before the son of Heaven; a dignitary, being a Great officer, by keeping in his mind the observing of the laws (which he had learned); and an officer, by keeping in his mind that he must not fail in the duties of his office.

In this way, when they clearly understood the meaning of those regulating measures, and were thus able to avoid all failure in their services, they were successful in their undertakings, and their character

---

the *K*âu Lî (射人, Book XXX, paragraphs 54–67, especially 57), the 3âu-yü was played or sung nine times; the Lî-shâu seven times; and the two other pieces five times. When the king was shooting therefore, he began to shoot after the fifth performance, and had all the previous time to prepare himself; a prince began to shoot after the third performance; and in the two other cases there was only the time of one performance for preparation.

[1] The 3âu-yü is the last piece in the 2nd Book of the first part of the Book of Poetry; supposed to celebrate the benevolence of the king; here seen in his delight at every office being rightly filled. The Lî-shâu, 'Fox's Head,' or 'Wild Cat's Head,' has not come down to us;—see note 2, page 124. The 3hâi-pin and 3hâi-fân are the fifth and second pieces of the same Book and same part of the Shih as the 3âu-yü. The regulating the discharge of the arrows by the playing of these pieces was part of the moral discipline to which it was sought to make the archery subservient.

and conduct were established. When their characters were established, no such evils as oppression and disorder occurred; and when their undertakings were successful, the states were tranquil and happy. Hence it is said that 'the archery served to show the completeness of (the archer's) virtue.'

4. Therefore, anciently, the son of Heaven chose the feudal lords, the dignitaries who were Great officers, and the officers, from their skill in archery. Archery is specially the business of males, and there were added to it the embellishments of ceremonies and music. Hence among the things which may afford the most complete illustration of ceremonies and music, and the frequent performance of which may serve to establish virtue and good conduct, there is nothing equal to archery: and therefore the ancient kings paid much attention to it.

5. Therefore, anciently, according to the royal institutes, the feudal princes annually presented the officers who had charge of their tribute to the son of Heaven, who made trial of them in the archery-hall. Those of them whose bodily carriage was in conformity with the rules, and whose shooting was in agreement with the music, and who hit the mark most frequently, were allowed to take part at the sacrifices. When his officers had frequently that privilege, their ruler was congratulated; if they frequently failed to obtain it, he was reprimanded. If a prince were frequently so congratulated, he received an increase to his territory; if he were frequently so reprimanded, part of his territory was taken from him. Hence came the saying, 'The archers shoot in the interest of their princes.' Thus, in the states, the rulers and their officers devoted

themselves to archery, and the practice in connexion with it of the ceremonies and music. But when rulers and officers practise ceremonies and music, never has it been known that such practice led to their banishment or ruin.

6. Hence it is said in the ode (now lost),

'The long-descended lord
Presents your cups of grace.
His chiefs and noble men
Appear, all in their place;
Small officers and Great,
Not one will keep away.
See them before their prince,
All in their full array.
They feast, and then they shoot,
Happy and praised to boot.'

The lines show how when rulers and their officers earnestly devoted themselves together to archery, and the practice in connexion with it of ceremonies and music, they were happy and got renown. It was on this account that the son of Heaven instituted the custom, and the feudal lords diligently attended to it. This was the way in which the son of Heaven cherished the princes, and had no need of weapons of war (in dealing with them); it furnished (also) to the princes an instrument with which they trained themselves to rectitude.

7. (Once), when Confucius was conducting an archery meeting in a vegetable garden at *K*io-hsiang, the lookers-on surrounded it like a wall. When the proceedings reached the point when a Master of the Horse should be appointed, he directed 3ze-lû to take his bow and arrows, and go

out to introduce those who wished to shoot, and to say, 'The general of a defeated army, the Great officer of a ruler-less state, and any one who (has schemed to be) the successor and heir of another, will not be allowed to enter, but the rest may all enter.' On this, one half went away, and the other half entered.

After this, (wishing to send the cup round among all the company), he further directed Kung-wang *Kh*iû and Hsü Tien to raise the horns of liquor, and make proclamation. Then Kung-wang *Kh*iû raised his horn, and said, 'Are the young and strong (here) observant of their filial and fraternal duties? Are the old and men of eighty (here) such as love propriety, not following licentious customs, and resolved to maintain their characters to death? (If so), they may occupy the position of guests.' On this, one half (of those who had entered) went away, and the other half remained.

Hsü Tien next raised his horn, and proclaimed, 'Are you fond of learning without being tired? are you fond of the rules of propriety, and unswerving in your adherence to them? Do those of you who are eighty, ninety, or one hundred, expound the way (of virtue) without confusion or error? If so, you can occupy the position of visitors.' Thereupon hardly any remained[1].

8. To shoot means to draw out to the end, and some say to lodge in the exact point. That draw-

[1] The authenticity of what is related in this paragraph, which is not in the expurgated edition of the Lî *K*î, may be doubted. But however that be, it is evidently intended to be an illustration of what did, or might, take place at meetings for archery in the country. *K*io-hsiang is understood to be the name of some place in Lû.

ing out to the end means every one unfolding his own idea; hence, with the mind even-balanced and the body correctly poised, (the archer) holds his bow and arrow skilfully and firmly. When he so holds them, he will hit the mark. Hence it is said, 'The father (shoots) at the father-mark; the son, at the son-mark; the ruler, at the ruler-mark; the subject, at the subject-mark.' Thus the archer shoots at the mark of his (ideal) self; and so the Great archery of the son of Heaven is called shooting at (the mark of) the feudal prince. 'Shooting at the mark of the feudal prince' was shooting to prove himself a prince. He who hit the mark was permitted to be (that is, retain his rank as) a prince; he who did not hit the mark was not permitted to retain his rank as a prince[1].

9. When the son of Heaven was about to sacrifice, the rule was that he should celebrate the archery at the pool, which name suggested the idea of selecting the officers (by their shooting)[2]. After

[1] In this paragraph we have a remarkable instance of that punning or playing on words or sounds, which Callery has pointed out as a 'puerility' in Chinese writers, and of which we have many examples in the writers of the Han dynastry. The idea in the paragraph is good, that when one realises the ideal of what he is, becoming all he ought to be, he may be said to hit the mark. But to bring out this from the character (射), which is the symbol of shooting with the bow, the author is obliged to give it two names,—yî (射 = 繹, drawing out or unwinding the thread of a cocoon, or clue of silk, to the end) and shê (射 = 舍, a cottage or booth, a place to lodge in). The latter is the proper name for the character in the sense of shooting.

[2] Here there is another play on names,—ʒeh, in Pekinese *k*âi (澤), 'a pond or pool,' suggesting the character 擇, which has the same name, and means 'to choose, select.' There were two

the archery at the pool came that in the archery hall. Those who hit the mark were permitted to take part in the sacrifice; and those who failed were not permitted to do so. (The ruler of those) who did not receive the permission was reprimanded, and had part of his territory taken from him. The ruler of those who were permitted was congratulated, and received an addition to his territory. The advancement appeared in the rank; the disapprobation, in the (loss of) territory.

10. Hence, when a son is born, a bow of mulberry wood, and six arrows of the wild raspberry plant (are placed on the left of the door), for the purpose of shooting at heaven, earth, and the four cardinal points. Heaven, earth, and the four points denote the spheres wherein the business of a man lies. The young man must first give his mind to what is to be his business, and then he may venture to receive emolument, that is, the provision for his food.

11. Archery suggests to us the way of benevolence. (The archer) seeks to be correct in himself, and then discharges his arrow. If it miss the mark, he is not angry with the one who has surpassed himself, but turns round and seeks (for the cause of failure) in himself[1]. Confucius said, 'The student of virtue has no contentions. If it be said that he cannot avoid them, shall this be in archery? (But) he bows complaisantly to his competitor, ascends

places for the archery, one called the *K*âi Kung, 'Palace or Hall by the pool,' and the other, Shê Kung, 'Palace or Hall of Archery,' which was, says Callery, 'a vast gallery in the royal college.'

[1] Compare above, page 307, paragraph 40, where we have 'the way of the superior man' instead of 'the way of benevolence, or perfect virtue.'

(the hall), descends (again), and exacts the forfeit of drinking. In his contention, he is still the superior man [1].'

12. Confucius said, 'How difficult it is to shoot! How difficult it is to listen (to the music)! To shoot exactly in harmony with the note (given) by the music, and to shoot without missing the bull's-eye on the target:—it is only the archer of superior virtue who can do this! How shall a man of inferior character be able to hit the mark? It is said in the Book of Poetry (II, viii, ode 6, 1),

'"Now shoot," he says, "and show your skill."
The other answers, "Shoot I will,
And hit the mark;—and when you miss,
Pray you the penal cup to kiss."'

'To pray' is to ask. The archer seeks to hit that he may decline the cup.' The liquor in the cup is designed (properly) to nourish the aged, or the sick. When the archer seeks to hit that he may decline the cup, that is declining what should serve to nourish (those that need it).

[1] See Confucian Analects, III, vii.

BOOK XLIV. YEN Î

OR

THE MEANING OF THE BANQUET[1].

1. Anciently, among the officers of the kings of *K*âu, there was one called the shû-ȝze. He was charged with the care of the sons of the feudal lords, the high dignitaries who were the Great officers, and (other) officers,—the eldest sons who occupied the next place to their fathers. He managed (the issuing) to them of (all) cautions and orders; superintended their instruction in all they had to learn and (the art of self-)government; arranged them in their different classes; and saw that they occupied their correct positions. If there were any grand solemnity (being transacted) in the kingdom, he conducted them—these sons of the state—and placed them under the eldest son, the heir-apparent, who made what use of them he thought fit. If any military operations were being undertaken, he provided for them their carriages and coats of mail, assembled for them the companies of a hundred men and of five men (of which they should have charge), and appointed their inferior officers, thus training them in the art of war:—they were not under the jurisdiction of the minister of War. In all (other) governmental business of the state, these sons of it were left free, their fathers' eldest sons, without public occupation,

---

[1] See introductory notice, vol. xxvii, pages 57, 58.

and were made to attend to the cultivation of virtuous ways. In spring, (the shû-ȝze) assembled them in the college; and in autumn, in the archery (hall), that he might examine into their proficiency, and advanced or degraded them accordingly.

2. The meaning of the ceremony of the banquet at the feudal courts (may be thus described):—The ruler stood on the south-east of (his own) steps on the east, having his face towards the south, fronting the ministers or dignitaries who were nearest to him. They and all the (other) Great officers came forward a little, taking each his proper station. The ruler's mat is placed at the top of the eastern steps:—there is the station of the host. The ruler alone goes up and stands on his mat; with his face to the west he stands there by himself:—showing that no one presumes to place himself on a par with him.

3. Guests and host having been arranged, according to the rules for the ceremony of drinking in the country districts, (the ruler) makes his chief cook act for him in presenting (the cup):—a minister may not presume to take on himself any usage proper to the ruler. None of the (three) kung and no high minister has the place of a guest; but the Great officers are among the guests,—because of the doubts that might arise, and to show the jealousy (which such great men in that position might create).

When the guests have entered to the middle of the courtyard, the ruler descends a step and bows to them:—thus courteously receiving them.

4. The ruler sends the cup round among the guests in order; and when he has given a special cup to

any, they all descend, and bow twice, laying at the same time their heads to the ground; after which they ascend, and complete their bowing:—thus showing the observance due from subjects. The ruler responds to them, for every act of courtesy must be responded to:—illustrating the observances due from the ruler and superiors. When ministers and inferiors do their utmost to perform service for the state, the ruler must recompense them with rank and emoluments. Hence all officers and inferiors endeavour with their utmost strength and ability to establish their merit, and thus the state is kept in tranquillity, and the ruler's mind is at rest.

(The principle) that every act of courtesy must be responded to, showed that rulers do not receive anything from their inferiors without sufficient ground for doing so. The ruler must illustrate the path of rectitude in his conduct of the people; and when the people follow that path and do good service (for the state), then he may take from them a tenth part (of their revenues). In this way he has enough, and his subjects do not suffer want. Thus harmony and affection prevail between high and low, and they have no mutual dissatisfactions. Such harmony and rest are the result of the ceremonial usages. This is the great idea in the relation between ruler and subject, between high and low:—hence it is said that the object of the banquet was to illustrate the idea of justice between ruler and subject.

5. The mats were arranged so that the dignitaries of smaller rank occupied the place next (in honour) to those of higher; the Great officers, the place next to the lower dignitaries. The officers and sons of

concubines[1] (also) took their places below in their regular order. The cup being presented to the ruler, he begins the general pledging, and offers the cup to the high dignitaries[2]. They continue the ceremony, and offer the cup to the Great officers, who offer it in turn to the (other) officers, and these finally offer it to the sons of concubines. The stands and dishes, with the flesh of the animals[3], and the savoury viands, were all proportioned to the differences of rank in the guests:—and thus the distinction was shown between the noble and the mean.

---

[1] This is a common meaning of the phrase shû-ʒze. We cannot suppose that there is a reference to the officer so called in paragraph 1. He was of too high a rank to be placed after the officers, who ranked below the Great officers. Nor can we suppose that it denotes here 'the sons of the state' under his charge.

[2] The ruler did this by his deputy, the chief cook, who officiated for him on the occasion. All the different offerings are said to have been made by him indeed; but that is not the natural interpretation of the text.

[3] *Kh*ăn Hâo says these were dogs; see above, page 443, paragraph 17.

BOOK XLV. PHING Î

OR

THE MEANING OF THE INTERCHANGE OF MISSIONS BETWEEN DIFFERENT COURTS[1].

1. According to the ceremonies in missions, a duke of the highest grade sent seven attendants with (his representative); a marquis or earl, five; and a count or baron, three. The difference in number served to show the difference in rank of their principals[2].

2. The messages (between the visitor and the host) were passed through all the attendants, from one to another. A superior man, where he wishes to do honour, will not venture to communicate directly and in person. This was a high tribute of respect.

3. The message was transmitted (only) after the messenger had thrice declined to receive (the courtesies offered to him at the gate); he entered the gate of the ancestral temple after thrice in the same way trying to avoid doing so; thrice he exchanged bows with his conductor before they arrived at the steps; and thrice he yielded the precedence offered to him before he ascended the hall:—so did he carry to

---

[1] See introductory notice, vol. xxvii, pages 58, 59.

[2] If the ruler went in person on the mission, he had in every case, according to his rank, two attendants more than the number specified for his representative.

the utmost his giving of honour and yielding courtesy.

4. The ruler sent an officer to meet (the messenger) at the border (of the state), and a Great officer to offer him the customary presents and congratulations (after the toils of the journey) in the suburb (near the capital); he himself met him and bowed to him inside the great gate, and then received him in the ancestral temple; with his face to the north he bowed to him when the presents (which he brought) were presented, and bowed again (when his message was delivered), in acknowledgment of its condescension:—in this way did he (on his part) testify his respect.

5. Respectfulness and yielding courtesy mark the intercourse of superior men with one another. Hence, when the feudal lords received one another with such respectfulness and yielding courtesy, they would not attack or encroach on one another.

6. A high minister is employed as principal usher (for the messenger), a Great officer as the next, and (ordinary) officers acted as their attendants. (When he had delivered his message), the ruler himself showed him courtesy, (and presented to him the cup of new liquor). He had his private interviews (with the dignitaries and Great officers of the court), and also with the ruler [1]. (After this), supplies of animals, slaughtered and living, were sent (to his hotel). (When he was about to take his departure), the jade-symbols (by which he was accredited) were returned to him, and the return

[1] At these interviews, after he had discharged his mission and presented the gifts from his ruler, he presented other gifts on his own account.

gifts (of silk and other things) presented at the same time. He had been entertained and feasted. All these observances served to illustrate the idea underlying the relations between ruler and minister in receiving visitors and guests[1].

7. Therefore it was a statute made by the son of Heaven for the feudal lords, that every year they should interchange a small mission, and every three years a great one:—thus stimulating one another to the exercise of courtesy. If the messenger committed any error in the exchange of his mission, the ruler, his host, did not personally entertain and feast him:—thereby making him ashamed, and stimulating him.

When the princes thus stimulated one another to the observance of the ceremonial usages, they did not make any attacks on one another, and in their states there was no oppression or encroachment. In this way the son of Heaven cherished and nourished them; there was no occasion for any appeal to arms, and they were furnished with an instrument to maintain themselves in rectitude.

8. (The commissioners) carried with them their jade-symbols, the sceptre and half-sceptre:—showing the importance of the ceremony. On the completion of their mission, these were returned to them:—showing the small importance to be attached to their value, and the great importance of the ceremony. When the princes thus stimulated one another, to set light by the value of the articles, and recognise the importance of the ceremony, the people learned to be yielding and courteous.

[1] The entertainment took place in the open court; the banquet in the banqueting chamber.

9. The prince of the state to which the mission was sent treated his guests in this way:—Till their departure from their coming, they were supplied from the three stores (provided for such purposes). Living animals were sent to them at their lodging. A provision of five sets of the three animals for slaughter was made inside. Thirty loads of rice, the same number of grain with the straw, and twice as many of fodder and firewood were provided outside. There were five pairs of birds that went in flocks every day. All the attendants had cattle supplied to them for their food. There was one meal (a day in the court), and two (spare) entertainments (in the temple). The banquets and occasional bounties were without any definite number. With such generosity was the importance of the ceremony indicated[1].

10. They could not always be so profuse as this in antiquity in the use of their wealth; but their employment of it thus liberally (in connexion with these missions) showed how they were prepared to devote it to the maintenance of the ceremonies. When they expended it as they did on the ceremonies, then in the states ruler and minister did not encroach on one another's rights and possessions, and different states did not attack one another. It was on this account that the kings made their statute about these missions, and the feudal lords did their utmost to fulfil it[2].

[1] The particulars here briefly mentioned and many others are to be found in great detail in the 8th division of the Î Lî, Books 15–18, which are on the subject of these missions.

[2] About twenty years ago, when I had occasion to accompany a mandarin from Canton to a disturbed district in the interior, he

11. The archery in connexion with these missions was a very great institution. With the early dawn they commenced it, and it was nearly midday before the whole of the ceremonies were concluded:—it required men of great vigour and strength to go through with it.

And further, when such men were about to engage in it, though the liquor might be clear and they were thirsty, they did not venture to drink of it; though the stalks of flesh were dry (and ready to their hand), and they were hungry, they did not venture to eat of them; at the close of the day, when they were tired, they continued to maintain a grave and correct deportment. So they carried out all the details of the ceremonies; so they maintained correctly the relation between ruler and subject, affection between father and son, and harmony between seniors and juniors. All this it is difficult for the generality of men to do, but it was done by those superior men; and on this account they were called men possessed of great ability in action. The ascribing to them such ability in action implied their possession of the sense of righteousness; and their possession of that sense implied that they were valiant and daring. The

introduced one day in conversation the subject of these missions, saying that they must have been a great drain on the revenues of the ancient states, and that in the same way in the present day the provincial administrations were burdened with many outlays which should be borne by the imperial treasury. As resident ambassadors from foreign nations had then begun to be talked about, he asked whether China would have to pay their expenses, or the countries which they represented would do so, and was greatly relieved when I told him that each nation would pay the expenses of its embassy.

most valuable quality in a man who is bold and daring is that he can thereby establish his sense of righteousness; the most valuable quality in him who establishes that sense is that he can thereby show his great ability in action; the most valuable quality in him who has that ability is that he can carry all ceremonies into practice. In this way, the most valuable quality in valiant daring is that its possessor dares to carry into practice the rules of ceremony and righteousness.

It follows from this that such men, bold and daring, full of vigour and strength, when the kingdom was at peace, employed their gifts in the exercise of propriety and righteousness; and, when there was trouble in the kingdom, employed them in the battle-field and in gaining victory. When they employed them to conquer in battle, no enemies could resist them; when they employed them in the exercise of propriety and righteousness, then obedience and good order prevailed. No enemies abroad, and obedience and good order at home:—this was called the perfect condition for a state. But when men, so endowed, did not use their valour and strength in the service of propriety and righteousness, and to secure victory, but in strifes and contentions, then they were styled men of turbulence or disorder. Punishments were put in requisition throughout the kingdom, and the (first) use of them was to deal with those same men, and take them off. In this way (again), the people became obedient and there was good order, and the state was tranquil and happy.

12. Ȝze-kung asked Confucius, saying, 'Allow me to ask the reason why the superior man sets

a high value on jade, and but little on soapstone? Is it because jade is rare, and the soapstone plentiful?'

13. Confucius replied, 'It is not because the soapstone is plentiful that he thinks but little of it, and because jade is rare that he sets a high value on it. Anciently superior men found the likeness of all excellent qualities in jade. Soft, smooth, and glossy, it appeared to them like benevolence; fine, compact, and strong,—like intelligence; angular, but not sharp and cutting,—like righteousness; hanging down (in beads) as if it would fall to the ground,—like (the humility of) propriety; when struck, yielding a note, clear and prolonged, yet terminating abruptly,—like music; its flaws not concealing its beauty, nor its beauty concealing its flaws,—like loyalty; with an internal radiance issuing from it on every side,—like good faith; bright as a brilliant rainbow,—like heaven; exquisite and mysterious, appearing in the hills and streams,—like the earth; standing out conspicuous in the symbols of rank,—like virtue; esteemed by all under the sky,—like the path of truth and duty. As is said in the ode (I, xi, ode 3, 1),

"Such my lord's car. He rises in my mind,
Lovely and bland, like jade of richest kind."

This is why the superior man esteems it so highly!'

BOOK XLVI. SANG FÛ SZE *K*IH

OR

THE FOUR PRINCIPLES UNDERLYING THE DRESS OF MOURNING[1].

1. All ceremonial usages looked at in their great characteristics are the embodiment of (the ideas suggested by) heaven and earth; take their laws from the (changes of the) four seasons; imitate the (operation of the) contracting and developing movements in nature; and are conformed to the feelings of men. It is on this account that they are called the Rules of Propriety; and when any one finds fault with them, he only shows his ignorance of their origin.

2. Those usages are different in their applications to felicitous and unfortunate occurrences; in which they should not come into collision with one another:—this is derived from (their pattern as given by) the contracting and developing movements in nature.

3 The mourning dress has its four definite fashions and styles, the changes in which are always according to what is right:—this is derived from the (changes of the) four seasons.

Now, affection predominates; now, nice distinctions; now, defined regulations; and now, the consideration of circumstances:—all these are

[1] See the introductory notice, vol. xxvii, pp. 59, 60.

derived from the human feelings. In affection we have benevolence; in nice distinctions, righteousness; in defined regulations, propriety; and in the consideration of circumstances, knowledge. Benevolence, righteousness, propriety, and knowledge;—these make up the characteristic attributes of humanity.

4. Where the affection has been great, the mourning worn is deep. On this account the sackcloth with jagged edges is worn for the father for three years:—the regulation is determined by affection.

5. In the regulation (of the mourning) within the family circle, the affection throws the (duty of public) righteousness into the shade[1]. In the regulation (of that which is) beyond that circle, the (duty of public) righteousness cuts the (mourning of) affection short[1]. The service due to a father is employed in serving a ruler, and the reverence is the same for both:—this is the greatest instance of (the conviction of the duty of) righteousness. In all the esteem shown to nobility and the honour done to the honourable. Hence the sackcloth with jagged edges is worn (also) for the ruler for three years:—the regulation is determined by righteousness.

6. The eating after three days; the washing the head after three months; the sacrifice and change of dress at the end of the first year; the not carrying the emaciation to such an extent as to affect life:—these regulations were to avoid doing harm to the living

[1] A son, on his father's death, is exempted from official duties for a time; but this exemption is suspended on occasions of pressing exigency.

(by the mourning) for the dead. Not protracting the mourning rites beyond three years; not mending even the coarsest sackcloth; making no addition to the mound (raised at first) over the grave; fixing the day for the sacrifice at the end of the second year; playing (at first, on the conclusion of the rites) on a plain, unvarnished lute:—all these things were to make the people aware of the termination (of the several rites), and constituted the defined regulations.

The service due to a father is employed in serving a mother, and the love is the same for both. (But) in the sky there are not two suns, nor in a land two kings, nor in a state two rulers, nor in a family two equally honourable:—one (principle) regulates (all) these conditions. Hence, while the father is alive, the sackcloth with even edges is worn (for a mother), (and only) for a year,—showing that there are not (in the family) two equally honourable.

7. What is meant by the use of the staff? It is (a symbol of) rank. On the third day it is given to the son; on the fifth day, to Great officers; and on the seventh day, to ordinary officers;—(at the mourning rites for a ruler). Some say that it is given to them as the presiding mourners; and others, that it is to support them in their distress.

A daughter (not yet fully grown) and a son (while but a lad), do not carry a staff;—(being supposed) not to be capable of (extreme) distress.

When all the array of officers is complete, and all things are provided, and (the mourner) cannot speak (his directions), and things must (still) proceed, he is assisted to rise. If he be able to speak, and things will proceed (as he directs), he rises by the help of the staff. Where (the mourner) has himself to take part in what is to be done, he will have his face grimed (as if black with sorrow). Women who are bald do not use the coiffure; hunchbacks do not unbare their arms; the lame do not leap; and the old and ill do not give up the use of liquor and flesh. All these are cases regulated by the consideration of circumstances.

8. After the occurrence of the death, the (wailing for) three days, which left no leisure for anything else; the not taking off (the headband or girdle) for three months; the grief and lamentation for a whole year; and the sorrow on to the three years:—(in all these things) there was a gradual diminution of the (manifestation of) affection. The sages, in accordance with that diminution of the natural feeling, made their various definite regulations.

9. It was on this account that the mourning rites were limited to three years. The worthiest were not permitted to go beyond this period, nor those who were inferior to them to fall short of it. This was the proper and invariable time for those rites, what the (sage) kings always carried into practice.

When it is said in the Shû (Part IV, Book VIII, i, 1), that Kâo Ȝung, while occupying the mourning shed, for three years did not speak, this expresses approval of that sovereign. But the kings all observed this rule;—why is the approval only expressed in connexion with him? It may be replied, 'This Kâo Ȝung was Wû Ting.' Wû Ting was a worthy sovereign of Yin. He had come to the throne in the due order of succession, and was thus loving and good in his observance of the mourning rites. At this time Yin, which had been decaying, revived again; ceremonial usages, which had been neglected, came again into use. On this account the approval of him was expressed, and therefore it was recorded in the Shû, and he was styled Kâo (The Exalted), and designated Kâo 3ung (The Exalted and Honoured Sovereign). (The rule was that), during the three years' mourning, a ruler should not speak; and that the Shû says, 'Kâo 3ung, while he occupied the mourning shed, for the three years did not speak,' was an illustration of this. When it is said (in the Hsiâo King, chapter 18th), 'They speak, but without elegance of phrase,' the reference is to ministers and inferior (officers).

10. According to the usages, when wearing the sackcloth with jagged edges (for a father), (a son) indicated that he heard what was said to him, but did not reply in words; when wearing that with even edges (for a mother), he replied, but did not speak (of anything else); when wearing the mourning of nine months, he might speak (of other things), but did not enter into any discussion; when wearing that of five months, or of three, he might discuss, but did not show pleasure in doing so.

11. At the mourning rites for a parent, (the son) wore the cap of sackcloth, with strings of cords, and sandals of straw; after the third day, he (began to) take gruel; after the third month, he washed his head; at the end of the year, in the thirteenth month, he put on the mourning silk and cap proper after the first year; and when the three years were completed, he offered the auspicious sacrifice.

12. When one has completed these three regulated periods, the most animated with the sentiment

of benevolence (or humanity) can perceive the affection (underlying the usages); he who has (most) knowledge can perceive the nice distinctions pervading them; and he who has (most) strength can perceive the (force of) will (required for their discharge). The propriety that regulates them, and the righteousness that maintains their correctness, may be examined by filial sons, deferential younger brothers, and pure-minded virgins.

INDEX

TO THE

TEXTS OF CONFUCIANISM,

PARTS I, II, III, IV,

VOLUMES III, XVI, XXVII, XXVIII.

INDEX OF SUBJECTS.

The references refer to the parts and the pages.

INDEX OF PROPER NAMES.

TRANSLITERATION OF ORIENTAL ALPHABETS ADOPTED FOR THE TRANSLATIONS OF THE SACRED BOOKS OF THE EAST.

CONSONANTS.	MISSIONARY ALPHABET. I Class.	II Class.	III Class.	Sanskrit.	Zend.	Pehlevi.	Persian.	Arabic.	Hebrew.	Chinese.
Gutturales.										
1 Tenuis	k	...	...	क	𐬐	[illegible]	ک	ك	כּ	k
2 „ aspirata	kh	...	...	ख	𐬑	[illegible]	...	...	כ	kh
3 Media	g	...	...	ग	𐬔	[illegible]	گ	...	גּ	...
4 „ aspirata	gh	...	...	घ	𐬖	[illegible]	...	...	ג	...
5 Gutturo-labialis	q	...	...	...	...	...	ق	ق	ק	...
6 Nasalis	ṅ (ng)	...	...	ङ	𐬣 (ng) / 𐬧 (N)	...	...	...	...	...
7 Spiritus asper	h	...	...	ह	𐬵 (𐬓 *hv*)	[illegible]	ه	ه	ה	h, hs
8 „ lenis	’	...	...	...	...	...	ا	ا	א	...
9 „ asper faucalis	‘h	...	...	...	...	...	ح	ح	ח	...
10 „ lenis faucalis	’h	...	...	...	...	...	ع	ع	ע	...
11 „ asper fricatus	...	‘*h*	...	...	...	...	خ	خ	ח	...
12 „ lenis fricatus	...	’*h*	...	...	...	...	...	...	...	...
Gutturales modificatae (palatales, &c.)										
13 Tenuis	...	*k*	...	च	𐬗	[illegible]	چ	...	...	*k*
14 „ aspirata	...	*kh*	...	छ	...	...	...	...	...	*kh*
15 Media	...	*g*	...	ज	𐬘	[illegible]	ج	ج	...	...
16 „ aspirata	...	*gh*	...	झ	...	...	غ	غ	...	...
17 „ Nasalis	ñ	...	...	ञ	...	...	...	...	...	...

CONSONANTS (*continued*).	MISSIONARY ALPHABET. I Class.	II Class.	III Class.	Sanskrit.	Zend.	Pehlevi.	Persian.	Arabic.	Hebrew.	Chinese.
18 Semivocalis	y	...	...	य	𐬌𐬌, 𐬫 (init.)	[illegible]	ي	ي	י	y
19 Spiritus asper	...	(ẙ)	...	...	...	...	...	...	...	...
20 „ lenis	...	(ẏ)	...	...	...	...	...	...	...	...
21 „ asper assibilatus	...	*s*	...	श	𐬱	[illegible]	ش	ش	...	...
22 „ lenis assibilatus	...	*z*	...	...	𐬲	[illegible]	ژ	...	...	*z*
Dentales.										
23 Tenuis	t	...	...	त	𐬙	[illegible]	ت	ت	תּ	t
24 „ aspirata	th	...	...	थ	𐬚	...	...	...	ת	th
25 „ assibilata	...	...	TH	...	...	...	ث	ث	...	...
26 Media	d	...	...	द	𐬛	[illegible]	د	د	דּ	...
27 „ aspirata	dh	...	...	ध	𐬜	...	...	...	ד	...
28 „ assibilata	...	...	DH	...	...	...	ذ	ذ	...	...
29 Nasalis	n	...	...	न	𐬥	[illegible]	ن	ن	נ	n
30 Semivocalis	l	...	...	ल	...	[illegible]	ل	ل	ל	l
31 „ mollis 1	...	*l*	...	ळ	...	...	...	...	...	...
32 „ mollis 2	...	...	L	...	...	...	...	...	...	...
33 Spiritus asper 1	s	...	...	स	𐬯	[illegible]	س (ث)	س	שׂ	s
34 „ asper 2	...	...	s (ʃ)	...	...	...	...	...	ס	...
35 „ lenis	z	...	...	...	𐬰	[illegible]	ز (ذ)	ز	ז	z
36 „ asperrimus 1	...	...	z (ʒ)	...	...	...	ص	ص	צ	ʒ, ʒh
37 „ asperrimus 2	...	...	ẓ (ʒ̣)	...	...	...	ض	...	...	...

Dentales modificatae (linguales, &c.)										
38 Tenuis	...	*t*	....	ट	....	...	ط	ط	ט	...
39 „ aspirata	...	*th*	....	ठ	....	...	ظ	ظ	...	...
40 Media	...	*d*	....	ड	[illegible]	[illegible]	...	...	...	...
41 „ aspirata	...	*dh*	....	ढ	....	...	...	ض	...	...
42 Nasalis	...	*n*	....	ण	[illegible]	...	...	...	...	...
43 Semivocalis	r	...	....	र	[illegible]	[illegible]	ر	ر	ר	...
44 „ fricata	...	*r*	....	...	....	...	...	...	...	*r*
45 „ diacritica	...	...	R	...	....	...	...	...	...	...
46 Spiritus asper	sh	...	....	ष	[illegible]	[illegible]	...	...	...	sh
47 „ lenis	zh	...	....	...	....	...	...	...	...	...
Labiales.										
48 Tenuis	p	...	....	प	[illegible]	[illegible]	پ	...	פּ	p
49 „ aspirata	ph	...	....	फ	....	...	...	...	פ	ph
50 Media	b	...	....	ब	[illegible]	[illegible]	ب	ب	בּ	...
51 „ aspirata	bh	...	....	भ	....	...	...	...	ב	...
52 Tenuissima	...	*p*	....	...	....	...	...	...	...	...
53 Nasalis	m	...	....	म	[illegible]	[illegible]	م	م	מ	m
54 Semivocalis	w	...	....	...	[illegible]	...	...	...	...	w
55 „ aspirata	hw	...	....	...	....	...	...	...	...	...
56 Spiritus asper	f	...	....	...	[illegible]	[illegible]	ف	ف	...	*f*
57 „ lenis	v	...	....	व	[illegible]	[illegible]	و	و	ו	...
58 Anusvâra	...	*m*	....	अं	[illegible] ã	...	...	...	...	...
59 Visarga	...	*h*	....	अः	....	...	...	...	...	...

VOWELS.	MISSIONARY ALPHABET. I Class.	II Class.	III Class.	Sanskrit.	Zend.	Pehlevi.	Persian.	Arabic.	Hebrew.	Chinese.
1 Neutralis	0	...	...	...	...	...	...	...	ְ	ă
2 Laryngo-palatalis	ĕ	...	...	...	...	...	...	...	...	...
3 „ labialis	ŏ	...	...	...	...	𐮀 fin.	...	...	...	...
4 Gutturalis brevis	a	...	...	अ	𐬀	𐮀 init.	ـَ	ـَ	ַ	a
5 „ longa	â	(*a*)	...	आ	𐬁	𐮀	ـَا	ـَا	ָ	â
6 Palatalis brevis	i	...	...	इ	𐬌	...	ـِ	ـِ	ִ	i
7 „ longa	î	(*i*)	...	ई	𐬍	𐮉	ـِي	ـِي	ִי	î
8 Dentalis brevis	*li*	...	...	ऌ	...	...	...	...	...	...
9 „ longa	*lî*	...	...	ॡ	...	...	...	...	...	...
10 Lingualis brevis	*ri*	...	...	ऋ	...	...	...	...	...	...
11 „ longa	*rî*	...	...	ॠ	...	...	...	...	...	...
12 Labialis brevis	u	...	...	उ	𐬎	...	ـُ	ـُ	ֻ	u
13 „ longa	û	(*u*)	...	ऊ	𐬏	𐮅	ـُو	ـُو	וּ	û
14 Gutturo-palatalis brevis	e	...	...	...	𐬈(e) 𐬆(*e*)	...	...	...	ֶ	e
15 „ longa	ê (a)	(*e*)	...	ए	𐬉, 𐬇	𐮉	...	...	ֵ	ê
16 Diphthongus gutturo-palatalis	âi	(*ai*)	...	ऐ	...	...	ـَيْ	ـَيْ	...	âi
17 „ „	ei (ĕ)	...	...	...	...	...	...	...	...	ei, êi
18 „ „	oi (ŏ)	...	...	...	...	...	...	...	...	...
19 Gutturo-labialis brevis	o	...	...	...	𐬊	...	...	...	ָ	o
20 „ longa	ô (a)	(*o*)	...	ओ	𐬋	𐮅	...	...	וֹ	...
21 Diphthongus gutturo-labialis	âu	(*au*)	...	औ	𐬃 (*au*)	...	ـَوْ	ـَوْ	...	âu
22 „ „	eu (ĕu)	...	...	...	...	...	...	...	...	...
23 „ „	ou (ŏu)	...	...	...	...	...	...	...	...	...
24 Gutturalis fracta	ä	...	...	...	...	...	...	...	...	...
25 Palatalis fracta	ï	...	...	...	...	...	...	...	...	...
26 Labialis fracta	ü	...	...	...	...	...	...	...	...	ü
27 Gutturo-labialis fracta	ö	...	...	...	...	...	...	...	...	...